Introduction
to Research
in Education

Introduction to Research in Education

Second Edition

Donald Ary
Northern Illinois University

Lucy Cheser Jacobs
Indiana University

Asghar Razavieh
Shiraz University,
Shiraz, Iran

Holt, Rinehart and Winston
New York   Chicago   San Francisco   Dallas
Montreal   Toronto   London   Sydney

Library of Congress Cataloging in Publication Data

Ary, Donald.
   Introduction to research in education.

   Includes index.
   1. Educational research.   I. Jacobs, Lucy Cheser, joint author.
II. Razavieh, Asghar, joint author. III. Title.
LB1028.A7 1979   370′.78   78-10653
ISBN 0-03-020606-5

Printed in the United States of America

2 3 4   039 9 8 7 6 5

To Sheila, Marion, and Nasrin

Preface

Our goals in preparing the first edition of *Introduction to Research in Education* were to provide a book that would enable readers to master the basic competencies necessary (1) to understand and evaluate the research of others and (2) to plan and conduct their own research with a minimum of assistance. The reception the first edition has received is an indication that we have been reasonably successful in achieving these goals. We hope both students and colleagues will find this second edition even more useful. The latter have provided suggestions we found very helpful in our attempts to provide a clearer and more complete text. For example, in response to many suggestions we have added study exercises for each chapter.

The sequence of topics discussed in this book begins with a general description of the scientific approach and the relevance of this approach to the search for knowledge in education. We assume that the reader is not familiar with the concepts, assumptions, and terminology of the scientific approach; therefore, these are explained as they are introduced. We have expanded the discussion of the roles deductive reasoning and inductive reasoning play in science. From this basis we proceed to suggestions for translating general problems into questions amenable to scientific inquiry. A section on the identification of the population and variables of interest has been added to the guidelines for developing problems for research.

Next we describe the role of previous research in the planning of a research project. We have updated the sources of related literature with particular emphasis on data bases that provide efficient access to relevant research and theory. We then proceed to investigate the ways in which theory, experience, observations, and related literature lead to hypothesis formation.

The more useful descriptive and inferential statistical procedures are included, with the emphasis on the role these procedures play in the research process and on their interpretation. The role of systematic observation and measurement is explored, and examples of useful measurement procedures are included. The chapter on validity and reliability has been extensively revised.

Following this, we discuss the various types of research that have proven useful in education, pointing out the advantages and disadvantages of various approaches without espousing any particular one as being superior to the others. The chapter on ex post facto research has been revised in order to show more clearly the strengths and weaknesses of this type of research.

We conclude by presenting the general rules for interpreting the results of research and the accepted procedures for reporting such results. We have added sections on procedures for meeting ethical and legal requirements in research and on the use of computers.

The focus of this edition remains the provision of a text designed for use in an introductory course in educational research. Its aim is to familiarize the beginning researcher with the procedures for conducting an original research project. We focus on the typical and practical problems encountered in research, beginning with the formulation of the question and continuing through the preparation of the final report.

Although *Introduction to Research in Education* is directed toward the beginning student in educational research, it is hoped that others who wish to learn more about the philosophy, tools, and procedures of scientific inquiry in education will find it useful. The principal criterion used in determining what to include has been the potential usefulness of various aspects of educational research to the educational practitioner.

To all of those teachers who used the first edition and have made very valuable suggestions for improving and updating the second edition, we are deeply grateful. We also thank Linda Burke for her many contributions. We are indebted to the Literary Executor of the late Sir Ronald A. Fisher, F.R.S., for permission to reprint Table A.5 in the Appendix from the book *Statistical Methods for Research Workers*. We are also indebted to the aforementioned and to Dr. Frank Yates, F.R.S., for permission to reprint Tables A.3 and A.7 (also in the Appendix) from their book *Statistical Tables for Biological, Agricultural, and Medical Research*.

D. A.
L. C. J.
A. R.

Contents

Part

3

Statistical Analysis

Part

4

Tools of Research

Part

5

Research Methods

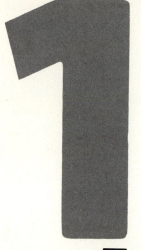

Part

Foundations

The Scientific Approach in Education

Educators are, by necessity, decision makers. Daily, in the course of carrying out the educative process, we are faced with the task of making decisions about how to plan learning experiences, how to teach, how to guide students, how to organize a school system, and a myriad of other matters.

Unlike unskilled workers who are told what to do and how to do it, professionals must plan for themselves. It is assumed that they have the knowledge and skills necessary to make valid decisions about what to do and how. But how are educators to know what is the right answer in a particular situation? Although there are other sources of knowledge, such as experience, authority, and tradition, it is scientific knowledge about the educational process that makes the most valuable contribution to decision making in education. Educators can turn to this source for reliable information and suggestions to be used in a decision-making situation. This fund of knowledge has been made available to educators as a result of scientific inquiry into educational problems. Education has not always been influenced by the results of such careful and systematic investigations. In fact, it might be said that the development of an educational science is at a comparatively early stage.

Sources of Knowledge

Before we pursue further the role of scientific inquiry in education, let us review the ways in which human beings throughout history have sought answers to their questions. The sources of knowledge may be categorized under the five headings: (1) experience, (2) authority, (3) deductive reasoning, (4) inductive reasoning, and (5) the scientific approach.

EXPERIENCE

Experience is a familiar and well-used source of knowledge. After trying several routes from home to work, one learns which route takes the least time or is the most free of traffic or is the most scenic. By personal experience one can find the answers to many of the questions one faces. Much of the wisdom that is passed from generation to generation is the result of experience. If we were not able to profit from experience, progress would be severely retarded. In fact, this ability to learn from experience is generally considered a prime characteristic of intelligent behavior.

Yet, for all its usefulness, experience has its limitations as a source of truth. How one is affected by an event depends upon who one is. Two people will have very different experiences in the same situation. The same woods that is a delightful sanctuary to one may be a menacing wilderness to another. Two supervisors observing the same classroom at the same time could truthfully compile very different reports if one focused on and reported the things that went right and the other focused on and reported the things that went wrong.

Another shortcoming of experience is that one so frequently needs to know things that one as an individual cannot learn by experience. A child turned loose to figure out arithmetic alone might figure out the technique of addition but would be unlikely to find an efficient way to compute square roots. A teacher could learn through experience the population of a classroom on a particular day but could not personally count the population of the United States.

AUTHORITY

For those things that are difficult or impossible to know by personal experience, one frequently turns to authority; that is, one seeks the answers to questions from someone who has had experience with the problem or has some other source of expertise. We accept as truth the word of those recognized as authorities. To know the population of the United States, one turns to the U.S. Census Bureau reports. A student looks up the correct pronunciation of a word in the dictionary. The superintendent consults a lawyer concerning a legal problem in the school. A beginning teacher asks an experienced one for suggestions. The new teacher may try a certain technique for teaching reading because the supervisor suggests that it is effective.

Throughout history one can find examples of reliance upon authority for truth, particularly during the Middle Ages when ancient scholars, such as Plato and Aristotle, and the early Fathers of the church were preferred as sources of truth—even over direct observation or experience. Although authority is one of our very useful sources of knowledge, one must not lose sight of the question, How does authority know? In earlier days an authority was assumed to be right simply because of the position held, such as that of king, chief, or high priest. Today we are reluctant to rely upon an individual as an authority merely because of position or rank. We are inclined to accept the assumptions of an authority only when that authority bases its assertion on experience or other recognized sources of knowledge.

Closely related to authority are custom and tradition, which we depend on for answers to many of the questions related to our professional as well as everyday problems. In other words, one often asks, How has this been done in the past? and then uses the answer as a guide for his or her actions. Custom and tradition have been especially prominent influences in the school setting, where educators often rely on past practices as a dependable guide. However, an examination of the history of education reveals that many traditions that had prevailed for years were later found to be erroneous and had to be rejected. It is wise to appraise custom and tradition carefully before one accepts them as truth.

As a source of truth, authority has shortcomings that one must consider. In the first place, authorities can be wrong; they have no claim to infallibility. Also, one may find that authorities are in disagreement among themselves on issues, indicating that their authoritative statements are often more personal opinion than fact.

DEDUCTIVE REASONING

Perhaps the first significant contribution to the development of a systematic approach for discovering truth was made by the ancient Greek philosophers. Aristotle and his followers introduced the use of deductive reasoning, which can be described as a thinking process in which one proceeds from general to specific statements using prescribed rules of logic. It is a system for organizing known facts in order to reach a conclusion. This is done through a series of statements called a syllogism, containing (a) the major premise, (b) the minor premise, and (c) the conclusion. An example of syllogistic reasoning is: (a) all men are mortal (major premise); (b) Socrates is a man (minor premise); therefore, (c) Socrates is mortal (conclusion).

In deductive reasoning, if the premises are true, the conclusion is necessarily true. Deductive reasoning enables one to organize premises into patterns that provide conclusive evidence for the validity of a conclusion. Mystery fans will recall that Sherlock Holmes frequently would say, "I deduce . . ." as he combined previously unconnected facts in such a way as to imply a previously unsuspected conclusion.

However, deductive reasoning does have its limitations. We must begin with true premises in order to arrive at true conclusions. The conclusion of a syllogism can never exceed the content of the premises. Since deductive conclusions are necessarily elaborations on previously existing knowledge, scientific inquiry cannot be conducted through deductive reasoning alone because of the difficulty involved in establishing the universal truth of many statements dealing with scientific phenomena. Deductive reasoning can organize what is already known and can point up new relationships as one proceeds from the general to the specific, but it is not sufficient as a source of new truth.

In spite of its limitations, deductive reasoning is useful in the research process. It provides a means for linking theory and observation. It enables researchers to deduce from existing theory what phenomena should be observed. Deductions from theory can provide hypotheses, which are a vital part of scientific inquiry.

INDUCTIVE REASONING

The conclusions of deductive reasoning are true only if the premises on which they are based are true. But how is one to know if the premises are true? In the Middle Ages dogma was often substituted for true premises, with the result that invalid conclusions were reached. It was Francis Bacon (1561–1626) who first called for a new approach to knowing. He held that thinkers should not enslave themselves by accepting premises handed down by authority as absolute truth. He believed that an investigator should establish general conclusions on the basis of facts gathered through direct observation. Bacon advised the seeker of truth to observe nature directly and to rid the mind of prejudice and preconceived ideas, which he called "idols." For Bacon, obtaining knowledge required that one observe nature itself, gather particular facts, and formulate generalizations from these findings. The importance of observation is seen in the following anecdote attributed to Bacon.

> In the year of our Lord 1432, there arose a grievous quarrel among the brethren over the number of teeth in the mouth of a horse. For 13 days the disputation raged without ceasing. All the ancient books and chronicles were fetched out, and wonderful and ponderous erudition, such as was never before heard of in this region, was made manifest. At the beginning of the 14th day, a youthful friar of goodly bearing asked his learned superiors for permission to add a word, and straightway, to the wonderment of the disputants, whose deep wisdom he sore vexed, he beseeched them to unbend in a manner coarse and unheard-of, and to look in the open mouth of a horse and find an answer to their questionings. At this, their dignity being grievously hurt, they waxed exceedingly wroth; and, joining in a mighty uproar, they flew upon him and smote him hip and thigh, and cast him out forthwith. For, said they, surely Satan hath tempted this bold neophyte to declare unholy and unheard-of ways of finding truth contrary to all the teachings of the fathers. After many days more of grievous strife the dove of peace sat on the assembly, and they as one man, declaring the problem to be an everlasting mystery because of a grievous dearth of historical and theological evidence thereof, so ordered the same writ down.[1]

The youth in this story was calling for a new way of seeking truth, namely, to seek the facts rather than depend upon authority or upon sheer speculation. This was to become the fundamental principle of all science.

In Bacon's system observations were made on particular events in a class, and then, on the basis of the observed events, inferences were made about the whole class. This approach is known as inductive reasoning, which is the reverse of the processes employed in the deductive method. The difference between deductive and inductive reasoning may be seen in the following examples:

A. Deductive: Every mammal has lungs.
　　　　　　　All rabbits are mammals.
　　　　　　　Therefore, every rabbit has lungs.
B. Inductive: Every rabbit that has ever been observed has lungs.
　　　　　　　Therefore, every rabbit has lungs.

Note that in deductive reasoning the premises must be known before a conclusion can be reached, but in inductive reasoning a conclusion is reached by observing examples and generalizing from the examples to the whole class. In order to be absolutely certain of an inductive conclusion, the investigator must observe all examples. This is known as perfect induction under the Baconian system; it requires that the investigator examine every example of a phenomenon. In the example

---

[1]Quoted from C. E. Kenneth Mees, "Scientific Thought and Social Reconstruction," *General Electric Review* 37 (1934)113–19.

above, to be absolutely sure that every rabbit had lungs, the investigator would have to have observations on all rabbits presently alive as well as all past and future rabbits. In practice this is usually not feasible; therefore one generally must rely on imperfect induction based on incomplete observation.

Inductive conclusions can be absolute only when the group about which they are asserted is small. For example, one might observe that all the red-haired pupils in a particular class make above-average grades in spelling, and could legitimately assert that the red-haired children presently enrolled in the class have above-average spelling grades. But one could not draw legitimate conclusions concerning the spelling grades of red-haired children in other classes or in one's future classes.

Since one can make perfect inductions only on small groups, we commonly use imperfect induction, a system in which one observes a sample of a group and infers from the sample what is characteristic of the entire group. An example of a conclusion based on imperfect induction is the present thinking concerning the physical characteristics of very intelligent children. For many years it was generally believed that exceptionally bright children were prone to be poor physical specimens. Even today cartoonists usually portray the bright child as a scrawny creature with thick spectacles. Terman, a pioneer in the field of mental testing, was interested in the characteristics of exceptionally bright youngsters.[2] He made an intensive study of over 1,000 California children who scored above 140 on the Stanford-Binet Intelligence Test. He found the average height, weight, and general physical health of these children to be slightly above average for children of their age. From this study it has been concluded that bright children, far from being the traditionally expected scrawny specimens, are a little more likely to be above average in physical development than children with average IQ scores.

Note that this conclusion has not been positively proved. It is simply highly probable that it is true. To be positively sure about this conclusion, one would have to have physical measures for all children with IQ scores of 140 or more on the Stanford-Binet. Even then one could only be positive about the characteristics of such children today and could not be 100 percent sure that the same would be true of such children in the future. Although imperfect induction does not enable us to reach infallible conclusions, it can provide reliable information upon which one can make reasonable decisions.

THE SCIENTIFIC APPROACH

Exclusive use of induction resulted in the accumulation of isolated knowledge and information that made little contribution to the advancement of knowledge. Furthermore, it was found that many problems could not be solved by induction alone. It was inevitable that scholars would soon learn to integrate the most important aspects of the inductive and deductive methods into a new technique, namely,

---

[2]Lewis M. Terman et al., *The Mental and Physical Traits of a Thousand Gifted Children*, vol. 1 (Stanford, Calif.: Stanford University Press, 1926).

the inductive-deductive method or the scientific approach. Charles Darwin, in the development of his theory of evolution, is generally recognized as the first to apply this method in the pursuit of knowledge. Darwin reports that he spent a long period of time making biological observations, hoping to establish some generalizations concerning evolution. He describes how he arrived at a new approach:

> My first note-book (on evolution) was opened in July 1837. I worked on true Baconian principles, and without any theory collected facts on a wholesale scale, more especially with respect to domesticated productions, by printed enquiries, by conversation with skillful breeders and gardeners, and by extensive reading. When I see the list of books of all kinds which I read and abstracted, including whole series of Journals and Transactions, I am surprised at my industry. I soon perceived that selection was the keystone of man's success in making useful races of animals and plants. But how selection would be applied to organisms living in a state of nature remained for some time a mystery to me.
>
> In October 1838, that is, fifteen months after I had begun my systematic enquiry, I happened to read for amusement "Malthus on Population," and being well prepared to appreciate the struggle for existence which everywhere goes on from long-continued observation of the habits of animals and plants, it at once struck me that under these circumstances favourable variations would tend to be preserved, and unfavourable ones to be destroyed. The result of this would be the formation of new species. Here then I had at last got a theory by which to work.[3]

Darwin's procedure, involving only observation, was unproductive until reading and further thought led him to formulate a tentative hypothesis to explain the facts that he had gathered through observation. He then proceeded to test this hypothesis by making deductions from it and gathering additional data to determine whether these data would support the hypothesis. From this method of inquiry, Darwin was able to develop his theory of evolution. This use of both inductive and deductive reasoning is characteristic of modern scientific inquiry, which is regarded as the most reliable method for obtaining knowledge.

The scientific approach is generally described as a process in which investigators move inductively from their observations to hypotheses and then deductively from the hypotheses to the logical implications of the hypotheses. They deduce the consequences that would follow if a hypothesized relationship is true. If these deduced implications are compatible with the organized body of accepted knowledge, they are then further tested by the gathering of empirical data. On the basis of the evidence, the hypotheses are accepted or rejected.

The use of the hypothesis is a principal difference between the scientific approach and inductive reasoning. In inductive reasoning one makes observations first and then organizes the information gained. In the scientific approach one reasons what one would find if a hypothesis is true and then makes systematic observations in order to confirm or fail to confirm the hypothesis.

It is generally considered helpful to present the scientific approach as a series of steps to be followed. The exact formulation of the steps will be found to vary from

[3]Francis Darwin, ed., *The Life and Letters of Charles Darwin,* vol. 1 (New York: Appleton, 1899), p. 68.

author to author. However, the names given to the steps are not important. What is important is to convey the idea that the scientific approach is a systematic process of inquiry involving interdependent parts. It is a method of inquiry that developed gradually over time and has been maintained because it has proved to be a successful method for understanding our complex natural world.

The five steps in the scientific approach are as follows:

Definition of the Problem

A scientific inquiry originates from a problem or a question in need of solution. In order to be subject to scientific investigation, a question must have one essential characteristic: It must be possible to formulate it in such a way that observation or experimentation in the natural world can provide an answer. Questions involving choice or values cannot be answered on the basis of factual information alone. Consider the question, Do children who are introduced to reading through the Initial Teaching Alphabet (i/t/a) score higher on reading achievement after they have made the transition to conventional letters and spelling than children who are introduced to reading through the sight method? This could be investigated empirically by comparing scores on a criterion of reading achievement for two groups who are equivalent except that one group was introduced to reading through i/t/a and the other, through sight reading. However, the question, Is training with i/t/a good for students? could not be investigated scientifically without knowing what ''good for students'' means or how to observe or measure ''goodness.'' Value judgments are out of place in science, so words that imply value judgments should not be included in the definition of a problem.

Statement of a Hypothesis

The next step is to formulate a hypothesis that provides a tentative explanation of the problem. This stage will require a review of the related literature and much further thought. Using the example above, one might hypothesize: Introducing reading through i/t/a produces greater reading achievement than introducing reading through the sight method.

Deductive Reasoning

Through the process of deductive reasoning, the implications of the suggested hypothesis—that is, what should be observed if the hypothesis is true—are determined. *If* it is true that introducing reading through i/t/a produces greater reading achievement than introducing reading through the sight method, *then* one should observe higher reading achievement scores among those students who were introduced to reading through i/t/a than among equivalent students who were introduced to reading through the sight method.

Collection and Analysis of Data

The hypothesis, or, more precisely, its deduced implications, is tested by collecting data relevant to it through observation, testing, and experimentation.

Confirmation or Rejection of the Hypothesis

Once the data have been collected, the results are analyzed in order to determine whether the investigation has produced evidence that supports the hypothesis. In the scientific approach one does not claim to prove the hypothesis; this would be dealing in terms of absolute truth, which is not characteristic of this approach. One merely concludes that the evidence does or does not support the hypothesis.

Although the various steps of the scientific approach are conceptually separable, it is well to remember that in practice they are closely related activities that will overlap continuously rather than always follow a rigid, strictly prescribed sequence.

AN EXAMPLE OF THE SCIENTIFIC APPROACH

Pirsig provides a vivid and succinct description of the scientific approach by comparing it to the process of maintaining a motorcycle in good working order:

> Two kinds of logic are used, inductive and deductive. Inductive inferences start with observations of the machine and arrive at general conclusions. For example, if the cycle goes over a bump and the engine misfires, and then goes over another bump and the engine misfires, and then goes over another bump and the engine misfires, and then goes over a long smooth stretch of road and there is no misfiring, and then goes over a fourth bump and the engine misfires again, one can logically conclude that the misfiring is caused by the bumps. That is induction: reasoning from particular experiences to general truths.
>
> Deductive inferences do the reverse. They start with general knowledge and predict a specific observation. For example, if, from reading the hierarchy of facts about the machine, the mechanic knows the horn of the cycle is powered exclusively by electricity from the battery, then he can logically infer that if the battery is dead the horn will not work. That is deduction.
>
> Solution of problems too complicated for common sense to solve is achieved by long strings of mixed inductive and deductive inferences that weave back and forth between the observed machine and the mental hierarchy of the machine found in the manuals. The correct program for this interweaving is formalized as scientific method.
>
> Actually I've never seen a cycle-maintenance problem complex enough really to require full-scale formal scientific method. Repair problems are not that hard. When I think of formal scientific method an image sometimes comes to mind of an enormous juggernaut, a huge bulldozer—slow, tedious, lumbering, laborious, but invincible. It takes twice as long, five times as long, maybe a dozen times as long as informal mechanic's techniques, but you know in the end you're going to *get* it. There's no fault isolation problem in motorcycle maintenance that can stand up to it. When you've hit a really tough one, tried everything, racked your brain and nothing works, and you know that this time Nature has really decided to be difficult, you say, "Okay, Nature, that's the end of the *nice* guy," and you crank up the formal scientific method.
>
> For this you keep a lab notebook. Everything gets written down, formally, so that you know at all times where you are, where you've been, where you're going and where you want to get. In scientific work and electronics technology this is necessary because otherwise the problems get so complex you get lost in them and confused and forget what you know and what you don't know and have to give up. In cycle maintenance things are not that involved, but when confusion starts it's a good idea to hold it down by making

everything formal and exact. Sometimes just the act of writing down the problems straightens out your head as to what they really are.

The logical statements entered into the notebook are broken down into six categories: (1) statement of the problem, (2) hypotheses as to the cause of the problem, (3) experiments designed to test each hypothesis, (4) predicted results of the experiments, (5) observed results of the experiments, and (6) conclusions from the results of the experiments. This is not different from the formal arrangement of many college and high-school lab notebooks but the purpose here is no longer just busywork. The purpose now is precise guidance of thoughts that will fail if they are not accurate.

The real purpose of scientific method is to make sure Nature hasn't misled you into thinking you know something you don't actually know. There's not a mechanic or scientist or technician alive who hasn't suffered from that one so much that he's not instinctively on guard. That's the main reason why so much scientific and mechanical information sounds so dull and so cautious. If you get careless or go romanticizing scientific information, giving it a flourish here and there, Nature will soon make a complete fool out of you. It does it often enough anyway even when you don't give it opportunities. One must be extremely careful and rigidly logical when dealing with Nature: one logical slip and an entire scientific edifice comes tumbling down. One false deduction about the machine and you can get hung up indefinitely.

In Part One of formal scientific method, which is the statement of the problem, the main skill is in stating absolutely no more than you are positive you know. It is much better to enter a statement "Solve Problem: Why doesn't cycle work?" which sounds dumb but is correct, than it is to enter a statement "Solve Problem: What is wrong with the electrical system?" when you don't absolutely *know* the trouble is *in* the electrical system. What you should state is "Solve Problem: What is wrong with cycle?" and *then* state as the first entry of Part Two: "Hypothesis Number One: The trouble is in the electrical system." You think of as many hypotheses as you can, then you design experiments to test them to see which are true and which are false.

This careful approach to the beginning questions keeps you from taking a major wrong turn which might cause you weeks of extra work or can even hang you up completely. Scientific questions often have a surface appearance of dumbness for this reason. They are asked in order to prevent dumb mistakes later on.

Part Three, that part of formal scientific method called experimentation, is sometimes thought of by romantics as all of science itself because that's the only part with much visual surface. They see lots of test tubes and bizarre equipment and people running around making discoveries. They do not see the experiment as part of a larger intellectual process and so they often confuse experiments with demonstrations, which look the same. A man conducting a gee-whiz science show with fifty thousand dollars' worth of Frankenstein equipment is not doing anything scientific if he knows beforehand what the results of his efforts are going to be. A motorcycle mechanic, on the other hand, who honks the horn to see if the battery works is informally conducting a true scientific experiment. He is testing a hypothesis by putting the question to nature. The TV scientist who mutters sadly, "The experiment is a failure; we have failed to achieve what we had hoped for," is suffering mainly from a bad scriptwriter. An experiment is never a failure solely because it fails to achieve predicted results. An experiment is a failure only when it also fails adequately to test the hypothesis in question, when the data it produces don't prove anything one way or another.

Skill at this point consists of using experiments that test only the hypothesis in question, nothing less, nothing more. If the horn honks, and the mechanic concludes that the whole electrical system is working, he is in deep trouble. He has reached an illogical conclusion. The honking horn only tells him that the battery and horn are working. To design an experiment properly he has to think very rigidly in terms of what directly causes what. This you know from the hierarchy. The horn doesn't make the cycle go. Neither does the battery, except in a very indirect way. The point at which the electrical system *directly* causes the engine to fire is at the spark plugs, and if you don't test here, at the output of the electrical system, you will never really know whether the failure is electrical or not.

To test properly the mechanic removes the plug and lays it against the engine so that the base around the plug is electrically grounded, kicks the starter lever and watches the spark-plug gap for a blue spark. If there isn't any he can conclude one of two things: (a) there is an electrical failure or (b) his experiment is sloppy. If he is experienced he will try it a few more times, checking connections, trying every way he can think of to get that plug to fire. Then, if he can't get it to fire, he finally concludes that *a* is correct, there's an electrical failure, and the experiment is over. He has proved that his hypothesis is correct.

In the final category, conclusions, skill comes in stating no more than the experiment has proved. It hasn't proved that when he fixes the electrical system the motorcycle will start. There may be other things wrong. But he does know that the motorcycle isn't going to run until the electrical system is working and he sets up the next formal question: "Solve problem: what is wrong with the electrical system?"

He then sets up hypotheses for these and tests them. By asking the right questions and choosing the right tests and drawing the right conclusions the mechanic works his way down the echelons of the motorcycle hierarchy until he has found the exact specific cause or causes of the engine failure, and then he changes them so that they no longer cause the failure.

An untrained observer will see only physical labor and often get the idea that physical labor is mainly what the mechanic does. Actually the physical labor is the smallest and easiest part of what the mechanic does. By far the greatest part of his work is careful observation and precise thinking. That is why mechanics sometimes seem so taciturn and withdrawn when performing tests. They don't like it when you talk to them because they are concentrating on mental images, hierarchies, and not really looking at you or the physical motorcycle at all. They are using the experiment as part of a program to expand their hierarchy of knowledge of the faulty motorcycle and compare it to the correct hierarchy in their mind. They are looking at underlying form.[4]

The Nature of Science

It might also be mentioned at this point that all sciences, though they may differ from one another in material or in specialized techniques, have in common this general method for arriving at reliable knowledge. It is this method of inquiry that determines whether a discipline is a science. Perhaps science is best described as a *method* of inquiry that permits investigators to examine the phenomena of interest to

[4]Robert M. Pirsig, *Zen and the Art of Motorcycle Maintenance: An Inquiry into Values* (New York: Morrow, 1974), pp. 107–11. Copyright © 1974 by Robert M. Pirsig and reprinted by permission of William Morrow & Company.

them. In addition to the method followed by scientists as they seek reliable knowledge, there are certain other aspects of the scientific approach, which we will examine briefly. These are (1) assumptions made by scientists, (2) attitudes of scientists, and (3) culmination of scientific theory in terms of theoretical formulations.

ASSUMPTIONS MADE BY SCIENTISTS

A fundamental assumption made by scientists is that the events they investigate are lawful or ordered—no event is capricious. Science is based upon the belief that all natural phenomena have antecedent factors, which can be found through observation. This assumption is sometimes referred to as universal determinism. Primitive people proposed supernatural causes for most of the events they observed. Modern science did not develop until people began to look beyond supernatural explanations and began to depend upon the observation of nature itself to provide answers.

This assumption underlies any statement that declares that under specified conditions certain events will occur. For example, the chemist is able to state that when a mixture of potassium chlorate and manganese dioxide is heated, oxygen will be produced. Behavioral scientists likewise assume that the behavior of organisms is lawful and predictable.

Related to this first assumption is the belief that the events in nature are, at least to a degree, orderly and regular and that this order and regularity of nature can be discovered through the scientific method.

A second assumption is that truth can ultimately be derived only from direct observation. Reliance upon empirical observation differentiates science from nonscience. The scientist does not depend upon authority as a source of truth but insists upon gathering the relevant evidence for himself. In the history of science we find many examples of scientists who rejected the prevailing notions of their day and proceeded with their observations and experimentation. Galileo's early experiments with falling bodies resulted in new knowledge that contradicted notions held by the authorities of his day.

A corollary of this assumption is the belief that only phenomena that can actually be seen to exist are within the realm of scientific investigation.

ATTITUDES OF SCIENTISTS

Scientists recognize certain characteristic attitudes which they acquire as they pursue their work.

1. Scientists are essentially doubters, who maintain a highly skeptical attitude toward the data of science. Findings are regarded as tentative and are not accepted by scientists unless they can be verified. Verification requires that others must be able to repeat the observations and obtain the same results. Scientists want to test opinions and questions concerning the relationships among natural phenomena.

Furthermore, they make their testing procedures known to others in order that they may verify, or fail to verify, their findings.

2. Scientists are objective and impartial. In conducting observations and interpreting data, scientists are not trying to prove a point. They take particular care to collect data in such a way that any personal biases they may have will not influence their observations. They seek truth and accept the facts even when they are contrary to their own opinions. If the accumulated evidence upsets a favorite theory, then they either discard that theory or modify it to agree with the factual data.

3. Scientists deal with facts, not values. They do not indicate any potential moral implications of their findings; they do not make decisions for us about what is good or what is bad. Scientists provide data concerning the relationship that exists between events, but we must go beyond these scientific data if we want a decision about whether or not a certain consequence is desirable. Thus, while the findings of science may be of key importance in the solution of a problem involving a value decision, the data themselves do not furnish that value judgment.

4. Scientists are not satisfied with isolated facts but seek to integrate and systematize their findings. They want to put the things known into an orderly system. Thus scientists aim for theories that attempt to bring together empirical findings into a meaningful pattern. However, they regard these theories as tentative or provisional, subject to revision as new evidence is found.

SCIENTIFIC THEORY

The last aspect of the scientific approach to be considered is the construction of theory. Scientists, through empirical investigation, gather many facts. But as these facts accumulate, there is need for integration, organization, and classification in order to make the isolated findings meaningful. Significant relationships must be identified in the data and explained. In other words, theories must be formulated. A theory is defined as ''a set of interrelated constructs (concepts), definitions, and propositions that presents a systematic view of phenomena by specifying relations among variables, with the purpose of explaining and predicting the phenomena.''[5]

Theories knit together the results of observations, enabling scientists to make general statements about variables and the relationships among variables. For example, it can be observed that if pressure is held constant, hydrogen gas expands when its temperature is increased from 20° to 40° C. It can be observed that if pressure is held constant, oxygen gas contracts when its temperature is decreased from 60° to 50° C. A familiar theory, Charles's law, summarizes the observed effects of temperature changes on the volumes of all gases by the statement, When pressure is held constant, as the temperature of a gas is increased its volume is increased and as the temperature of a gas is decreased its volume is decreased. The theory not only summarizes previous information but predicts other phenomena by telling us what to expect of any gas under any temperature change.

[5]Fred N. Kerlinger, *Foundations of Behavioral Research,* 2nd ed. (New York: Holt, Rinehart and Winston, 1973), p. 9.

The ultimate goal of science is theory formation. This statement will sound strange to those who think of theory as vague conjecture or impractical speculation. However, a scientific theory is a tentative explanation of phenomena. From such explanations we can proceed to prediction and, finally, to control. As soon as a statement (theory) could be made about the relationship between the *Anopheles* mosquito and malaria in humans, we could (1) explain why malaria was endemic in some areas and not in others, (2) predict how changes in the environment would be accompanied by changes in the incidence of malaria, and (3) control malaria by making changes in the environment. Although the basic goal of science is theory building, scientific endeavor provides (1) explanation, (2) prediction, and (3) control.

Types of Theories

A theory that is developed primarily to explain previous observations is known as an inductive theory. For example, after a series of experiments concerning memory, Ebbinghaus summarized his observations by stating that the proportion of material remembered can be described as a decelerating curve (shown in Figure 1.1), in which the initial rate of forgetting is more rapid than the rate at later stages.[6]

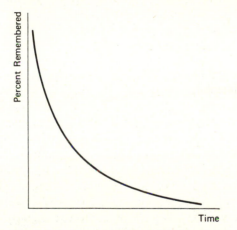

Figure 1.1   General outline of Ebbinghaus's curve

Although Ebbinghaus's observations were limited to one subject, himself, his theory has been confirmed by subsequent investigations.

A theory that is developed when little or no observations have been made concerning the phenomena is classified as a hypothetical-deductive theory. It typically consists of a set of hypotheses, which form a deductive system. That is, the theory is composed of a set of hypothetical propositions and then a series of deductions logically derived from the higher-order hypotheses. Such theories can be generated

[6]H. Ebbinghaus, *Memory,* trans. H. A. Ruger and C. E. Bussenius (New York: Teachers College, Columbia University, 1913). First published in German in 1885.

in a number of ways. One method is to deduce what would be the state of affairs if a relationship in one class of phenomena were also true in another class of phenomena. For example, it is known that mammalian embryos begin as a single cell, resembling the most primitive form of animal life, and pass through stages resembling the evolutionary progress of their species. The theory summarizing these phenomena states that the embryonic development of the young of a species re-capitulates the history of that species. It has been hypothesized that a similar theory would account for the social growth of children, and thus the recapitulation theory of child development was formed, which stated that the growth of social behavior in children would follow the social history of mankind; that is, in the early stages of their development children would behave like savages and then progress through barbarian and half-civilized stages on their way toward becoming civilized. (Despite the descriptions of classes one frequently hears in teachers' lounges, the recapitula-tion theory of child development has not proved useful in explaining the social growth of children and seems to have been abandoned.)

Most theories are neither purely inductive nor purely hypothetical-deductive but are formed when some observations have been made and a theory is needed to summarize these observations and to guide future observations.

Purposes of Theories

There are several purposes to be served by theory in the development of a science. In the first place, theory summarizes and puts in order the existing knowl-edge in a particular area. A theory of learning, for instance, brings together in a consistent manner the results of many separate investigations into the learning process. Furthermore, a theory clarifies and gives meaning to the previously isolated empirical findings.

Theory provides a provisional explanation for observed events and relationships. It does so by showing what variables are related and how they are related. A theory of learning would explain the relationship among the speed and efficiency of learn-ing and such variables as motivation, reward, practice, and so on. On the basis of the explanatory principles embodied within the theory, deductions from the theory permit prediction of the occurrence of phenomena, some as yet unobserved. From theory astronomers predicted the existence of the outermost planets long before they were actually observed.

Theory stimulates the development of new knowledge by providing leads for further inquiry. From the theory the scientist makes deductions about what will happen in certain situations under specified conditions. From reinforcement theory one could make a deduction concerning the effects of rewarding a response regu-larly versus occasionally. These deductions provide hypotheses for scientific studies, the outcome of which leads to acceptance, rejection, or modification of the theories they were designed to test. In this way scientists use what they know as a springboard for new advances. Conant says that ''the history of science dem-onstrates beyond a doubt that the really revolutionary and significant advances come not from empiricism but from new theories.''[7]

[7]James B. Conant, *Modern Science and Modern Man* (New York: Garden City Books, 1953), p. 53.

It can be seen that the relationship between fact and theory is one of reciprocal contribution. A theory can be built from observed facts and must, in turn, be tested by further observed facts. A theory is verified through evidence gathered by observation or experimentation. Thus the scientist uses facts both as the building blocks for theory and as a way of verifying the theory. Theory stimulates and guides scientific inquiry and explains the meaning of its findings; scientific inquiry, on the other hand, serves to test existing theories and to provide a basis for the development of new ones. Furthermore, this two-way relationship is a continuing one; the investigations that are stimulated by theory may raise new theoretical issues, which in turn lead to further investigations, and so on. As Conant says, ''Science is an interconnected series of concepts and conceptual schemes that have developed as a result of experimentation and observation and are fruitful of further experimentation and observations . . . emphasis is on the word 'fruitful.' ''[8]

Characteristics of Theories

A theory, if it is to serve its purpose in science, must satisfy certain criteria. The following are some of the characteristics of a sound theory:

1. A theory must be able to explain the observed facts relating to a particular problem; it must be able to propose the ''why'' concerning the phenomena under consideration. This explanation of the events should be in the simplest form possible. A theory that has fewer complexities and assumptions is favored over a more complicated one. This statement is known as the principle of parsimony.

2. A theory must be consistent with observed facts and with the already established body of knowledge. We look for the theory that provides the most probable or the most efficient way of accounting for the accumulated facts.

3. A theory must provide means for its verification. That is, a theory must permit deductions to be made in the form of hypotheses that state the consequences that one can expect to observe if the theory is true. The scientist can then investigate or test these hypotheses empirically in order to determine whether the data support the theory. It must be emphasized that it is inappropriate to speak of the truth or falsity of a theory. The acceptance or rejection of a theory depends primarily upon its *utility*. A theory is useful or not useful, depending upon how efficiently it leads to predictions concerning observable consequences, which are then confirmed when the empirical data are collected. Even then, any theory is considered tentative and subject to revision as new evidence accumulates.

4. A theory should stimulate new discoveries and indicate further areas in need of investigation.

The goal of theory formation has been achieved to a far greater extent in the physical sciences than in the social sciences, which is not surprising since they are older sciences. In the early days of a science the emphasis, typically, is upon empiricism. Scientists are concerned with collecting facts in particular problem areas. Only with maturity does science begin to integrate the isolated knowledge into a theoretical framework.

Education in particular has suffered from an absence of theoretical orientations;

---

[8]James B. Conant, *Science and Common Sense* (New Haven: Yale University Press, 1951), p. 25.

the main emphasis has been upon empiricism. Educators have been critized for their continued concern with ''getting the facts'' rather than finding out the ''why.'' This concern is reflected in the vast number of facts that have been accumulated through educational studies, but without the accompanying integration into theories to help explain educational phenomena. Education needs to focus more attention on theory development in order to obtain more perspective into educational problems as well as to guide its efforts at the empirical level.

Although there are marked differences in the number and power of the theories that have been established in the physical and social sciences, theory has the same role to play in the progress of any science. Regardless of the subject matter, theory works in essentially the same way. It serves to summarize existing knowledge, to explain observed events and relationships, and to predict the occurrence of unobserved events and relationships. It can be said that theories represent our best efforts to understand the basic structure of the world in which we live.

LIMITATIONS OF THE SCIENTIFIC APPROACH IN THE SOCIAL SCIENCES

In spite of their use of the scientific approach and accumulation of a large quantity of reliable knowledge, education and the other social sciences have not attained the scientific status typical of the natural sciences. The social sciences have not been able to establish generalizations equivalent to the theories of the natural sciences in scope of explanatory power or in capacity to yield precise predictions. Frequently there is lack of agreement among researchers in the social sciences as to what the established facts are or what explanations are satisfactory for the assumed facts. Perhaps the social sciences will never realize the objectives of science as completely as the natural sciences. Certainly it must be stressed that the use of the scientific approach is not in itself a sufficient condition for scientific achievement. There are several limitations involved in the application of the scientific approach in education and the other social sciences.

Complexity of Subject Matter

A major obstacle is the inherent complexity of subject matter in the social sciences. Natural scientists deal with physical and biological phenomena. A limited number of variables that can be measured precisely are involved in the explanation of many of these phenomena and it is possible to establish universal laws. For example, Boyle's law on the influence of pressure on the volume of gases, which deals with relatively uncomplicated variables, formulates relations between phenomena that are apparently unvarying throughout the universe.

On the other hand, social scientists deal with the human subject. They are concerned with the subject's behavior and development both as an individual and as a member of a group. There are so many variables, acting independently and in interaction, that must be considered in any attempt to understand complex human behavior. Each individual is unique in the way he or she develops, in mental equipment, in social and emotional behavior, and in total personality. The behavior of humans in groups and the influence of the behavior of group members on an individual must also be dealt with by social scientists. A group of first graders in one situation will not behave like the first graders in another situation. There are learners, teachers, and environments, each with variables that contribute to the behavioral phenomena observed in a setting. Thus researchers must be extremely cautious about making generalizations, since the data obtained in one group situation may not be valid for other groups and other settings.

Difficulties in Observation

Observation, the *sine qua non* of science, is more difficult in the social sciences than in the natural sciences. Observation in the social sciences is more subjective because it more frequently involves interpretation on the part of the observers. For example, the subject matter for investigation is often a person's responses to the behavior of others. Motives, values, and attitudes are not open to inspection. Observers must make subjective interpretations when they decide that behaviors observed indicate the presence of any particular motive, value, or attitude. The problem is that social scientists' *own* values and attitudes may influence both the observations and the assessment of the findings on which they base their conclusions. Natural scientists study phenomena that require less subjective interpretation.

Difficulties in Replication

The chemist can objectively observe the reaction between two chemicals in a test tube. The findings can be reported and the observations can be easily replicated by others. This replication is much more difficult to achieve in the social sciences. An American educator cannot reproduce the conditions of a Russian educator's experimental teaching method with the same precision of replication as that with which an American chemist can reproduce a Russian chemist's experiment. Even within a single school building one cannot reproduce a given situation in its entirety and with precision. Social phenomena are singular events and cannot be repeated for purposes of observation.

Interaction of Observer and Subjects

An additional problem is that mere observation of social phenomena may produce changes that might not have occurred otherwise. Researchers may think that X is causing Y, when in fact it may be their observation of X that causes Y. For example, in the well-known Hawthorne experiments changes in the productivity of workers were found to be due not to the varying working conditions but to the mere fact that the workers knew they had been singled out for investigation. Investigators are human beings and their presence as observers in a situation may change the behavior of their human subjects. The use of hidden cameras and tape recorders may help minimize this interaction in some cases, but much of social science research includes the responses of human subjects to human observers.

Difficulties in Control

The range of possibilities for controlled experiments on human subjects is much more limited than in the natural sciences. The complexities involved in research on human subjects present problems in control that are unparalleled in the natural sciences. In the latter, rigid control of experimental conditions is possible in the laboratory. Such control is not possible with human subjects; the social scientists must deal with many variables simultaneously and must work under conditions that are much less precise. They try to identify and control as many of these variables as possible, but the task is sometimes very difficult.

Problems of Measurement

Experimentation must provide for measurement of the factors involved. The tools for measurement in the social sciences are much less perfect and precise than the tools of the natural sciences. We have nothing that can compare with the precision of the ruler, the thermometer, or the numerous laboratory instruments. We have already pointed out that an understanding of human behavior is complicated by the large number of determining variables acting independently and in interaction. The multivariate statistical devices available for analyzing data in the social sciences take care of relatively few of the factors that obviously are interacting. Furthermore, these devices permit one to attribute the variance only to factors operating at the time of measurement. Factors that have influenced development in the past are not measurable in the present, and yet they have significantly influenced the course of development.

Since social science research is complicated by these factors, researchers must exercise caution in making generalizations from their studies. It will often be necessary to conduct several studies in an area before attempting to formulate generalizations. If initial findings are consistently confirmed, then one would have more confidence in making broad generalizations.

Despite the handicaps, education and the social sciences have made great progress, and their scientific status can be expected to increase as scientific investigation and methodology become more systematic and rigorous.

The Nature of Research

At this point, it may be well to ask the question, What is research? Research may be defined as the application of the scientific approach to the study of a problem. It is a way to acquire dependable and useful information. Its purpose is to discover answers to meaningful questions through the application of scientific procedures. An investigation must involve the scientific approach that has been described in the previous section in order to be classified as research. Although it may take place in different settings and may utilize different methods, research is universally a systematic and objective search for reliable knowledge.

EDUCATIONAL RESEARCH

When the scientific approach is applied to the study of educational problems, educational research is the result. Educational research is the way in which one acquires dependable and useful information about the educative process. Travers defines educational research as ''an activity directed toward the development of an organized body of scientific knowledge about the events with which educators are concerned.''[9] Its goal is to discover general principles or interpretations of behavior that can be used to explain, predict, and control events in educational situations—in other words, scientific theory.

The acceptance of the scientific approach in education and the other social sciences has lagged far behind its acceptance in the physical sciences. In 1897 Rice, a pioneer in educational research, found himself in a situation similar to that described in the quotation attributed to Bacon. Rice asked the educators at the annual meeting of the Department of Superintendence if it would be possible to determine whether students who are given forty minutes of spelling each day learn more than students given ten minutes each day. He reports:

> . . . to my great surprise, the question threw consternation into the camp. The first to respond was a very popular professor of psychology engaged in training teachers in the West. He said, in effect, that the question was one which could never be answered; and he gave me a rather severe drubbing for taking up the time of such an important body of educators in asking them silly questions.[10]

Rice did, in fact, collect empirical evidence on his question and found that the differences in achievement between those spending ten minutes a day and those spending forty minutes a day were negligible. He also pointed out that many of the words children had to learn to spell were of little practical value. His work led other investigators, such as Edward L. Thorndike, to use documentary analysis to determine the frequency of use of words in our language. Their work in turn led to improvements in our language arts texts and curricula.

Even in our own time we find educators who deny that there is a systematic body of knowledge in education. In 1966 a college president, explaining that there would be no education courses in his college, declared, ''We would love to teach education if we could find anyone who knew anything about it. This would be the greatest breakthrough since the time of the Greeks.''[11]

However, although educational research is a young science, it has made progress since its beginnings in the late nineteenth century. The American government appropriated $269 million for research in education in fiscal 1978. Although this sum is minuscule in relation to the appropriations for defense research and other research endeavors, it does demonstrate that educational research is no longer only a spare-time activity.

[9]Robert M. W. Travers, *An Introduction to Educational Research,* 3rd ed. (New York: Macmillan, 1969), p. 5.

[10]Joseph M. Rice, *Scientific Management in Education* (New York: Hinds, Noble and Eldredge, 1912), pp. 17–18.

[11]Ronald C. Nairn, as quoted in *Time*, September 23, 1966, p. 43.

As a science, educational research uses investigative methods that are consistent with the basic procedure and operating conceptions of science. As such, research involves a number of stages.

TYPICAL STAGES IN RESEARCH

Selecting a Problem

Researchers begin with a question that, to them, deals with issues of sufficient consequence to warrant investigation. It must be a question that can be answered through scientific investigation. It must be a question for which the answer is not already available, but for which the means for finding answers through collecting and analyzing data are available.

There are meaningful questions that cannot be answered through the use of scientific procedures. Should we provide sex education in the elementary school? is an example of this type of question; the answer is a matter of belief and values. As was mentioned earlier, research would not provide a direct answer to this type of question.

Analytical Stage

After the problem has been identified, the next stage is the analytical phase of the study which requires an exhaustive study of all previous research that may have been done on the problem. This review of related research is necessary to give insight into the problem and to provide a background for formulating the hypothesis of the study, which is the prominent feature of the analytic phase. The best guide to an intelligent hypothesis is careful analysis of the available data bearing on the problem.

In this stage the researchers crystallize the definitions of the terms they will use.

Selecting Research Strategy and Developing Instruments

The problem will indicate the research method to follow. Certain problems require experimentation; others may be attacked with one of the descriptive strategies. Choice of the research method then influences the details of the design of the study and of the procedures for measuring variables. Instruments for measuring variables may already be available as standardized instruments or they may have to be developed by the researcher.

Collecting and Interpreting the Data

The deduced consequences of the hypotheses of the study must be tested. This stage therefore involves data collection, which includes the routine aspects of administering instruments, keeping records, scheduling, and so on. Contrary to popular belief, this stage usually takes much less time than the previous planning stages of a study.

After collection, data must then be analyzed, usually statistically, and appropriate interpretations made of the findings.

Reporting the Results

Researchers must make their procedures, findings, and conclusions available in an intelligible form to others who may be interested. This involves a clear, concise presentation of the steps in the study.

Each of the foregoing stages of a research study is discussed in detail in later chapters of this volume. It is probably rare for researchers to follow such a rigid sequence as described in the preceding paragraphs. These activities overlap continuously and there may be a moving back and forth from one stage to another. Often a review of the literature may change the investigators' view of a problem, and the problem and hypotheses may have to be restated.

QUESTIONS ASKED BY EDUCATIONAL RESEARCHERS

The specific question chosen for research will, of course, depend upon the area that interests the researchers, their background, and the particular problem confronting them. However, we may classify questions in educational research as theoretical, that is, having to do with fundamental principles; or practical, that is, designed to solve immediate problems of the everyday situation.

Theoretical Questions

Questions of a theoretical nature are those asking, What is it? or How does it occur? or Why does it occur? In educational research the "what" questions are formulated more specifically as, What is intelligence? or What is creativity? Typical "how" questions are, How does the child learn? or How does personality develop? "Why" questions might ask, Why does one forget? Why are some children more achievement-oriented than other children?

Research with a theoretical orientation may be directed toward either developing theories or testing existing theories. The former involves a type of study in which researchers attempt to discover generalizations about behavior with the aim of clarifying the nature of the relationships existing among variables. They may believe that certain variables are related and thus conduct their research in order to describe the nature of the relationship. From the findings they may begin to formulate a theory about the phenomenon. Theories of learning have been developed in this way as investigators have been able to show the relationships among certain methods, individual and environmental variables, and the efficiency of the learning process.

Probably more common in educational research are studies that aim to test already existing theories. It may be overambitious, especially for beginning researchers in education, to have as a goal the development of a theory. It is usually more realistic to attempt to deduce hypotheses from existing theories of learning, personality, motivation, and so forth, and to test these hypotheses. If the hypotheses are logical deductions from the theory, and the empirical tests provide evidence that supports the hypotheses, then this evidence also provides support for the theory itself.

Practical Questions

Many questions in educational research are of a directly practical nature, aimed at solving specific problems that may be encountered by educators in their everyday activities. They are relevant questions for educational research because they deal with actual problems at the level of practice. Such questions are, How effective is programmed instruction in teaching second grade spelling? or What is the effect of using the i/t/a on reading achievement in first grade? or What is the relative effectiveness of the problem-discussion method as compared with the lecture method in teaching high school social studies? The answers to such questions may be quite valuable in helping teachers make practical decisions.

These practical questions can be investigated just as scientifically as the theoretical problems. The two types of questions are differentiated primarily on the basis of the goals they help to achieve rather than the level of sophistication of the study.

BASIC AND APPLIED RESEARCH

Another system of classification is sometimes used for the research dealing with these two types of questions. The classification is based on the goal or objective of the research. The first type of research—which has as its aim obtaining the empirical data that can be used to formulate, expand, or evaluate theory—is called basic research. This type of study is not oriented in design or purpose toward the solution of practical problems. Its essential aim is to expand the frontiers of knowledge without regard to practical application. Of course, the findings may eventually be applied to practical problems that have social value. For example, advances in the practice of medicine are dependent upon basic research in biochemistry and microbiology. Likewise, progress in educational practice has been related to progress in the discovery of general laws through basic psychological, educational, and sociological research.

The primary concern of basic research, however, is the discovery of knowledge solely for the sake of knowledge. Its design is not hampered by considerations of the social usefulness of the findings.

The second type of research, which aims to solve an immediate practical problem, is referred to as applied research. It is research performed in relation to actual problems and under the conditions in which they are found in practice. Through applied research, educators are often able to solve their problems at the appropriate level of complexity, that is, in the classroom teaching-learning situation. We may depend upon basic research for the discovery of the more general laws of learning, but applied research must be conducted in order to determine how these laws operate in the classroom. This approach is essential if scientific changes in teaching practices are to be effected. Unless educators undertake to solve their own practical problems of this type, no one else will.

It should be pointed out that applied research also uses the scientific method of inquiry. We find that there is not always a sharp line of demarcation between basic and applied research. Certainly applications are made from theory to help in the solution of practical problems. We attempt to apply the theories of learning in the classroom. On the other hand, basic research may depend upon the findings of applied research to complete its theoretical formulations. A classroom learning experiment could shed some light on learning theory. Furthermore, observations in a practical situation serve to test theories and may lead to the formulation of new theories.

Research Methodologies in Education

Research method refers to the general strategy followed in gathering and analyzing the data necessary for answering the question at hand. It is the plan of attack for the problem under investigation.

Four generally used categories for classifying educational research are:

1. Experimental: "a scientific investigation in which an investigator manipulates and controls one or more independent variables and observes the dependent variable or variables for variation concomitant to the manipulation of the independent variables."[12] Its major purpose is to determine what may be.
2. Ex post facto: similar to the experimental research except the investigator cannot directly manipulate the independent variables.
3. Descriptive: "describes and interprets what is. It is concerned with conditions or relationships that exist; practices that prevail; beliefs, points of view, or attitudes that are held; processes that are going on; effects that are being felt; or trends that are developing."[13] Its major purpose is to tell what is.
   There are several subcategories of descriptive research:

   a. Case studies
   b. Surveys
   c. Developmental studies
   d. Follow-up studies
   e. Documentary analysis
   f. Trend studies
   g. Correlational studies

4. Historical: "involves a procedure supplementary to observation, a process by which the historian seeks to test the truthfulness of the reports of observations made by others."[14] Its major purpose is to tell what was.

None of these methods is necessarily superior to the others. The method used in a research study is dictated by the nature of the problem and the kinds of data required. Often there is a logical order in which one type of research will follow another. Sometimes researchers may profitably begin with a historical study to ascertain what has been done in the past. Next a descriptive study would supply information on the current status of the problem in education. With this background,

[12]Kerlinger, *Foundations of Behavioral Research*, p. 315.
[13]John W. Best, *Research in Education*, 2nd ed. (Englewood Cliffs, N.J.: Prentice-Hall, 1970), p. 315.
[14]Travers, *Introduction to Educational Research*, p. 183.

the researchers could begin experimentation to determine the relationship among variables that may have been suggested by the other types of research.

The Language of Research

Any scientific discipline has need for a specific language for describing and summarizing the observations in that area. Scientists need terms at the empirical level in order to describe particular observations; they also need terms at the theoretical level for referring to hypothetical processes that may not be subject to direct observation. Scientists may use words taken from everyday language, but they often ascribe to them new and specific meanings not commonly found in ordinary usage. Or perhaps they must introduce new technical terms that are not a part of the everyday language. The purpose of this section is to introduce the reader to some of the general terms used in educational research.

The terms that scientists use at both the descriptive and theoretical levels are labels for concepts and constructs.

CONCEPTS AND CONSTRUCTS

A concept is an abstraction from observed events; it is a word that represents the similarities or common aspects of objects or events that are otherwise quite different from one another. Words such as *chair, dog, tree, liquid,* and thousands of others in our language represent common aspects of otherwise diverse things. The purpose of a concept is to simplify thinking by including a number of events under one general heading. Some concepts are quite close to the events they represent. Thus, for example, the meaning of the concept *tree* may be easily illustrated by pointing to specific trees. The concept is an abstraction of the characteristics all trees have in common—characteristics that are directly observable.

However, terms such as *motivation, justice,* and *problem-solving ability* cannot be easily illustrated by pointing to specific objects or events. These higher-level abstractions are referred to as constructs. People have put together or constructed more complex abstractions from their concepts. In the same way that we construct a house by putting together wood and other materials in a purposeful pattern, we create constructs by combining concepts and less complex constructs in purposeful patterns. For example, such concepts as visual acuity, symbol discrimination, left-to-right orientation, listening vocabulary, and others are combined in a purposeful manner to produce the construct *reading readiness*. Constructs are useful in interpreting empirical data and in building theory. They are used to account for observed regularities and relationships.

Constructs are created in order to summarize observations and to provide explanations. A construct is abandoned when a better way of explaining and summarizing observations replaces it. For example, the observations that (*a*) some materials burn while others do not and (*b*) some materials burn more intensely than others were once summarized by the construct *phlogiston,* which was believed to be a necessary constituent of all combustible materials which was released in the burning process. This construct was abandoned when more useful explanations of the process of burning were developed.

SPECIFICATION OF MEANING

The further removed one's concepts or constructs are from the empirical facts or phenomena they are intended to represent, the greater the possibility for misunderstanding and the greater the need for precise definition. The meaning of the words in the scientist's vocabulary must be established. Concepts must be defined both in abstract terms, which give the general meaning they are supposed to have, and in terms of the operations by which they will be measured in the particular study. Margenau[15] calls the former type of definition a constitutive definition; the latter is known as an operational definition.

Constitutive Definition

A constitutive definition refers to a more formal type of definition in which a term is defined by using other terms. For example, intelligence is defined as the ability to think abstractly. This type of definition helps to convey the general nature of the phenomenon in which the investigator is interested, as well as to show its relation to other studies using similar concepts and to theory. A constitutive definition elucidates a term and perhaps gives one some insight into the phenomenon described by the term. However, if one is to carry out research, one must translate concepts into observable events.

Operational Definition

An operational definition is one which ascribes meaning to a concept or construct by specifying the operations that must be performed in order to measure the concept. This type of definition is essential in research since data must be collected in terms of observable events. Scientists may deal on a theoretical level with constructs such as learning, motivation, anxiety, or achievement, but before they can study them empirically, they have to decide on some kinds of observable events to represent those constructs. When defining a concept or construct operationally, scientists choose discriminable events as indicators of the abstract concept and devise operations to obtain data relevant to the concept.

An operational definition thus refers to the operations by which investigators may measure a concept. For example, intelligence quotient may be defined operationally as the scores on the X intelligence test. Achievement may be defined as the scores on the X achievement test. An operational definition of creativity may refer to the scores made on the Minnesota Test of Creativity, and so on.

[15]H. Margenau, *The Nature of Physical Reality* (New York: McGraw-Hill, 1950).

Although investigators are guided by their own experience and knowledge and the reports of other investigators, the operational definition of a concept is to some extent an arbitrary procedure. Often we choose from a variety of possible operational definitions those that best represent our approach to the problem. Certainly an operational definition does not exhaust the full scientific meaning of any concept. It is very specific in meaning; its purpose is to delimit a term, to insure that everyone concerned understands the particular way in which a term is being used. Operational definitions are considered adequate if their procedures gather data that constitute acceptable indicators of the concepts they are intended to represent. Often it is a matter of opinion as to whether or not this result has been achieved.

Operational definitions are essential to research because they permit investigators to measure abstract concepts and constructs and permit scientists to move from the level of constructs and theory to the level of observation, upon which science is based. By using operational definitions, researchers are able to proceed with investigations that might not otherwise be possible. It is important to remember that, although researchers report their findings in terms of abstract constructs and relate these to other research and to theory, what they have actually found is a relationship between two sets of observable and measurable data that were selected to represent the constructs. For example, an investigation of the relation of the construct creativity and the construct intelligence in practice will relate scores on an intelligence test to scores on a measure of creativity.

VARIABLES

A variable is an attribute, which is regarded as reflecting or expressing some concept or construct. A variable takes on different values. Height is one example of a variable; it can vary in an individual from one time to another, between individuals at the same time, between the averages for groups, and so on. Social class, sex, vocabulary level, intelligence quotient, and spelling test scores are other examples of variables. Educational researchers are interested in determining how such variables are related to one another. In a study concerned with the relation of vocabulary level to science achievement among eighth graders, the variables of interest would be the measures of vocabulary and the measures of science achievement. The concept of grade level, although by definition a variable, is not in this study a variable since all subjects are eighth graders. Thus the concepts that are of interest in a study become the variables for investigation.

When subjects are classified by sorting them into groups, the attribute on which the classification is based is termed a *categorical variable*. Home language, county of residence, father's principal occupation, and school in which enrolled are examples of categorical variables. The simplest type of categorical variable has only two classes and is called a *dichotomous variable*. Male-female, citizen-alien, pass-fail are dichotomous variables. Some categorical variables have more than two classes; some examples are educational level, religious affiliation, state of birth.

Other attributes are termed *continuous variables*. A continuous variable can take on an infinite number of values within a range. As a child grows in height from 40 inches to 41 inches, he or she passes through an infinite number of heights. Height, weight, age, and distance are examples of continuous variables.

Types of Variables

There are several ways to classify variables. The most important classification is on the basis of their *use* within the research under consideration, when they are classified as independent variables or dependent variables.

Some variables are antecedent to other variables. We may know this empirically or we may hypothesize on the basis of some theory that one variable is antecedent to another. For instance, to be able to read, it is presumed, an individual needs to have some degree of intelligence. That is, the variable *intelligence* is antecedent to the variable *reading*. To a certain extent reading ability is a consequence of the variable *intelligence;* it is dependent upon the individual's intelligence level. In research, variables that are a consequence of or dependent upon antecedent variables are called *dependent variables*. Variables that are antecedent to the dependent variable are called *independent variables*. For example, a child's height (dependent variable) would be dependent to a certain extent upon his age (independent variable). We often use these terms even in the absence of empirical or theoretical reasons for considering one to be the antecedent and the other to be the consequence. They are used to indicate the direction of prediction—from the individual's position on the independent variable to his or her position on the dependent variable.

In research studies the dependent variable is the phenomenon that is the object of study and investigation. It is the one that must always be assessed. The independent variable is the factor that is measurably separate and distinct from the dependent variable, but may relate to the dependent variable. Many factors that may function as independent variables—such as social class, home environment, and classroom conditions—are discriminable aspects of the environment. In addition, such personal characteristics as, for example, age, sex, intelligence, and motivation may be independent variables that can be related to the dependent variable.

Later, when we discuss the experimental method of research, we will define the independent variable as the variable that is manipulated or changed by the experimenters. The variable upon which the effects of the manipulation are observed is called the dependent variable. It is so named because its value depends upon and varies with the value of the independent variable. For example, to study the relative effectiveness of programmed instruction, as opposed to drill, in teaching spelling, the investigators manipulate the method of instruction, the independent variable, and then observe the effect upon spelling achievement, the dependent variable. After the relationship between the variables has been established through research, one may predict *from* an independent variable *to* the dependent variable. In educational research, teaching methods and procedures are probably the most frequently used independent variables. Others include age, sex, social class, attitudes, intelligence, and motivation. The most common dependent variable is school achievement or learning.

It is possible for a variable to be an independent variable in one study and a dependent variable in another. Whether a variable is considered independent or dependent depends upon the purpose of the study. If the effect of motivation on achievement is investigated, then motivation is considered the independent variable. However, if one wished to determine the effect of testing procedures, classroom grouping arrangements, or grading procedures on students' motivation, then motivation becomes the dependent variable. Intelligence is generally treated as an independent variable since we are interested in its effect on learning, the dependent variable. However, in studies investigating the effect of nursery school experience on the intellectual development of children, intelligence is the dependent variable.

A classification of independent variables can be made on the basis of whether or not the independent variable is one that can be manipulated by the investigators. According to this classification, there are two types of variables, active and attribute.

An active variable is defined as one that can be directly manipulated by the researchers. For instance, method of teaching, method of grouping, and reinforcement procedures are all variables that can be manipulated and are thus called active variables.

An attribute variable is one that cannot be actively manipulated by the researchers. Such variables, sometimes called assigned variables, are characteristics of individuals and cannot be manipulated at will. For example, aptitude, sex, race, age, and social class are typical attribute variables. Investigators can incorporate attribute variables into their research by assigning subjects to groups on the basis of such preexisting variables.

History of Educational Research

Educational research as a discipline is a fairly recent development—it is less than 80 years old. You may recall that the scientific era began in the physical sciences in the seventeenth and eighteenth centuries. But it was not until near the end of the nineteenth century that education began to take on the methodology of science. The late emergence of education as a science was due not only to the complexity of the phenomena to be studied, but also to the slow progress in the development of tools for observation and measurement. Before real advances could occur in the development of educational research, it was necessary to have scientific instruments for measuring those variables of interest to educators. It can be said that measurement became the cornerstone of the research movement. Let us first look briefly at some of the significant developments in the history of measurement that furnished a background for the educational research movement.

THE BEGINNINGS OF MEASUREMENT

The seeds of the research movement were planted in 1879, when Wilhelm Wundt established the first laboratory for experimental psychology in Leipzig, Germany. Early studies were primarily centered around the measurement of sensory acuity, reaction time, and motor skills. Wundt's laboratory represented a real advance in the scientific study of human behavior. Prescientific studies, in such forms as phrenology, astrology, and physiognomy, began to fade. From this early experimental psychology came a number of research procedures as well as a respect for careful experimental method and precision of techniques that was to have an influence on educational research.

The development of educational research was also greatly influenced by Sir Francis Galton (1822–1911), who studied individual differences among people. This British man of genius was also interested in the development of statistical tools for analyzing and describing his data on individual differences. Galton pioneered in the use of the method of correlation. The statistical techniques developed by the British were later employed in the study of educational problems.

In the United States James McKeen Cattell, who had studied in Germany with Wundt and was also influenced by Galton, began a systematic investigation of individual differences in reaction time in sensory-motor functions in relation to human intelligence. In 1890 Cattell wrote a now classic article called "Mental Tests and Measurements," in which the term "mental test" was first introduced into the literature. Cattell emphasized the need for standardization of test procedures in order to obtain comparable measurements from subjects. Cattell's beginnings led to the systematic study of individual differences in other human functions, including the measurement of intelligence.

THE BEGINNINGS OF EDUCATIONAL RESEARCH

Joseph M. Rice is generally recognized as the pioneer in the educational research movement. In 1897 he published two articles reporting the results of his rather lengthy investigation of the spelling achievement of schoolchildren in the United States.[16] This work is usually taken as the beginning of the modern movement for the objective study of educational problems. Rice's investigations tended to show that the methods of teaching spelling used during his day, which mainly emphasized drill, were largely ineffective. He aroused a great deal of opposition from educators, who thought it foolish to try to evaluate teaching methods by finding out how well children could spell. Rice investigated teaching methods in other areas and tried to point out the weaknesses in the educational theories prevalent in the nineteenth century. One can see in Rice's work the unfolding of a point of view that would accord to research a significant place in the total scheme of thought about educa-

[16]Joseph M. Rice, "The Futility of the Spelling Grind," *Forum* 23 (April 1897): 163–72, and (June 1897): 409–19.

tion—a place in assessing the strengths and weaknesses of educational practices and suggesting the way toward improvement.

The growth of educational research may conveniently be divided into three periods.

THE PIONEERING PERIOD: 1900–1920

Although it is difficult to pinpoint the formal beginnings of educational research, most authorities concur in suggesting 1900 as the start of a true scientific era in education. The period from 1900 to 1920 was one of exploration and of development of the measuring instruments needed by researchers. In 1905 Alfred Binet published the first workable intelligence scale, which was eagerly sought in this country. Binet's tests were translated and produced in several versions, of which the most important was the Stanford-Binet Intelligence Test, developed by Terman in 1916.

Edward L. Thorndike became a strong influence in the spread and development of standardized educational tests. He published his handwriting scale in 1910, which is often referred to as the first scientifically calibrated instrument for measuring an educational product. Among the other early achievement tests were Stone's arithmetic test, Buckingham's spelling test, and Trabue's language test.

Group intelligence tests had their beginnings during World War I due largely to the work of Otis, and subsequently became widely used tools in educational research. By 1920 individual and group tests were available for measuring both verbal and nonverbal intelligence. Aptitude tests, such as the Seashore Test of Musical Talent, also emerged during this period.

Although the emphasis was on the development of scientific devices for measurement, other activities were also taking place to promote the scientific study of education. Studies utilizing statistics began to appear. The principal stimulus to the use of statistical methods in educational research was Thorndike's teaching and writing. It was his *Notes on Child Study,*[17] published in 1901, and *Introduction to the Theory of Mental and Social Measurements,* published in 1904,[18] that established the statistical type of study in education. Early statistical studies were conducted by Thorndike (1907), Ayres (1909), and Strayer (1911) on children's progress in the school situation. As a result of their investigations, it became possible to establish national norms of achievement for all grades and to evaluate children's progress according to these norms.

Another major theme of the pioneer period was the school survey. Still one of the most popular types of research, the school survey involves a description and evaluation of one or more aspects of a school situation. The first formal school survey was conducted in 1910 in Boise, Idaho, by the superintendent of schools of In-

---

[17]Edward L. Thorndike, *Notes on Child Study* (New York: Macmillan, 1901).

[18]Edward L. Thorndike, *Introduction to the Theory of Mental and Social Measurements* (New York: Science Press, 1904).

dianapolis. Other early surveys were made of the schools in Montclair, New Jersey, and in New York City. In the latter survey, conducted in 1911–12, standardized tests were employed on a large scale for the first time. With the increased emphasis on testing in surveys, there arose a great debate concerning the propriety of obtaining such data. Gaining a favorable opinion among educators as to the value of standardized measuring was one of the major problems facing test makers from the beginning of this period. Educators continued to voice strong objections to the use of tests, and it required a great deal of effort on the part of educational leaders in the research movement to get them accepted. A debate of considerable significance was staged at the National Council of Education meeting in 1915 on the use of tests. Tests were defended by the prominent educational leaders of the day. At this same meeting, the American Educational Research Association (AERA) was born, one of its objectives being "the promotion of the practical use of educational measures in all educational research." It was at about this time that Thorndike enunciated his now famous dictum. In an address at the First Annual Conference on Educational Measurement, meeting at Indiana University in 1914, he declared: "If a thing exists, it exists in some amount; if it exists in some amount, it can be measured." This dictum served as a stimulus for the growth of the budding educational research movement. Researchers were encouraged to employ quantitative methods to obtain needed data on various aspects of education.

THE PERIOD OF EXPANSION: 1920–1945

The period from 1920 to 1945 was one of rapid expansion for educational research. The number of measuring instruments available to researchers increased tremendously during this time. Commercial publishers began to supply tests. Buros began publication of the *Mental Measurements Yearbook,* containing critical reviews of the available standardized tests.

Educational research was established as a field of study in universities. Graduate programs in education began to require such a course. Universities and large city school systems established bureaus or institutes for the conduct of educational research. Public and private experimental schools and teacher-training laboratory schools conducted a great deal of research and also promoted the application of research findings.

As research procedures and techniques were developed, the number of investigations increased. The famous Eight-Year Study, under the auspices of the Progressive Education Association, was conducted in the 1930s. Experimentation became more popular as a method of research. McCall's *How to Experiment in Education,* published in 1923, was one of the first books to deal with the problem of control in educational experimentation.[19] It has been suggested that the real breakthrough in educational research came in 1935 when Fisher developed his multivariate statistical

[19]W. A. McCall, *How to Experiment in Education* (New York: Macmillan, 1923).

designs that made possible an adequate attack on the complex problems characteristic of education.

Many journals designed to disseminate educational research findings began publication during this period. The AERA founded several publications of which four have provided a major contribution over the years. They began the *Educational Research Bulletin* in 1920 and the *Review of Educational Research* in 1931. The *Journal of Educational Research* was first published in 1920, and the first edition of the *Encyclopedia of Educational Research* appeared in 1940.

THE PERIOD OF CRITICAL APPRAISAL: 1945 TO THE PRESENT

Since 1945 attempts have been made to reevaluate educational research in the light of improvements that research has brought about in the educational process. This critical appraisal has greatly strengthened research in education.

Methods and procedures have been refined with the aim of attaining more reliable information. Many early studies in education were frequently defective in design and methodology and made little contribution to the body of organized knowledge. More sophisticated statistical procedures have permitted a more realistic attack on educational problems.

Educational research has been greatly expanded in scope. Every year vast numbers of investigations are concerned with determining the effectiveness of all aspects of the curriculum, teaching methods, guidance, and administrative practices. Educational research is no longer just a fact-finding enterprise. Although many feel it is still somewhat deficient in theoretical foundation, a sufficient body of theory has now been developed to permit sound approaches to many of the more practical problems of education.

In the 1960s we witnessed unprecedented government support of research in education and a great optimism concerning the use of research to solve problems in education. But disappointment followed this optimism, because frequently the knowledge gained did not lead directly to the solution of pressing problems. We now seem to be moving toward a balanced view of research in education. On the one hand, research is seen as an activity that adds to the knowledge that can lead to the improvement of our procedures and our institutions. On the other hand, we do not expect growth of that knowledge to lead inevitably and immediately to the solution of educational problems. In some fields, such as medicine, research findings on occasion lead to dramatic solutions. The effect of research on education has been less dramatic and more gradual.

This brief outline has presented only some of the highlights in the history of educational research. The whole spectrum of developments would defy discussion in this limited treatment. The reader is referred to the *Encyclopedia of Educational Research* or to issues of the *Review of Educational Research* for a summary of the accomplishments in particular areas of educational research.

Summary

Human beings have attempted to answer questions through experience, authority, deductive reasoning, inductive reasoning, and the scientific approach. Each method requires certain assumptions. The correctness of the answers depends upon the correctness of the assumptions underlying the method employed.

The scientific approach rests on two basic assumptions: (1) that truth can be derived from observation; and (2) that phenomena conform to lawful relationships.

Scientific inquirers seek not absolute truth but rather theories that explain and predict phenomena in a reliable manner. They seek theories that are parsimonious, testable, and consistent, as well as theories that are themselves stimuli for further research. The scientific approach incorporates self-correction, inasmuch as every theory is considered tentative and may be set aside if a new theory better fits the criteria.

The scientific approach has been employed to explain, predict, and control physical phenomena for centuries but has only recently been employed in education. The complexity of educational variables and the difficulties encountered in making reliable observations have impeded scientific inquiry in education. However, since the beginning of the movement at the turn of the century scientific inquiry in education has enjoyed increasing acceptance and increasing success both in theoretical and practical research.

Scientific inquiry in education, as in other fields is concerned with relationships among variables—that is, attributes that can take on different values. Independent variables are manipulated to determine their relationship to measures on dependent variables.

The general steps in scientific inquiry are (1) definition of the problem, (2) statement of a hypothesis, (3) deducing consequences of the hypothesis, (4) collection and analysis of data, and (5) confirmation or rejection of the hypothesis.

Exercises

1. Identify the source of knowledge—*deductive reasoning, inductive reasoning,* or *the scientific approach*—most prominently utilized in the following examples:
   a. After extensive observation of reactions, Lavoisier concluded that combustion is a process in which a burning substance combines with oxygen. His work was the death blow to the old phlogiston theory of burning.
   b. Dalton, after much reflection, concluded that matter must be composed of small particles called atoms. His early assumptions were the basis for the atomic theory.
   c. Later scientists took Dalton's assumptions, made deductions from them, and proceeded to gather data which confirmed these assumptions. Support was found for the atomic theory.
   d. Knowing that radioactive substances constantly give off particles of energy without apparently

reducing their mass, Einstein developed the formula $E = mc^2$ for converting matter into energy.

   e. Accepting Einstein's theory, Fermi carried on experimentation which resulted in the splitting of the atom.

   f. After studying reinforcement theory, a teacher hypothesizes that programmed learning techniques will lead to superior achievement in arithmetic. She devises a study in which programmed materials are used with two third grade classes, while conventional materials are used with two other third grade glasses.

2. What is the role of theory in scientific inquiry?
3. What is the difference between an inductive theory and a hypothetical-deductive theory?
4. Based on the title of the study, classify the following research as *basic* or *applied:*
   a. "The Effect of RNA (Ribonucleic Acid) Injections on the Transfer of Skills from Trained Animals to Untrained Animals"
   b. "Programmed Instruction versus Usual Classroom Procedures in Teaching Boys to Read"
   c. "Conditioning as a Function of the Interval between the Conditioned and Original Stimulus"
   d. "Teaching Geometry to Cultivate Reflective Thinking: An Experimental Study"
5. Using the designations *active, assigned,* or *may be either,* classify the following variables:
   a. amount of drug administered   c. socioeconomic background
   b. anxiety   d. teaching method
6. Which characteristic attitudes of scientists are violated in the following statement?
   a. This study was undertaken to prove that the use of marijuana is detrimental to academic achievement.
   b. It proved conclusively that this is the case.
   c. The results show that marijuana is evil.
7. What are the characteristics of a useful theory?
8. In a study designed to determine the effect of inhalation of varying amounts of marijuana on the learning of nonsense syllables
   a. What is the independent variable?
   b. What is the dependent variable?
9. Classify the following variables as *categorical* or *continuous:*
   a. achievement
   b. phonics method of reading versus look-say method of reading
   c. Spanish-speaking, English-speaking, French-speaking
   d. muscle prowess
   e. music aptitude
10. What are the characteristics of the operational definitions?
11. Listed below are the titles of research articles published in various journals. Classify the research methodology indicated by the titles, using *experimental, ex post facto, descriptive,* or *historical.*
   a. "The Child in Pedagogy and Culture: Concepts of American Preadolescence as Revealed in Teaching Theories and as Related to the Culture, 1900–1914"
   b. "Effect of Early Father Absence on Scholastic Aptitude"
   c. "A Comparative Study of Conventional Instruction and Individual Programmed Instruction in the College Classroom"
   d. "College Students' Views and Ratings of an Ideal Professor"

e. "Consistency and Variability in the Growth of Intelligence from Birth to Eighteen Years"

12. Why is each of the following people important in the history of educational research?

a. Alfred Binet
b. Joseph M. Rice
c. Lewis M. Terman
d. Sir Francis Galton
e. Wilhelm Wundt
f. James McKeen Cattell

13. Give examples of the use of authority and experience as sources of knowledge.

14. Give an example of how basic research in the biological sciences has improved the practice of medicine.

15. Give an example of how basic research in learning has improved the practice of teaching.

16. Give an example of an applied research study completed in your own field of interest. List other areas where additional research needs to be done in your field. What variables might be investigated in such studies?

17. Select a theory from your field of interest and use deductive reasoning to develop a specific testable hypothesis. What effect would confirmation of the hypothesis have on the theory?

Answers

1. a. inductive reasoning
   b. deductive reasoning
   c. scientific approach
   d. deductive reasoning
   e. scientific approach
   f. scientific approach

2. Theory integrates findings, summarizes information, provides leads for new research, and enables us to explain and predict phenomena.

3. An inductive theory serves to explain previous observations while a hypothetical-deductive theory is developed before extensive observations have been made.

4. a. basic   b. applied   c. basic   d. applied

5. a. active   b. may be either   c. assigned   d. active

6. a. The scientist is objective and impartial.
   b. The scientist is skeptical and regards findings as tentative.
   c. The scientist deals with facts not values.

7. A useful theory explains the phenomena in the simplest form possible; is consistent with observation and the established body of knowledge; provides means for its verification; and stimulates new investigation.

8. a. amount of marijuana inhaled
   b. number of nonsense syllables learned

9. a. continuous
   b. categorical
   c. categorical
   d. continuous
   e. continuous

10. Acceptable definitions state a clear-cut procedure for determining the existence of the phenomenon and its extent.

11. a. historical
    b. ex post facto
    c. experimental
    d. descriptive—survey
    e. descriptive—developmental study

12. a. published first workable intelligence test

b. pioneered in objective study of educational problems
c. developed Stanford-Binet test
d. studied individual differences among people
e. established first laboratory for experimental psychology
f. pioneered in study of individual differences and in the measurement of intelligence

Part

Research
Background

The Research Problem

Systematic research begins with a problem. John Dewey[1] spoke of the first step in the scientific method as the recognition of a felt difficulty, an obstacle or problem that puzzles the researchers.

Selecting and formulating a problem is one of the most important aspects of doing research in any field. Beginning researchers are often surprised to find that this initial stage often takes up a large part of the total time invested in a research project. There is no way to do research until a problem is recognized, thought through, and formulated in a useful way.

A researcher must first of all decide on the general subject of investigation. Such choices are necessarily very personal but should lead to an area that holds deep interest or about which there is real curiosity. Otherwise, the motivation to carry the research through to its end may be difficult to muster. The researcher's own knowledge, experience, and circumstances generally determine these choices: An elementary-school teacher may feel a need to investigate some aspect of the teaching of reading; or a junior high school teacher may be interested in the effectiveness of multimedia programs in the teaching of science.

Once chosen, the general subject is then narrowed down to a very specific research problem. The researcher must decide on a specific question to be answered and must state precisely what is to be done to reach an answer. Much of this chapter focuses on this aspect of research in education.

Most beginning researchers find this task of formulating a researchable problem or question a difficult one. The difficulty is not due to a shortage of researchable problems in education. In fact, there are so many questions begging for answers that beginners usually have trouble choosing among them. One common difficulty is that a problem must be selected and a question formulated very early, when the beginner's understanding of how to do research is most limited. In addition, uncertainties about the nature of research problems, the isolation of a problem, the criteria for acceptability, and how to solve the problem often seem overwhelming. Even experienced researchers usually find it necessary to make several attempts before arriving at a research problem that meets generally accepted criteria. A first selection or formulation may on closer examination be found to be unfeasible or not worth doing. Skill in doing research is to a large extent a matter of making wise choices about what to investigate. The skill takes time and repeated effort to develop but can be developed by the willing beginner.

Unlikely as it may seem, once a problem is selected and a question clearly formulated, one of the most difficult phases of the research process is accomplished.

[1]John Dewey, *How We Think* (Boston: Heath, 1933), pp. 106–18.

The Nature of Problems

Research problems in education are questions about states of affairs in the field. Although there are different types of research problems, all involve a question whose answer is being sought in the research. For example, experimental and ex post facto research involve a question about the relationship existing between two or more variables. A typical problem in experimental research would ask a question about the relationship between method of instruction and mastery of a skill. Such a study might be made more elaborate by introducing other variables into the question. For instance, one might ask the effect of the method of instruction at different levels of intelligence.

Descriptive research, on the other hand, asks questions about the nature, incidence, or distribution of educational variables. An example of this type of research problem is the question, What do high school sophomores know about the process through which political parties select candidates for president?

The Sources of Problems

The first question most students ask is, How do I find a research problem? Although there are no set rules for locating a problem, certain suggestions have been found to be helpful. Three important sources of problems are experience, deductions from theory, and related literature.

EXPERIENCE

Among the most fruitful sources for beginning researchers are their own experiences as educational practitioners. Decisions must be made daily about the probable effects of educational practices on pupil behavior. If these decisions are to be sound, educators must make critical inquiry into the validity of their assumptions concerning the relationship between learning experiences and pupil change.

There are decisions to be made about teaching methods. Certainly teaching methods are susceptible to and in need of scientific investigation. The scientific approach to educational practice holds that decisions about how to do things in education should be based on empirical evidence rather than upon hunches, impressions, feelings, or dogma. For instance, primary teachers may question the effectiveness of their methods of teaching reading. They may want to evaluate their usual methods or any of several other well-known methods in order to decide what is the most effective approach to use. Secondary teachers might ask whether the problem–discussion method or the lecture method is more effective in the teaching of high school economics. Biology teachers may want to investigate the contribution of the Biological Science Curriculum Studies (BSCS) course to the development of their students' critical thinking ability: Is BSCS more effective than other biology curricula?

Observations of certain relationships for which no satisfactory explanations exist are yet another source of problems for investigation. A teacher may notice an increase in overt signs of anxiety in students at certain times. To investigate this, the teacher can structure various tentative explanations of the origin of the anxiety and then proceed to test them empirically. This investigation may not only solve the immediate problem but also make some small contribution to an understanding of the causes of classroom anxiety.

Similarly, there are decisions to be made about practices that have become routine in the school situation and are in some instances based mainly upon tradition or authority with little or no support from scientific research. Why not evaluate some of these practices—for instance, the annual testing program? Are there alternative tests that would be more valid for the purpose intended than those now being used?

Educators' everyday experiences can yield worthwhile problems for investigation and, in fact, most of the research ideas developed by beginning educational researchers tend to come from their personal experiences. They may have hunches about new relationships or about alternative ways of accomplishing certain objectives and thus, through a kind of intuitive process, arrive at ideas for research. These studies will be mainly of a type leading to the solution of an immediate problem, but sometimes such problems are nevertheless more appropriate and meaningful for beginning researchers than those arrived at through a process of logical deduction from theory. In addition, such studies can often be justified on the basis of their contribution to the improvement of educational practice.

DEDUCTIONS FROM THEORY

The deductions that can be made from various educational and behavioral theories with which the researcher is familiar provide an excellent source of problems. Theories involve general principles whose applicability to specific educational problems is only hypothetical until they are empirically confirmed. It is only through research that one determines whether the generalizations embodied in theories can be translated into specific recommendations for educational practice.

From a theory the researcher can generate hypotheses stating the expected findings in a particular practical situation. That is, the researcher asks, What relationships between variables will be observed if the theory correctly summarizes the state of affairs? and then conducts systematic inquiry to ascertain whether the empirical data do or do not support the hypothesis and hence the theory.

There are learning theories, personality theories, sociological theories, theories of social development, and many others whose validity, scope, and practicality might be profitably tested in educational situations. Reinforcement theory might be a particularly useful starting point for classroom research. Consider the implications for classroom testing that could be deduced from just one postulate of reinforcement theory, namely, Reinforcement of responses leads to an increment in response rate and strength. Of course, we know that this theory has stimulated a great deal of research already, but there are still many deductions to be made and tested under classroom conditions. For instance, there has not been sufficient research concerning the effect of a lack of overt reinforcement or of nonreinforcement on correct student responses in classroom situations. We know from experimental laboratory studies with animals that each withholding of reinforcement decreases the probability of that response and eventually results in its extinction. Can this finding be extrapolated to the classroom? That is, can the teacher assume that correct student responses that are not overtly reinforced will weaken and become extinct? At the present time, we do not have sufficient classroom research testing the applicability of this principle.

Among other theories that appear to be fruitful sources of hypotheses for investigation are Stern's need-press cultural theory,[2] Festinger's cognitive-dissonance theory,[3] Pervin's transactional approach,[4] the various self-theories, theories of achievement motivation, role theory, and phenomenological theory.

Kipnis, for example, used Festinger's theory of social comparison processes as the basis for research on the relationship between perception of others and the process of changing self-concept.[5] Festinger's theory postulates that self-evaluations are formulated through comparison between the self and others.[6] A number of hypotheses were deduced from the theory stating the expected changes in self-concept in relation to perception of and comparison with important others. The subjects of the study were 87 students living together in a university dormitory. Their evaluations of their own personality traits were examined in relation to their perceptions of their best friends. All the hypotheses were supported by the data and Kipnis concluded that interpersonal perception and self-perception are closely-related.

This approach to research problems results in studies that are easily integrated since they are all based on a common theory. Such interrelated research is especially productive as a means for expanding knowledge in a particular area.

RELATED LITERATURE

Another valuable source of problems is the literature in one's own area of interest. In reading about previous research, we are exposed to examples of research problems and the way in which research is conducted. Also authors often conclude their studies with suggestions about further research that is needed to follow up the reported work. It is useful to see if the procedures employed in previous research

---

[2]G. G. Stern, *People in Context* (New York: Wiley, 1970).

[3]L. Festinger, *A Theory of Cognitive Dissonance* (New York: Harper & Row, 1957).

[4]L. A. Pervin, ''Performance and Satisfaction as a Function of Individual Environmental Fit,'' *Psychological Bulletin* 69 (1968): 56–68.

[5]Dorothy M. Kipnis, ''Change in Self-Concepts in Relation to Perceptions of Others,'' *Journal of Personality* 29 (1961): 449–65.

[6]L. Festinger, ''A Theory of Social Comparison Process,'' *Human Relations* 7 (1954): 117–40.

can be adapted to solving other problems, or whether a similar study could be conducted in a different field or subject area or with different groups of subjects.

For example, one reads a study investigating the effectiveness of a multimedia approach in teaching chemistry. Perhaps a similar study could be conducted in biology or in another subject area. Or a study involving secondary school students might serve as a guide to the elementary teacher who is interested in determining whether the same relationships between variables prevail at the elementary level.

One of the essential characteristics of a scientific research study is that it should be replicable, so that the findings can be verified. Replication of a study with or without variation may be a profitable and worthwhile activity for a beginning researcher. Repeating a study increases the extent to which the research findings can be generalized and provides additional evidence of the validity of the findings. In many educational experiments, it is not possible to select subjects at random, but rather we must use classroom groups as they are already organized. This, of course, limits the extent to which the findings can be generalized. However, as experiments are repeated at different times and in different places with the expected relations supported in each study, the confidence that can be placed in the scientific validity of the findings increases. Mere repetition of other studies is not the most challenging of research activities, but with educational problems there is frequently need for confirmation and extension of the findings.

In most cases replications of previous studies are not exact ones. Variation is introduced in order to clarify some aspect of the findings, to test how far the findings can be generalized, or to investigate factors not included in the original study.

For example, numerous replications of Piaget's studies of the development of moral judgment in children have been conducted in other countries.[7] These studies have used Piaget's basic approach but have investigated the development of moral judgment in children of different socioeconomic classes, in children of the same chronological age but differing in intelligence level, in children differing in the extent of their participation in their own age-groups, in children differing in the nature of parental discipline, and in both boys and girls. Recently, other investigators have used techniques that were different from Piaget's in their attempts to confirm his findings and conclusions. In general, the large body of research originating from Piaget's investigations has supported his original conclusions. Thus a single research study, if it deals with a significant problem and if its findings are exciting, can be the inspiration for many other studies.

Often in an investigation there is a next logical step that readily suggests itself. Readers may also be able to detect contradictions and inconsistencies in the published studies or may be dissatisfied with their findings.

Let us illustrate how dissatisfaction with previous research findings can stimulate additional research. In 1928 Hartshorne and May challenged the existing theory that honesty was a unified character trait.[8] They correlated the behavior of several

[7]Jean Piaget, *The Moral Judgment of the Child* (Glencoe, Ill.: Free Press, 1932).
[8]H. Hartshorne and M. A. May, *Studies in the Nature of Character,* vol. 1, *Studies in Deceit* (New York: Macmillan, 1928).

thousand school children in various temptation situations. They concluded from the low correlations among the temptation measures that honesty was not a general inner trait; rather it was specific and influenced by the situation in which individuals were placed.

Burton (1963) replicated this study because he questioned Hartshorne's and May's emphasis on situational factors in honesty behavior.[9] Burton used a factor analysis approach and found evidence for intra-individual consistency across the tasks presented to the children. He concluded that there probably was an underlying trait of honesty which a person shows in resisting temptation situations, but agreed with Hartshorne and May in rejecting an ''all or none'' formulation about a person's character.

In 1965 Hunt replicated Burton's study but used analysis of variance as the statistical technique instead of factor analysis.[10] Hunt argued that personality differences, situations, and the interaction between persons and situations should be considered as sources of variation in honesty behavior, and found support for the interaction hypothesis.

Nelsen, Grinder, and Mutterer (1969) replicated and extended all of the studies above.[11] They compared the alternative methodological approaches to the problem and concluded that temptation behavior is only moderately consistent across a variety of tasks. Thus their findings agree with the early Hartshorne and May study in spite of a time difference of over forty years in the data collection periods of the two studies and in spite of different populations, tasks, and methodological procedures.

Often one is aware of obvious gaps in the organized knowledge in an area. Research could be planned that would help to fill these gaps and result in more reliable knowledge. For students conferences with professors in their major field of study may be helpful with this step. Thus, with some critical analysis of published research in their field and a bit of creativity, students should be able to find several potentially researchable problems. An understanding of the theoretical and empirical aspects of the subject area enables them to read critically and choose a good problem.

NONEDUCATION SOURCES

Our experiences and observations in the world at large, as well as our professional activities, can be fruitful sources of research problems. Theories or procedures encountered in other fields might be adapted to apply to education. Often movements that originate outside our profession lead us to new paths of research.

[9]R. V. Burton, ''Generality of Honesty Reconsidered,'' *Psychological Review* 70 (1963): 481–99.

[10]J. McV. Hunt, ''Traditional Personality Theory in the Light of Recent Evidence,'' *American Scientist* 53 (1965): 80–96.

[11]E. A. Nelsen, R. E. Grinder, and M. L. Mutterer, ''Sources of Variance in Behavioral Measure of Honesty in Temptation Situations: Methodological Analysis,'' *Developmental Psychology* 1 (1969): 265–79.

The women's movement has led us to study sex stereotyping in educational materials, the influence of schools in the learning of sex roles, sex differences in personality, and so forth. The civil rights movement led to many studies about the education of minority children. The kidnapping of Patricia Hearst focused attention on brainwashing and the psychological process through which an individual identifies himself with a group. The inspiration for much valuable research in education has come from such noneducation sources.

Evaluating the Problem

After a problem has been tentatively selected, it must be evaluated. The researcher must be confident that the problem area is of sufficient importance to warrant investigation, although this is not always easy to determine. Judging the worth of a problem is often a matter of individual values and subjective opinion. However, there are certain criteria that should be used in this process of evaluating a problem's significance.

1. *Ideally, the problem should be one whose solution will make a contribution to the body of organized knowledge in education.* The researcher should show that the study is likely to fill in gaps in present knowledge or to help resolve some of the inconsistencies in previous research. Perhaps the study can improve upon earlier studies in such a way that more reliable knowledge would be made available. Most scholars agree that the problems that are rooted in theory have greater potential for satisfying this criterion. The investigator might ask whether the study will yield knowledge about new relationships or will replicate previously established findings.

Certain studies may make contributions to both theory and practice. However, if the problem lacks apparent theoretical implications, then it must, at least, have some practical implications. Researchers should be able to answer the question, So what? with respect to their studies. Would the solution of the problem make any difference to educational practice? Would other educators be interested in the findings? Would the findings be useful in an educational decision-making situation? Would they have wide generalizability? Unless these questions can be answered clearly and affirmatively, the problem should be abandoned. Since there are so many problems with theoretical or practical implications in need of solution, there is little justification for spending time and effort on petty or unimportant questions. An attempt should be made to estimate the probable information yield from the study for theory or practice. *Avoid the obviously trivial problem,* that is, the one whose solution would have little usefulness to educators.

Sometimes in their effort to locate a problem, students will select a question involving rather trivial relationships. For example, What is the relationship between popularity with one's peers and reading speed? would be considered a trivial problem because it has little or no significance for educational practice, has little relationship to other studies, and has no consequences for theory. A question such as, What is the correlation between intelligence and reading achievement? would also be considered trivial because we already have sufficient data on this relationship and thus additional research is probably unnecessary.

Many proposed studies should be rejected because their methodology would contribute little to either educational theory or practice. For example, a researcher seeking to evaluate the comparative merits of phonics and sight reading in beginning reading instruction might propose to survey the attitudes of primary teachers on this question. Such a survey would not yield a meaningful answer concerning the relative merits of the two systems because it would provide only the opinions of a sample of teachers who may be just as ignorant of the answer as the researcher. A superior approach would involve a controlled experiment comparing the progress of students taught under one system with that of students of equivalent ability taught under the other system. The ease of surveying opinion tempts many to use this procedure when it is inappropriate for answering the question being asked.

Similarly the strictly local problem, which is peculiar to a particular school situation, usually lacks significance since the results would not have application in other areas and would have little interest to anyone else. For example, studies investigating the cafeteria eating habits of seniors at X high school, the use of audiovisual aids in schools in a particular county or the proportion of the seniors at X high school who read the local newspaper, are typical local problems and would be criticized on the basis of this first criterion.

2. *The problem should be one that will lead to new problems and so to further research*. If researchers begin by linking their problem to organized knowledge and give some consideration to the type of study that might logically follow their own, they are much more likely to satisfy this criterion. A good study, while arriving at an answer to one question, usually generates a number of other questions that need investigation. This has been true of the studies dealing with reinforcement theory in the classroom. In contrast, much descriptive research fails to satisfy this second criterion.

In connection with this criterion, we suggest that the beginning student in research might give some consideration to the selection of a problem that could possibly be expanded or followed up later in a master's thesis or even a doctoral study.

3. *The problem must be one that is researchable*. Although this criterion would seem self-evident, in practice many problems do not involve questions that can be subjected to scientific investigation. To be researchable, a problem must be concerned with the relation existing between two or more variables that can be defined and measured. Many interesting questions in education cannot be subjected to empirical research but must be investigated through philosophic inquiry. Such questions as, Is it good to have sex education in the elementary schools? Should we teach about communism in the high school? Do democratic procedures improve the learning environment for children? are philosophical issues and cannot be answered by scientific investigation. Although these questions as worded cannot be attacked

empirically, they might be reformulated into workable research questions. For instance, we might restate the first question above as, What is the effect of sex education in the elementary schools on the attitudes of junior high school students toward premarital sex? A study could be designed to obtain information on this type of question. Although philosophical questions as such are not appropriate for scientific research, the information provided by research can be used in developing solutions to philosophical and ethical questions. That is, the data arrived at through scientific research on a problem can be useful to educators as they make decisions involving rights and values.

The researcher must also give some attention to the definition and measurement of the variables involved in the question. A problem such as What is the effect of the new morality on American adolescents? would seem to elude scientific determination. Defining the term *new morality* in such a way that its effect could be measured would be difficult.

4. *The problem must be suitable for the particular researcher*. The problem may be excellent from the point of view of the criteria mentioned but inappropriate for the individual. Some of the personal aspects to be considered here are:

a. The problem should be one in which you, the researcher, have a genuine interest and about which you can be enthusiastic. It should be a problem whose solution is personally important because of the contribution it could make to one's own knowledge in an area or to the improvement of one's performance as an educational practitioner. Unless the problem is meaningful and interesting, it is doubtful whether one would be willing to expend the time and energy to do a thorough job.

b. The problem should be in an area in which one has both knowledge and some experience. One needs to be familiar with the existing theories, concepts, and established facts in order to identify a worthwhile problem. Furthermore, one needs to consider whether one has the necessary skills and competencies that may be required to carry the study through to completion. Instruments may have to be developed and validated or complex statistical analyses may be required.

c. The problem must be one that is feasible in the situation in which you, the researcher, find yourself. One must ascertain whether or not the data necessary to answer the question are or will be available. One must check to make sure that the necessary subjects will be available or that the appropriate school records will be accessible. School administrators are quite often opposed to the conduct of research in their schools. They will not give student researchers permission to carry out their studies. So unless one is employed in a school situation at the time, one is quite likely to be left without the means to solve the research problem. One of the authors found it necessary to visit four school systems before permission could be obtained to conduct an educational experiment.

d. The problem must be one that can be investigated and completed in the allotted time. One should not select a problem that is too big or too involved, and should allow adequate time for constructing the instruments, administering the instruments, analyzing the data, and writing the report.

Stating the Problem

After the problem has been selected and its significance decided, there is still the task of formulating or stating the problem in a form amenable to investigation. A good statement of the problem must (1) clarify exactly what is to be determined or solved and (2) restrict the scope of the study to a specific question. We cannot overemphasize the importance of a clear, concise statement of the question. Beginning researchers often have a general idea of the problem but have trouble formulating it as a workable research question. They find that their initial general ideas, although adequate for communication and understanding, are not sufficiently specific to permit an empirical attack on the problem. They cannot make progress until they can state a concrete question amenable to research.

To illustrate, a beginning researcher states that he or she is interested in studying the effectiveness of the new science curriculum in the secondary schools. As stated, one could understand in a broad sense what he or she wants to do and could communicate about it in a general way. But the researcher must specify the problem with much greater clarity if a method for investigating it is to be found.

An essential step involves a definition of the terms involved. What is meant by *effectiveness, science curriculum,* and *secondary schools?* The definitions required for research will not usually be supplied by a dictionary. For example, effectiveness is defined as "producing the intended or expected result." This definition describes the general construct effectiveness but is not sufficiently precise for research purposes. One needs to be able to specify exactly what indicator of effectiveness one will use or what one will do to assess the presence or absence of the phenomenon denoted by the concept *effectiveness*. The same is true for the other terms. In other words, one must define the variables of the problem operationally. To define concepts operationally, one must designate some kind of overt behavior or event that is directly observable and measurable by oneself and others to represent those concepts. As mentioned in chapter 1, an operational definition is one that defines a concept in terms of the operation or processes that will be used to measure the concept.

In this study, the researcher might choose to define effectiveness as the improvement made in scores on a test of critical thinking or on a standardized science test. The term *curriculum* would be defined as the BSCS course offered to high school sophomores. *Secondary schools* might refer to those high schools that have certain specified characteristics. The original problem now might become, What is the effect of the BSCS course on the comprehension of biological concepts in beginning biology students at the sophomore level? The operational definitions serve to focus the scope of a general question to specific observable variables.

Now that the work is indicated with some clarity and focus, the researcher can proceed to design an experimental study that compares the scores made on pre- and post-tests of comprehension of biological concepts by students having the BSCS course with those of similar students having an alternative biology curriculum. The researcher can now begin to gather some objective evidence concerning a particular curriculum in a particular situation that will shed light on the more general original question.

Furthermore, in stating the problem, the researcher must strive for a balance between generality and specificity. If the stated problem is too broad and too general, one is faced with a vague area with no clear indication of the direction the research is to take. For instance, a question such as, What is the effect of programmed instruction on scientific achievement in the high school? is too general. It would be much better to ask, What is the effect of the use of programmed textbooks on the biology achievement of sophomores at Washington High School in Indianapolis? This statement indicates immediately the subjects to be included, the variables involved, and the type of data that will be gathered.

On the other hand, the problem must not be so narrow that it becomes trivial and meaningless. One wants a problem that is broad enough to be significant according to the criteria discussed, yet specific enough to be feasible in one's particular situation.

It is suggested that the problem be presented as a question rather than a statement. Although there is no general agreement that this format is essential, the authors prefer the question form since it is simple and straightforward. Psychologically it seems to orient the researcher to the task at hand—namely, to plan a method of finding the answer to the question. A mere statement, such as ''the adjustment of children to the Head-Start Program,'' does not tell us precisely what it is the researcher wants to know.

The problem presented in question form should ask the relationship between two or more variables. However, this does not mean that the *exact* words *What is the relationship between* _____ *and* _____ have to appear in the statement. The question may appear in that form or the relationship may only be implied. Students are often confused on this point. For instance, the problems, What is the effect of vocabulary instruction on social studies achievement? and What is the relative effectiveness of reading Method A as compared with Method B in teaching slow learners? ask a question about the *relationship between* variables but without using those precise words.

State the problem in such a way that research into the question is possible. Avoid philosophical issues, as well as value or judgmental questions that cannot be answered by scientific investigation.

Identifying Population and Variables

A good strategy for shaping a felt problem, or a vague notion of what one wants to investigate, into a researchable problem is to think in terms of population and variables.

For example, let us consider Ms. Burke, an elementary principal whose felt difficulty is, *Does individual tutoring by upper grade students have a positive effect on below-average readers?*

It is usually easiest to identify the population, that is, those people about whom one wishes to learn something. The population is below-average readers. Reading ability is not a variable in this question since all the children being considered have been diagnosed as below-average readers. Having identified below-average readers as the population in the original statement, Ms. Burke should now ask herself, Is that really the population I want? She will probably decide that below-average readers are too broad a category and she should confine herself to a particular age, below-average second-grade readers.

Now she is ready to look for variables in the remainder of her original statement. *Individual tutoring* can be made into a variable either by varying the type of tutoring used, or by varying the amount of tutoring time, or by having some children receive the tutoring while others do not. Ms. Burke decides that the last alternative is what she really wants to know, so she rewrites the relevant part of the question as, Does receiving a specified amount of individual tutoring versus no tutoring . . . Thus tutoring is the independent variable because it is antecedent to reading achievement, and the principal is predicting that the tutoring will have an effect on reading achievement, the dependent variable.

Now it becomes obvious that the word *tutoring* is too general. Unless all subjects receive the same type and amount of tutoring the results of the study will be meaningless. Ms. Burke decides to use word flash drill as the specific type of tutoring and to specify fifteen minutes per day as the amount of time.

The phrase, *have a positive effect on,* seems quite vague until she looks at it in terms of her independent variable. Does word flash drill have an effect on . . . what? She knows it has an effect on word flash recall. But she wants to study its effects on other aspects of reading behavior that might be observed: expressive oral reading, silent reading, positive feelings toward reading, number of books read, comprehension, and so forth. But she is afraid that teachers may rate good word callers as comprehending more and being more positive toward reading while they view the poorer word callers as more inferior on these variables than they really are. She wants a dependent variable that is independent of teacher judgment, and decides to use reading scores from the California Achievement Test (CAT) as the dependent variable.

Ms. Burke's revised statement of the problem now reads, *Among below-average second-grade readers is there a difference in CAT reading scores between those who have received 15 minutes per day of individual word flash drill by upper-grade students and those who have received no word drill?* This question tells whom she is studying, what will be done differently for some than for others, and what she expects differential treatment to influence. Note also that the value judgment *positive effect* has dropped out of the question.

It is often useful to follow this procedure in a formal manner similar to that used for diagramming a sentence. One can begin by drawing a vertical line and writing ''Population'' to the left and ''Variables'' to the right. These elements in the study are then listed below the horizontal line. In our example the diagram would be:

Population	Variables
Below-average second-grade readers	Word flash drill for 15 minutes daily by upper-grade students versus no word flash drill (independent) Reading scores on CAT (dependent)

Let us take another question, What is the effect of having experienced or not having experienced a preschool program on the reading achievement of first graders?

Population	Variables
First graders	Having experienced or not having experienced a pre-school program (independent) Reading achievement (dependent)

This question is complete in that it has an identified population and two variables. Since *preschool programs* precedes *reading achievement of first graders,* the former can be identified as an independent variable and the latter as a dependent variable.

Let us look at another example, Does high school driver education do any good? As it stands, the question has neither a population nor variables. An investigator starting with this question might first decide to compare 19-year-old drivers who have had high school driver education with those who have not. We now have a population statement and an independent variable. Now we can turn our attention to selecting a dependent variable. What effect might having or not having driver education have on 19-year-old drivers? It is decided that accident rate would be a suitable dependent variable. Putting these elements into a diagram we have:

Population	Variables
19-year-old drivers	Have had or have not had high school driver education (independent) Accident rate (dependent)

A complete question can now be stated: Do 19-year-old drivers who have had high school driver education have a lower accident rate than 19-year-old drivers who have not had high school driver education?

The question, What is the relationship of dogmatism to political attitudes among college freshmen? illustrates another point.

Population	Variables
College freshmen	Dogmatism Political attitudes

This question is complete with a population and two variables. But we cannot label the variables as independent and dependent since it cannot be determined which is antecedent to the other.

If a study is conducted to investigate *status quo* rather than a relationship between variables, it may be complete with only one variable. For example, one might study the opinions of college seniors concerning legalization of marijuana. In this case the population is college seniors and the single variable is their opinions on the subject.

Different methods are employed to answer the different types of research questions. Whenever an independent variable can be manipulated by the researcher, the experimental method is the appropriate one to use (see chapter 9). The first example in this section involving the influence of word flash drill on CAT reading scores is experimental research. Many variables in education cannot be manipulated and thus the experimental method cannot be used in research on these variables. The research problem involving a comparison of the accident rate of 19-year-old drivers who had had or had not had driver training would require the ex post facto method (see chapter 10). The independent variable (driver education or lack of driver education) was not manipulated by the researcher.

For some research problems either the experimental or the ex post facto method is appropriate depending upon how the study is designed. The research example above on the effect of preschool programs on reading achievement could employ either method, depending upon whether the investigator chose to manipulate the independent variable of preschool programs or to select subjects who already had or had not had preschool training.

Other research problems are concerned with describing the nature or incidence of one or more educational variables. The descriptive method is the appropriate one for this type of problem (see chapter 11). The example involving the question of the relationship between dogmatism and political attitudes among college freshmen is descriptive research. Surveys seeking opinions on issues such as legalization of marijuana also represent descriptive research.

Summary

The first task facing researchers is the selection and formulation of a problem. A research problem is a question about the relationship between variables. In attempting to find a researchable problem, investigators may look to their personal experiences, to theories from which questions may be deduced, or to the current literature in some area of interest. They must evaluate the significance of the proposed problem in terms of specific criteria, asking the questions: Will the problem contribute to the present body of knowledge? Does it have potential for leading to further research? Is it testable—that is, can the variables be observed and measured? How appropriate is the problem with respect to my interests, experience, and knowledge in the area? Do I have access to the data required by the problem, and are instruments available, or could they be constructed, to measure the variables? Can the data be analyzed and interpreted within the time available? The question should not directly involve philosophical issues nor should it be so general that a research undertaking is impossible. The statement of the question should identify the population of interest and the variables to be investigated.

Exercises

1. Find a research report published in a journal and answer the following questions based on your reading:
   a. What problem is investigated in the study?
   b. What is/are the hypothesis(es)?
   c. What are the independent and dependent variables?
   d. Where did you find the problem and hypothesis(es) stated in the report?
   e. Were the problem and hypothesis(es) stated with sufficient clarity so that you knew exactly what was being investigated in the study?
2. Select a broad area in which you might be interested in doing research. Choose a particular aspect of this broad area and then identify a research problem that you would be interested in pursuing. State this problem in a form for research.
3. The following examples are inadequate statements of research problems. Restate each so that it becomes a specific question suitable for research.
   a. effects of different ways of learning science concepts
   b. anxiety and academic achievement
   c. attitudes of culturally disadvantaged children
   d. counseling and underachievers
   e. effectiveness of the Cuisenaire method of teaching elementary arithmetic
4. Evaluate the following research problems:
   a. Has the permissive child-rearing philosophy of Dr. Spock had an adverse effect on American education?
   b. What is the relationship between the preferred method of leg-crossing and the intelligence of American college women?
   c. Considering recent empirical studies on math achievement, should "modern" mathematics be abandoned in the elementary school and replaced by traditional math?
   d. How do students perceive the role of the principal at Central Middle School?
5. State the most likely independent variable and dependent variable of each study:
   a. "An Experimental Study of the Effect of Three Speech Variables on Listener Comprehension" (*Speech Monograph* 21 [1954]: 248–53)
   b. "Effects of Logical and Scrambled Sequences in Mathematical Materials in Learning with Programmed Instruction Materials" (*Journal of Educational Psychology* 61 [1970]: 41–45)
   c. "Competition for Grades and Graduate Student Performance" (*Journal of Educational Research* 62 [1969]: 351–54)
   d. "Children's Perceptions of Their Teacher's Feelings toward Them Related to Self-Perception, School Achievement Behavior" (*Journal of Experimental Education* 29 [1960]: 107–18)
   e. "An Experimental Study of the Relationship of Homework to Pupil Success in Fractions" (*School Science and Math* 71 [1971]: 339–46)

Answers

3. a. Is there a difference between the Science Research Associates (SRA) science achievement scores of sixth graders who have had one year of the Elementary Science Study (ESS) science program and the scores of those who have had one year of a textbook-centered science course?
   b. Among high school students, is there a relationship between composite Stanford Achievement Test scores and Manifest Anxiety Scale scores?
   c. One needs to specify which attitudes of children are being investigated and then compare these with attitudes of a suitable control group (perhaps nondisadvantaged children), or hypothesize the relationship between types of attitudes and other behavior. For example, do culturally disadvantaged children with positive attitudes toward school have higher grades than those with negative attitudes toward school?
   d. What is the effect of a counseling program on the attitudes of middle school underachievers toward school?
   e. Do the math achievement scores of third graders who have had one year of the Cuisenaire method of teaching elementary arithmetic differ from the scores of those who have had an alternate method of teaching?

4. a. This question involves a value judgment that is impossible to investigate empirically.
   b. This question is trivial and answering it would make little contribution to knowledge.
   c. Research cannot answer questions of value; it can only provide information on which decisions can be based.
   d. Though the question could be researched, it is too local in scope to be generalized to other situations.

5. a. independent: three speech variables
      dependent: listener comprehension
   b. independent: logical sequences and scrambled sequences in programmed instruction materials
      dependent: a measure of learning of the mathematics concepts covered
   c. independent: competition for grades
      dependent: graduate students' grades
   d. independent: children's perceptions of their teacher's feelings toward them
      dependent: self-perception and school achievement
   e. independent: assigning or not assigning homework
      dependent: a measure of achievement in fractions

Related Literature

Once a topic has been selected, the investigator is naturally eager for action. However, it is a mistake to rush headlong into planning and carrying out the study before making a thorough survey of what is already known in the area of interest. The topic must be related to relevant knowledge in the field. It is as important for educators, as it is for others engaged in research, to know how to locate, organize, and use the literature in their field.

This chapter discusses (1) the role of related literature in a research project, (2) reference sources in education, and (3) the task of organizing the related literature for presentation in the report.

The Role of Related Literature in a Research Project

The search for related literature should be completed before the actual conduct of the study begins. This stage serves several important functions.

1. *A knowledge of related research enables investigators to define the frontiers of their field.* To use an analogy, an explorer might say, "We know that beyond this river there are plains for 2,000 miles west and beyond those plains a range of mountains, but we do not know what lies beyond the mountains. I propose to cross the plains, go over the mountains, and proceed from there in a westerly direction." So the researcher in a sense says, "The work of A, B, and C has discovered this much about my question; the investigations of D have added this much to our knowledge. I propose to go beyond D's work in the following manner."

2. *An understanding of theory in the field enables researchers to place their question in perspective.* One should determine whether one's endeavors would be likely to add to knowledge in a meaningful way. In general, those studies that determine whether the hypotheses generated by a theory can be confirmed are more useful than studies that proceed completely independent of theory. The latter tend to produce isolated bits of information that are of limited usefulness.

3. *Through studying related research, investigators learn which procedures and instruments have proved useful and which seem less promising.* As one proceeds through the related literature and develops increasing sophistication, one may soon find oneself seeing ways in which the studies could have been improved. Of course, hindsight is always better than foresight, so perhaps it is inevitable that early studies in a field often seem crude and ineffective. This point illustrates a major reason for

emphasizing the related-literature portion of research studies; both the successes and the failures of past work provide insight for designing one's own study. If researchers build carefully on past investigations, we can expect increasing sophistication in our knowledge about education.

4. *A thorough search through related research avoids unintentional replication of previous studies.* Frequently a researcher develops a worthwhile idea only to discover that a very similar study has already been made. In such a case the researcher must decide whether deliberately to replicate the previous work or to change the proposed plans and investigate a different aspect of the problem.

5. *The study of related literature places researchers in a better position to interpret the significance of their own results.* Becoming familiar with theory in the field and with previous research prepares researchers for fitting the findings of their research into the body of knowledge in the field.

Reference Sources in Education

It is clearly essential for scholars and researchers to know how to find previous work in their areas. To do this, one should know (1) the sources of previous work, (2) what agencies collect such information and organize it into data bases, (3) what form these data bases take, and (4) efficient ways of finding the information one needs. The basic sources are (1) information storage and retrieval systems, computerized data bases (of which the Educational Resources Information Center, or ERIC, System is the most likely to be of help to researchers in education), (2) indexes to periodicals, (3) other periodicals, (4) books, and (5) dissertations.

In order to use these sources, one must become familiar with available library facilities and services. Many libraries have printed guides describing their services and regulations, or will schedule orientation tours. It is especially important to learn how the card catalog is organized and where needed periodicals can be found. One should also find out whether the library can obtain books and other documents through interlibrary loan.

EDUCATIONAL RESOURCES INFORMATION CENTER

One of the most important landmarks in the history of educational research was the establishment, in 1964, of the Educational Resources Information Center (ERIC) by the U.S. Office of Education (USOE) to collect, store, and disseminate information on education. The ERIC System has become a vital part of the American educational scene.

Before the ERIC System was established, reports submitted to USOE by its contractors and grantees received an initial scattered distribution and then disappeared, as did reports from other sources. ERIC was intended to correct this chaotic situation, to collect and preserve unpublished "fugitive" materials of interest to educators, and to make this store of information available to the public.

The ERIC System, now sponsored by the National Institute of Education (NIE), is a network of approximately sixteen clearinghouses, each devoted to collecting, evaluating, and abstracting resource material in its own area of specialization. In addition, there is a central processing facility which is in charge of storage and dissemination of materials. The results of this work are made available through the periodicals *Current Index to Journals in Education*[1] and *Resources in Education,*[2] plus other publications.

A carefully developed system of indexing is used for providing access to ERIC documents. This system is described in the *Thesaurus of ERIC Descriptors* (1970), which is available in most libraries or can be ordered from the publishers, the Macmillan Information Corporation.[3] The *ERIC* thesaurus is a useful source for planning a comprehensive search for related studies in one's area.

Current Index to Journals in Education

The monthly journal *Current Index to Journals in Education (CIJE)* is compiled from the work of the specialists of the ERIC clearinghouses. Articles from over 700 journals are classified and indexed according to the system developed in the *ERIC* thesaurus.

CIJE is divided into four sections: (1) subject index, (2) author index, (3) main entry section, and (4) journal contents index. One can find articles of interest by first looking in the subject index for the titles and numbers of relevant articles, then using these numbers to find the entries in the main entry section. If you cannot find your topic of interest in the subject index, look for synonyms for the topic. The vocabulary of the ERIC thesaurus is deliberately limited to provide a more systematic indexing system. The separate author index is useful to those wishing to find the work of a particular researcher. The journal contents index indicates the journals covered and the contents of each issue.

Figure 3.1 is a typical article description taken from the main entry section, with explanation of its various parts, as provided by *CIJE* to illustrate the type of information in each entry.

The annotation is particularly useful since it gives a brief description of the article. Note that in the example in Figure 3.1 the title alone gives only a partial idea of what the article is about. Before January 1970, when *CIJE* began including annotations, researchers endured extensive frustration in their search for articles whose titles were misleading or insufficiently revealing and which on inspection proved to be unrelated to the topic of interest. If the title of an article is considered to be sufficient to convey the main thrust of the article, the abstractors do not include an annotation. Publication of *CIJE* was begun in 1969. The Journal is cumulated semiannually and annually.

An efficient approach to the use of *CIJE* falls into six stages:

[1]*Current Index to Journals in Education,* Macmillan Information Corporation, 866 Third Avenue, New York, N.Y. 10022.

[2]*Resources in Education,* Superintendent of Documents, U.S. Government Printing Office, Washington, D.C. 20402.

[3]Macmillan Information Corporation, 866 Third Avenue, New York, N.Y. 10022.

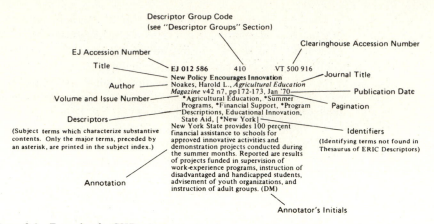

Figure 3.1   Example of a *CIJE* entry

1. Determine the key words under which articles relevant to your study might be listed. These key words will always include the population and the variables you have identified in your problem statement.
2. Check the *Thesaurus of ERIC Descriptors* to find which of your key words are used as descriptors. You may need to find synonyms for the key words you have listed.
3. Begin your search with the most recent issues of *CIJE* and work back through earlier issues.
4. Copy from *CIJE* the entire reference given for any title which may be useful. This procedure simplifies the task of finding the original articles.
5. Search out the articles in their journals. If your library does not have the journal, the librarian may be able to obtain a Xerox copy of the article through inter-library loan.
6. Read the abstract first—if one accompanies the journal article—to determine whether or not it will be useful to read the entire article. If there is no abstract, start with the summary and conclusion sections.

Resources in Education

Abstracts of research reports from sources other than journals are indexed and published monthly by ERIC in *Resources in Education (RIE)*. A semiannual cumulative edition of the index sections is also published. Each clearinghouse collects materials related to its field of specialization, and then catalogs the documents and prepares indexes and abstracts. The original documents, together with the abstracts prepared by each clearinghouse, are sent on a regular basis to the Processing Facility, where they become part of the central data base on which users of the ERIC System can draw. The Processing Facility is responsible for collecting the input of all clearinghouses and publishing the combined abstracts monthly in *RIE*.

The sources covered by the specialized clearinghouses include reports of all federally funded educational research, abstracts, pamphlets, curriculum guides, significant papers from the proceedings of learned societies and institutes, bibliographies, exemplary course-related materials, teachers' guides and program outlines, as well as various other research proposals and project reports. With such a far-ranging coverage it is clear that the documents in the ERIC collections are of vital interest to practitioners as well as researchers in education. Over 120,000 documents are now included, and the collection is growing at a rate of 14,000 documents per year.

Each abstract is assigned its own accession number for the purposes of identification, and for ordering copies of the original documents. Three indexes are provided: author, institution, and subject. Using the appropriate index, one finds the titles of documents and their accession numbers which one then uses to locate the individual abstracts.

The procedure for using *RIE* is similar to that used for *CIJE*. One typically begins with the most recent copy and works backward, looking under the subject or subjects of interest.

Figure 3.2 is an example of an entry in the main entry section of *RIE*.

The ERIC Document Collection

Microfiche copies of most of the original documents can be obtained as required, or a standing order may be placed with ERIC to receive all documents as they become available. Many libraries have such an arrangement with ERIC, thus making available to their users the entire document collection in a convenient location.

Most documents are available in two forms, hard copy and microfiche. In most libraries microfiche is preferred, as it is less expensive and requires less storage space. The cost of each ERIC document is listed in *RIE* for both microfiche and hard copy.

The microfiche technique is a photographic process that reduces pages of printed text to small images. One 4-inch by 6-inch microfiche sheet contains up to 60 pages of text. An entire book or an extensive file of reports can be reduced to a few sheets of microfiche. The entire ERIC collection in microfiche occupies the space of a few file cabinets.

A machine called a microfiche reader is used to enlarge the images of the pages onto a built-in screen and to allow the user to proceed from page image to page image. Most libraries and universities have such equipment available. Since their cost is moderate (from about $75 to $400), even small libraries often have these readers available. Some libraries also have machines that reproduce blown-up microfiche pages on paper.

All projects funded by the USOE are automatically included in the ERIC System, and complete copies of reports of these projects are available through ERIC. Where publication is first made under copyright privileges, reference is made to the source; however, copies are usually not available through ERIC. The same is true for books and other materials prepared for sale. ERIC is invaluable to the field of education because it collects and abstracts, from a wide range of sources, relevant material for educational researchers, much of which was previously almost impossible to obtain.

SAMPLE RESUME ENTRY

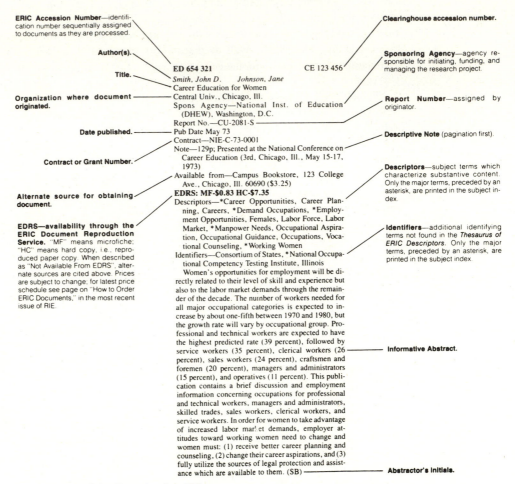

ERIC Accession Number—identification number sequentially assigned to documents as they are processed.

Author(s).

Title.

Organization where document originated.

Date published.

Contract or Grant Number.

Alternate source for obtaining document.

EDRS—availability through the ERIC Document Reproduction Service. "MF" means microfiche; "HC" means hard copy, i.e., reproduced paper copy. When described as "Not Available From EDRS", alternate sources are cited above. Prices are subject to change; for latest price schedule see page on "How to Order ERIC Documents," in the most recent issue of RIE.

Clearinghouse accession number.

Sponsoring Agency—agency responsible for initiating, funding, and managing the research project.

Report Number—assigned by originator.

Descriptive Note (pagination first).

Descriptors—subject terms which characterize substantive content. Only the major terms, preceded by an asterisk, are printed in the subject index.

Identifiers—additional identifying terms not found in the *Thesaurus of ERIC Descriptors*. Only the major terms, preceded by an asterisk, are printed in the subject index.

Informative Abstract.

Abstractor's Initials.

ED 654 321   CE 123 456

Smith, John D.   Johnson, Jane
Career Education for Women
Central Univ., Chicago, Ill.
Spons Agency—National Inst. of Education (DHEW), Washington, D.C.
Report No.—CU-2081-S
Pub Date May 73
Contract—NIE-C-73-0001
Note—129p; Presented at the National Conference on Career Education (3rd, Chicago, Ill., May 15-17, 1973)
Available from—Campus Bookstore, 123 College Ave., Chicago, Ill. 60690 ($3.25)
EDRS: MF-$0.83 HC-$7.35
Descriptors—*Career Opportunities, Career Planning, Careers, *Demand Occupations, *Employment Opportunities, Females, Labor Force, Labor Market, *Manpower Needs, Occupational Aspiration, Occupational Guidance, Occupations, Vocational Counseling, *Working Women
Identifiers—Consortium of States, *National Occupational Competency Testing Institute, Illinois

Women's opportunities for employment will be directly related to their level of skill and experience but also to the labor market demands through the remainder of the decade. The number of workers needed for all major occupational categories is expected to increase by about one-fifth between 1970 and 1980, but the growth rate will vary by occupational group. Professional and technical workers are expected to have the highest predicted rate (39 percent), followed by service workers (35 percent), clerical workers (26 percent), sales workers (24 percent), craftsmen and foremen (20 percent), managers and administrators (15 percent), and operatives (11 percent). This publication contains a brief discussion and employment information concerning occupations for professional and technical workers, managers and administrators, skilled trades, sales workers, clerical workers, and service workers. In order for women to take advantage of increased labor market demands, employer attitudes toward working women need to change and women must: (1) receive better career planning and counseling, (2) change their career aspirations, and (3) fully utilize the sources of legal protection and assistance which are available to them. (SB)

Figure 3.2   Example of an *RIE* entry

The ERIC clearinghouses prepare annotated bibliographies on selected topics. Before preparing your own bibliography, it is a good idea to write to the clearinghouse dealing with your field of interest to see if the clearinghouse staff already has a bibliography that will be of value to you in preparing your own.

A more complete description of the ERIC System and how to use it will be found in the booklet *ERIC: What It Can Do for You, How to Use It,* which is available in many libraries.[4]

---

[4]James W. Brown, Maxine K. Sitts and Judith Yarborough, *ERIC: What It Can Do for You, How to Use It* (Syracuse, N.Y.: ERIC Clearinghouse on Information Sources, 1975).

The clearinghouses of the ERIC network wish to make their collections as comprehensive as possible and ask educators to submit relevant materials. In the booklet we are urged:

> If you have prepared a report, speech or paper which you would like to have considered for national dissemination through ERIC, send one copy to:
>
> Educational Resources Information Center
> National Institute of Education
> 400 Maryland Avenue, S.W.
> Washington, D.C. 20208

Computer Access to the ERIC System

A generation ago a thorough search of 500 journals and 100,000 other documents for material relevant to a given research problem was a task of major proportions. Today, computerized access to the ERIC System makes it possible to conduct such searches by means of a single letter or telephone call.

The contents of *CIJE* and *RIE* are available on computer tapes. Computer searches of the ERIC System can be made with these tapes. For example, to identify journal articles and *RIE* documents that deal with the use of programmed materials to teach French, the computer is instructed to identify all documents and journal articles that have been given both the descriptor *programmed instruction* and the descriptor *French*. Some computer programs print out only the ED and EJ accession numbers, but most programs print out complete *CIJE* entries (see Figure 3.1) and complete *RIE* entries (see Figure 3.2) for every article and document that have both descriptors.

Over 900 institutions have the ERIC tapes and can run computer searches. Most of the 50 state departments of education have the ERIC tapes and will run computer searches free of charge for educators within their state. Most of these departments have information retrieval specialists who will work with clients to translate general requests for help into the form needed for the computer to retrieve the desired information from the ERIC System. Many universities provide similar services to their students. Some of the ERIC clearinghouses and some school systems also provide search services.

Some search services also buy tapes from other information systems, such as the National Literature Analyses and Retrieval System National Library of Medicine (MEDLARS) and the National Technical Information Service (NTIS), and offer to search these data bases also. These data bases function similarly to ERIC but use their own indexing system. Several different computer programs of varying sophistication are now available for carrying out searches. The most advanced provide full-text searching of the titles and abstracts, thus bypassing the indexing system altogether. At present, however, few agencies can afford this type of program, and most rely on programs using the ERIC descriptors and other appropriate indexing systems for access.

A good start for a search for related literature is to inquire at your local school, university, library, or state department of education to find which agencies will provide you with a free search of the ERIC System. If you do not have access to such a service, a number of agencies provide searches for a fee. For example, Lockheed Information Systems will provide a search of *RIE, CIJE, Exceptional Child Education Resources, Psychological Abstracts,* and other data bases for approximately $40.[5]

A search of the ERIC System is an important step in the quest for related liberature, but one can *not* assume that when this step is finished the quest is completed. Material relevant to one's question may not have entered the ERIC System. There are many other important sources of related literature.

OTHER INDEXES

In addition to *CIJE* and *RIE,* other periodicals are useful for locating up-to-date information on research, theory, and contemporary opinion in education. These publications, which are issued in successive parts at regular intervals, serve as guides for locating information that is widely dispersed in journals and other sources.

One of the standard reference works in the field of education is *Education Index*, which has been published regularly since 1929 by the H. W. Wilson Company of New York.[6] This publication, which is similar to *CIJE,* though smaller in scope, lists the titles of all articles in more than 200 periodicals, yearbooks, bulletins, proceedings, and monographic series in the field of education.

The procedure for using *Education Index* is similar to that employed with *CIJE.* However, since annotations are not provided in *Education Index,* one is likely, on occasion, to lose considerable time in following up articles that prove to be unrelated to one's topics. *Education Index* is the best source for journal articles prior to the establishment of *CIJE* in 1969, as well as very recent articles, as it typically lists articles about six months before *CIJE* does.

The *Readers Guide to Periodical Literature* indexes articles in popular magazines.[7] Prior to the establishment of *Education Index,* many education journals were covered in *Readers Guide*. Specialized indexes similar to *Education Index* are also available for business education, industrial arts, agriculture, and a variety of other fields, and may be of great help to researchers whose topics touch on such fields.

Journals of abstracts are produced in a number of subject areas. Those most likely to be of interest to educators are *Child Development Abstracts and Bibliography, Exceptional Child Education Resources* (formerly *Exceptional Child Education*

---

[5]Lockheed Information Systems, Lockheed Information Retrieval Service, 3251 Hanover Street, Palo Alto, Calif. 94304.

[6]*Education Index* (New York: H. W. Wilson, 1929–   ).

[7]*Readers Guide to Periodical Literature* (New York: H. W. Wilson, 1900–   ).

Abstracts), and *Psychological Abstracts.*[8] These publications include abstracts of the articles indexed. These abstracts present a clear summary of the content of the article, thus enabling one to determine immediately whether or not an article is relevant.

The *Review of Educational Research,*[9] published quarterly by the AERA, summarizes research findings in education and related fields. From 1931 until 1970 the *Review* concentrated on one of fifteen broad areas in education for each review. An issue chairman, chosen for each topic, was responsible for soliciting reviews in his area of expertise. Thus each topic was reviewed once every three years and an educator could depend upon having available relatively recent reviews of research in his field.

In June 1970 the *Review of Educational Research* abandoned this policy and began publishing unsolicited reviews; each issue now contains reviews covering an assortment of topics. In an attempt to provide summaries of research within broad areas in the profession, the editorial board of AERA launched publication of the series *Review of Research in Education* in 1973.[10]

Psychological studies that may also be interest to educators are summarized in the *Annual Review of Psychology.*[11]

Dissertation Abstracts International, published by University Microfilms, contains the original authors' abstracts of all doctoral dissertations accepted by over 150 universities in the United States and Canada.[12] These abstracts are classified by subject, institution, and author. *Dissertation Abstracts International* is published monthly and indexed annually.

One can seek related dissertations following the same procedure as that employed with *CIJE.* If one needs more information than is contained in the abstract, a microfilm copy of the entire dissertation can be obtained from University Microfilms at a nominal cost.

A more efficient way to find related dissertations is to use the DATRIX II service of University Microfilms. DATRIX II users fill out a request form on which they identify the relevant dimensions of their question. The information on a completed form enables University Microfilms to identify and provide abstracts of all relevant dissertations through the use of a computer search. Over 125,000 dissertations are

---

[8]*Child Development Abstracts and Bibliography* (Chicago, Ill.: Society for Research in Child Development, 1927–   ); *Exceptional Child Education Resources* (Reston, Va.: Council for Exceptional Children, 1969–   ); *Psychological Abstracts* (Washington, D.C.: American Psychological Association, 1927–   ).

[9]*Review of Educational Research* (Washington, D.C.: American Educational Research Association, 1931–   ).

[10]Fred N. Kerlinger, ed., *Review of Research in Education I* (Itasca, Ill.: Peacock, 1972); Fred N. Kerlinger and John B. Carroll, eds., *Review of Research in Education II* (Itasca, Ill.: Peacock, 1974); Fred N. Kerlinger, ed., *Review of Research in Education III* (Itasca, Ill.: Peacock, 1975); Lee S. Shulman, ed., *Review of Research in Education IV* (Itasca, Ill.: Peacock, 1976); idem., *Review of Research in Education V* (Itasca, Ill.: Peacock, 1977).

[11]*Annual Review of Psychology* (Palo Alto, Calif.: Annual Reviews, Inc., 1950–   ).

[12]*Dissertation Abstracts International* (Ann Arbor, Mich.: University Microfilms, Inc.).

now available through this computer sorting routine. The cost of the DATRIX II service is modest, especially when compared with the time involved in searching through *Dissertation Abstracts International* on one's own. The most serious drawback to using these sources is the two-year time lag between the submission of a dissertation and its appearance in *Dissertation Abstracts International*.

Since 1962 University Microfilms has also published abstracts of selected masters theses in *Masters Abstracts*.[13] Complete theses in microfilm or Xerox copies can be purchased.

Phi Delta Kappa's *Research Studies in Education* lists both completed and ongoing dissertations in the field of education classified by subject field. Silvey's *Master's Theses in Education* lists masters theses from several universities.[14]

Social Sciences Citation Index,[15] published in three volumes a year by the Institute for Scientific Information Inc., can tell you which authors have been cited during the year in all areas of social science including education, what topics have been covered, and the necessary bibliographic information for both citing and cited authors. This information is made available by way of four indexes:

1. The Source Index provides an alphabetical list of all authors publishing during the year, with complete bibliographic information, including an alphabetical list of the references provided by the source author's bibliography. This index is cross-referenced to secondary authors.
2. The Citation Index takes the names cited by the authors in the Source Index and presents them alphabetically so that the researcher can find where a particular paper has been cited. Bibliographic references are provided for each cited item. A corporate author citation index and an index for anonymously authored papers are also provided. This index enables one to follow ideas forward in time.
3. The Permuterm Subject Index takes every significant word and pairs it with every other significant word in each title. Each word in a title is then listed as a primary term combined with each of the other terms as co-terms. An alphabetical listing of the names of authors whose titles contain the words is provided for each pair of primary and co-terms. Bibliographic information can then be found for each author in the Source Index.
4. The Corporate Address Index is an alphabetical listing of organizations to which authors publishing during the year are affiliated. Under each entry is an alphabetical list of authors with complete bibliographic information. Coauthors from different institutions are listed under both institutions but under the first author's name only.

---

[13]*Masters Abstracts* (Ann Arbor, Mich.: University Microfilms, Inc., 1962–).

[14]*Research Studies in Education* (Itasca, Ill.: Phi Delta Kappa, Inc., Peacock); H. M. Silvey, *Master's Theses in Education* (Cedar Falls, Iowa: Research Publications).

[15]*Social Sciences Citation Index* (Philadelphia: Institute for Scientific Information Inc., 1973–).

BOOKS

Certain books have proved especially useful to those who are engaged in educational research. Woodbury's *A Guide to Sources of Educational Information* is a comprehensive guide to locating information relating to education and educational affairs.[16] It contains detailed descriptions of more than 700 published and institutional sources, plus backup chapters on how to locate them and how and when to use them. Sheehy's *A Guide to Reference Books* describes and evaluates several thousand references.[17] This publication is kept up to date by means of biennial supplements.

The *Mental Measurements Yearbooks,* compiled by Buros, are considered the standard references on commercially available psychological, educational, and vocational tests.[18] Each volume includes independent evaluations of the tests listed, as well as details concerning publisher, price, and grade level. Buros's *Tests in Print II*[19] serves as an index and supplement to the *Mental Measurements Yearbooks*. Buros has also organized the material in the *Mental Measurements Yearbooks* and *Tests in Print II* into specialized monographs on tests of personality, reading, intelligence, vocational and business skills, English, foreign languages, mathematics, science, and social studies.[20] Shaw and Wrights *Scales for the Measurement of Attitudes* describes many attitudinal measures, including several that are not available commercially but which may be obtained from the investigators who developed them for their own research.[21]

The 33,000 entries and cross-references in Good's *Dictionary of Education* provide definitions of terms in the field.[22]

The *Encyclopedia of Educational Research,* an AERA project, presents useful summaries and evaluations of research on a wide variety of topics in the field of education. A new edition is published at the end of each decade. The most recent edition was published in 1969.[23]

[16]Marda Woodbury, *A Guide to Sources of Educational Information* (Washington, D.C.: Information Resources Press, 1976).

[17]Eugene Sheehy, ed., *A Guide to Reference Books* (Chicago: American Library Association, 1976).

[18]Oscar K. Buros, *Mental Measurements Yearbooks* (Highland Park, N.J.: Gryphon, vol. 1, 1938; vol. 2, 1940; vol. 3, 1949; vol. 4, 1953; vol. 5, 1959; vol. 6, 1965; vol. 7, 1972; vol. 8, 1978).

[19]Oscar K. Buros, *Tests in Print II* (Highland Park, N.J.: Gryphon, 1974).

[20]Oscar K. Buros, *Personality Tests and Reviews II* (Highland Park, N.J.: Gryphon, 1975); *Reading Tests and Reviews II* (Highland Park, N.J.: Gryphon, 1975); *Intelligence Tests and Reviews* (Highland Park, N.J.: Gryphon, 1975); *Vocational Tests and Reviews* (Highland Park, N.J.: Gryphon, 1975); *English Tests and Reviews* (Highland Park, N.J.: Gryphon, 1975); *Foreign Language Tests and Reviews* (Highland Park, N.J.: Gryphon, 1975); *Mathematics Tests and Reviews* (Highland Park, N.J.: Gryphon, 1975); *Science Tests and Reviews* (Highland Park, N.J.: Gryphon, 1975); *Social Studies Tests and Reviews* (Highland Park, N.J.: Gryphon, 1975).

[21]Marvin E. Shaw and Jack M. Wright, *Scales for the Measurement of Attitudes* (New York: McGraw-Hill, 1967).

[22]Carter V. Good, ed., *Dictionary of Education,* 3rd ed. (New York: McGraw-Hill, 1973).

[23]Robert Ebel, ed., *Encyclopedia of Educational Research* (New York: Macmillan, 1969).

Sometimes research results are reported in book form. For example, Alschuler reported the results of his study on increasing achievement motivation in his book *Motivating Achievement in High School Students: Education for Human Growth*.[24]

THE SMITHSONIAN SCIENCE INFORMATION EXCHANGE

The Smithsonian Science Information Exchange (SIE) provides a clearinghouse for information about work currently in progress, classified not only by subject matter but also by location, chief investigators, and source of funding. All fields of the behavioral, social, biological, and medical sciences are included, and the research project summaries received each year total over 100,000, about 80 percent of which are supported by the federal government.

One can request current research notices by subject content, by state or country, institution or company, specific school, supporting agency, period of time, individual investigator, or any combination of these. The result of such a request is a list of projects giving complete data, plus a 200-word abstract on each project. Fees for this service are based on the type of search required, and the number of abstracts sent.

Written requests should be sent to:

Smithsonian Science Information Exchange, Suite 300
1730 M Street, N.W.
Washington, D.C. 20036

Or one can telephone (202) 381-5511 for general information or (202) 381-5721 for inquiries relating to education and other behavioral sciences.

Organizing the Related Literature

Once one is satisfied that a reasonably comprehensive study of the literature in the field has been carried out, one can proceed to the task of organizing it. A useful approach is to arrange the studies by topic and determine how each of these topics relates to one's own study.

The literature should be presented in such a way as to justify carrying out the study by showing what is known and what remains to be investigated in the topic of concern. The hypotheses provide a framework for such organization. Like an explorer proposing an expedition, the researcher maps out the known territory and points the way to the unknown territory to be explored. If the study includes several facets, or investigates more than a single hypothesis, the organization process is done separately for each one.

One should avoid the temptation to present the literature as a series of abstracts.

[24]A. S. Alschuler, *Motivating Achievement in High School Students: Education for Human Growth* (Englewood Cliffs, N.J.: Educational Technology Publications, 1972).

Rather, it should be presented in such a way as to lay a systematic foundation for the study.

It is almost inevitable that a number of the reports one has carefully studied and included in one's notes will, on reflection, prove to be only peripherally related to the topic. It is neither necessary nor desirable to include in a proposal every study encountered in a search through the literature. One's readers will not be impressed by mere quantity. Relevance and organization of the material are of prime importance.

The researcher who fails to approach the task of assembling the related literature in a systematic manner from the beginning can become very disorganized. The following suggestions may be of assistance.

1. *Begin with the most recent studies in your field and then work backward through earlier volumes.* One obvious advantage of this approach is that you start with studies that have already incorporated the thoughts and findings of previous research. Earlier misunderstandings have been corrected and unprofitable approaches have been avoided. Another advantage is that these studies will include references to earlier works and, therefore, direct you to sources you might not otherwise encounter. In fact, accumulating a network of references in this way is rather like pulling up crabgrass. As you pull out one, its roots lead you to others that when pulled out lead you to still others, *ad nauseam!* Obviously, limits must be set to the process of gathering related research. On the one hand, laying meaningful groundwork for a study entails including all the important works in the field. On the other hand, devoting excessive time to this endeavor could result in boring the readers of your own report with superfluous detail. Make sure that the related literature serves, but does not dominate, your own work.

2. *Read the abstract or summary sections of a report first to determine whether it is relevant to your question.* Doing so can save much time that might be wasted reading unhelpful articles.

3. *Before taking notes, skim the report quickly to find those sections that are related to your question*—another way to save reading time.

4. *Make notes directly on file cards as they are easier to sort and organize than sheets of paper, backs of envelopes, and so on.* Many prefer 4-inch by 6-inch file cards, which provide a reasonable space for notes but are small enough to fit in a pocket or purse.

5. *Write out a complete bibliographic reference for each work.* If you know which style manual will be used in the finished report, you can save time by using that reference form while note-taking. Add the library call number also to facilitate finding the work again, should it be necessary.

6. *To facilitate sorting and organizing, do not put more than one reference on each card.* It is not possible to arrange your references alphabetically or in any other way unless you record them singly.

7. *Be sure to indicate which parts of the notes are direct quotations from the author and which are your own paraphrases.* Failure to make this distinction can lead to inadvertent plagiarism. It is also wise to clearly separate an author's evaluation of his research from your own.

Table 3.1   Sources of Related Literature in Education

Source	Content
Current Index to Journals in Education	Titles, authors, and journal citations of journal articles related to education, with annotations where needed. Classification by subject, by author, and by journal. No abstracts.
Resources in Education	Abstracts of research reports and other documents acquired by ERIC clearinghouses.
Thesaurus of ERIC Descriptors	System for classifying and indexing ERIC documents.
ERIC Microfiche Collection	Complete documents, the abstracts of which are in *Resources in Education*.
Education Index	Titles, authors, and journal citations of journal articles related to education. Indexed by subject and title. No abstracts.
Readers Guide to Periodical Literature	Titles, authors, and journal citations of articles in popular journals. Indexed by subject and title. No abstracts.
Child Development Abstracts and Bibliography	Abstracts of journal articles in the field of child development.
Exceptional Child Education Resources	Abstracts of journal articles in special education.
Psychological Abstracts	Abstracts of journal articles in psychology.
Review of Educational Research	Before June 1970: Review of research in selected topics in education in a three-year cycle. Beginning June 1970: Unsolicited reviews on various topics in each issue.
Encyclopedia of Educational Research	Summaries and evaluations of research in education, published at the end of each decade.
Dissertation Abstracts International	Abstracts of doctoral dissertations in the United States and Canada.
DATRIX II	Computerized sorting system for finding relevant dissertations listed in *Dissertation Abstracts International*.
Mental Measurements Yearbooks	Information and evaluations of commercially available tests.
Tests in Print II	Index and supplement to the first seven *Mental Measurements Yearbooks*
Scales for the Measurement of Attitudes	Describes and illustrates attitudinal measures not listed in the *Mental Measurements Yearbook*.
Smithsonian Science Information Exchange	Information retrieval system for work currently in progress.
Social Sciences Citation Index	Bibliographic information for cited authors and topics.

Summary

If the compiler-researcher covers the avenues to information in the area as suggested, a reasonably complete picture of the place the study occupies within the field should result.

Table 3.1 summarizes the most important sources of related literature in education and their content.

Exercises

1. State three important roles of related literature in a research project.
2. Compare the merits of *CIJE* and *Education Index.*
3. What is DATRIX II, and how might it be useful in research projects?
4. At what point during the research project should the researcher survey the literature and research concerning the chosen question?
5. What is an annotation?
6. Which of the sources of related literature in Table 3.1 are available in libraries that are accessible to you?

Answers

1. A knowledge of related research enables the researcher to define the frontiers of the field, place the question in perspective, and avoid unintentional replication of previous studies.
2. *CIJE* is computer indexed; lists of articles can be found by computer as well as by hand search. *Education Index* provides a means of locating articles published from 1929 to the present. *CIJE* covers more journals and provides annotations, whereas *Education Index* lists articles more quickly than *CIJE*.
3. DATRIX II is a computer search service for dissertations offered by University Microfilms. It is an efficient means of finding dissertations on topics related to the researcher's area of interest.
4. The researcher surveys the related literature as soon as the research problem has been selected and delineated.
5. An annotation is a brief description of an article. It can aid the researcher in selecting articles on his topic.

The Hypothesis

The hypothesis is a powerful tool in scientific inquiry. It enables us to relate theory to observation and observation to theory. Today the use of hypotheses enables us, in our search for knowledge, to employ both the ideas of the inductive philosophers, with their emphasis on observation, and the logic of the deductive philosophers, with their emphasis on reason. The use of hypotheses has united experience and reason to produce a powerful tool for seeking truth.

After finding and stating the problem and examining the literature, the researcher is ready to structure a hypothesis. A hypothesis may be precisely defined as a tentative proposition suggested as a solution to a problem or as an explanation of some phenomenon. It presents in simple form a statement of the researcher's expectations relative to a relationship between variables within the problem. It is then tested in a research study. Hence it is presented only as a suggested solution to the problem, with the understanding that the ensuing investigation may lead either to its retention or to its rejection.

For instance, one may begin with the question, What is the role of children's perceptions of themselves in the process of learning to read? One might then hypothesize that there is a positive relationship between children's perceptions of themselves and their achievement in reading in the first grade. Or one may begin with a question such as, What is the effect of preschool training upon the achievement of culturally disadvantaged children in first grade? The hypothesis might read: Culturally disadvantaged children who have had preschool training achieve at a higher level in first grade then culturally disadvantaged children who have not had preschool training. In both examples, it can be seen that the hypothesis is a proposition relating two variables. In the first hypothesis the variables are self-perception and reading achievement; in the second, they are preschool training and achievement in first grade.

The hypothesis must be structured before the data-gathering phase of the study for two reasons: (1) A well-grounded hypothesis indicates that the researcher has sufficient knowledge in the area to undertake the investigation. (2) The hypothesis gives direction to the collection and interpretation of the data; it tells the researcher what procedure to follow and the type of data to gather and thus may prevent a great deal of wasted time and effort on the part of the researcher. It should be emphasized that this is true for all types of research studies, not just the experimental.

The purposes served by the hypothesis are:

1. *The hypothesis provides a tentative explanation of phenomena and facilitates the extension of knowledge in an area.* In order to arrive at reliable knowledge about educational problems, one must go beyond a mere gathering of isolated facts to seek

generalizations and interrelations existing among those facts. These interrelations and generalizations provide the patterning significant for an understanding of the problem. Such patterning is not likely to become apparent as long as data gathering is without direction. Well-planned hypotheses provide direction and propose explanations. Because they can be tested and validated through scientific inquiry, they permit us to extend knowledge.

2. *The hypothesis provides the investigator with a relational statement that is directly testable in a research study.* Questions cannot be tested directly. An investigation begins with a question, but only the proposed relationship between the variables can be tested. For instance, one does not test the question, Do teachers' comments on students' papers cause a significant improvement in student performance? Instead, one tests the hypothesis that the question implies: Teachers' comments on students' papers result in a significant improvement in performance, or more specifically, The performance scores of students who have had teacher comments on previous papers will exceed those of students who have not had teacher comments on previous papers. One then proceeds to investigate the relationship between the two variables, teachers' comments and student performance.

3. *The hypothesis provides direction to the research.* The hypothesis represents a specific objective and thus determines the nature of the data needed to test the proposition. Very simply, the hypothesis tells the researcher what to do. Facts must be selected and observations made as they have relevance to a particular question and it is the hypothesis that determines the relevancy of these facts. The hypothesis provides a basis for selecting the sample and the research procedures to be used, and suggests the statistical analysis needed and the relationship to be tested. Furthermore, the hypothesis helps to keep the study restricted in scope, preventing it from becoming too broad or unwieldy.

For example, consider again the hypothesis concerning preschool training of culturally disadvantaged children and their achievement in first grade. This hypothesis indicates the research method required and the sample to use, and it even directs the researcher to the statistical test that would be necessary for analyzing the data. It is clear from the statement of the hypothesis that the researcher must conduct an experimental study that compares the first grade achievement of a sample of culturally disadvantaged children who went through a preschool program and a similar group of children who were not given preschool training. Any difference in the mean achievement of the two groups could be analyzed for statistical significance by the *t*-test or analysis-of-variance technique. (These procedures are discussed in chapter 6.)

4. *The hypothesis provides a framework for reporting the conclusions of the study.* The researcher will find it very convenient to take each hypothesis separately and state the conclusions that are relevant to it. That is, the researcher can organize this section of the written report around the provision of answers to the original hypotheses, thereby making a more meaningful and readable presentation.

Suggestions for Deriving Hypotheses

How does the researcher go about deriving a hypothesis? As explained in chapter 2, one's study might have its origin in a practical problem, in some observed behavioral situation in need of explanation, in previous research, or even more profitably in some educational, psychological, or sociological theory. Thus hypotheses are derived inductively from observations of behavior or deductively from theory or from the findings of previous research.

INDUCTIVE HYPOTHESES

In the inductive procedure the researcher formulates a hypothesis as a generalization from observed relationships. That is, the researcher makes observations of behavior, notices trends or probable relationships, and then hypothesizes an explanation for this observed behavior. Of course, this reasoning process should be accompanied by an examination of previous research to determine what findings other investigators have reported on the question. The inductive procedure is a particularly fruitful source of hypotheses for classroom teachers. Teachers observe student behavior every day and attempt to relate it to their own behavior, to the behavior of other students, to the teaching methods used, to changes in the school environment, and so on. On the basis of their experience and knowledge of behavior in a school situation, teachers may inductively formulate a generalization that attempts to explain the observed relationship. The validity of this explanation must be determined, however, and thus it can become the hypothesis for a scientific investigation.

Perhaps a teacher has observed a high degree of anxiety that is aroused by classroom tests and believes that this has an adverse effect on students' performance. Furthermore, the teacher has noted that when students are given an opportunity to write comments about objective questions, their test performance seems to improve. The teacher reasons that this freedom to make comments must somehow serve to reduce anxiety and, as a result, the students make better scores. This observation suggests a hypothesis: Students who are encouraged to write comments about test items on their answer sheets will make higher test scores than students who have no opportunity to make comments. Our teacher could then design an experiment to test the validity of this hypothesis. Note that the hypothesis expresses the teacher's belief concerning the relationship between two variables: writing comments about test items and the performance on the test. Note also that the variable anxiety that was part of the deductive chain leading to the hypothesis is not part of the final hypothesis. Therefore, the results of the investigation would provide information concerning only the relation between writing comments and test performance. The relationships between anxiety and comments, and anxiety and test performance, could be subjects for subsequent hypotheses to be investigated. Frequently one will find that an original idea involves a series of relationships that cannot be directly observed. One then reformulates the question in order to focus on relationships that are amenable to direct observation.

The following are some other simple examples of hypotheses that might result from a teacher's observations: Teacher comments on student papers lead to improvement on later papers; Utilization of the problem-discussion method as compared with the lecture method, results in greater group achievement in consumer economics; A counselor's use of authoritative advice rather than nondirective counseling increases a counselee's self-disclosure; Teaching the commutative property increases the speed with which addition combinations are learned; Children make higher scores on final measures of first grade reading achievement when they are taught in small groups rather than large groups. In the inductive process, the researcher makes observations, thinks about the problem, turns to the literature for clues, makes additional observations, and then formulates a hypothesis that attempts to account for the observed behavior. The hypothesis is then tested under controlled conditions in order to examine scientifically the teacher's assumption concerning the relationship between the variables.

The investigation of inductive hypotheses that derive from everyday problems can often be helpful in indicating solutions to such problems. Because they are generated from specific local problems, however, the results of such hypotheses often lead to a series of findings which, although worthwhile, have limited explanatory power.

DEDUCTIVE HYPOTHESES

In contrast to hypotheses that are formulated as generalizations from observed relationships, there are those that are derived by deduction from theory. These hypotheses have the advantage of leading to a more general system of knowledge, as the framework for incorporating them meaningfully into the body of knowledge already exists within the theory itself. A science cannot develop efficiently if each study remains an isolated effort: It becomes cumulative by building on the existing body of facts and theories. A hypothesis derived from a theory is known as a deductive hypothesis.

As discussed in chapter 1, a theory states in the simplest possible form the relations believed to prevail in a comprehensive body of facts. Most theories are not mere speculations but are built on previously known facts. A good theory organizes what is known and provides a framework for the prediction of what is not yet known. Then through deductive reasoning from a theory, hypotheses are formulated. At the hypothesis-forming stage one does not know whether these deductions are correct or not. Empirical data must be obtained concerning the hypothesis. If the data support the hypothesis, the findings can then be incorporated into the theory. This process serves as a technique for testing the adequacy of a theory.

One may begin a study by selecting one of the theories in one's own area of interest. Once the theory has been chosen, one proceeds to derive a hypothesis from this theory. The most widely used approach is to utilize deductive reasoning to arrive at the logical consequences of the theory. These deductions then become the hypotheses in research studies.

For example, one of the postulates of McClelland's theory of motivation is that "the intensity of the achievement motive is a directly proportional function of the education to independence and self-sufficiency."[1] From this postulate, one can deduce as a logical consequence the hypothesis: Children whose parents greatly restrict their freedom, when compared with children whose parents do not restrict their freedom, make lower scores on a task where the amount of work done is a function of their motivation.

Piaget has suggested that children pass through various stages in their mental development, one of which is the stage of concrete operations, which begins at age 7 or 8 and marks the transition from dependence on perception to an ability to use some logical operations. These operations are on a concrete level but do involve symbolic reasoning.[2] Using this theory as a starting point, one might therefore hypothesize: The proportion of 9-year-old children who will be able to answer correctly the transitive inference problem, Frank is taller than George; George is taller than Robert; who is the tallest? will be greater than the proportion of 6-year-olds who are able to answer it correctly.

In a study designed to test a deduction from a theory, it is extremely important to check for any logical gaps intervening between theory and hypothesis. The researcher must ask the question, Does the hypothesis logically follow from the theory? If the hypothesis does not really follow from the theory, then the researcher cannot reach valid conclusions about the adequacy of the theory. If the hypothesis is supported, but not rigorously deduced from the theory, the researcher cannot say that the findings furnish credibility to the theory. Conversely, if the hypothesis is not supported by the data, the theory from which it originated will not necessarily be any less credible.

It is true that many of the hypotheses that can be deduced from the better-known theories have already been tested, but many such deductions remain to be made and tested. Also a previously researched deduction could be used to generate hypotheses in more widely varied circumstances in order to extend the application of the theory.

Characteristics of the Usable Hypothesis

After the hypothesis has been tentatively formulated, but before any actual empirical testing is attempted, the potential of the hypothesis as a research tool must be assessed. A hypothesis must meet certain criteria of acceptability. The final worth of a hypothesis cannot be judged prior to empirical testing, but there are certain criteria

---

[1] D. McClelland et al., *The Achievement Motive* (New York: Appleton, 1953), p. 288.
[2] Jean Piaget, *Six Psychological Studies* (New York: Vintage Books, 1968), pp. 61–62.

that characterize worthwhile hypotheses and the researcher should use them to judge the adequacy of the proposed hypothesis.

A HYPOTHESIS MUST HAVE EXPLANATORY POWER

A hypothesis must be a possible explanation of what it is attempting to explain. This is an obvious but important criterion. To illustrate, suppose you attempt to start your car and nothing happens. A hypothesis stating that the car will not start because you left the water running in the bathroom sink is not a possible explanation. A hypothesis stating that the battery is dead is a possible explanation and would be worth testing.

A HYPOTHESIS MUST STATE THE EXPECTED RELATIONSHIP BETWEEN VARIABLES

A hypothesis should conjecture the relationship between two or more variables. In our example, it would be unprofitable to state, The car will not start and it has a wiring system, because no relationship between variables is specified and, consequently, there is no proposed relationship to test. A fruitful hypothesis would be: The car will not start because of a fault in the wiring system. This criterion may seem patently obvious, but consider the following statement: If children differ from one another in self-concept, they will differ from one another in social studies achievement. The statement appears to be a hypothesis until you note that there is no statement of an expected relationship. An expected relationship could be described as: Higher self-concept is a likely antecedent to *higher* social studies achievement. This hypothesis would then be stated, There will be a *positive* relationship between self-concept and social studies achievement. If the opposite is predicted, that is, Higher self-concept leads to *lower* social studies achievement, then the hypothesis would be, There will be a *negative* relationship between self-concept and social studies achievement. Either statement would meet our second criterion.

A HYPOTHESIS MUST BE TESTABLE

It is said that the most important characteristic of a ''good'' hypothesis is testability. A testable hypothesis is verifiable; that is, deductions, conclusions, or inferences can be drawn from the hypothesis in such a way that empirical observations can be made that will either support or not support the hypothesis. If the hypothesis is true, then certain predictable results should be manifest. A testable hypothesis enables the researcher to determine by observation whether or not those consequences that are deductively implied actually do or do not occur. Otherwise, it would be impossible either to confirm or not to confirm the hypothesis. In our example, the hypothesis, The car's failure to start is a punishment for my sins, is apparently untestable in this world.

Many hypotheses or propositions as they may initially be stated are essentially untestable. For instance, the hypothesis, The Head-Start Program promotes the all-around adjustment of the preschool child, would be hard to test because of the difficulty of defining and measuring all-around adjustment. Another example of an untestable hypothesis is, The use of ditto work in school art stifles the child's artistic creativity. In this case, the problem would be one of defining and measuring artistic creativity as well as setting up the criteria to determine whether or not a stifling of creativity has occurred.

To be testable, a hypothesis must relate variables that are capable of being measured. If there are no means available for measuring the variables, then it would be impossible to gather the data necessary to test the validity of the hypothesis. This cannot be emphasized too strongly. Unless it is possible to define specifically the indicators of each variable and subsequently to measure these variables, then the hypothesis is not testable.

The indicators of the variables are referred to as operational definitions. An operational definition, as explained earlier, is one that defines a variable by stating the ''operations'' or procedures necessary to measure that variable. For instance, consider the hypothesis: There is a positive relationship between a child's self-esteem and his reading achievement in first grade. In order for this hypothesis to meet the criteria of acceptability, it is necessary to define the variables operationally. Self-esteem might be defined as the scores made on the Coopersmith Self-Esteem Scale[3] and reading achievement, as scores on the California Reading Test or first grade teachers' ratings of reading achievement.

A primary consideration in formulating a hypothesis is to make sure that the variables can be given operational definitions. Avoid the use of constructs for which it would be difficult or impossible to find adequate measures. Constructs such as creativity, authoritarianism, democracy, and the like have acquired such diverse meanings that agreement on operational definitions of such concepts would be difficult, if not impossible. Remember that the variables must be defined in terms of identifiable and observable behavior.

It is important to avoid value statements in hypotheses. A statement such as, A counseling program in the elementary school is desirable, cannot be investigated in a research study. However, one could test the hypothesis, Elementary pupils who have had counseling will verbally express greater satisfaction with their school than those who have not had counseling. One can measure verbal expressions of satisfaction, but whether they are desirable or not is a value judgment.

A HYPOTHESIS SHOULD BE CONSISTENT WITH THE EXISTING BODY OF KNOWLEDGE

Hypotheses should not contradict previously well-established hypotheses, theories, and laws. The hypothesis, My car will not start because the fluid in the battery has changed to gold, satisfies the first three criteria but is so contrary to what

[3]Stanley Coopersmith, *The Antecedents of Self-Esteem* (San Francisco: Freeman, 1967).

is known about the nature of matter that one would not pursue it. The hypothesis, The car will not start because the fluid in the battery has evaporated to a low level, is consistent with previous knowledge and therefore is worth pursuing. It would probably be unprofitable to hypothesize an absence of relationship between the self-concept of adolescent boys and girls and their rate of physical growth because the preponderance of evidence supports such a relationship.

In the history of science, it is found that people like Einstein, Newton, Darwin, Copernicus, and others developed truly revolutionary hypotheses which conflicted with what was accepted knowledge in their time, but it must be remembered that the work of such pioneers was not really so much a denial of previous knowledge as it was a reorganization of that knowledge into more satisfactory theory. In most cases, and especially for the beginning researcher, it is safe to suggest that the hypothesis should be in agreement with the knowledge already established in the field. Again, this points up the necessity for a thorough review of the literature so that hypotheses will be formulated on the basis of previously reported research in the area.

A HYPOTHESIS SHOULD BE STATED AS SIMPLY AND CONCISELY AS POSSIBLE

Stating the hypothesis in a simple manner not only makes testing of the hypothesis much easier, but also provides a basis for a clear and easily comprehended report at the conclusion of the study. It is often necessary to break a broad general hypothesis into several specific ones in order to allow for testability and clarity. For instance, Tuma and Livson considered these very general hypotheses: "The socioeconomic status of the family plays a part in determining the degree of conformity experienced by an adolescent in various social contexts," and "The various components of this social status differ in the extent of their effects upon his attitudes to authority." To promote clarity and testability, they broke these general hypotheses into specific ones, such as the following: (1) "There is a significant negative relationship between the attitude toward authority experienced by the male adolescent at home and the socioeconomic status of his family"; (2) "There is a significant negative relationship between the attitude toward authority experienced by the male adolescent at school and the socioeconomic status of his family"; (3) "There is a significant negative relationship between the attitude toward authority experienced by the male adolescent when with peers and the socioeconomic status of his family"; (4) "There is a significant negative relationship between adolescent boys' attitudes toward authority and fathers' education"; (5) "There is a significant negative relationship between adolescent boys' attitudes toward authority and mothers' education"; and so on.[4] These hypotheses would need to be restated to reflect expectations as far as female adolescents are concerned. Stating the hypotheses in this very specific form also facilitates a reporting of the findings and conclusions. The experimenter can consider each hypothesis separately and can indicate the findings and conclusions relevant to each.

[4]Elias Tuma and Norman Livson, "Family Socioeconomic Status and Adolescent Attitude to Authority," *Child Development*, 31 (1960): 387–99.

Thus it can be seen that several hypotheses may be needed in any one study. Generally it is recommended that the researcher state a hypothesis for every sub-aspect of the problem or for every data-gathering device that will be used. For example, an investigator might begin with the hypothesis, Students taught mathematics by means of a programmed textbook will show greater learning and retention of mathematical concepts than those using traditional textbooks. Since it will be necessary to report results for both learning and retention, the original hypothesis must be restated as two separate hypotheses. These hypotheses would read: (1) Students taught mathematics by means of a programmed textbook will show greater learning of mathematical concepts than those using traditional textbooks, and (2) Students taught mathematics by means of a programmed textbook will show greater retention of mathematical concepts than those using traditional textbooks. In this way, it is possible to show whether the data obtained support each particular aspect of the general question. The data may indicate the effectiveness of the programmed textbook for original learning but not for retention. One need not worry about the verbal redundancy obvious in stating multiple hypotheses. Remember that the goals of testability and clarity will be served better by the more specific hypotheses.

It is also recommended that the language or terms used in the hypothesis be the simplest that would be acceptable for the purpose of conveying the intended meaning; the use of vague constructs must be avoided. Use terms in the way that is generally accepted for referring to the phenomenon. When two hypotheses are of equal explanatory power, the simpler one is to be preferred since it will provide the necessary explanation with fewer assumptions and variables to be defined. Remember that the principle of parsimony is important in evaluating hypotheses.

Many of the hypotheses that are formulated are rejected after empirical testing. They are predictions that are not supported by the data. In the history of scientific research, hypotheses that failed to be supported have greatly outnumbered those that have been supported. Experienced researchers realize that unconfirmed hypotheses are an expected and useful part of the scientific experience. They can lead to reconsideration of theory and often bring us closer to a correct explanation of the state of affairs. "I have steadily endeavored," Darwin wrote, "to keep my mind free so as to give up any hypothesis, however much beloved (and I cannot resist forming one on every subject), as soon as facts are shown to be opposed to it. Indeed, I have had no choice but to act in this manner, for with the exception of the Coral Reefs, I cannot remember a single first-formed hypothesis which had not after a time to be given up or greatly modified."[5] Even an unsupported hypothesis can be useful in that it points up the need to consider other aspects of a problem and thus may bring the investigator a step closer to an acceptable explanation. In formulating a hypothesis, one's chief concern should be the avoidance of vagueness or ambiguity.

Even though one finds support for a hypothesis, except in cases of perfect induction, the hypothesis is not *proved* to be true. A hypothesis is never proved or

[5]Darwin, *Life and Letters of Charles Darwin,* p. 83.

disproved; it is only supported or not supported. Hypotheses are essentially probabilistic in nature; empirical evidence can lead one to conclude that the explanation is probably true, or that it is reasonable to accept the hypothesis, but it never proves the hypothesis.

Stating the Hypothesis

It has already been stressed that if hypotheses are to be evaluated, they must be stated in a testable form. This form requires a simple, clear statement of the specific relationship between two variables. This type of hypothesis, with which we usually begin, is called the research or substantive hypothesis. It reflects the researcher's expectations based on theory or previous research findings. An example of a research hypothesis is, Children with high IQs will exhibit more anxiety than children with low IQs.

Research hypotheses are sometimes further classified as being directional or nondirectional. As the label indicates, a *directional* hypothesis is one that specifies the direction of the expected findings. This type of statement is made when the experimenter has definite reasons for expecting certain relationships or certain differences to occur between groups. The research hypothesis, Children with high IQs will exhibit more anxiety than children with low IQs, is a directional hypothesis because it stipulates the direction of the difference between groups.

A research hypothesis that does not specify the direction that expected differences or relationships may take is termed a *nondirectional* hypothesis. Stated as a nondirectional hypothesis, our example would read, There is a difference in the anxiety level of children of high IQ and those of low IQ. Although the hypothesis indicates that a difference is expected, the direction of the difference is not specified. These two different forms of research hypotheses require different types of statistical tests. A discussion of these tests is given in Chapter 6.

Generally, the experimenter formulates a statistical or *null hypothesis,* which is one that states that there is no relationship between the variables of the problem. For example, the foregoing hypothesis stated in null form reads, There is no difference in the anxiety scores made by children of high IQ and those of low IQ—in other words, there is no relationship between the variables intelligence and anxiety. The null hypothesis states a negation of what the experimenter would expect or predict. It is used because it enables researchers to compare their findings against chance expectations through statistical methods. The nature and purpose of this type of hypothesis are explained more fully in Chapter 6.

Testing the Hypothesis

After hypotheses are formulated and evaluated according to the criteria discussed earlier, they are subjected to an empirical study. Hypotheses must pass an empirical test as well as a logical one. Even the best ideas, expert opinions, and deductions can sometimes be misleading. They must be tested ultimately by the careful gathering of data.

To test a hypothesis, a researcher (1) deduces the consequences that should be observable if the hypothesis is correct, (2) selects the research methods that will permit the observation, experimentation, or other procedures necessary to show whether or not these consequences do occur, and (3) applies this method and gathers the data that can be analyzed to indicate whether or not the hypothesis is supported.

AN EXAMPLE OF TESTING A HYPOTHESIS

An example may help to illustrate better this process of empirically testing a hypothesis. Assume that an investigator is interested in testing the hypothesis that praise or encouragement results in heightened motivation on the part of students. If this hypothesis is correct, it should be logical to assume that teachers' encouraging comments on test papers (praise) would be followed by improvement in student performance, which implies the assumption that heightened motivation is indicated by improved test performance. (Step 1) This deduced implication may be stated as follows: Teachers' comments on students' papers result in an improvement in pupils' performance on tests. It is the relationship between the two variables, teachers' comments and pupil performance, that must be tested.

This type of hypothesis can be tested by means of an experiment. (Step 2) The researcher could randomly select a number of classes to use in the study. Within each class, students would be randomly assigned to two groups: For those students assigned to Group A, their teachers would write encouraging comments concerning their test performance. (These comments would simply be words of encouragement to the student, such as ''Excellent,'' ''Keep up the good work,'' or ''You're doing better.'' These comments should have nothing to do with content or the correction of particular student errors; otherwise, the improvement could be attributed to the educational usefulness of such comments rather than to increased motivation.) The students assigned to Group B would receive no comments at all on their test papers.

The teachers would administer an objective test covering a certain unit of content. The tests would be scored and the experimental treatment introduced as described above. Then the teachers would administer a second test covering a unit comparable in difficulty to the previous unit and taught after the first test and the experimental treatment. The change from the first test to second test would be ascertained for each student as well as the average gain for the group. It would then be possible through analysis of the data to determine whether average gains on the second test were related to the experimental treatment (teacher comments on papers). (Step 3) If it is found that, as a group, the students who had received comments, Group A, achieved significantly higher gains than the group that did not receive comments, Group B, then the results would support the hypothesis that teachers' comments on students' papers result in an improvement in pupils' performance on tests.

PILOT STUDY

Before the research plan is prepared, it may be helpful to try out the proposed procedures on a few subjects. This trial run or pilot study will, first of all, help the researcher to decide whether or not the study is feasible and whether or not it is worthwhile to continue. It provides an opportunity to assess the appropriateness and practicality of the data collection instruments. It permits a preliminary testing of the hypothesis, which may give some indication of its tenability and suggest whether or not further refinement is needed.

The pilot study will also demonstrate the adequacy of the research procedures and the measures that have been selected for the variables. Unanticipated problems that appear may be solved at this stage, thereby saving time and effort later. A pilot study is well worth the time required and is especially recommended for the beginning researcher.

The Research Plan

After the question and the hypothesis have been formulated, one is ready to complete the tentative research plan. One needs to write out in detail what one proposes to do and just how one plans to do it.

Developing the research plan is essential. It forces one to set down ideas in a concrete form. Many initial ideas seem promising until one has to spell them out in black and white; then the difficulties or the inadequacies become obvious.

The written form can also be given to others for their comments and criticism. It is much easier for another to detect flaws and errors in a proposal when it is written out than when it is communicated by word of mouth.

Typically the research plan is at this stage only a preliminary proposal and many changes will probably be needed before the final, formal proposal is written. However, it is helpful to keep in mind that the more complete and detailed this initial proposal is, the more useful it will be to the researcher and the more time will be saved later.

The research plan includes the following elements.

THE PROBLEM

The plan begins with a clear statement of the question the research is supposed to answer. The problem gives the research its purpose. A brief description of the background of the problem should also be included.

THE HYPOTHESIS

The question is followed by a concise statement of the hypothesis or hypotheses to be tested. The hypothesis gives the research its direction. All subsequent plans for the research project depend on the statement of the hypothesis. It is imperative that the researcher state the hypotheses and the supporting rationale with the greatest clarity. This section of the plan should include operational definitions of the variables involved.

THE RESEARCH DESIGN

The next section of the plan presents a description of the research design—that is, a description of the procedures to be followed in testing the hypotheses. It is very important that an appropriate testing method be chosen. An experimental question cannot be answered by using descriptive methods and vice versa. This section should also include a listing of the measures or instruments to be used in gathering the data. Investigators must locate appropriate tests, scales, and other tools required to measure the variables and must assess the reliability and validity of these operations. The aim is to choose measures that are as objective and reliable as possible, without sacrificing the adequacy of their ''fit'' with the concepts they are supposed to represent.

THE SAMPLE

The plan must include a description of the population of concern in the study—that is, the type of subjects to be included. The researcher must have given some attention to the availability of these subjects. It is also necessary to describe the sampling procedures to be followed. The universe to be sampled must be specified as well as the techniques to be followed in drawing the sample and the proposed sample size.

THE STATISTICAL ANALYSIS

This section will include the researcher's plan for the statistical analysis of the data. Before one begins to collect data, one must identify the statistical test that will permit an answer to the research question or a test of the hypothesis. First, one will need to describe or summarize the data collected from the sample studied. Then one must be able to estimate the reliability or accuracy of the inferences and generalizations made from the sample findings to the total populations. Statistical methods serve both of these functions. The function of summarizing the obtained data is accomplished by descriptive statistics. Inferential statistics enables one to make inferences from sample data.

Many experienced researchers, as well as those who are just learning the process, find it necessary to consult with someone with expertise in statistics before completing their research plan. A brief discussion of the role statistical analysis plays in testing hypotheses is presented in chapter 6.

Summary

In order to proceed with the confirmatory phase of a research study, it is important to have one or more clearly stated hypotheses. The hypothesis is the researcher's prediction about the outcome of the study. Hypotheses are derived inductively from observation or deductively from a known theory. Experience and knowledge in the area and familiarity with previous research are important factors in the formulation of a satisfactory hypothesis.

The hypothesis serves a multipurpose function in research. Since it proposes an explanation that can be empirically tested, it serves to extend knowledge. The hypothesis provides direction to the researcher's efforts since it determines the research method and the type of data relevant to the solution of the problem. It also provides a framework for interpreting the results and for stating the conclusions of the study.

A good hypothesis must satisfy certain criteria: (1) it must have explanatory power; (2) it must be testable, which means that it relates variables that can be measured; (3) it must be in agreement with the preponderance of existing data; (4) it must be stated as clearly and concisely as possible; and (5) it must state the expected relationship between the variables.

After the formulation of the hypothesis, the next step is to write out a plan for the research including a statement of the problem and the hypothesis, as well as a description of the research design, the sample, and the statistical analysis to be applied. This initial written plan affords an opportunity for both the investigator and others to determine whether a feasible program for testing the hypothesis can be implemented.

Once formulated and evaluated in terms of these criteria, the hypothesis is subjected to an empirical test. It is important to remember that a hypothesis cannot be proved or disproved, but only supported or not supported. Even if it is not supported, a hypothesis may still serve a useful purpose since it can lead the researcher to reevaluate his rationale and procedures and to consider other approaches to the problem.

Exercises

1. What is the purpose of hypotheses?
2. What is the difference between an inductive and a deductive hypothesis?
3. State a hypothesis based on each of the research questions listed below:
    a. What would be the effect of using the Cuisenaire method in teaching elementary arithmetic?
    b. Is there a relationship between the sex of the tutor and the gains made in reading achievement by black male elementary students?
    c. Does living in interracial housing affect one's attitude toward members of another race?

d. Is there any relationship between the type of reinforcement (tangible or intangible) and the amount of learning achieved by socioeconomically disadvantaged children?

e. Does preschool training reduce the educational gap separating advantaged and disadvantaged children before they enter first grade?

f. Do teacher expectations of children's intellectual performance have any effect on their actual performance?

4. Rewrite the following hypothesis in null form: Children who read below grade level will express less satisfaction with school than those who read at or above grade level.

5. Evaluate the adequacy of each of the following hypotheses. If an hypothesis is inadequate, state the reason for the inadequacy.

a. Teachers deserve higher pay than administrators.

b. Students who take a middle school government course will be capable of more enlightened judgments concerning local political affairs than will those who do not take the course.

c. Traditional math is better than the new math for slow learners.

d. If students differ in their socioeconomic status, they will differ in their English proficiency scores.

e. Children who show high achievement motivation will show high anxiety as measured by the Children's Manifest Anxiety Scale.

f. Positive verbal reinforcement of student responses by the teacher will lessen the probability of future responses.

6. Write a directional and a nondirectional hypothesis based on the research question, What is the relationship between the maturational status of adolescent boys and their self-concepts?

Answers

1. The purpose of hypotheses is to provide a tentative proposition suggested as a solution to a problem or as an explanation of some phenomenon.

2. With an inductive hypothesis, the researcher makes observations of relationships and then hypothesizes an explanation for the observed behavior. With a deductive hypothesis, the researcher formulates a hypothesis based on known theory, accompanied by a rationale for the particular proposition.

3. a. Elementary students taught by the Cuisenaire method will score higher on an arithmetic test than students not taught by the Cuisenaire method.

b. Black male elementary students tutored by another male will achieve higher reading scores than will black male elementary students tutored by a female.

c. People living in interracial housing will express more favorable attitudes toward those of another race than will people living in segregated housing.

d. Lower-class children reinforced with tangible rewards will exhibit greater learning achievement than will lower-class children reinforced with intangible rewards.

e. Advantaged and disadvantaged children of preschool age receiving preschool training will be separated by a smaller educational gap than will advantaged and disadvantaged children of preschool age not receiving preschool training.

f. Children whose teachers evidence high expectations of their intellectual performance will perform at a higher level than will children whose teachers evidence low expectations of their intellectual performance.

4. There is no difference in the satisfaction with school expressed by children who read below grade level and children who read at or above grade level.

5. a. The hypothesis is inadequate because it is a value statement and cannot be investigated in a research study. A legitimate hypothesis would be: Teachers who receive higher pay than their administrators will express greater job satisfaction than will teachers who do not receive higher pay than their administrators.

   b. The hypothesis is inadequate because "enlightened judgments" is a value term and there is no independent variable. An acceptable hypothesis would be: Students who take a middle school government course will evidence more knowledge concerning local political affairs than will students who do not take a middle school government course.

   c. The hypothesis is inadequate because it is a value statement and lacks clear and concise operational definitions. A testable hypothesis would be: Those students performing below grade level in math who receive instruction in traditional math will score higher on a math test than will those performing below grade level in math who receive instruction in the new math.

   d. The hypothesis is inadequate because there is no statement of an expected relationship between variables. An acceptable hypothesis would be: There is a positive relationship between socioeconomic status and scores on an English proficiency exam.

   e. The hypothesis is inadequate because there are no independent or dependent variables. An acceptable hypothesis would be: Children who show high achievement motivation will have higher scores on the Children's Manifest Anxiety Scale than children with low achievement motivation.

   f. The hypothesis is inadequate because it is inconsistent with the existing knowledge of positive reinforcement and its effect on student responses.

6. Directional hypothesis: Boys who mature at a faster rate will exhibit more positive self-concepts than will boys who mature at a slower rate.
   Nondirectional hypothesis: There is a difference in the self-concepts of early and late maturing adolescent boys.

Part

3

Statistical Analysis

Descriptive Statistics

Statistical procedures are basically methods of handling quantitative information in such a way as to make that information meaningful. These procedures have two principal advantages for researchers. First, they enable us to describe and summarize our observations. Such techniques are called *descriptive statistics*. Second, they help us determine how reliably we can infer that those phenomena observed in a limited group, a *sample,* will also occur in the unobserved larger population of concern, from which the sample was drawn—in other words, how well we can employ inductive reasoning to infer that what we observe in the part will be observed in the whole. For problems of this nature we will need to employ *inferential statistics*.

A knowledge of some basic statistical procedures is essential for those proposing to carry out research, so that they can analyze and interpret their data and communicate their findings to others. In addition, it is desirable that educators who need to keep abreast of research and to make use of research findings be familiar with statistical procedures in order that they can understand and evaluate research studies conducted by others. The proper administration and interpretation of tests used in our schools also require some understanding of statistical procedures. Teachers who are unfamiliar with these procedures may have difficulty in evaluating their students' abilities and achievement. They also find it difficult to review research in their areas of specialization and to acquire up-to-date information.

Scales of Measurement

A fundamental step in the conduct of research is measurement. Measurement is the process through which observations are translated into numbers. S. S. Stevens stated, "In its broadest sense, measurement is the assignment of numerals to objects or events according to rules."[1] Researchers begin with variables, then use rules to determine how these variables will be expressed in numerical form. The variable *religious preference* may be measured according to the numbers indicated by students who are asked to select one among (1) Catholic, (2) Jewish, (3) Protestant, or (4) Other. The variable *weight* may be measured as the numbers observed when subjects step on a scale. The variable *social maturity* may be measured as the scores of subjects who have taken the Vineland Social Maturity Scale.

The nature of the measurement process that produces the numbers determines the interpretation that can be made from them and the statistical procedures that can be

[1]S. S. Stevens, "Mathematics, Measurement, and Psychophysics," in S. S. Stevens (ed.), *Handbook of Experimental Psychology* (New York: Wiley, 1951), p. 1.

meaningfully used with them. The most widely quoted taxonomy of measurement procedures is Stevens'[2] "Scales of Measurement" in which he classifies measurement as nominal, ordinal, interval, and ratio.

NOMINAL SCALE

The most primitive scale of measurement is *nominal* measurement. Nominal measurement involves the placing of objects or individuals into categories which are qualitatively rather than quantitatively different. Measurement at this level only requires that one be able to distinguish two or more relevant categories and know the criteria for placing individuals or objects into one or another category. The required empirical operation at this level involves recognizing that a given object or individual belongs in a given mutually exclusive category or that it does not. The only relationship between the categories is that they are *different* from each other; there is no suggestion that they represent "more" or "less" of the characteristic being measured. Classifying students according to sex, male or female, would constitute nominal measurement.

Numbers are often used at the nominal level, but only in order to identify the categories. The numbers arbitrarily assigned to the categories serve merely as labels or names. All the members of a category are assigned the same number and no two categories are assigned the same number. For example, in preparing data for a computer, the numeral 0 might be used to represent a male and the numeral 1 to represent a female. There is no empirical relationship among the numbers used in nominal measurement that corresponds to the mathematical relation between the numbers. The 1 does not indicate more of something than the 0. The numbers could be interchanged without affecting anything but the labeling scheme used.

The numbers used in a nominal scale do not represent absolute or relative amounts of any characteristic. They merely serve to identify the members of a given category. For example, the numbers assigned to football players constitute a nominal scale. We would not say that the player with number 48 on his jersey is necessarily a better player than the one with 36 on his jersey. Nor could we say that the difference in playing ability between players with the numbers 40 and 48 is equal to the difference between players with the numbers 50 and 58. The statement that the player with number 36 is three times as good as the player with number 12 is likewise meaningless.

The identifying numbers in a nominal scale can never, of course, be arithmetically manipulated through addition, subtraction, multiplication, or division. One may use only those statistical procedures based on mere counting, such as reporting the number of observations in each category.

ORDINAL SCALE

The next highest scale of measurement is *ordinal*. In ordinal measurement, one determines the relative position of objects or individuals with respect to some

[2]Ibid., pp. 1–49.

attribute, but without indicating the distance between positions. The essential requirement for measurement at this level is an empirical criterion for ordering objects or events with respect to the attribute—that is, some procedure for determining, for each thing being measured, whether that individual or object has more, the same amount, or less of the attribute in question. Ordinal measurement occurs, for example, when teachers rank students on certain characteristics, such as their social maturity, leadership abilities, cooperativeness, and so on. Students are frequently ranked according to their academic achievement or according to their performance in a music or athletic contest.

In ordinal measurement, the empirical procedure used for ordering objects must satisfy a criterion known as the *transitivity postulate*. This postulate is written: If $(a > b)$ and $(b > c)$, then $(a > c)$; it means that the relationship must be such that if object a is greater than object b, and object b is greater than object c, then object a is greater than object c. Of course, other words may be substituted for "greater than"; these might include "stronger than," "precedes," "has more of some attribute," and so on.

The empirical operation in ordinal measurement involves only direct comparison of the objects or individuals in terms of the extent to which they possess the attribute in question. Thus, when numbers are assigned to the objects, the only information considered is that *order* of the objects. Consequently, the only characteristic of the numbers having meaning is their order. The numbers assigned in ordinal measurement indicate only the order of position and nothing more. Neither the difference between the numbers nor their ratio has meaning. When the numbers 1, 2, 3, and so on, are used in ordinal measurement there is no implication that rank 1 is as much higher than rank 2 as 2 is than 3, and so on. The distance between the child with a rank of 1 and the child with a rank of 2 may be the same, less than, or greater than the distance between children with rankings of 2 and 3. There is simply no basis for interpreting the magnitude of differences between the numbers or the ratio of the numbers. In an untimed footrace, we may know who came in first, second, third, and so on, but we would not know how much faster one runner was than another. The difference between the first and second would not necessarily be the same as the difference between the second and third, or the third and fourth. Neither could one say that the runner who came in second was twice as fast as the runner who came in fourth.

A good example of an ordinal scale is the scale of hardness of minerals. Minerals are arranged according to their ability to scratch one another. If mineral A can scratch mineral B, then mineral A is said to be harder than mineral B. On this basis a diamond is ranked as the hardest, since it can scratch all other known minerals but cannot be scratched by any others. A set of ten minerals ranging in hardness from the softest to the hardest was selected as a standard and assigned the numbers from 1 to 10, with 1 indicating the softest mineral and 10 the hardest. Other minerals are assigned numbers on the basis of the scratch test. Thus, we know the order of hardness of minerals, but we do not know how much harder one mineral is than another. We may not assume that a mineral assigned a value of 4 is twice as hard as a mineral with a value of 2, or that the difference in hardness between minerals 2 and 4 is the same as the difference in hardness between minerals with values 1 and 3.

The arithmetical operations of addition, subtraction, multiplication, and division cannot be used with ordinal scales. The statistics appropriate for an ordinal scale are limited. Since the size of the interval between the categories is unknown, one cannot use any statistical procedure that assumes equal intervals. Statistics that indicate the points below which certain percentages of the cases fall are appropriate with an ordinal scale. Statistics appropriate for the nominal scale may also be used with an ordinal scale.

INTERVAL SCALE

An interval scale is one which provides equal intervals from an arbitrary origin. An interval scale not only orders objects or events according to the amount of the attribute they represent but also establishes equal intervals between the units of measure. Equal differences in the numbers represent equal differences in the attribute being measured. The Fahrenheit and Centigrade thermometers are examples of interval scales.

On an interval scale, both the order and distance relationships among the numbers have meaning. We may assert that the difference between 50 and 51 degrees Centigrade is equal to the difference between 30 and 31 degrees Centigrade. We could not say, however, that 50 degrees is twice as hot as 25 degrees. This is because there is no true zero point on an interval scale. A zero point is established by convention, as in the Centigrade scale which assigns the value 0 degrees to the freezing point of water.

Likewise, the zero point on a psychological or educational test is arbitrary. For example, there is no zero intelligence; there is no way in our standardized intelligence tests to identify an individual of zero intelligence. A student may occasionally receive a score of zero on a statistics test, but this does not mean that he has zero knowledge of statistics. If we had three students who made scores of 15, 30, and 45 on a statistics quiz, we could not say that the score of 30 represents twice as much knowledge of statistics as the score of 15 or that the score of 45 represents three times as much knowledge as the score of 15. To understand the reason why this is so, let us assume that 15 very simple items are added to the quiz so that all three students are able to answer them correctly. The three scores would now become 30, 45 and 60 for the three students. If we attempted to form ratios between the values on this interval type scale, we would mistakenly report that the student with a score of 60 had twice as much knowledge of statistics as the student with a score of 30, whereas in the earlier ratio we had incorrectly assumed that the same student had three times as great a knowledge of statistics as the other student.

Thus, because the zero is arbitrary, multiplication and division of the numbers are not appropriate; as we have seen, ratios between the numbers on an interval scale are meaningless. However, the difference between positions on an interval scale may be reported or the numbers may be added. Any statistical procedures based on adding may be used with this level scale along with the procedures appropriate for the lower level scales. These include most of the common statistical procedures.

It is important to point out that in most of the cases where we use interval scales, the intervals are equal in terms of the measuring instrument itself but not necessarily in terms of the ability we are measuring. To illustrate, consider a spelling test with the following words: *cat, dish, ball, loquacious, schizophrenia, pneumonia.* Here the distance between 1 correct and 3 correct is the same as the distance between 3 correct and 5 correct. However, when considered in terms of spelling ability, the difference between 3 and 5 correct suggests a greater difference in ability than does the difference between 1 and 3 correct. Unless one can say that the distance between 3 and 5 on the spelling test represents the same amount of spelling ability as does the distance between 1 and 3, then these scores indicate only the rank order of the students.

However, through careful construction one can produce an instrument where the intervals observed between scores on the test give a reasonable approximation of ability intervals. The better intelligence tests are an example of this. The difference in ability between an IQ of 90 and an IQ of 95 may not be precisely the same as the difference between an IQ of 105 and an IQ of 110, but we will not be greatly misled if we assume that the two differences are approximately equal.

RATIO SCALE

A ratio scale, the highest type, is one which provides a true zero point as well as equal intervals. Ratios can be formed between any two given values on the scale. A yardstick used to measure length in units of inches or feet is a ratio scale, for the origin on the scale is an absolute zero corresponding to no length at all. Thus, it is possible to state that a stick 6 feet long is twice as long as a stick 3 feet long. With a ratio scale, it is possible to multiply or divide each of the values by a certain number without changing the properties of the scale. For example, we can multiply 2 pounds by 16 to change the unit of measurement to 32 ounces or we can multiply 6 feet by 12 to change the unit to inches. We can multiply and maintain the same ratio as before the multiplication. For example, we can multiply 4 quarts of milk and 2 quarts of milk by 2 and change the unit of measurement to pints. In pints, 8 pints is still twice as much as 4 pints.

Only a few variables of interest in education are ratio in nature. These are largely confined to motor performance and other physiological measures. While we may say that a person 6 feet tall is twice as tall as a person 3 feet tall, we cannot say that a person with an IQ of 150 is twice as intelligent as a person with an IQ of 75.

All types of statistical procedures are appropriate with a ratio scale.

Organizing Research Data

Describing data that have not been arranged in some kind of order is very difficult, if not impossible. Therefore, organizing research data is a fundamental step in descriptive statistics. Two frequently used ways of organizing data are (1) arranging the measures into frequency distributions and (2) presenting them in graphic form.

FREQUENCY DISTRIBUTIONS

A systematic arrangement of individual measures from lowest to highest is called a frequency distribution. The use of this technique merely involves making a list of the individual measures in a column, with the highest measure at the top, the next highest second from the top, and continuing down until the lowest measure is recorded at the bottom of the column. It is often found that several identical scores will occur in a distribution. Instead of listing these scores separately, it is customary to add a second column where the frequency of each measure is recorded. In Table 5.1 the scores of a group of 105 students in a statistics test are shown. In Section A of the table the scores are listed in an unorganized form. In Section B the same scores are arranged into a frequency distribution.

From a frequency distribution it is possible to examine the general "shape" of the distribution. With the scores so organized one can determine their spread, whether they are distributed evenly or tend to cluster, and where clusters occur in the distribution. For example, looking over the frequency distribution of the scores presented in Table 5.1, it is easy to see that they range from 21 to 35, that 29 is the most frequent score, and that there is a tendency for scores to cluster more near the top of the distribution than the bottom. None of this would be apparent if the scores had not been organized. Organizing data into frequency distributions also facilitates the computation of various useful statistics.

GRAPHIC PRESENTATION OF DATA

It is often helpful and convenient to present research data in graphic form. Among various types of graphs the most widely used are the *histogram* and the *frequency polygon*. The initial steps in constructing the histogram and the frequency polygon are identical:

1. Lay out the score points on a horizontal dimension (abscissa) from the lowest value on the left to the highest on the right. Leave enough space for an additional score at both ends of the distribution.

Table 5.1   The Test Scores of 105 Students in a Statistics Test

A. Unorganized Scores

33,	29,	30,	30,	33,	29,	33,	32,	28,	24,	34,	31,	27,	29,	23,
25,	29,	24,	27,	26,	33,	33,	26,	30,	28,	26,	29,	32,	32,	31,
28,	34,	30,	31,	33,	21,	29,	31,	30,	32,	35,	30,	31,	27,	29,
26,	29,	33,	32,	29,	28,	28,	30,	28,	27,	30,	31,	34,	33,	22,
30,	29,	27,	29,	24,	30,	21,	31,	31,	33,	28,	21,	31,	29,	31,
31,	33,	22,	29,	31,	32,	32,	31,	28,	29,	30,	22,	33,	30,	30,
32,	33,	31,	33,	28,	29,	27,	33,	27,	21,	30,	29,	28,	27,	33

B. Frequency distribution

Scores (X)	Tallies	Frequency (f)
35	/	1
34	///	3
33											15
32	||| ///	8
31	||| ||| ////	14
30	||| ||| ////	14
29	||| ||| ||| /	16
28								10
27	||| ///	8
26	////	4
25	/	1
24	///	3
23	/	1
22	///	3
21	////	4
		$N = \overline{105}$

2. Lay out the frequencies of the scores or intervals on the vertical dimension (ordinate), numbering up from zero.
3. Place a dot above each score at the level of the frequency of that score.

From this point one can construct either a histogram or a polygon.

In constructing a histogram one should draw through each dot a horizontal line equal to the width representing a score, as shown in Figure 5.1.

To construct a polygon, the adjacent dots are connected and the two ends of the resulting figure are connected to the base (zero line) at the points representing one less than the lowest score and one more than the highest score, as shown in Figure 5.2.

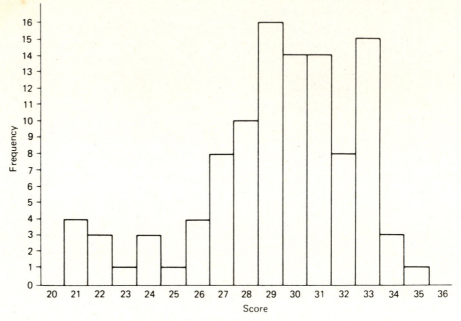

Figure 5.1   Histogram of 105 statistics scores from Table 5.1

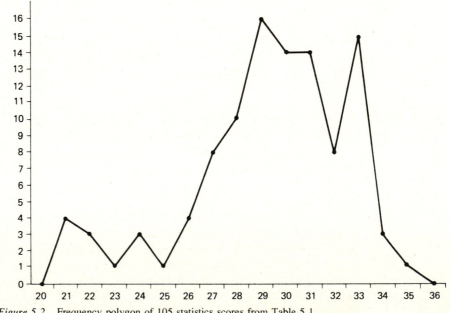

Figure 5.2   Frequency polygon of 105 statistics scores from Table 5.1

Measures of Central Tendency

A convenient way of summarizing data is to find a single index that can represent a whole set of measures. For example, finding a single score that can give an indication of the performance of a group of 300 students on an IQ test would be useful for comparative purposes. In statistics three indices are available for such use. They are called measures of central tendency or averages. To most laymen the term *average* means the sum of the scores divided by the number of scores. To a statistician the average can be this measure, known as the *mean,* or one of the other two measures of central tendency, known as the *mode* and the *median*. Each of these three can serve as an index to represent a group as a whole.

THE MODE

The mode is that value in a distribution that occurs most frequently. It is the simplest to find of the three measures of central tendency since it is determined by inspection rather than by computation. Given the distribution of scores

$$14 \quad 16 \quad 16 \quad 17 \quad 18 \quad 19 \quad 19 \quad 19 \quad 21 \quad 22$$

one can readily see that the mode of this distribution is 19 because it is the most frequent score.

Sometimes there is more than one mode in a distribution. For example, if the scores had been

$$14 \quad 16 \quad 16 \quad 16 \quad 18 \quad 19 \quad 19 \quad 19 \quad 21 \quad 22$$

we would have two modes: 16 and 19. This kind of distribution is called bimodal.

The mode is not often a useful indicator of central value in a distribution for two reasons. In the first place, it is unstable. For example, two random samples drawn from the same population may have quite different modes. In the second place, a distribution may have more than one mode. In published research the mode is seldom reported as an indicator of central tendency. Its use is largely limited to inspectional purposes. A mode may be reported for any of the scales of measurement, but it is the only measure of central tendency that may legitimately be used with nominal scales.

THE MEDIAN

The median is defined as that point in a distribution of measures below which 50 percent of the cases lie (which means that the other 50 percent will be above this point). For example, given the distribution of scores

$$14 \quad 16 \quad 16 \quad 17 \quad 18 \quad 19 \quad 19 \quad 19 \quad 21 \quad 22$$

the point below which 50 percent of the cases fall is halfway between 18 and 19. Thus, the median of this distribution is 18.5. Note that to find this value, we first placed the ten scores of the distribution in rank order (that is, from the lowest to the highest), and then found the point below which one-half of the scores lie. This point, 18.5, which exactly separates the two values 18 and 19, is called in statistical terminology the *upper limit* of the score 18 and the *lower limit* of the score 19. In computing the median, each score is thought of as representing a range or interval from halfway between that score and the next lowest score up to halfway between that score and the next highest score. Thus, in the example, 18 is thought of as representing an interval from 17.5 to 18.5 while 19 represents an interval from 18.5 to 19.5.

It is important to note that the median does not always fall on the border line between two values. In fact it is often located somewhere between the upper limit and the lower limit of an interval. For the purpose of establishing the median we must picture a recorded score as representing the range between its lower and upper limits rather than a single point. Consider the following example:

$$23 \quad 24 \quad 25 \quad 26 \quad 26 \quad 26 \quad 26 \quad 27$$

In this distribution, the median falls between two of the scores of 26. Note the frequency of the score 26. There are four of these scores in the distribution, one of which is located below the midpoint and three above the midpoint. In this case, to find the median we must subdivide the interval 25.50–26.50 into four parts. The distance between each of these four scores would thus be 0.25 of the interval. Each of these scores is therefore thought of as representing a range covering 0.25 of the distance between 25.50 and 26.50, which are the upper and lower limits of the score 26. The following is an illustration of this concept, showing the position and value of the median:

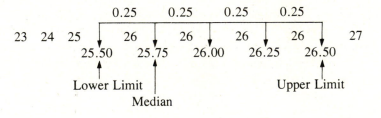

It is easier to use a formula for finding the median rather than to go through this process each time.

$$Md = L + \left(\frac{\frac{N}{2} - cfb}{fw} \right) i \qquad (5.1)$$

where

Md = the median

N = the number of cases in the distribution

L = the lower limit of the interval within which the median lies

cfb = the cumulative frequency in all intervals below the interval containing the median

fw = the frequency of cases within the interval containing the median

i = the interval size

The value i becomes necessary only when the size of the interval is other than 1. For example, if we are working with achievement test grade level scores that are expressed in decimal units such as 3.4 and 5.9, the interval size is 0.1.

In the foregoing example L is 25.50, N is 8, cfb is 3, fw is 4, and i is 1.

$$\underset{cfb\,=\,3}{\underline{23 \quad 24 \quad 25}} \Big| \underset{fw\,=\,4}{\underline{26 \quad 26 \quad 26 \quad 26}} \quad 27$$
$$L = 25.50$$

Putting these values in the formula we obtain

$$Md = 25.50 + \left(\frac{\frac{8}{2} - 3}{4} \right) 1 = 25.75$$

A frequency distribution can be used to compute the median efficiently. Table 5.2 shows the same data as Table 5.1 and includes an additional column labeled *cumulative frequency (cf)*, which is used for locating the median. Cumulative frequencies show the frequencies of the values up to and including any given interval in a distribution. For example, the frequency of scores up to and including the interval of the score 30 in Table 5.2 is 64 as shown in the *cf* column. This column enables us to locate the interval within which the median lies. Since the median is that point in the distribution below which 50 percent of the cases fall, the interval containing the median will be the one with a cumulative frequency containing the value of $N/2$. In other words, we divide the N of the distribution by 2 and look for the interval that contains this value.

In the distribution of scores shown in Table 5.2, the number of cases, or N, equals 105, and thus the value of $N/2$ is 52.50. Looking up the *cf* column, we see that there are 50 cases up to and including the score 29, and 64 cases up to and including the score 30; thus the median is located within the interval represented by the score of 30. It is possible now to apply formula (5.1) and find the median of the distribution. The value of L in this example is 29.50 because the interval that contains the median represents a range from 29.50, the lower limit, to 30.50, the upper limit. The value of cfb (that is, the frequency of the values below the interval that contains the median) is 50. The frequency of the values within the interval represented by the

Table 5.2 Computation of the Median with a Frequency Distribution of Scores of 105 Students in a Statistics Test

Scores (X)	Frequency (f)	Cumulative Frequency (cf)
35	1	105
34	3	104
33	15	101
32	8	86
31	14	78
30	14 fw	64
29	16	50
28	10	34
27	8	24
26	4	16
25	1 cfb = 50	12
24	3	11
23	1	8
22	3	7
21	4	4

$$Md = 29.50 + \left(\frac{\frac{105}{2} - 50}{14} \right) 1 = 29.678$$

score 30 (that is, the value of fw) is 14. The interval size, or the value of i, in this distribution is 1 because each score represents an interval width of 1. Using the formula we find that the median of the distribution is 29.678.

Notice that the median does not take into account the size of individual scores. In order to find it we arrange our data in rank order and find the point that divides the distribution into two equal halves. The median is an ordinal statistic since it is based on rank. We can compute a median from interval or ratio data, but we do not use the interval characteristic of the data.

One circumstance when the median may be the preferred measure of central tendency arises when there are some extreme scores in the distribution. In this case the use of a measure of central tendency that takes into account the size of each score results in either overestimation or underestimation of the typical score. The median, because of its insensitivity to extreme scores, is the most appropriate index to be applied when one wants to find the typical score. For illustration consider the following distribution:

$$50 \quad 51 \quad 53 \quad 54 \quad 55 \quad 70 \quad 89$$

The score of 54, which is the median of this distribution, is the most typical score. An index that takes into account the individual values of the scores 70 and 89 will certainly result in an overestimation of the typical score.

THE MEAN

The most widely used measure of central tendency is the mean, which is popularly known as the average or *arithmetic average*. It is the sum of all the values in a distribution divided by the number of cases. In terms of a formula it is

$$\bar{X} = \frac{\Sigma X}{N} \qquad (5.2)$$

where
$\bar{X}$ = the mean
Σ = the sum of
X = each of the values in the distribution
N = the number of cases

Applying formula (5.2) to the following IQ scores, we find that the mean is 111.

IQ Score: 112   121   115   101   119   109   100

$$\bar{X} = \frac{112 + 121 + 115 + 101 + 119 + 109 + 100}{7} = \frac{777}{7} = 111$$

Note that in this computation the scores were not arranged in any particular order. This procedure is unnecessary when the mean of a set of measures is to be found.

Since the mean is an arithmetic average, it is classified as an interval statistic. Its use is appropriate for interval or ratio data but not for nominal or ordinal data.

Computing the Mean from a Frequency Distribution

If the data have been arranged into a frequency distribution, the sum of the scores can be computed by multiplying each score by its frequency and summing these products, as shown in Table 5.3, which simplifies the computation of the mean.

COMPARISON OF THE THREE INDICES OF CENTRAL TENDENCY

Since the mean is an interval or ratio statistic, it is generally a more precise measure than the median (an ordinal statistic) or the mode (a nominal statistic). It takes into account the value of *every* score. It is also the most stable of the three measures of central tendency in that if a number of samples are randomly drawn from a parent population, the means of these samples will vary less from one another than will their medians and their modes. For these reasons the mean is more frequently used in research than the other two measures.

The mean is the best indicator of the combined performance of an entire group. However, the median is the best indicator of *typical* performance. Consider, for example, a school board whose members have the following annual incomes: $33,000, $10,000, $8,000, $6,000, $6,000. The mean, $12,600 indicates the total income in relation to number of members, but it is higher than all but one of the board members' incomes. The median, $8,000, gives a better picture of the typical income in the group.

Table 5.3   Computation of the Mean for Frequency Distribution of Scores of 105 Students in a Statistics Test

X	f	fX
35	1	35
34	3	102
33	15	495
32	8	256
31	14	434
30	14	420
29	16	464
28	10	280
27	8	216
26	4	104
25	1	25
24	3	72
23	1	23
22	3	66
21	4	84
	$N = \overline{105}$	$\Sigma fX = \overline{3076}$

$$\bar{X} = \frac{3076}{105} = 29.30$$

Shapes of Distributions

If a distribution of measures is symmetrical, the values of the mean and the median coincide. If such a distribution has a single mode, rather than two or more modes, the three indices of central tendency will coincide, as shown in Figure 5.3.

If a distribution is not symmetrical, it is described as being *skewed*. In skewed distributions the values of the measures of central tendency differ. In such distributions the value of the mean, because it is influenced by the size of extreme scores, is pulled toward the end of the distribution in which the extreme scores lie, as shown in Figures 5.4 and 5.5. The effect of extreme values is less on the median since this index is influenced not by the size of scores, but by their frequency. Extreme values have no impact on the mode since this index, because of its nature, has no relation

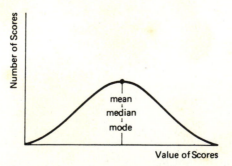

Figure 5.3   A symmetrical distribution

with either of the ends of the distribution. When the distribution is skewed toward the lower end, or negatively skewed, the mean is *always* smaller than the median and the median is *usually* smaller than the mode (Figure 5.4). When a distribution is skewed toward the higher end, or positively skewed, the mean is *always* greater than the median and the median is *usually* greater than the mode (Figure 5.5). The skew of a distribution can be identified by comparing the mean and the median without necessarily constructing a histogram or polygon.

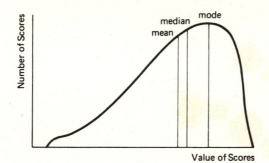

Figure 5.4   A negatively skewed distribution

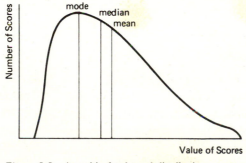

Figure 5.5   A positively skewed distribution

Measures of Variability

Although indices of central tendency help us describe data in terms of average value or typical measure, they do not give us the total picture of a distribution. The mean values of two distributions may be identical, but the degree of dispersion or variability of their scores might be quite different. In one distribution the scores might cluster around the central value; in the other they might be scattered. For illustration consider the following distributions of scores:

$$(A) \;\; 24, \; 24, \; 25, \; 25, \; 25, \; 26, \; 26 \qquad \bar{X} = \frac{175}{7} = 25$$

$$(B) \;\; 16, \; 19, \; 22, \; 25, \; 28, \; 30, \; 35 \qquad \bar{X} = \frac{175}{7} = 25$$

The value of the mean in both of these distributions is 25, but the degree of scattering of the scores differs considerably. The scores in distribution (A) are obviously much more homogeneous than those in distribution (B). There is clearly a need for an index that can describe distributions in terms of *variation* of scores. In statistics, several indices are available for this purpose. The four most commonly used are *range, quartile deviation, variance,* and *standard deviation.*

RANGE

The simplest of all indices of variability is the range. It is the distance between the highest and the lowest scores in a distribution and is found by subtracting the smallest value from the highest. For example, the range of distribution (A) above is 2 and of distribution (B) is 19.

The range is an unreliable index of variability in that it is based on only two scores, the highest and the lowest. It is not a stable indicator of the nature of the spread of the measures around the central value. For this reason the use of range is mainly limited to inspectional purposes. In some research reports, reference is made to the range of distributions, but such references are usually used in conjunction with other measures of variability, such as quartile deviation and standard deviation.

QUARTILE DEVIATION

The quartile deviation (QD) is half the difference between the upper and lower quartiles in a distribution. The upper quartile (Q_3) is the point in a distribution below which 75 percent of the cases lie. The lower quartile (Q_1) is the point below which 25 percent of the cases lie. The upper quartile is also referred to as the seventy-fifth percentile and the lower quartile as the twenty-fifth percentile.

The procedure for finding Q_1 and Q_3 is similar to that used for finding the median. The median is, in fact, the second quartile. In the case of Q_3 the formula becomes

$$Q_3 = L + \left(\frac{\frac{3N}{4} - cfb}{fw} \right) i \tag{5.3}$$

and for Q_1 the formula is

$$Q_1 = L + \left(\frac{\frac{N}{4} - cfb}{fw} \right) i \tag{5.4}$$

where
Q_3 = the upper quartile
Q_1 = the lower quartile
 N = the number of cases in the distribution
 L = the lower limit of the interval within which the quartile lies
cfb = the cumulative frequency below the interval containing the quartile
fw = the frequency of cases within the interval containing the quartile
 i = the interval size

Once the values of the first and third quartiles have been found, the quartile deviation can be computed as follows:

$$QD = \frac{Q_3 - Q_1}{2} \qquad (5.5)$$

For example, if the upper and the lower quartiles in a distribution of scores are 35 and 15, respectively, the value of the quartile deviation would be 10.

$$QD = \frac{35 - 15}{2} = 10$$

The quartile deviation provides a measure of one half of that range of scores within which lie the middle 50 percent of the cases. If the spread of scores is great, the value of the quartile deviation will be higher than it will be if the spread is small. The quartile deviation is a more useful value than the range since it is more stable.

The quartile deviation belongs to the same statistical family as the median because it is an ordinal statistic. It is most often used in conjunction with the median. It is also called the *semi-interquartile range*.

VARIANCE AND STANDARD DEVIATION

Variance and standard deviation are very useful measures of variability. They are based on the mean as the point of reference and take into account the size and location of each individual score.

The basic ingredient of both statistics is the *deviation score*. This score (symbolized by x) is the difference between a raw score and the mean. Symbolically this is shown as $x = X - \bar{X}$. Raw scores below the mean will have negative deviation scores and raw scores above the mean will have positive deviation scores. By definition, the sum of the deviation scores in a distribution is always zero.

For this reason in order to use the deviation scores to generate an index of variability, one must square each of them. As the squares of both negative and positive numbers are positive, the sum of the squared deviation scores will be greater than zero. The sum of these squares can be employed to indicate the variability of the scores in a distribution. The mean of the squared deviation scores ($\Sigma x^2 / N$), called the *variance*, is sometimes used as an index of variability. The definition of variance in mathematical form is

$$\sigma^2 = \frac{\Sigma x^2}{N} \qquad (5.6)$$

where
σ^2 = the variance
Σ = the sum of
x = the deviation of each score from the mean ($X - \bar{X}$), otherwise known as the deviation score
N = the number of cases in the distribution

Since each of the deviation scores is squared, the variance is necessarily expressed in units that are squares of the original units of measure. For example, we might find the variance of the heights of children in a class is 9 square inches. This would tell us that this class is more heterogeneous in height than a class with a variance of 4 square inches and more homogeneous than a class with a variance of 16 square inches.

In many cases educators prefer an index that summarizes the data in the same unit of measurement as the original data. *Standard deviation* (σ), the square root of variance, provides such an index. It is by far the most commonly used measure of variability. By definition the standard deviation is the square root of the mean of the squared deviation scores. Rewriting this definition using symbols, we obtain

$$\sigma = \sqrt{\frac{\Sigma x^2}{N}} \tag{5.7}$$

For an illustration, consider Table 5.4. Column (1) in this table shows the distribution of the test scores of seven individuals. The mean of this distribution is 6. Column (2) presents the deviations for each of the scores. For example, the deviation of the score 8 from the mean is $+2$, the deviation of the score 5 from the mean is -1, and so forth. Column (3) shows the squares of each of these deviation scores. The sum of these squared deviation scores is 28. Putting this value in the formula and dividing by 7, the number of cases, we arrive at 4, which is the mean of the squared deviation scores. The square root of this value is 2, which is the standard deviation of this distribution.

The foregoing procedure is convenient when the mean of the distribution is a round number, which it is not in most cases. Therefore, the following formula has been developed to eliminate the tedious task of working with fractional deviation scores. The use of this formula gives the same result with much less labor. (Table A.1 in the Appendix gives the squares and square roots of numbers from 1 to 1,000 to facilitate computations.)

$$\sigma = \sqrt{\frac{\Sigma X^2 - \frac{(\Sigma X)^2}{N}}{N}} \tag{5.8}$$

where

σ = the standard deviation

ΣX^2 = the sum of the squares of each score (that is, each score is first squared, then these squares are summed)

$(\Sigma X)^2$ = the sum of the scores squared (the scores are first summed, then this total is squared)

N = the number of cases

Table 5.5 shows the computation of the standard deviation of the data in Table 5.4 using formula (5.8). The first column in this table shows the scores and their sum. The second column shows the square of each score and the sum of these squares. The rest of the table shows the application of formula (5.8) to find the value of the standard deviation. Note that the resulting value is the same as that found by applying formula (5.7) to the same data.

The standard deviation belongs to the same statistical family as the mean; that is, like the mean, it is an interval or ratio statistic and its computation is based on the size of individual scores in the distribution. It is by far the most frequently used measure of variability and is used in conjunction with the mean.

Table 5.4   Computation of the Standard Deviation

(1) X	(2) $x = X - \bar{X}$	(3) $x^2 = (X - \bar{X})^2$
9	+3	+9
8	+2	+4
7	+1	+1
6	0	0
5	−1	+1
4	−2	+4
3	−3	+9
$\Sigma X = 42$		$28 = \Sigma x^2$

$$\bar{X} = \frac{42}{7} = 6$$

$$\sigma = \sqrt{\frac{28}{7}} = \sqrt{4} = 2$$

Table 5.5   Computation of the Standard Deviation Using Formula (5.8)

X	X^2	
9	81	$\sigma = \sqrt{\dfrac{280 - \dfrac{(42)^2}{7}}{7}}$
8	64	
7	49	
6	36	
5	25	$= \sqrt{\dfrac{280 - 252}{7}}$
4	16	
3	9	$= \sqrt{4}$
$42 = \Sigma X$	$280 = \Sigma X^2$	$= 2$

Standard Scores

We often wish to make a comparison between the relative positions of one individual on two different tests. It is only possible to do this meaningfully if the two tests have the same means and the same standard deviations, but this seldom happens in practice. To overcome this difficulty we can translate measures into standard scores. A widely used standard score that plays an important role in statistical analyses is the z-score, which is defined as the distance of a score from the mean, as measured by standard deviation units. The formula for finding a z-score is

$$z = \frac{X - \bar{X}}{\sigma} = \frac{x}{\sigma} \tag{5.9}$$

where

X = the raw score
$\bar{X}$ = the mean of the distribution
σ = the standard deviation of the distribution
x = the deviation score $(X - \bar{X})$

Applying this formula, a score exactly one standard deviation above the mean becomes a z of $+1$, a score exactly one standard deviation below the mean becomes a z of -1, and so on. A score with the same numerical value as the mean will have a z-score value of zero. For illustration, suppose a student's score on a psychology test is 72 where the mean of the distribution is 78 and the standard deviation equals 12. Suppose also that the same student has made a score of 48 on a statistics test where the mean is 51 and the standard deviation is 6. If we subsitute these figures for the appropriate symbols in formula (5.9), we can derive a z-score for each test.

Psychology   Statistics

$$z_1 = \frac{72 - 78}{12} = -0.50 \qquad z_2 = \frac{48 - 51}{6} = -0.50$$

Both these standard scores belong to the z-distribution, where by definition the mean is zero and the standard deviation is one, and therefore they are directly comparable. It is apparent in this example that the score of 72 on the psychology test and the score of 48 on the statistics test are equivalent. That is, both scores are indicative of the same relative level of performance. In other words, the standing of the student who has obtained these scores is the same in both tests when compared with the performance of the other students. It would be very difficult to make such a comparison without employing the z-score technique.

Let us use another example: Suppose a student who has taken these same tests has obtained a score of 81 on the psychology test and a score of 53 on the statistics test. As before, it is difficult to compare these raw scores to show on which test this student has done better. Converting the scores to z-scores makes the comparison easy. Using formula (5.9), we find the values of z_1 and z_2 in this case to be

$$z_1 = \frac{81 - 78}{12} = +0.25 \qquad z_2 = \frac{53 - 51}{6} = +0.33$$

This rather surprising result shows that the score of 53 on the statistics test actually indicates a slightly better relative performance than the score of 81 on the psychology test. Compared with the other students, this student has done somewhat better in statistics than in psychology.

A disadvantage of z-scores is that we have to deal with negative values and decimal fractions. To overcome these difficulties we can use Z-scores when comparisons between the scores in various distributions are to be made. The Z-distribution has by definition a mean of 50 and a standard deviation of 10. To transform z-scores to Z-scores we multiply the z-value by 10 and add 50. The Z-score formula is:

$$Z = 10z + 50 = 10\left(\frac{X - \bar{X}}{\sigma}\right) + 50 \tag{5.10}$$

Suppose a student's score on a Spanish test is 21. Given that the mean of the scores in this test is 27 and the standard deviation is 6, the z-score will be $(21 - 27)/6$, which can be inserted directly into the Z-score formula as follows:

$$Z = 10\left(\frac{21 - 27}{6}\right) + 50 = 40$$

The transformation of z-scores into Z-scores not only enables one to work with whole numbers, but it also avoids the adverse psychological implications of describing subjects' performances with negative numbers.

Teachers who wish to compare the standings of their students on successive tests, or to add all the scores obtained on different tests in the same course to make a general distribution, can convert the students' raw scores to z-scores or Z-scores in order to give equal weight to each set of scores. Adding and averaging scores that belong to different distributions and have different means and different standard deviations, without converting them to some kind of standard score, is not statistically justified.

Z-scores, being transformations of z-scores, are a type of standard score. Other standard scores, such as those for the College Entrance Examination Board (CEEB) and the Army General Classification Test (AGCT), are transformations of z-scores. The mean of CEEB has been arbitrarily set at 500 with an arbitrary standard deviation of 100, whereas the mean of the AGCT distribution has been set at 100 and its standard deviation set at 20. To convert a raw score to CEEB we first determine its z-value, then multiply this z-score by 100, the size of the standard deviation, and add 500, the arbitrary mean. To transform a raw score to AGCT we convert it to a z-score, then multiply the z-value by 20 and add 100 to the result.

The Normal Curve

It has been found that the distribution of many physical and psychological measures takes the shape of a bell when plotted as a frequency polygon. For example, if we measure American boys on their tenth birthday, we will find many boys whose height is near the mean and several boys who are slightly above or below the mean. The further we get from the mean, the fewer boys we will find at each height. A polygon showing this distribution closely resembles a theoretical polygon known as the normal curve. This theoretical curve is a model which was deductively derived from mathematical theory through use of the formula

$$Y = \frac{1}{\sigma\sqrt{2\pi}} e^{-x^2/2\sigma^2} \tag{5.11}$$

where

Y = the ordinate for any value of x

π = a mathematical constant, equal to 3.1416

e = another constant, equal to 2.7183

x = the deviation of each score from the mean

σ = the standard deviation of the distribution

By the use of formula (5.11) it is possible to determine the ordinate of each value in the distribution and construct the normal curve. Such an operation requires considerable calculation, but fortunately this is not necessary since tables of the ordinates and the areas of the normal curve have already been computed. The areas are shown in Table A.2 in the Appendix.

This hypothetical polygon indicates the expected (that is, theoretical) frequencies of all possible z-scores. It indicates that z-scores near zero will be expected to occur more frequently than other z-score values, and the farther from zero a z-score is, the less frequently it will be expected to occur.

Inasmuch as so many naturally occurring distributions resemble the normal curve, this theoretical model has proved to be highly useful. Whenever actual data are known or believed to resemble the normal curve in distribution, we can deduce many useful estimates from the theoretical properties of the normal curve.

The normal curve is a symmetrical distribution of measures with the same number of cases at specified distances below the mean as above the mean. Its mean is the point below which exactly 50 percent of the cases fall and above which the other 50 percent of the cases are located. The median and the mode in such a distribution are identical values and coincide with the mean. In a normal curve most of the cases concentrate near the mean. The frequency of cases decreases as we proceed away from the mean in either direction. Approximately 34 percent of the cases in a normal distribution fall between the mean and one standard deviation above or below the mean. The area between one and two standard deviations from the mean on either side of the distribution contains about 14 percent of the cases. Only about 2 percent of the cases fall between two and three standard deviations from the mean, and only

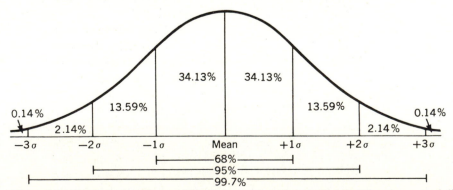

Figure 5.6 The percentage of cases falling between successive standard deviations in a normal distribution

about 0.1 percent of the cases fall above or below three standard deviations from the mean. This is illustrated in Figure 5.6.

It is possible to determine the percentage of the cases below and above each z-score in the normal distribution by consulting Table A.2 in the Appendix, which gives the areas of the normal curve. Column (1) of the table contains different z-values. Column (2) gives the area under the curve between the mean and each z-value. Column (3) shows the remaining area from each z-score to the end of the curve. Therefore the areas in column (2) and column (3) add up to .5000. Finally, column (3) contains the area beyond each z-score in the direction opposite to the mean. Take as an example the z-value of $+0.70$. The area between this z-value and the mean can be found in column (2); it is .2580. This figure indicates that more than 25 percent of the cases fall between this z-value and the mean of the distribution. Since the mean of the normal distribution coincides with the median, 50 percent of the cases lie below the mean. We add .50 to the .2580, and the result tells us that we can expect 75.8 percent of the cases to fall below the z-value of $+0.70$. Column (3) indicates that 24.2 percent of the cases fall above the z-value of $+0.70$.

This procedure is reversed when the z-value is negative; that is, instead of adding the percentage of the cases between the mean and the given z-value to 50 percent, we subtract it from 50 percent. Suppose we want to find the percentage of cases below the z-value of -0.70. The area between the mean and a z-score of 0.70 is .2580 or, in terms of percentage, 25.8 percent of the cases. Subtracting 25.8 from 50, we obtain 24.2. This result would indicate that only about 24 percent of the scores lie below a z-value of -0.70 in a normal distribution. This value can also be found in column (3) of the table, which gives a value of 0.2420 for a z-score of 0.70.

Correlation

Our discussion of statistical techniques so far has been concerned with describing single distributions of scores. We want now to discuss a method of indicating the relationship between pairs of scores.

Statistical techniques for determining relationships between pairs of scores are known as correlational procedures. Typically measurements on two variables are available for each member of a group and one determines if there is a relationship between these paired measurements. The relationship is concisely described by statistical indices known as correlation coefficients. These coefficients show the extent to which change in one variable is associated with change in another variable. For example, we know that achievement and intelligence are related and so we would expect students with high IQs to earn above-average scores on achievement tests. A simple way of showing this relationship is to plot the intelligence test scores and achievement test scores of a number of individuals in a two-dimensional table called a scattergram. Scores on one variable are plotted on the horizontal axis, with the lowest number on the left and the highest on the right.

Scores on the other variable are plotted on the vertical axis, with the lowest at the bottom and the highest at the top. The position of each individual on the two tests is then indicated by a single point in the scattergram. The achievement test scores of 30 tenth graders are plotted against their intelligence test scores in Figure 5.7. An examination of this figure reveals that there is a tendency for achievement scores to be high when the intelligence tests scores are high.

Plotting a scattergram enables us to see both the *direction* and the *strength* of a relationship. Direction refers to whether the relationship is positive or negative. In Figure 5.7 the dots form a pattern going from lower left to upper right as low scores on one variable (intelligence) are associated with low scores on the other variable (achievement) and high scores on one variable are associated with high scores on the other. (By convention, scores of the independent variable [X] are plotted along the horizontal axis and scores of the dependent variable [Y] are plotted on the vertical axis.) Such a relationship between variables is said to be positive because high scores are associated with high scores and low scores with low scores.

The relationship between two variables is not always positive. Some variables are negatively related. For example, birthrate and socioeconomic level have been found to be negatively related; that is, birthrate decreases as the socioeconomic level increases. With a negative relationship high scores on one variable are associated with low scores on the other variable and the dots on the scattergram go from upper left to lower right.

A scattergram of z-scores also reveals the strength of the relationship between variables. If the dots in the scattergram form a narrow band, so that when a straight line is drawn through the band the dots will be near the line, there is a strong relationship between the variables. However, if the dots in the z-score scattergram scatter widely, the relationship between he variables is relatively weak. The scattergrams in Figure 5.8 show various positive and negative and strong and weak relationships.

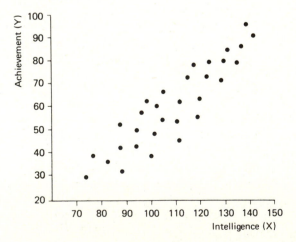

Figure 5.7   A scattergram showing the relationship between intelligence and achievement

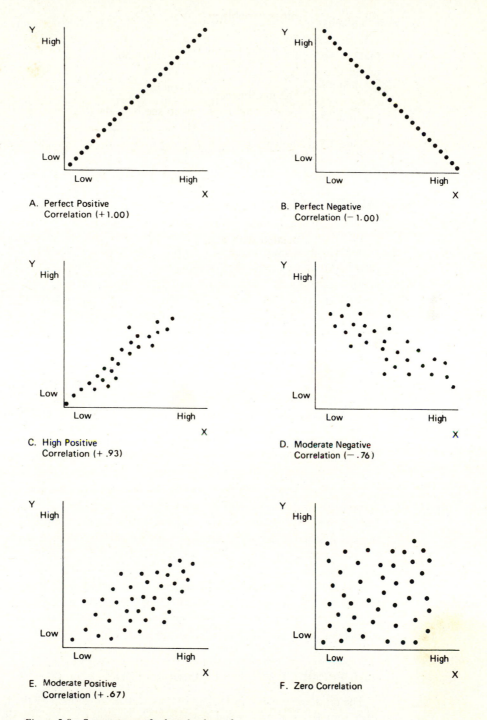

A. Perfect Positive
   Correlation (+1.00)

B. Perfect Negative
   Correlation (−1.00)

C. High Positive
   Correlation (+.93)

D. Moderate Negative
   Correlation (−.76)

E. Moderate Positive
   Correlation (+.67)

F. Zero Correlation

Figure 5.8   Scattergrams of selected values of *r*

An important use of correlation is in prediction. When correlational analysis indicates some degree of relationship between two variables, we can use the information about one of them to make predictions about the other. For example, having found that intelligence and achievement are correlated we can make predictions about the future achievement of schoolchildren from the results of an intelligence test given at the beginning of the school year. The accuracy of such prediction is a function of the degree of relationship between the variables being investigated, that is, the strength of the correlation between them. The higher the correlation in either a positive or a negative direction, the more accurate the predictions will be.

Correlation Coefficient

Statistical indices have been developed which indicate both the direction (negative or positive) and the strength of a relationship between variables. These indices are called correlation coefficients. Calculation of a correlation coefficient between two variables results in a value that ranges from -1.00 to $+1.00$. A correlation coefficient of -1.00 indicates a perfect negative relationship, a value of $+1.00$ implies a perfect positive relationship, and the midpoint of this range, zero, indicates no relationship at all. A perfect positive correlation results when each individual's z-score on one variable is identical in size and sign to the z-score on the other variable. A perfect negative correlation, on the other hand, results when each individual's z-scores are the same in size but opposite in sign. A zero correlation results when no such trends are present, that is, when positions on one variable are not associated with positions on the other. A coefficient of correlation near unity, either -1.00 or $+1.00$, indicates a high degree of relationship. Such high relationships enable one to make accurate predictions about one variable on the basis of information about the other. A negative correlation coefficient is just as good for prediction as a positive correlation.

In Figure 5.8 the coefficient of correlation for each of the sets of data in z-score form is given. Note that where the correlation is perfect all the scores fall on a straight line. The nearer to zero the coefficient of correlation is, the greater the deviation of the scores from a straight line. In the example with zero correlation (F) the scores are scattered over the surface of the graph and do not take any shape in any direction.

Correlation coefficients in educational and psychological measures, because of the complexity of these phenomena, seldom reach the maximum points of $+1.00$ and -1.00. For these measures, any coefficient that is more than .90 plus or minus is usually considered to be very high.

THE PRODUCT MOMENT CORRELATION

The product moment coefficient of correlation, developed by the English statistician Karl Pearson and called Pearson r, is the most commonly used correlation index. This coefficient is used when the scale of measurement is of either the interval or the ratio type. It is defined as the mean of the z-score products; that is, each individual's z-score on one variable (X) is multiplied by his or her z-score on the other variable (Y). These paired z-score products are added and the sum is divided by the number of pairs. The definition formula for Pearson r is:

$$r = \frac{\Sigma z_x z_y}{N} \qquad (5.12)$$

where

r = the Pearson product moment coefficient of correlation
$\Sigma z_x z_y$ = the sum of the z-score products
N = the number of paired scores

Because of the way z-scores are defined mathematically, when each individual has the same z-score on X that he has on Y, the sum of the $z_x z_y$ products will be equal to the number of pairs and the mean z-score product (the Pearson product moment correlation) will be $+1$. If there is a perfect positive correspondence between z-scores, the product moment correlation will be $+1$. If the z-scores are numerically identical but of opposite sign, the product will be negative and the Pearson product moment correlation will be -1. In both cases all the scores will fall along a straight line when plotted on a scattergram. Let us now use formula (5.12) to compute the correlation between the scores of fourteen subjects on two tests, X (descriptive statistics) and Y (inferential statistics), as shown in Table 5.6.

Columns (2) and (3) present the subjects' raw scores (X) and deviation scores (x), respectively, on the descriptive statistics test. Columns (5) and (6) present the subjects' raw scores (Y) and deviation scores (y) on the inferential statistics test. Columns (4) and (7) show the squared deviation scores used for calculating the standard deviations. Columns (8) and (9) present the z-scores of the X- and Y-scores computed using formula (5.9). Column (10) shows the products of $z_x z_y$ values. The sum of these products is 11.50. It is now possible to find the Pearson product moment coefficient of correlation between the two sets of scores by applying formula (5.12).

$$r = \frac{\Sigma z_x z_y}{N}$$

$$= \frac{11.50}{14} = +.82$$

The process of converting scores to z-scores becomes tedious when a large number of cases is being used. It is possible to eliminate this step and work directly with the raw scores by using a computation formula that is mathematically equivalent to formula (5.12):

Table 5.6 Computation of Pearson r between Two Sets of Scores (X and Y)

(1) Subject	(2) X-scores	(3) x	(4) x^2	(5) Y-scores	(6) y	(7) y^2	(8) z_x	(9) z_y	(10) $z_x z_y$
1	18	+3	9	28	4	16	+1.5	+1	+1.50
2	18	+3	9	30	6	36	+1.5	+1.5	+2.25
3	17	+2	4	30	6	36	+1	+1.5	+1.50
4	17	+2	4	26	2	4	+1	+0.5	+0.50
5	16	+1	1	28	4	16	+0.5	+1	+0.50
6	16	+1	1	24	0	0	+0.5	0	0
7	15	0	0	22	−2	4	0	−0.5	0
8	15	0	0	20	−4	16	0	−1	0
9	14	−1	1	26	2	4	−0.5	+0.5	−0.25
10	14	−1	1	22	−2	4	−0.5	−0.5	+0.25
11	13	−2	4	24	0	0	−1	0	0
12	13	−2	4	18	−6	36	−1	−1.5	+1.50
13	12	−3	9	20	−4	16	−1.5	−1	+1.50
14	12	−3	9	18	−6	36	−1.5	−1.5	+2.25
	210		56	336		224			11.50

$$\bar{X} = \frac{\Sigma X}{N} = \frac{210}{14} = 15 \qquad \bar{Y} = \frac{\Sigma Y}{N} = \frac{336}{14} = 24$$

$$\sigma x = \sqrt{\frac{\Sigma x^2}{N}} = \sqrt{\frac{56}{14}} = 2 \qquad \sigma y = \sqrt{\frac{\Sigma y^2}{N}} = \sqrt{\frac{224}{14}} = 4$$

$$r = \frac{\Sigma XY - \dfrac{(\Sigma X)(\Sigma Y)}{N}}{\sqrt{\left[\Sigma X^2 - \dfrac{(\Sigma X)^2}{N}\right]\left[\Sigma Y^2 - \dfrac{(\Sigma Y)^2}{N}\right]}} \qquad (5.13)$$

where
  r = Pearson r
  ΣX = the sum of scores in X-distribution
  ΣY = the sum of scores in Y-distribution
  ΣXY = the sum of the products of paired X- and Y-scores
  ΣX^2 = the sum of the squared scores in X-distribution
  ΣY^2 = the sum of the squared scores in Y-distribution
  N = the number of paired X- and Y-scores (subjects)

Using the same raw-score data as before, let us use formula (5.13) to compute the Pearson product moment coefficient of correlation. The necessary figures and calculations are provided in Table 5.7. Substituting the values from this table in formula (5.13), we can calculate Pearson r.

$$r = \frac{5132 - \frac{(210)(336)}{14}}{\sqrt{\left[3206 - \frac{(210)^2}{14}\right]\left[8288 - \frac{(336)^2}{14}\right]}} = +.82$$

Note that by applying this formula not only was it unnecessary to convert the scores to z-scores, but also computation of the means and standard deviations of the two distributions was eliminated.

Table 5.7   Computation of Pearson r Using the Raw-Score Formula

(1) Subjects	(2) X	(3) Y	(4) X²	(5) Y²	(6) XY
1	18	28	324	784	504
2	18	30	324	900	540
3	17	30	289	900	510
4	17	26	289	676	442
5	16	28	256	784	448
6	16	24	256	576	384
7	15	22	225	484	330
8	15	20	225	400	300
9	14	26	196	676	364
10	14	22	196	489	308
11	13	24	169	576	312
12	13	18	169	324	234
13	12	20	144	400	240
14	12	18	144	324	216
$N = 14$	$\Sigma X = 210$	$\Sigma Y = 336$	$\Sigma X^2 = 3,206$	$\Sigma Y^2 = 8,288$	$\Sigma XY = 5,132$

The product moment coefficient of correlation belongs to the same statistical family as the mean. Its computation takes into account the size of each score in both distributions, X and Y. Like the mean and the standard deviation, it is an interval statistic which can also be used with ratio data.

An assumption underlying the product moment coefficient of correlation is that the relationship between the two variables (X and Y) is a linear one; that is, a straight line provides a reasonable expression of the relationship of one variable to the other. If a curved line is needed to express this relationship, the relationship is said to be curvilinear.

A practical way of finding out whether or not the relationship between two variables is linear or curvilinear is to examine the scattergram of the data. Figure 5.9 shows two diagrams, one of which (A) indicates a linear relationship and the other (B), a curvilinear one.

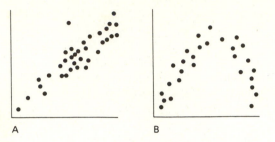

Figure 5.9 (A) Linear and (B) curvilinear relationships

If the relationship between the variables is curvilinear, the computation of Pearson r will result in a misleading underestimation of the degree of relationship. In this case another index, such as the correlation ratio, should be applied.

INTERPRETATION OF PEARSON *r*

We have seen that when two variables are highly related in a positive way the correlation between them approaches $+1$. When they are highly related in a negative way, the correlation approaches -1. When there is little relation between variables, the correlation will be near zero. Pearson r provides a meaningful index for indicating relationship, with the sign of the coefficient indicating the direction of the relationship, and the difference between the coefficient and zero indicating the degree of the relationship.

However, in interpreting the coefficient of correlation one should have the following points in mind.

1. *Correlation does not necessarily indicate causation*. When two variables are found to be correlated this indicates that relative positions in one variable are *associated* with relative positions in the other variable. It does not necessarily mean that changes in one variable are *caused* by changes in the other variable. In our example we found a correlation of $+.82$ between scores in a test on descriptive statistics and another test on inferential statistics. This correlation coefficient tells us that a person with an above-average score on one test will probably obtain an above-average score on the other test. We cannot say that a high performance on one test *causes* a high performance on the other. Scores on both tests may be the result of other causes, such as the numerical aptitude of the persons who take these tests.

Using another example, suppose we find a high positive correlation between the wealth of families and intelligence of the children of those families. Such high correlation is by no means indicative of a cause-and-effect relationship between these two variables. Wealth does not necessarily result in intelligence, nor does intelligence necessarily create wealth for intelligent individuals.

2. *The size of correlation is in part a function of the variability of the two distributions to be correlated*. Restricting the range of the scores to be correlated

reduces the observed degree of relationship between two variables. For example, it has been observed that success in playing basketball is related to height: that is to say, the taller an individual is, the more probable it is that that person will do well in this sport. This statement is true about the population at large, where there is a wide range of heights. However, within a basketball team whose members are all tall, there may be little or no correlation between height and success since the range of the heights is restricted.

In a college that accepts students with a wide range of scores on a scholastic aptitude test, we would expect a correlation between the test scores and college grades. In a college that accepts only students with very high scholastic aptitude scores, we would expect very little correlation between the test scores and grades because of the restricted range of the test scores in this situation.

3. *Correlation coefficients should not be interpreted in terms of percentage of perfect correlations.* Since correlation coefficients are expressed as fractions, individuals who are not trained in statistics sometimes interpret correlation coefficients as a percentage of perfect correlation. An r of .80 does *not* indicate 80 percent of a perfect relationship between two variables. This interpretation is erroneous since, for example, an r of .8 does not express a relationship that is twice as great as an r of .4. One way of determining the degree to which one can predict one variable from the other is to calculate an index called the *coefficient of determination*. The coefficient of determination is the square of the correlation coefficient. It gives the percentage of variance in one variable that is associated with the variance in the other. For example, if we find a correlation of $+.80$ between achievement and intelligence, 64 percent of the variance in achievement is associated with variance in intelligence test scores. Probably the best way to give meaning to the size of the correlation coefficient is to picture the degree of scatter implied by correlations of different sizes (as illustrated in Figure 5.8) and to become familiar with the size of correlations commonly observed between variables of interest.

4. *Avoid interpreting the coefficients of correlation in an absolute sense.* In interpreting the degree of correlation, keep in mind the purpose for which it is being used. For example, a coefficient of correlation equal to $+.50$ might be satisfactory when predicting the future performance of a group of individuals, but it might not be wise to use this coefficient of correlation for predicting the performance of one person in a future task. That is, the coefficient of $+.50$ is not an absolute value with the same implication in both cases.

THE RANK CORRELATION COEFFICIENT

The Pearson product moment coefficient of correlation is the statistical index used for finding the relationship between two sets of linearly distributed interval data. In research we sometimes wish to find the coefficient of correlation between two sets of measures that are rank-ordered, that is, ordinal rather than interval data. For example, we might want to correlate the ranks assigned by two teachers to a group of students with respect to originality. The index employed in such cases is the Spearman rho (rank) correlation coefficient (ρ), which is calculated by means of the formula

$$\rho = 1 - \frac{6\Sigma D^2}{N(N^2 - 1)} \qquad (5.14)$$

where
   ρ = the Spearman rho correlation coefficient
ΣD^2 = the sum of the squares of the differences between ranks
   N = the number of cases

For illustration, consider Table 5.9 which shows the ranking of eleven students by two teachers. Columns (2) and (3) of Table 5.9 present the rankings of teacher one and teacher two, respectively. Column (4) shows the differences between these ranks. For example, the difference between the ranking of student A by these teachers is -3, of student B is -1, and so forth. The sum of the values in this column is always zero. Column (5) gives the square of these differences. The sum of the D^2 values is 26 and the number of cases is 11. When these values are substituted into formula (5.14), the computation gives a Spearman rank correlation of $+.88$.

Table 5.9   The Computation of the Correlation Coefficient between Two Sets of Ranks

(1)	(2) First Teacher's Rank R_1	(3) Second Teacher's Rank R_2	(4) Difference D	(5) D^2
Student				
A	1	4	-3	9
B	2	3	-1	1
C	3	1	2	4
D	4	2	2	4
E	5	5	0	0
F	6	6	0	0
G	7	8	-1	1
H	8	9	-1	1
I	9	7	2	4
J	10	11	-1	1
K	11	10	1	1
			0	26

$$\rho = 1 - \frac{(6)(26)}{11(121 - 1)} = +.88$$

When ranking individuals or objects for the purpose of finding a correlation between two sets of ranks, you are likely to find that two or more will have been assigned to the same rank. For example, when two individuals are tied for rank 3, they are in fact the third and fourth in the series and the next person will be assigned to position 5. In such cases, it is necessary to assign both the average position—in this example, 3.5.

Sometimes one wants to find the relationship between a set of ranks and a set of interval measures, such as a group of test scores. To do this, one first converts the scores into ranks and then applies the Spearman rho formula. Consider, as an example, Table 5.10. Column (2) of the table shows a teacher's prediction of the ranks of a group of students in an examination prior to the administration of the test. Column (3) shows the actual scores of these students on the examination. To determine the relationship between predicted ranks and actual ranks, the teacher will have to convert the students' test scores to ranks. Column (4) shows the ranking of the students on the basis of their test scores. Note that both Linda and Dick made scores of 17 and thus tied for the third and fourth places; consequently they are given an equal rank of 3.5, which is the average of ranks 3 and 4. The situation is similar for Tom, John, and David who all made a score of 15 and share the fifth, sixth, and seventh places. A rank of 6, which is the average for ranks 5, 6, and 7, is assigned to each of the three. The procedure for finding the values for D and D^2 is exactly like that shown in Table 5.9. The coefficient of correlation between these sets of data is $+.95$.

Table 5.10   The Computation of Rank Correlation between a Set of Ordinal and a Set of Interval Data

(1) Students	(2) Rank 1	(3) Scores	(4) Rank 2	(5) D	(6) D^2
Jack	1	19	1	0	0
Linda	2	17	3.5	−1.5	2.25
Lucy	3	18	2	1	1
Dick	4	17	3.5	0.5	0.25
Tom	5	15	6	−1	1
Marsha	6	14	8	−2	4
John	7	15	6	1	1
David	8	15	6	2	4
Joan	9	12	10	−1	1
Ann	10	13	9	1	1
George	11	8	11	0	0
Sue	12	5	12	0	0
				0	15.5

$$\rho = 1 - \frac{(6)(15.5)}{12(144 - 1)} = +.95$$

The Spearman rho rank correlation coefficient is part of the same statistical family as the median. It is an ordinal statistic designed for use with ordinal data. Like the Pearson product moment coefficient of correlation, it ranges from -1 to $+1$. When each individual has the same rank on both variables, the rank correlation will be $+1.00$, and when their ranks on one variable are exactly the opposite of their ranks on the other variable, rho will be -1.00. If there is no relationship at all between the rankings, the rank correlation coefficient will be zero. Spearman rho is interpreted in the same way as Pearson r.

Summary

Descriptive statistics serve to describe and summarize observations. The descriptive technique to be employed is selected according to the purpose the statistic is to serve and the scale of measurement used in recording the data.

Scales of measurement are means of quantifying observations and are of four types: nominal scales classify observations into mutually exclusive categories; ordinal scales sort objects or classes of objects on the basis of their relative standing; interval scales use equal intervals for measurement and indicate the degree to which a person or an object possesses a certain quality; ratio scales use equal intervals for measurement and measure from an absolute zero point.

Once observations are quantified, the data—either raw or grouped—can be arranged into frequency distributions and shown graphically in histograms or polygons.

Measures of central tendency—the mode, the median, and the mean—provide a single index to represent the average value of a whole set of measures. The mode, which is a nominal statistic, is the least stable and least useful measure in educational research. The median is an ordinal statistic that takes into account the ranks of scores within a distribution, and not the size of the individual scores. The mean, which is an interval (or ratio) statistic, is the most stable and most widely used index of central tendency.

Another way of describing observations is to indicate the variation or spread of the values within a distribution. The range, the quartile deviation, and the standard deviation are three indices used for this purpose. The range gives the distance between the highest and the lowest values in a distribution. It is a nominal statistic. Quartile deviation gives the half-distance between the upper and the lower quartiles. It is an ordinal statistic. The standard deviation is the square root of the mean of the squared deviations of values from the mean. It is an interval (or ratio) statistic and is the most widely used index of variability.

Standard scores are used to indicate the position of a single score in a distribution. The most widely used is the z-score, which converts values into standard deviation units. Using the characteristics and the areas of the normal curve, we can approximate the percentage of cases below and above each z-score in a normal distribution.

Finally, correlation techniques enable us to describe the relationship between two sets of measures. Product moment correlation (Pearson r) and rank correlation (Spearman rho) are two widely used indices of relationship. Pearson r is used with interval or ratio data, and for ordinal data Spearman rho is used to find the relationship between two sets of ranks. Table 5.11 summarizes these statistics.

Table 5.11   Summary of Descriptive Statistics Presented in This Chapter

	Nominal	Ordinal	Interval
Indices of central tendency	mode	median	mean
Indices of variability	range	quartile deviation	variance and standard deviation
Indices of location	label or classification	percentile rank	z-score, Z-score, and other standard scores
Correlation indices		Spearman rho	Pearson r

Exercises

1. Identify the type of measurement scale—*nominal, ordinal, interval,* or *ratio*—suggested by each statement:
   a. John finished the math test in 35 minutes, while Jack finished the same test in 25 minutes.
   b. Jack speaks French, but John does not.
   c. Jack is taller than John.
   d. John is 6 feet, 2 inches tall.
   e. John's IQ is 120, while Jack's IQ is 110.
2. Draw a histogram and a frequency polygon for the following frequency distribution:

X	f	X	f	X	f	X	f
80	1	76	6	73	20	70	7
79	2	75	15	72	17	69	3
78	3	74	22	71	9	68	1
77	10						

3. Given the following distribution: 15, 14, 14, 13, 11, 10, 10, 10, 8, 5
   a. Calculate the mean.
   b. Determine the value of the median.
   c. Determine the value of the mode.
4. Briefly explain the relationship between the skewness of a distribution of scores and the resulting values of the mean, median, and mode.

5. Identify the measure—*mode, mean,* or *median*—that best suits each type of scale:
   a. ordinal   b. nominal   c. interval
6. Identify the measure—*mode, mean,* or *median*—that each term defines:
   a. the middle score
   b. the arithmetic average
   c. the most frequently occurring score
7. The scores below represent the vocabulary test scores from a seventh grade class of 20 pupils. Calculate the range, standard deviation, and quartile deviation and discuss the benefits and disadvantages of each as a measure of the variability of the scores.

X	f	fX	X^2	fX^2
16	1	16	256	256
15	0	0	225	0
14	0	0	196	0
13	0	0	169	0
12	2	24	144	288
11	0	0	121	0
10	2	20	100	200
9	1	9	81	81
8	1	8	64	64
7	1	7	49	49
6	4	24	36	144
5	2	10	25	50
4	1	4	16	16
3	1	3	9	9
2	4	8	4	16

8. To minimize the effect of an extreme score, should one choose the *quartile deviation* or *standard deviation* as the index of variability?
9. The mean score on a test is 40 and the standard deviation is 4. Express each of the following raw scores as a z-score:
   a. 41   b. 30   c. 48   d. 36   e. 46
10. Describe the relationship shown by these scattergrams. Then estimate the correlation coefficients.

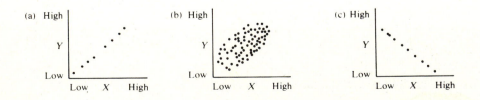

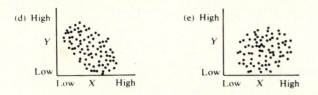

11. The following data are scores obtained by ten students on an Abstract Reasoning Test and their cumulative grade-point averages in philosophy. Calculate the Pearson r for these data.

Student	Abstract Reasoning	Grade-Point Average
A	15	1.5
B	20	2.5
C	30	3.0
D	35	2.0
E	25	3.0
F	40	3.5
G	35	4.0
H	5	1.0
I	12	2.0
J	10	2.5

12. A researcher is interested in anxiety and how it might affect performance on intelligence tests. He has a clinical psychologist assess the anxiety of subjects by ranking them from 1 through 20. Then he administers a standardized intelligence test to each of the 20 subjects and converts their IQ scores to ranks. Which correlation coefficient should the researcher calculate for the data? Explain your answer.

13. A researcher demonstrated a correlation of +.60 between teacher attire and student academic performance across 150 grade schools in her state. She concluded that encouraging teachers to be properly attired will increase academic performance. Comment on her conclusion.

Answers

1. a. ratio   b. nominal   c. ordinal   d. ratio   e. interval
3. a. mean = 11   b. medium = 10.5   c. mode = 10
4. The three measures are not equal in a skewed distribution. The mean is pulled in the direction of the skewed side. Thus in a positively skewed distribution the mean is always higher than the median, and the mode is usually lowest in value. In a negatively skewed distribution the mean is always lower than the median and the mode is usually highest in value.

5. a. medium   b. mode   c. mean
6. a. median   b. mean   c. mode
7. range $= 16 - 2 = 14$

$$\sigma = \sqrt{\dfrac{1173 - \dfrac{(133)^2}{20}}{20}} = \sqrt{14.4275} = 3.798$$

$$QD = \frac{Q_3 - Q_1}{2} = \frac{9.5 - 3.5}{2} = \frac{6}{2} = 3$$

8. quartile deviation
9. a. .25   b. -2.5 c. 2   d. -1 e. 1.5
10. a. perfect positive, $+1.0$ b. positive, $+.75$ c. perfect negative, -1.0
    d. negative, $-.75$ e. no correlation, .0

11.

X	Y	XY	X^2	Y^2
15	1.5	22.5	225	2.25
20	2.5	50.0	400	6.25
30	3.0	90.0	900	9.00
35	2.0	70.0	1,225	4.00
25	3.0	75.0	625	9.00
40	3.5	140.0	1,600	12.25
35	4.0	140.0	1,225	16.00
5	1.0	5.0	25	1.00
12	2.0	24.0	144	4.00
10	2.5	25.0	100	6.25
$\Sigma 227$	25.0	641.5	6,469	70

$$r = \frac{\Sigma XY - \dfrac{(\Sigma X)(\Sigma Y)}{N}}{\sqrt{\left[\Sigma X^2 - \dfrac{(\Sigma X)^2}{N}\right]\left[\Sigma Y^2 - \dfrac{(\Sigma Y)^2}{N}\right]}}$$

$$\frac{641.5 - \dfrac{(227)(25)}{10}}{\sqrt{\left(6469 - \dfrac{(227)^2}{10}\right)\left(70 - \dfrac{(25)^2}{10}\right)}} = +.74$$

12. Since the researcher has ordinal or rank-order data, he should calculate the Spearman rank correlation coefficient.
13. The researcher has no justification for inferring a causal relationship merely on the basis of correlational evidence. Teacher attire and student academic performance could very well be functions of some other variable.

Sampling and Inferential Statistics

The statistics discussed in the previous chapter are used for organizing, summarizing, and describing data. In research, however, we often need to go further than describing data. After making observations of a sample, we employ induction or inference to generalize our findings to the entire population from which the sample was drawn. To do this we need techniques that enable us to make valid inferences from samples to whole populations.

Sampling

An important characteristic of inferential statistics is the process of going from the part to the whole. For example, we might study a randomly selected group of 500 students attending a university in order to make generalizations about the entire student body of that university.

The small group that is observed is called a *sample* and the larger group about which the generalization is made is called a *population*. A *population* is defined as "all members of any well-defined class of people, events or objects."[1] For example, in a study where American adolescents constitute the population of interest, one could define this population as all American boys and girls within the age range of 12–21. A sample is a portion of a population. For example, the students of Washington High School in Indianapolis constitute a sample of American adolescents. They are a portion of the large population in that they are both American citizens and within the age range of 12–21.

Statistical inference is a procedure by means of which one estimates *parameters*, characteristics of populations, from *statistics,* characteristics of samples. Such estimations are based on the laws of probability and are best estimates rather than absolute facts. In any such inferences a certain degree of error is involved.

RATIONALE OF SAMPLING

Inductive reasoning is an essential part of the scientific approach. The inductive method involves making observations and then drawing conclusions from these observations. If one can observe all instances of a population, one can with confidence base conclusions about the population on these observations (perfect induction). On the other hand, if one observes only some instances of a population then one can do no more than infer that these observations will be true of the population

[1]Fred N. Kerlinger, *Foundations of Behavioral Research* (New York: Holt, Rinehart and Winston, 1966), p. 52.

as a whole (imperfect induction). This is the concept of sampling, which involves taking a portion of the population, making observations on this smaller group, and then generalizing the findings to the large population.

Sampling is indispensable to the researcher. Usually the time, money, and effort involved do not permit a researcher to study all possible members of a population. Furthermore, it is generally not necessary to study all possible cases to understand the phenomenon under consideration. Sampling comes to our aid by enabling us to study a portion of the population rather than the entire population.

Since the purpose of drawing a sample from a population is to obtain information concerning that population, it is extremely important that the individuals included in a sample constitute a representative cross section of individuals in the population. That is, samples must be representative if one is to be able to generalize with confidence from the sample to the population. For example, the researcher might assume that the students at Washington High School are representative of American adolescents. However, this sample might not be representative if the individuals who are included have some characteristics that differ from the parent population. The location of their school, their socioeconomic background, their family situation, their prior experiences, and many other characteristics of this group might make them unrepresentative of American adolescents. This type of sample would be termed a *biased sample*. The findings of a biased sample cannot legitimately be generalized to the population from which it is taken.

Steps in Sampling

The first essential in sampling is the identification of the population to be represented in the study. If the researcher is interested in learning about the teachers in the St. Louis school system, all those who teach within that system constitute the target population. In a study of the attitudes and values of American adolescents, the target population would be all American boys and girls in the age range of 12–21, granted that adolescence is operationally defined as the period between ages 12 and 21.

However, since it is usually not possible to deal with the whole of the target population, one must identify that portion of the population to which one can have access—called the *accessible population*—and it is from this group that the researcher will take the sample for the study. The nature of the accessible population is influenced by the time and resources of the researcher. In a typical attitude study, for example, a researcher might designate all adolescent boys and girls in California or just those in San Francisco as the accessible population.

From the accessible population, one selects a sample in such a way that it is representative of that population. For example, the researcher would have to sample from adolescents all over the state of California if California adolescents are identified as the accessible population. Or if adolescents living in San Francisco are the accessible population, then the sample would be drawn from this particular group.

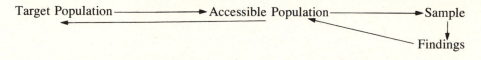

How safely can one generalize from a sample to the target population? If the sample selected is truly representative of the accessible population, then there is little difficulty in making this first step in the generalization process. The general principle is: If a sample has been selected so that it is representative of the accessible population, findings from the sample can be generalized to that population. For example, if one has selected a representative sample of California adolescents, then one could make generalizations concerning the attitudes and values of all adolescent boys and girls in California.

However, generalizing from the accessible population to the target population typically involves greater risk. The confidence that one can have in this step depends upon the similarity of the accessible population to the target population. In the example above, a researcher could have more confidence making generalizations about American adolescents if adolescents in several states throughout the country are designated as the accessible population rather than those in California alone. In this way all sections of the United States would be represented and a more adequate sampling of attitudes and values would be possible.

It is true that one must make an inferential ''leap of faith'' when estimating population characteristics from sample observations. The likelihood that such inferences will be correct is largely a function of the sampling procedure employed. Various sampling procedures are available to researchers for use in the selection of a subgroup of a population that will represent that population well and will avoid bias.

RANDOM SAMPLING

The best known of the sampling procedures is random sampling. The basic characteristic of random sampling is that all members of the population have an equal and independent chance of being included in the sample. That is, for every pair of elements X and Y, X's chance of being selected equals Y's chance, and the selection of X in no way affects Y's probability of selection. The steps in random sampling are:

1. Define the population.
2. List all members of the population.
3. Select the sample by employing a procedure where sheer chance determines which members on the list are drawn for the sample.

The most systematic procedure for drawing a random sample is to refer to a *table of random numbers,* which is a table containing columns of digits that have been mechanically generated, usually by a computer, to assure a random order. Table

A.6 in the Appendix is an example. The first step in drawing a random sample from a population is to assign each member of the population a distinct identification number. Then the table of random numbers is used to select the identification numbers of the subjects to be included in the sample.

Let us illustrate the use of this table to obtain a sample of adolescents from the population of students attending Washington High School. First it is necessary to enumerate all of the individuals included in the population. The principal's office could supply a list of all students enrolled in the school. One would then assign a number to each individual in the population for identification purposes. Assuming there were 800 students in the school, one might use the numbers 000, 001, 002, 003, . . . , 799 for this purpose. Then one would enter a table of random numbers to obtain numbers of three digits each, using only those numbers that are less than or equal to 799. For each number chosen, the corresponding element in the population falls in the sample. One continues the process until the desired number for the sample has been chosen. It is customary, in using a table of random numbers, to determine by chance the point at which the table is entered. One way is to touch the page blindly and begin wherever the page is touched.

The generally understood meaning of the word *random* is "without purpose or by accident." However, random sampling is purposeful and methodical. It is apparent that a sample selected randomly is not subject to the biases of the researcher. When researchers employ this method, they are committing themselves to selecting a sample in such a way that their biases are not permitted to operate. They are pledging themselves to avoid a deliberate selection of subjects who will confirm the hypothesis. They are allowing chance alone to determine which elements in the population will be in the sample.

One would expect a random sample to be representative of the parent population sampled. However, random selection, especially with small samples, does not absolutely guarantee a sample that will represent the population well. Random selection does guarantee that any differences between the sample and the parent population are only a function of chance and not a result of the researcher's bias. The differences between random samples and their parent population are not systematic. For example, the mean reading achievement of a random sample of sixth graders may be higher than the mean reading achievement of the parent population, but it is equally likely that the mean for the sample will be lower than the mean for the parent population. In other words, with random sampling the sampling errors are just as likely to be negative as they are to be positive.

Furthermore, statistical theorists have, through deductive reasoning, shown how much one can expect the observations derived from random samples to differ from what would be observed in the population. All of the procedures described in this chapter have this aim in mind. Remember that characteristics observed in a small sample are more likely to differ from population characteristics than are characteristics observed in a large sample. When random sampling is used, the researcher can employ inferential statistics to estimate how much the population is likely to differ from the sample. The inferential statistics in this chapter are all based on random sampling and apply only to those cases in which randomization has been employed.

Unfortunately, random sampling requires an enumeration of all the individuals in a finite population before the sample can be drawn—a requirement that often presents a serious obstacle to the use of this method in practice.

STRATIFIED SAMPLING

When the population consists of a number of subgroups or strata that may differ in the characteristics being studied, it is often desirable to use a form of sampling called stratified sampling. For example, if one were conducting a poll designed to assess opinions on a certain political issue, it might be advisable to subdivide the population into groups on the basis of age or occupation because one would expect opinions to differ systematically among various age or occupational groups. In stratified sampling one first identifies the strata of interest and then draws a specified number of subjects from each stratum. The basis for stratification may be geographical or it may involve characteristics of the population, such as income, occupation, sex, age, year in college, or teaching level. In the study of adolescents, for example, one may be interested not merely in surveying the attitudes of adolescents toward certain phenomena, but also in comparing the attitudes of adolescents who reside in small towns with those who live in medium-size and large cities. In such a case, one would divide the adolescent population into three groups, based on the size of the towns or cities in which they reside, and then randomly select independent samples from each stratum.

An advantage of stratified sampling is that it enables the researcher to determine to what extent each stratum in the population is represented in the sample. One may either take equal numbers from each stratum or select in proportion to the size of the stratum in the population. This latter procedure is known as *proportional stratified sampling;* that is, the stratum is represented in the sample in exact proportion to its frequency in the total population. If 10 percent of the voting population are college students, then 10 percent of one's sample of voters to be polled would be taken from this stratum. The procedure used will be chosen according to the nature of the research question. If the emphasis is on the types of differences among the strata, one selects equal numbers of cases from each. If the characteristics of the entire population are the main concern, proportional sampling is more appropriate.

When applicable, stratified sampling may give us a more representative sample than simple random sampling. In simple random sampling certain strata may by chance be over- or underrepresented in the sample. For example, in the simple random sample of high school students it would be theoretically possible (though highly unlikely) to obtain female subjects only. This could not happen, however, if males and females are listed separately and a random sample is then chosen from each group.

The major advantage of stratified sampling is that it guarantees representation of defined groups in the population.

CLUSTER SAMPLING

As mentioned earlier, it is very difficult, if not impossible, to list all the members of a target population and select the sample from among them. The population of American high school students, for example, is so large that one cannot list all its members for the purpose of drawing a sample. In addition, it would be a very expensive undertaking to study a sample that is scattered all around the United States. In this case it would be more convenient to study subjects in naturally occurring groups or clusters. That is, the researcher would choose a number of schools randomly from a list of schools and then include all the students in those schools in the sample. This kind of sampling is referred to as *cluster sampling* since the unit chosen is not an individual but a group of individuals who are naturally together. These individuals constitute a cluster insofar as they are alike with respect to characteristics relevant to the variables of the study. Let us assume a public opinion poll is being conducted in Atlanta. The investigator would probably not have access to a list of the entire adult population; thus it would be impossible to draw a simple random sample. A more feasible approach would involve the selection of a random sample of, say, fifty blocks from a city map, and then the polling of all the adults living on those blocks. Each block represents a cluster of subjects, similar in certain characteristics associated with living in proximity.

It is essential that the clusters actually included in the study be chosen at random from a population of clusters. If only a single cluster were used—for example, one elementary school in a large city—one could not generalize to the population. Another procedural requirement is that once a cluster is selected, *all* the members of the cluster must be included in the sample. The sampling error in a cluster sample is much greater than in true random sampling.

SYSTEMATIC SAMPLING

Still another form of sampling is called systematic sampling. This procedure involves drawing a sample by taking every kth case from a list of the population.

One first decides how many subjects one wants in the sample (n). Since one knows the total number of members in the population (N), one simply divides N by n and determines the sampling interval (k) to apply to the list. The first member is randomly selected from the first k members of the list and then every kth member of the population is selected for the sample. For example, let us assume a total population of 500 subjects and a desired sample size of 50; thus, $k = N/n = 500/50 = 10$.

One would start near the top of the list so that the first case could be randomly selected from the first ten cases, and then every tenth case thereafter would be selected. Say the third name or number on the list was the first to be selected. One would then add the sampling interval k, or 10, to 3—and thus the thirteenth person falls in the sample, as does the twenty-third, and so on—and would continue adding the constant sampling interval until the end of the list is reached.

Systematic sampling differs from simple random sampling in that the various choices are not independent. Once the first case is chosen, all subsequent cases to be included in the sample are automatically determined.

If the original population list is in random order, systematic sampling would yield a sample that could be statistically considered a reasonable substitute for a random sample. However, if the list is alphabetical, for example, it is possible that every kth member of the population might have some unique characteristic that would affect the dependent variable of the study and thus yield a biased sample. Systematic sampling from an alphabetical list would probably not give a representative sample of various national groups because certain national groups tend to cluster under certain letters and the sampling interval could omit them entirely or at least not include them to an adequate extent.

It should be noted that the various types of sampling that have been discussed are not mutually exclusive. Various combinations may be used. For example, one could use cluster sampling if one is studying a very large and widely dispersed population. At the same time, one may be interested in stratifying the sample to answer questions regarding its different strata. In this case one would stratify the population according to the predetermined criteria and then randomly select the clusters of subjects from among each stratum.[2]

THE SIZE OF THE SAMPLE

One of the first questions to be asked concerns the number of subjects that need to be included in the sample. Technically, the size of the sample depends upon the precision the researcher desires in estimating the population parameter at a particular confidence level. There is no single rule that can be used to determine sample size. An estimation of required sample size can be calculated algebraically if one defines precisely the variance of the population, the expected difference, and the desired probabilities of Type I and Type II errors (see 179–80). A number of statistics texts describe this procedure.

The best answer to the question of size is to use as large a sample as possible. A larger sample is much more likely to be representative of the population. Furthermore, with a large sample the data are likely to be more accurate and precise: which is to say, the larger the sample, the smaller the standard error. In general, the standard error of a sample mean is inversely proportional to the square root of n. Thus in order to double the precision of one's estimation, one must quadruple the sample size.

Some authors suggest that one include at least thirty subjects in a sample since this number permits the use of large sample statistics. In experimental research, one should select a sample that will permit at least thirty in each group. Descriptive research typically uses larger samples; it is sometimes suggested that one select 10 to 20 percent of the accessible population for the sample.

[2]For further discussion of specific sampling techniques, the reader is referred to W. G. Cochran, *Sampling Techniques,* 2nd ed. (New York: Wiley, 1963).

It must be emphasized, however, that size alone will not guarantee accuracy. Representativeness is the most important consideration in selecting a sample. A sample may be large and still contain a bias. The latter situation is well illustrated by the *Literary Digest* poll of 1936, which predicted the defeat of President Roosevelt. Although the sample included approximately two and a half million respondents, it was not representative of the voters; and thus an erroneous conclusion was reached. The bias resulted from the selection of respondents for the poll from automobile registrations, telephone directories, and the magazine's subscription lists. These subjects would certainly not be representative of the total voting population in 1936. Also, since the poll was conducted by mail, the results were biased by differences between those who responded and those who did not. Thus the researcher must recognize that sample size will not compensate for the bias that may be introduced through faulty sampling techniques. Representativeness must remain the prime goal in sample selection.

THE CONCEPT OF SAMPLING ERROR

When an inference is made from a sample to a population a certain amount of error is involved because even random samples can be expected to vary from one to another. The mean intelligence score of one random sample of fourth graders may be different from the mean intelligence score of another random sample of fourth graders from the same population. Such differences, called sampling errors, result from the fact that one has observed a sample and not the entire population.

Sampling error is defined as the difference between a population parameter and a sample statistic. For example, if one knows the mean of the entire population (symbolized μ) and also the mean of a random sample (symbolized $\bar{X}$) from that population, the difference between these two, $\bar{X} - \mu$, represents sampling error (symbolized e). Thus, $e = \bar{X} - \mu$. For example, if we know that the mean intelligence score for a population of 10,000 fourth graders is $\mu = 100$ and a particular random sample of 200 has a mean of $\bar{X} = 99$, then the sampling error is $\bar{X} - \mu = 99 - 100 = -1$. Because we usually depend on sample statistics to estimate population parameters, the notion of how samples are expected to vary from populations is a basic element in inferential statistics. However, instead of trying to determine the discrepancy between a sample statistic and the population parameter (which is not often known), the approach in inferential statistics is to estimate the variability that could be expected in the statistics from a number of different random samples drawn from the same population. Since each of the sample statistics is considered to be an estimate of the same population parameter, then any variation among sample statistics must be attributed to sampling error.

THE LAWFUL NATURE OF SAMPLING ERRORS

Given that random samples drawn from the same population will vary from one another, is using a sample to make inferences about a population really any better than just guessing? Yes, it is, because sampling errors behave in a lawful and predictable manner. The laws concerning sampling error have been derived through deductive logic and have been confirmed through experience.

Although we cannot predict the nature and extent of the error in a single sample, we can predict the nature and extent of sampling errors in general. Let us illustrate this with reference to sampling errors connected with the mean.

Sampling Errors of the Mean

Some sampling error can always be expected when a sample mean $\overline{X}$ is used to estimate a population mean μ. Although, in practice, such an estimate is based on a single sample mean, assume that one drew several random samples from the same population and computed a mean for each sample. We would find that these sample means would differ from one another and would also differ from the population mean (if it were known). This variation among the means is due to the sampling error associated with each random sample mean as an estimate of the population mean. Sampling errors of the mean have been studied carefully and it has been found that they follow regular laws.

The Expected Mean of Sampling Errors Is Zero. Given an infinite number of random samples drawn from a single population, the positive errors can be expected to balance the negative errors so that the mean of the sampling errors will be zero. For example, if the mean height of a population of college freshmen is 5 feet 9 inches, and several random samples are drawn from that population, we would expect some samples to have mean heights greater than 5 feet 9 inches and some to have mean heights less than 5 feet 9 inches. In the long run, however, the positive and negative sampling errors will balance. If we had an infinite number of random samples of the same size, calculated the mean of each of these samples, then computed the mean of all these means, the mean of the means would be equal to the population mean.

Since positive errors equal negative errors, a single sample mean is as likely to underestimate a population mean as to overestimate it. Therefore, we can justify saying that a sample mean is an unbiased estimate of the population mean, and is a reasonable estimate of the population mean.

Sampling Error Is an Inverse Function of Sample Size. As the size of a sample increases there is less fluctuation from one sample to another in the value of the mean. In other words, as the size of a sample increases the expected sampling error decreases. Small samples are more prone to sampling error than large ones. One would expect the means based on samples of 10 to fluctuate a great deal more than the means based on samples of 100. In our height example it would be much more likely that a random sample of four had three above-average freshmen and only one below-average freshman than that of a random sample of 40 had 30 above average and ten below. As sample size increases the likelihood that the mean of the sample is near the population mean also increases. There is a mathematical relationship between sample size and sampling error. We will show later how this relationship has been incorporated into inferential formulas.

Sampling Error Is a Direct Function of the Standard Deviation of the Population.   The more spread or variation we have among members of a population, the more spread or variation we expect in sample means. For example, the mean weights of random samples of 25 each selected from a population of professional jockeys would show relatively less sampling error than the mean weights of samples of 25 each selected from a population of school teachers. The weights of professional jockeys fall within a narrow range, the weights of school teachers do not. Therefore, for a given sample size, the expected sampling error for teachers' weights would be greater than the expected sampling error for jockeys' weights.

Sampling Errors Are Distributed in a Normal or Near Normal Manner around the Expected Mean of Zero.   Sample means near the population mean will occur more frequently than sample means far from the population mean. As we move farther and farther from the population mean we find fewer and fewer sample means occurring. Both theory and experience have shown that the means of random samples are distributed in a normal or near normal manner around the population mean.

Since a sampling error in this case is the difference between a sample mean and the population mean, the distribution of sampling errors is also normal or near normal in shape. The two distributions are by definition identical except that the distribution of sample means has a mean equal to the population mean while the mean of the sampling error is zero.

The distribution of sample means will resemble a normal curve even when the population from which the samples are drawn is not normally distributed. For example, in a typical elementary school we find about equal numbers of children of the various ages included, so a polygon of the children's ages would be basically rectangular. If we take random samples of 40 each from a school with equal numbers of children aged 6 through 11 we would find many samples with means near the population mean of 8.5, sample means of about 8 or 9 would be less common, and sample means as low as 7 or as high as 10 would be rare.

Standard Error of the Mean

Since the extent and the distribution of sampling errors can be predicted, we can use sample means with predictable confidence to make inferences concerning population means. However, we need an estimate of the magnitude of the sampling error associated with the sample mean when it is used as an estimate of the population mean. An important tool for this purpose is the *standard error of the mean*.

It has been stated that sampling error manifests itself in the variability of sample means. Thus, if one calculates the standard deviation of a collection of means from random samples from a single population, one would have an estimate of the amount of sampling error. It is possible, however, to obtain this estimate on the basis of only one sample. We have seen that two things affect the size of sampling error, the size of the sample and the standard deviation in the population. When these two things are known, one can predict the standard deviation of sampling errors. This expected standard deviation of sampling errors of the mean is called the standard error of the mean and is represented by the symbol $\sigma_{\bar{X}}$. It has been shown through deductive logic that the standard error of the mean is equal to the standard deviation of the population (σ) divided by the square root of the number in each sample ($\sqrt{n}$). In formula form:

$$\sigma_{\bar{X}} = \frac{\sigma}{\sqrt{n}} \qquad (6.1)$$

where:

$\sigma_{\bar{X}}$ = standard error of the mean
σ = standard deviation of the population
n = number in each sample

In chapter 5 we saw that standard deviation (σ) is an index of the degree of spread among individuals in a population. In the same way standard error of the mean ($\sigma_{\bar{X}}$) is an index of the spread expected among the means of samples drawn randomly from a population. As we will see, the interpretation of σ and $\sigma_{\bar{X}}$ is very similar.

Since the means of random samples have approximately normal distributions we can also use the normal curve model to make inferences concerning population means. Given that the expected mean of sample means is equal to the population mean, and that the standard deviation of these means is equal to the standard error of the mean, and that the means of random samples are distributed normally, one can compute a z-score for a sample mean and refer that z to the normal curve table to approximate the probability of a sample mean occurring through chance that far or farther from the population mean. The z is derived by subtracting the population mean from the sample mean and then dividing this difference by the standard error of the mean. In formula form this becomes:

$$z = \frac{\bar{X} - \mu}{\sigma_{\bar{X}}} \qquad (6.2)$$

To illustrate, let us consider a college admissions officer who wonders if his population of applicants is average or below average on the College Board examination. The national mean for College Board scores is 500 and the standard deviation is 100. He pulls a random sample of 64 from his population and finds the mean of the sample to be 470. He asks the question, "How probable is it that a random sample of 64 with a mean of 470 would be drawn from a population with a mean of 500?" Using formula (6.1), the admissions officer calculates the standard error of the mean as 12.5:

$$\sigma_{\bar{x}} = \frac{\sigma}{\sqrt{n}}$$

$$= \frac{100}{\sqrt{64}}$$

$$= 12.5$$

Calculating the z-score for his sample mean with formula (6.2) he has:

$$z = \frac{\bar{X} - \mu}{\sigma_{\bar{x}}}$$

$$= \frac{470 - 500}{12.5}$$

$$= -2.4$$

Thus, his sample mean deviates from the population mean by 2.4 standard error units. What is the probability of having a sample mean that deviates by this amount ($2.4\sigma_{\bar{x}}$'s) or more from the population mean? It is only necessary to refer to the normal curve in order to express this deviation (z) in terms of probability. Referring a z of -2.4 to the normal curve table, one finds that the probability of a z that low or lower is .0082. This means that a z-score that low or lower would occur by chance only about 8 times in 1,000. Since the probability of getting a sample mean that far from the population mean is remote, he concludes that his sample mean probably did not come from a population with a mean of 500 and therefore the mean of his population, applicants to his college, is probably less than 500.

The Strategy of Inferential Statistics

Inferential statistics is the science of making reasonable decisions with limited information. We use what we observe in samples and what is known about sampling error to reach fallible but reasonable decisions about populations. A basic tool of inferential statistics is the *null hypothesis*.

NULL HYPOTHESIS

Suppose we have 100 fourth graders available to participate in an experiment concerning the teaching of certain number concepts. We randomly assign 50 students to be taught these concepts by Method A and the other 50 to be taught by Method B. We arrange their environment in such a way that the two groups differ only in method of instruction. At the end of the experiment we administer an examination that is considered to be a suitable operational definition of mastery of the number concepts of interest. We find that the mean for those students taught by

Method B is higher than the mean for those taught by Method A. How do we interpret this difference?

Assuming we have been careful to make the learning conditions of the two groups equivalent except for the method of teaching, we could account for the difference by declaring that (1) the method of teaching caused the difference or (2) the difference occurred by chance. Even though the subjects were randomly assigned to the treatments, it is possible that through chance the Method B group had students who were more intelligent, more highly motivated, or for some other reason were more likely to learn the number concepts than the students in the Method A group, no matter how they were taught.

The difference between the groups therefore could be a result of a relationship between the variables—method of teaching and mastery of the concepts—or it could be the result of chance alone (i.e., sampling error). How are we to know which explanation is correct? In the ultimate sense we cannot know. What we do, then, is estimate the likelihood of chance alone being responsible for the observed difference and determine which explanation to accept as a result of this estimate.

The chance explanation is known as the *null hypothesis,* which, as you will recall from chapter 4, is a statement that there is *no* actual relationship between variables and that any observed relationship is only a function of chance. In our example the null hypothesis would state that there is no relationship between teaching method and mastery of the number concepts.

Another way of stating the null hypothesis in our example is to declare that the mean for all fourth graders taught by Method A is equal to the mean for all fourth graders taught by Method B. In formula form, using the symbol μ for population mean, this statement becomes

$$H_0: \mu_A = \mu_B$$

where
H_0 = the null hypothesis
μ_A = the mean of all fourth graders taught by Method A
μ_B = the mean of all fourth graders taught by Method B

Note that the assumption is made that the 50 pupils taught by Method A are a sample of all fourth graders who might be taught by Method A, and the 50 pupils taught by Method B are a sample of all those who might be taught by Method B. The investigator hopes to use the data from the experiment to infer what would be expected when other fourth graders are taught by Methods A or B.

In interpreting the observed difference between the groups, the investigator must choose between the chance explanation (null hypothesis) and the explanation that states that there is a relationship between variables (research hypothesis)—and must do so without knowing the ultimate truth concerning the populations of interest. This choice is based on incomplete information and is therefore subject to possible error.

TYPE I AND TYPE II ERRORS

The investigator will either retain or reject the null hypothesis. Either decision may be right or wrong. If the null hypothesis is true, the investigator is correct in retaining it and in error in rejecting it. The rejection of a true null hypothesis is labeled a Type I error.

If the null hypothesis is false, the investigator is in error in retaining it and correct in rejecting it. The retention of a false null hypothesis is labeled a Type II error. The four possible states of affairs are summarized in Table 6.1.

Table 6.1   Schematic Representation of Type I and Type II Errors

		The real situation (unknown to the investigator) is that the null hypothesis is:	
		true	false
The investigator, after making a test of significance, concludes that the null hypothesis is:	true	investigator is correct	investigator makes Type II error
	false	investigator makes Type I error	investigator is correct

Let us consider some possible consequences of the two types of errors in our example.

Type I

The investigator declares that there is a relationship between teaching method and the mastery of the numerical concepts and therefore recommends Method B as the better method. Schools discard textbooks and other materials based on Method A and purchase materials based on Method B. In-service training is instituted to train teachers to teach by Method B. After all this expenditure of time and money, the schools do not observe an increase in mastery of the numerical concepts. Subsequent experiments do not produce the results observed in the original investigation. Although the ultimate truth or falsity of the null hypothesis is still unknown, the evidence supporting it is overwhelming. The original investigator is embarrassed and humiliated.

Type II

The investigator concludes that the difference between the two groups may be attributed to luck and that the null hypothesis is probably true. He declares that one method is as good as the other.

Subsequent investigators conclude that Method B is better than Method A, and schools that change from Method A to Method B report impressive gains in student mastery. Although the ultimate truth still remains unknown, a mountain of evidence supports the research hypothesis. The original investigator is embarrassed (but probably not humiliated).

Type I errors typically lead to changes that are unwarranted. Type II errors typically lead to a maintenance of the status quo when a change is warranted. The consequences of a Type I error are generally considered more serious than the consequences of a Type II error, although there are certainly exceptions to this.

Level of Significance

Recall that all scientific conclusions are statements that have a high probability of being correct, rather than statements of absolute truth. How high must the probability be before an investigator is willing to declare that a relationship between variables exists? In other words, how unlikely must the null hypothesis be before one rejects it? The consequences of rejecting a true null hypothesis, a Type I error, vary with the situation. Therefore, investigators usually weigh the relative consequences of Type I and Type II errors and decide, before conducting their experiments, how strong the evidence must be before they would reject the null hypothesis. This predetermined level at which a null hypothesis would be rejected is called the *level of significance*.

Of course, one could avoid Type I errors by always retaining the null hypothesis or avoid Type II errors by always rejecting it. Neither of these alternatives is productive. If the consequences of a Type I error would be very serious but a Type II error would be of little consequence, the investigator might decide to risk the possibility of a Type I error only if the estimated probability of the observed relationship's being due to mere luck is one chance in a thousand or less. This is called testing the hypothesis at the .001 level of significance. In this case the investigator is being very careful not to declare that a relationship exists when there is no relationship. However, this decision means the acceptance of a high probability of a Type II error, declaring there is no relationship when in fact a relationship does exist.

If the consequences of a Type I error are judged to be not serious, the investigator might decide to declare that a relationship exists if the probability of an observed relationship's being due to mere luck is one chance in ten or less. This is called testing the hypothesis at the .10 level of significance. Here the investigator is taking only moderate precautions against a Type I error, yet is not taking a great risk of a Type II error.

The level of significance is the probability of a Type I error that an investigator is willing to risk in rejecting a null hypothesis. If an investigator sets the level of significance at .01, it means that the null hypothesis will be rejected if the estimated probability of the observed relationship's being a chance occurrence is one in a hundred. If the level of significance is set at .0001, the null hypothesis will be rejected only if the estimated probability of the observed relationship's being a function of mere chance is one in 10,000 or less. The most commonly used levels of significance in the field of education are the .05 and the .01 levels.

Traditionally, investigators determine the level of significance after weighing the relative seriousness of Type I and Type II errors, but before running the experiment. If the data derived from the completed experiment indicate that the probability of the null hypothesis being true is less than the predetermined acceptable probability, the results are declared to be statistically significant. If the probability is greater than the predetermined acceptable probability, the results are described as nonsignificant—that is, the null hypothesis is retained.

The familiar meaning of the word *significant* is ''important'' or ''meaningful.'' In statistics this word means ''less likely to be a function of chance than some predetermined probability.'' Results of investigations can be statistically significant without being inherently meaningful or important.

There are numerous ways of testing a null hypothesis. Among the most widely used are the *t*-test, analysis of variance, and the chi-square test.

Significance of the Difference between Two Means

THE *t*-TEST

We have shown that it is possible to make use of the normal probability curve to compare the mean of a sample with the population mean by using the *z*-score to see whether or not the sample mean is representative of the population mean. To demonstrate that point, we found the standard error of the mean for the sample distribution, then used the formula $(\bar{X} - \mu)/\sigma_{\bar{X}}$. Implied in using this procedure is the appropriateness of the normal probability curve.

However, it has been shown mathematically that the normal curve is appropriate for hypothesis testing only when the population standard deviation is known. In most research situations the population standard deviation is not known and must be estimated by the formula

$$s = \sqrt{\frac{\Sigma x^2}{n - 1}} \tag{6.3}$$

where
s = estimated population standard deviation
x^2 = sum of the squared deviations scores, $\Sigma(X - \bar{X})^2$
n = number in the sample

When this estimate (s) is substituted for the population standard deviation (σ) in the calculation of the standard error of the mean, it is customary to express Formula (6.1) as

$$s_{\bar{x}} = \frac{s}{\sqrt{n}} \text{ instead of } \sigma_{\bar{x}} = \frac{\sigma}{\sqrt{n}}$$

When $s_{\bar{x}}$ is used instead of $\sigma_{\bar{x}}$ each finite sample size has its own unique probability distribution. These distributions are known as the *t*-curves. These distributions become more and more similar to the normal curve as the size of the sample increases. A series of distributions called *t*-distributions has been developed for testing hypotheses concerning the population mean using small samples. When the sample size is infinite, the *t*-distribution is the same as the normal distribution. As the sample size becomes smaller, the *t*-distribution becomes increasingly different from the *z*-distribution. For our purposes it is not necessary to know how to calculate *t*-distributions since the most frequently needed results of these calculations are to be found in Table A.3 in the Appendix. The *t*-curve does not approach the base line as rapidly as does the normal curve. Some of the *t*-curves are shown in Figure 6.1 along with the normal curve, the solid line labeled "*df* = ∞."

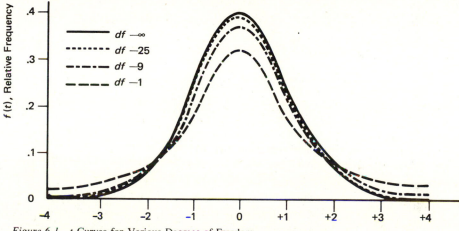

Figure 6.1   *t*-Curves for Various Degrees of Freedom

The *t*-curves are labeled according to their degrees of freedom, abbreviated "*df*." Before further discussion of the characteristics of *t*-curves, let us turn our attention to the concept of degrees of freedom.

Degrees of Freedom

The number of degrees of freedom refers to the number of observations free to vary around a constant parameter. To illustrate the general concept of degrees of freedom, suppose a teacher asks a student to name any five numbers that come into his head. The student would be free to name any five numbers he chooses. We would say that the student has five degrees of freedom. Now suppose the teacher tells the student to name five numbers but to make sure that the mean of these five numbers is equal to 20. The student now is free to name any numbers he chooses for the first four, but for the last number he must name the number that will make the total for the five numbers 100 in order to arrive at a mean of 20. If the student names, as his first four numbers, 16, 0.5, 1,000, and -65, then his fifth number must be -851.5. The student has five numbers to name and one restriction, so his degrees of freedom are five minus one equals four. We can show this in formula form as

$$
\begin{aligned}
df &= n - 1 \\
&= 5 - 1 \\
&= 4
\end{aligned}
$$

Now, suppose the teacher asks the student to name seven numbers in such a way that the first three have a mean of 10 and all seven have a mean of 12. Here we have seven numbers and two restrictions, so

$$
\begin{aligned}
df &= n - 2 \\
&= 7 - 2 \\
&= 5
\end{aligned}
$$

The concept of degrees of freedom is involved in most of the procedures in inferential statistics. There is an appropriate method of computing the degrees of freedom associated with each procedure.

The *t*-Test for Independent Samples

Research workers often draw two random samples from a population and assign a specific experimental treatment to each group. After being exposed to this treatment, the two groups are compared with respect to certain characteristics in order to find the effect of the treatments. A difference might be observed between the two groups after such treatments, but this difference might be statistically non-significant—that is, attributable to chance. The index used to find the significance of the difference between the means of the two samples in this case is called the *t-test for independent samples*. These samples are referred to as independent because they are drawn independently from a population without any pairing or other relationship between the two groups.

Let us use an example. Suppose a researcher is interested in finding out whether stress affects problem-solving performance. The first step is to randomly select two groups of 15 subjects from among the students in a course. The scores (X) on the dependent variable *problem-solving performance* are shown in Table 6.2, followed by the deviation scores (x) and the squared deviation scores (x^2). Since the members of the two groups are selected and assigned randomly, the mean performances of the two groups in a problem-solving task should not significantly differ prior to the treatment. After the treatment, however, the mean performance of the two groups should differ significantly if stress is actually related to problem-solving performance.

Table 6.2   The Computation of the t-Value for Two Sample Means

	Group 1 (Nonstress Condition)			Group 2 (Stress Condition)		
X_1	x_1	x_1^2		X_2	x_2	x_2^2
18	+4	16		13	+3	9
17	+3	9		12	+2	4
16	+2	4		12	+2	4
16	+2	4		11	+1	1
16	+2	4		11	+1	1
15	+1	1		11	+1	1
15	+1	1		10	0	0
15	+1	1		10	0	0
14	0	0		10	0	0
14	0	0		10	0	0
13	−1	1		9	−1	1
12	−2	4		9	−1	1
11	−3	9		8	−2	4
10	−4	16		7	−3	9
8	−6	36		7	−3	9

$$\Sigma X_1 = \overline{210} \qquad \Sigma x_1^2 = \overline{106} \qquad \Sigma X_2 = \overline{150} \qquad \Sigma x_2^2 = \overline{44}$$

$$n_1 \quad 15 \qquad\qquad\qquad\qquad\qquad n_2 \quad 15$$

$$\overline{X}_1 = 14 \qquad\qquad\qquad\qquad\qquad \overline{X}_2 = 10$$

The data presented in Table 6.2 are the performance scores of the members of the two groups, one of which worked under stress conditions and the other, under relaxed (nonstress) conditions. The table shows that the mean performance score of the subjects in the stress group is 10 and the mean performance score of the nonstress group is 14. Clearly there is a difference. Now we need to determine whether or not this difference could easily occur by chance.

In order to do this we must estimate how much difference between the groups would be expected through chance alone under a true null hypothesis. An appropriate procedure for doing this is to calculate the *standard error of the difference between two means* $(s_{\overline{X}_1 - \overline{X}_2})$. The formula for this in the case of independent samples is

$$S_{\overline{X}_1 - \overline{X}_2} = \sqrt{\frac{\Sigma x_1^2 + \Sigma x_2^2}{n_1 + n_2 - 2}\left(\frac{1}{n_1} + \frac{1}{n_2}\right)} \qquad (6.4)$$

where

$s_{\overline{X}_1 - \overline{X}_2}$ = the standard error of the difference between two means
n_1 = the number of cases in Group 1
n_2 = the number of cases in Group 2

$\Sigma x_1{}^2$ = the sum of the squared deviation scores in Group 1
$\Sigma x_2{}^2$ = the sum of the squared deviation scores in Group 2

The standard error of the difference between two means is sometimes referred to as the error term for the t-test. In our example this would be calculated as follows:

$$s_{\bar{X}_1 - \bar{X}_2} = \sqrt{\frac{106 + 44}{15 + 15 - 2}\left(\frac{1}{15} + \frac{1}{15}\right)}$$

$$= \sqrt{\frac{150}{28}\left(\frac{2}{15}\right)}$$

$$= \sqrt{0.714}$$

$$= 0.84$$

This calculation tells us the difference that would be expected through chance alone if the null hypothesis is true. In other words, the value 0.84 is the difference we would expect between the mean performance scores for our two groups if they are drawn at random from a common population and are *not* subjected to different treatments. Given an infinite number of samples in such circumstances, we would expect to observe a difference of less than 0.84 in 68 percent of the calculations of the differences between such random groups and a value of more than 0.84 in the other 32 percent. (It is beyond the scope of this text to discuss the reason why the application of the formula for the standard error of the difference between means yields the appropriate estimated difference that would be due to chance.)[3]

In our example for the data in Table 6.2 we should expect a difference of 0.84 through chance under a true null hypothesis. We observed a difference of 4.0. Is the observed difference sufficiently greater than the expected difference to enable us to reject the null hypothesis?

To answer this question we first make a ratio of the two numbers. This ratio is called the t-*ratio*. Its formula is

$$t = \frac{\bar{X}_1 - \bar{X}_2}{s_{\bar{X}_1 - \bar{X}_2}} \tag{6.5}$$

where
$\bar{X}_1 - \bar{X}_2$ = the observed difference between two means
$s_{\bar{X}_1 - \bar{X}_2}$ = the standard error of the difference between two means (expected difference between the two means when the null hypothesis is true)

We can write the t-ratio formula in more complete form by including the formula for the standard error for the difference between two means:

---

[3]For a discussion of the rationale of this procedure, see Donald Ary and Lucy C. Jacobs, *Introduction to Statistics* (New York: Holt, Rinehart and Winston, 1976).

$$t = \frac{\bar{X}_1 - \bar{X}_2}{\sqrt{\left(\dfrac{\Sigma x_1{}^2 + \Sigma x_2{}^2}{n_1 + n_2 - 2}\right)\left(\dfrac{1}{n_1} + \dfrac{1}{n_2}\right)}}$$

In our example the value of the t-ratio is

$$\frac{14 - 10}{0.84} = 4.76$$

Our observed difference is 4.76 times as large as the difference expected under a true null hypothesis. Is this large enough to reject the null hypothesis at the .05 level? To answer this we need only calculate the degrees of freedom and consult the t-table.

The degrees of freedom for an independent t-test are the number of cases in the first group plus the number of cases in the second group minus 2.

$$df = n_1 + n_2 - 2$$

In our example we have $15 + 15 - 2 = 28$ degrees of freedom. We can now use Table A.3 in the Appendix to determine the significance of our results. The first column in this table is labeled ''Degrees of Freedom.'' One finds the appropriate row in the table by locating the degrees of freedom in one's study. For our example we would consult the row for 28 degrees of freedom. The remaining columns show the t-values associated with certain probabilities. In the row for 28 degrees of freedom we find 1.701 in the column labeled .1, which tells us that with a true null hypothesis and 28 degrees of freedom a t-ratio of $+1.701$ or more or -1.701 or less will occur by chance one time in ten. The number 2.048 in the column labeled .05 indicates that under a true null hypothesis and 28 degrees of freedom a t-ratio of ± 2.048 or more will occur by chance 5 percent of the time.

Our observed ratio of 4.76 is greater than 2.048, which means that the difference between our groups is greater than the value required to reject the null hypothesis at the .05 level of significance. The estimated probability of the null hypothesis being true is less than 5 percent ($p < .05$). Although we do not know for certain that the variables *stress* and *problem-solving performance* are related, the evidence is significant enough according to our previously set criteria to enable us to conclude that the observed relationship is not just a chance occurrence. If the observed t-ratio had been less than 2.048, we would have concluded that the evidence was not good enough to lead us to declare that a relationship exists between the variables. In other words, we would have retained the null hypothesis.

Notice that as we proceed from left to right in the t-table we find the t-values required for rejecting the null hypothesis at increasingly rigorous levels of significance. For 28 degrees of freedom a value of 2.763 or greater would lead to the rejection of a null hypothesis at the .01 level. A value of 3.674 or greater would lead to the rejection of the null hypothesis at the .001 level. So our value of 4.76 is significant not only at the .05 level ($p < .05$) but also at the .01 level ($p < .01$) and the .001 level ($p < .001$).

The t-Test for Nonindependent Samples

So far our discussion has centered around comparing the means obtained from two independent samples. In an independent sample each member is chosen randomly from the population, and the composition of one group has no bearing on the composition of the other group. Sometimes, however, investigators may wish to match the subjects of their two groups on some qualities that are important to the purpose of their research, or they may wish to compare the means obtained by the same group under two different experimental conditions. In such cases the groups are no longer independent, inasmuch as the composition of one group is related to the composition of the other group. Also we would expect the dependent variable scores to be correlated. Therefore the t-test for nonindependent or correlated means must be used. The measure to be analyzed by the nonindependent t-test is the difference between the paired scores.

Let us consider an example. Suppose we wish to know whether taking a research course affects the attitudes of the students toward research. To investigate this we select a research class and obtain attitude measures toward research from the students on the first and last days of class. Let us suppose we have collected such data and the results are as presented in Table 6.3. Columns (2) and (3) show the scores of each student in the first and second tests. Column (4) presents the difference between the first and second scores of each student. The sum of these differences amounts to +30. The mean of the differences, +2, is found by dividing +30(ΣD) by n, the number of paired observations, or 15. Column (5) shows the squares of the differences.

The formula for the nonindependent t-test is

$$t = \frac{\bar{D}}{\sqrt{\dfrac{\Sigma D^2 - \dfrac{(\Sigma D)^2}{N}}{N(N-1)}}} \tag{6.7}$$

where
t = the t-value for nonindependent (correlated) means
D = the difference between the paired scores
$\bar{D}$ = the mean of the differences
ΣD^2 = the sum of the squared difference scores
N = the number of pairs

Substituting the values from Table 6.3, we obtain

$$t = \frac{\dfrac{30}{15}}{\sqrt{\dfrac{164 - \dfrac{(30)^2}{15}}{15(15-1)}}} = \frac{2}{\sqrt{\dfrac{164-60}{210}}} = \frac{2}{\sqrt{\dfrac{104}{210}}} = \frac{2}{\sqrt{0.4952}} = \frac{2}{0.704} = 2.8$$

Table 6.3   Before-and-After Scores of 15 Students in an Introduction to Research Class

(1) Subject Number	(2) Pretest	(3) Posttest	(4) D	(5) D^2
1	10	12	+2	+ 4
2	9	13	+4	+16
3	8	12	+4	+16
4	11	9	−2	+ 4
5	10	8	−2	+ 4
6	7	9	+2	+ 4
7	10	12	+2	+ 4
8	9	11	+2	+ 4
9	8	10	+2	+ 4
10	6	10	+4	+16
11	10	12	+2	+ 4
12	7	13	+6	+36
13	10	6	−4	+16
14	9	13	+4	+16
15	10	14	+4	+16
			$\Sigma D = +30$	$\Sigma D^2 = +164$

The t-ratio tells us that the observed difference is 2.84 times as great as the difference that would be expected under a true null hypothesis. We must now consult the Table of t-Values to determine the statistical significance of our observed ratio.

The number of degrees of freedom for the nonindependent t-test equals $N − 1$, N being the number of pairs of observations. In our example we have $15 − 1 = 14$ degrees of freedom. In the Table of t-Values we find that with 14 degrees of freedom a t-value of 2.145 is needed for the t to be significant at the .05 level and a t-value of 2.977, for significance at the .01 level. Our obtained value of 2.84 exceeds the given value for the .05 level but does not reach the given value for the .01 level. This means that the difference between the two means is significant at the .05 level but not at the .01 level. If we had set our level of significance at .05, we could conclude that taking a research course does change the attitude of the students toward research under the conditions present in our study.

The Logic of the t-Test

The numerator of the t-test is the actual difference that has been observed between two groups. The denominator $(s_{\bar{x}_1 - \bar{x}_2})$ is an estimate of how much these two groups would be expected to differ by chance alone; that is, it indicates the difference to be expected between two groups selected by a random procedure from a single parent population. This denominator is based on: (1) the number in the samples, $n_1 + n_2$ (the larger the number, the less random differences to be expected between sample means), and (2) the variation within the groups, s_1 and s_2 (the greater the variation *within* groups, the greater the random differences to be expected between groups). Since the denominator is a measure of how much apparent difference can be expected through chance alone, it is called the *error term* of the *t*-test.

If the ratio of observed difference (numerator) divided by error term (denominator) equals or exceeds the value indicated in the Table of *t*-Values, the null hypothesis can be rejected at the indicated level of significance.

Analysis of Variance

In *analysis of variance* (ANOVA), as in the *t*-test, a ratio of observed differences/error term is used to test hypotheses. This ratio, called the F-*ratio*, employs the variance (σ^2) of group means as a measure of observed differences among groups. This means that ANOVA is a more versatile technique than the *t*-test. A *t*-test can be used only to test a difference between *two* means. ANOVA can test the difference between two *or more* means. Some statisticians never use the *t*-test, since ANOVA can be used in any situation where a *t*-test can be used and, moreover, can do many things the *t*-test cannot do.

The general rationale of ANOVA is that the *total variance* of all subjects in an experiment can be analyzed into two sources, *variance between* groups and *variance within* groups.

Variance between groups is incorporated into the numerator in the *F*-ratio. Variance within is incorporated into the error term or denominator, as it is in the *t*-test. As variance between groups increases, the *F*-ratio increases. As variance within increases, the *F*-ratio decreases. The number of subjects influences the *F*-ratio; the larger the number, the larger the numerator becomes. When the numerator and denominator are equal, the differences between group means are no greater than would be expected by chance alone. If the numerator is greater than the denominator, one consults the Table of *F*-Values (2.4 in the Appendix) to determine whether the ratio is great enough to enable one to reject the null hypothesis at the predetermined level.

COMPUTATION OF *F*-RATIO (SIMPLE ANALYSIS OF VARIANCE)

Suppose we have the three experimental conditions of high stress, moderate stress, and no stress, and we wish to compare the performance of three groups of individuals, randomly assigned to these three conditions, in a simple problem-solving task. Assume that the data presented in Table 6.4 summarize our observations of the performance of these three groups and we are now to test the null hypothesis that there is no significant difference among these observations.

Table 6.4   Measures Obtained in Three Random Samples after Performance of a Task under Conditions of Moderate Stress, High Stress, and No Stress

Group 1 High Stress		Group 2 Moderate Stress		Group 3 No Stress	
X_1	X_1^2	X_2	X_2^2	X_3	X_3^2
19	361	22	484	15	225
18	324	20	400	14	196
17	289	19	361	14	196
16	256	18	324	13	169
15	225	17	289	13	169
15	225	16	256	12	144
14	196	16	256	12	144
13	169	15	225	11	121
12	144	14	196	11	121
11	121	12	144	10	100
150	2310	169	2935	125	1585
ΣX_1	ΣX_1^2	ΣX_2	ΣX_2^2	ΣX_3	ΣX_3^2

$$\bar{X}_1 = 15.0 \qquad \bar{X}_2 = 16.9 \qquad \bar{X}_3 = 12.5 \qquad \bar{\bar{X}} = 14.8$$

The means can be seen to differ from each other and from the overall mean for all 30 subjects. Are the differences among these means great enough to be statistically significant or is it likely that they occurred by chance? To answer this, we compute the F-ratio.

The first step is to find the sum of the squared deviation of each of the individual scores from the grand mean. This index is called the *total sum of squares* and is found by applying the formula

$$\Sigma x_t^2 = \Sigma X^2 - \frac{(\Sigma X)^2}{N} \tag{6.8}$$

In our example this value is

$$\Sigma x_t^2 = 6830 - \frac{(444)^2}{30} = 258.8$$

Then we find the part of the total sum of squares that is due to the deviations of the group means from the grand mean. This index is called the *sum of the squares between groups*. (To be grammatically correct, we should say the sum of squares *among* groups when more than two groups are involved. However, it is a long-standing tradition to use the term *sum of squares between groups,* and in order to be consistent with other texts, we are retaining this usage here.) This index is found by applying the formula

$$\Sigma x_b{}^2 = \frac{(\Sigma X_1)^2}{n_1} + \frac{(\Sigma X_2)^2}{n_2} + \cdots - \frac{(\Sigma X)^2}{N} \tag{6.9}$$

In our problem this value is

$$\Sigma x_b{}^2 = \frac{(150)^2}{10} + \frac{(169)^2}{10} + \frac{(125)^2}{10} - \frac{(444)^2}{30} = 97.4$$

Then we find the part of the total sum of squares that is due to the deviations of each individual score from its own group mean. This index is called the *sum of the squares within groups* and is found by applying the formula

$$\Sigma x_w{}^2 = \Sigma X_1{}^2 - \frac{(\Sigma X_1)^2}{n_1} + \Sigma X_2{}^2 - \frac{(\Sigma X_2)^2}{n_2} + \cdots \tag{6.10}$$

In our problem this value is

$$\Sigma x_w{}^2 = 2310 - \frac{(150)^2}{10} + 2935 - \frac{(169)^2}{10} + 1585 - \frac{(125)^2}{10} = 161.4$$

The sum of the squares within groups could also be found by subtracting the sum of squares between groups from the total sum of the squares, that is,

$$\Sigma x_w{}^2 = \Sigma x_t{}^2 - \Sigma x_b{}^2 \tag{6.11}$$

In our case

$$\Sigma x_w{}^2 = 258.8 - 97.4 = 161.4$$

The *F*-Test of Significance

Table 6.5 summarizes the results of our calculations so far, together with the results of further calculations. Column (1) of the table lists the three sources of variance: between-groups variance, within-groups variance, and total variance. Column (2) contains the sums of squares, which we have already calculated. Column (3) lists the number of degrees of freedom associated with each source of variance. The number of degrees of freedom for between-groups variance is equal to $(G - 1)$, G being the number of groups. In our example this value is $3 - 1 = 2$. The degrees of freedom for within-groups variance is $n_1 - 1 + n_2 - 1 + \cdots$. In our example this value is $10 - 1 + 10 - 1 + 10 - 1 = 27$. The number of degrees of freedom for total variance equals $N - 1$; in our example $30 - 1 = 29$. This last value could also be obtained by adding the between-groups and within-groups degrees of freedom.

Table 6.5   Summary of the Analysis of Variance of the Three Groups

(1) Source of Variance	(2) SS	(3) df	(4) MS	(5) F	(6) Level of Significance
Between groups	97.4	2	48.70	8.14	0.01
Within groups	161.4	27	5.98		
Total	258.8	29			

The next step, then, is to find the *between-groups mean square* and the *within-groups mean square*. These values are obtained by dividing the between-groups and within-groups sums of squares by their respective degrees of freedom. The resulting values are the mean squares. In our example the mean square between groups is $97.4/2 = 48.7$ and the mean square within groups is $161.4/27 = 5.98$. The mean square within groups is the error term for our F-ratio. By applying the following formula, we finally arrive at the end product of the analysis-of-variance procedure, the F-ratio:

$$F = \frac{MS_b}{MS_w} = \frac{SS_b/df_b}{SS_w/df_w} \qquad (6.12)$$

In our example this value is

$$F = \frac{48.70}{5.98} = 8.14$$

We now consult Table A.4 in the Appendix to determine whether the F-ratio we have obtained is statistically significant. We find the column headed by the between-groups (numerator) degrees of freedom of our experiment and go down this column to the row entry corresponding to the number of our within-groups (denominator) degrees of freedom. At this point in the column we find two values, one in roman type and one in boldface type. If our F-ratio is equal to or greater than the value given in lightface, our F-ratio is significant at the .05 level. If our obtained F-ratio is equal to or greater than the value given in boldface, it is also significant at the .01 level. In our example, with 2 and 27 degrees of freedom, we need an F-ratio of 3.35 to reject the null hypothesis at the .05 level and an F-ratio of 5.49 to reject the null hypothesis at the .01 level. Since our obtained F-ratio is greater than both of these values, it is significant at the .01 level and the null hypothesis is rejected at that level.

The assumption underlying the analysis-of-variance procedure is that if the groups to be compared are truly random samples from the same population, then the between-groups mean square should not differ from the within-groups mean square by more than the amount we would expect from chance alone. Thus under a true null hypothesis we would expect the F-ratio to be approximately equal to one. On the other hand, if the null hypothesis is false, the difference among group means should be greater than what is expected by chance, so the mean square between would exceed the mean square within. In such cases the F-ratio, the mean square between divided by the mean square within, will have a value greater than one. We then consult the Table of F-Values to determine whether the ratio for our data is sufficiently greater than 1.0 to enable us to reject the null hypothesis at our predetermined level. As the difference between these mean squares increases, the F-ratio increases and the probability of the null hypothesis being correct decreases.

When the null hypothesis is rejected as a result of this analysis-of-variance procedure, we cannot say more than that the measures obtained from the groups involved differ and the differences are greater than one would expect to exist by chance alone.

A significant F-ratio does not necessarily mean that all groups differ significantly from all other groups. The significant F may be a result of a difference existing between one group and the rest of the groups. For instance, in our problem it might be that Group 3 is significantly different from Group 1 and Group 2, but Groups 1 and 2 do not differ significantly from each other. There are several statistical tests that can be applied to find the location of significant differences. Those developed by Tukey and by Scheffé are particularly useful.[4]

In our example we selected our three groups randomly from the same population and thus we can assume that they did not differ beyond the chance expectation prior to our experimental treatments. The significance of the F-ratio indicates that the differences found between these groups *after* treatment are beyond chance expectation. We attribute this to our experimental treatment and conclude that the level of stress affects the performance of individuals in simple problem-solving tasks. This is as far as we can go in our interpretation of this F-ratio. If we need further statistical analysis, we can use Tukey's, Scheffé's, or other tests to determine the significance between pairs of individual measures. These techniques can tell us how specific stress conditions affect the performance and can answer such questions as, Is there any difference in performance scores under conditions of moderate and high stress? moderate and no stress? and high and no stress?

MULTIFACTOR ANALYSIS OF VARIANCE

We may wish to investigate the combined effect of stress level and task difficulty on performance in a problem-solving task. To investigate this problem we will vary both the level of stress and the difficulty of the task. The layout for an experiment

---

[4]See Gene V. Glass and Julian C. Stanley, *Statistical Methods in Education and Psychology* (Englewood Cliffs, N.J.: Prentice-Hall, 1970).

investigating the combined effects of two or more independent variables is called a *factorial design* and the results are analyzed by means of a *multifactor analysis of variance*.

Let us assume that we have carried out this experiment using five subjects in each group and that the data shown in Table 6.6 represent a summary of our observations of the performance of the subjects. Applying multifactor analysis of variance will enable us to find (1) whether there is a significant difference between the performance of the subjects under a moderate stress condition and under a high stress condition, (2) whether there is a significant difference between the performance of the subjects given an easy problem-solving task and those given a difficult task, and (3) whether or not the two variables, stress and task difficulty, have a combined effect on the performance of the subjects. The effects investigated by the first and second analyses are called *main effects,* whereas the third is referred to as the *interaction effect.* The end products of these analyses will be three *F*-ratios, two of which indicate the significance of the two main effects and the third, that of the interaction effect.

Table 6.6   Measures on Two Levels of Problem-Solving Tasks under Moderate and High Conditions of Stress

		Stress		
		Moderate	High	
Simple		20 20 Group 1 19 19 $\bar{X} = 19$ 17 ΣX 95	23 22 Group 3 21 20 $\bar{X} = 21$ 19 ΣX 105	$\Sigma X_{r_1} = 200$ $\bar{X}_{r_1} = 20.0$
Task				
Difficult		22 21 Group 2 20 19 $\bar{X} = 20$ 18 ΣX 100	18 16 Group 4 15 14 $\bar{X} = 15$ 12 ΣX 75	$\Sigma X_{r_2} = 175$ $\bar{X}_{r_2} = 17.5$

$$\Sigma X_{c_1} = 195 \qquad \Sigma X_{c_2} = 180 \qquad \Sigma X \text{ Total} = 375$$
$$\bar{X}_{c_1} = 19.5 \qquad \bar{X}_{c_2} = 18.0 \qquad \bar{\bar{X}} \text{ (Grand mean)} = 18.75$$

The computation of these *F*-ratios involves the following steps:

1. Find the total sum of squares, the sum of squares between groups, and the sum of squares within groups using the same procedures and formulas applied in simple analysis of variance. These values, derived from the data in Table 6.6, are

$$\Sigma x_t{}^2 = 7181 - \frac{(375)^2}{20} = 149.75$$

$$\Sigma x_b{}^2 = \frac{(95)^2}{5} + \frac{(105)^2}{5} + \frac{(100)^2}{5} + \frac{(75)^2}{5} - \frac{(375)^2}{20} = 103.75$$

$$\Sigma x_w{}^2 = 149.75 - 103.75 = 46.00$$

2. Break down the sum of the squares between groups into three separate sums of squares: (*a*) the sum of squares between columns, (*b*) the sum of squares between rows, and (*c*) the sum of squares for interaction between columns and rows:

a. The between-columns sum of squares represents the sum of the squared deviations due to the difference between the column means and the grand mean. It is found by using the formula

$$\Sigma x_{bc}^2 = \frac{(\Sigma X_{c1})^2}{n_{c1}} + \frac{(\Sigma X_{c2})^2}{n_{c2}} + \cdots - \frac{(\Sigma X)^2}{N} \tag{6.13}$$

Using this formula, the sum of squares between the columns for the data shown in Table 6.7 is

$$\Sigma x_{bc}^2 = \frac{(195)^2}{10} + \frac{(180)^2}{10} - \frac{(375)^2}{20} = 11.25$$

b. The between-rows sum of squares is the sum of the squared deviations due to the difference between the row means and the grand mean. It is found by applying the formula

$$\Sigma x_{br}^2 = \frac{(\Sigma X_{r1})^2}{n_{r1}} + \frac{(\Sigma X_{r2})^2}{n_{r2}} + \cdots - \frac{(\Sigma X)^2}{N} \tag{6.14}$$

For the data presented in Table 6.6 this value is

$$\Sigma x_{br}^2 = \frac{(200)^2}{10} + \frac{(175)^2}{10} - \frac{(375)^2}{20} = 31.25$$

c. The sum-of-squares interaction is the part of the deviation between the group means and the overall mean that is due neither to row differences nor to column differences. In other words, this is the difference between the total of the sum of squares between groups and the sum of squares between rows, that is,

$$\Sigma x_{int}^2 = \Sigma x_b^2 - (\Sigma x_{bc}^2 + \Sigma x_{br}^2) \tag{6.15}$$

Expressed in words, the interaction sum of squares is equal to the between-groups sum of squares minus the sum of the between-columns sum of squares and the between-rows sum of squares.

For the data presented in Table 6.6, this interaction value is

$$\Sigma x^2_{int} = 103.75 - (11.25 + 31.25) = 61.25$$

3. Determine the number of degrees of freedom associated with each source of variation. They are found as follows:

df for between-columns sum of squares $= C - 1$
df for between-rows sum of squares $= R - 1$
df for interaction $= (C - 1)(R - 1)$
df for between-groups sum of squares $= (G - 1)$
df for within-groups sum of squares $= \Sigma(n - 1)$
df for total sum of squares $= N - 1$

where
$C =$ the number of columns
$R =$ the number of rows
$G =$ the number of groups
$n =$ the number of subjects in one group
$N =$ the number of subjects in all groups

4. Find the mean-square values by dividing each sum of squares by its associated number of degrees of freedom.
5. Compute the F-ratios for the main and the interaction effects by dividing the between-groups mean squares by the within-groups mean square for each of the three components.

Table 6.7   Summary of a 2 × 2 Multifactor Analysis of Variance

Source of Variance	SS	df	MS	F	Level of Significance
Between columns (stress)	11.25	1	11.25	3.913	—
Between rows (task)	31.25	1	31.25	10.869	.01
Columns by rows (interaction)	61.25	1	61.25	21.304	.01
Between groups	103.75	3	34.583		
Within groups	46.00	16	2.875		
Total	149.75	19			

6. The results of the calculations based on the data presented in Table 6.6 are summarized in Table 6.7. Three F-ratios are listed in this table. To find the significance of each of these values we consult the Table of F-Values as before. To

enter this table we use the number of degrees of freedom associated with each F-ratio (df for the numerator) and the number of degrees of freedom associated with the within-groups mean square (df for the denominator). For example, our between-columns F-ratio is 3.913. Consulting the table, we see that, with 1 and 16 degrees of freedom, an F-ratio of 4.49 or more is needed for significance at the .05 level. Since our F-ratio is smaller than the value shown in the table, it is not significant.

To be significant, the F-ratio for between rows, with 1 and 16 degrees of freedom, should reach 4.49 (.05 level) or 8.53 (.01 level). Since our obtained value of F, 10.869, exceeds both of these values, it is significant at the .01 level.

For the interaction between columns and rows, with 1 and 16 degrees of freedom, an F-ratio of 4.49 (.05 level) or 8.53 (.01 level) is needed. Our obtained value of F, 21.304, exceeds both of these values and thus is significant at the .01 level.

Interpretation of the F-ratios

The first F-ratio (between columns) in Table 6.7 is not significant and shows that the stress conditions do not differ significantly from one another in their effect on the performance of the subjects in the experiment. This analysis is a comparison of the combined performance of Groups 1 and 2 with the combined performance of Groups 3 and 4. We could have arrived at the same conclusion by using the t-test procedure.

The second F-ratio (between rows), which is significant at the .01 level, is based on the comparison of the performance of the subjects in Groups 1 and 3 with those in Groups 2 and 4. From the significance of this F-ratio we can infer that the difference between the performance of those subjects given an easy problem-solving task and those given a difficult problem-solving task is beyond chance expectation. Examining the data presented in Table 6.7 we see that those groups who performed simple problem-solving tasks have obtained a combined mean of 20 as compared with a mean of 17.5 for those groups who performed difficult tasks. Since we have a significant F-ratio for the difference, we conclude that under conditions similar to those of our experiment, a higher level of task performance can be expected when the task is simple than when it is difficult.

The third F-ratio shows the interaction effect between the two variables, stress level and the degree of task difficulty. The significance of the F-ratio in this case means that the effect of stress level on performance in a problem-solving task depends on the degree of difficulty of the task. We can see this phenomenon more clearly if we compare the observed results with the results that would be expected if there had been no interaction between the two independent variables.

Let us calculate what we would expect the means of the four groups to be if there had been no interaction. The mean for all subjects is 18.75. The mean for the ten subjects under moderate stress, 19.5, is .075 greater than this figure, whereas the mean of the ten subjects under high stress is 0.75 less. The mean for the ten subjects doing the simple task, 20.0, is 1.25 greater than the mean for all subjects, whereas the mean for the ten subjects doing the difficult task is 1.25 less.

For each group we can calculate the mean that would be expected for this group if there had been no interaction. We do this by adding to the grand mean the difference for the column that group is in and the difference for the row that group is in. If there had been no interaction, what would we expect the mean of Group 1 to be? Beginning with the total mean, 18.75, we would add 0.75 because the subjects were under moderate stress and another 1.25 because they did an easy task. This gives a total of 20.75.

Following this procedure for each of the four groups, we would have the following expected values:

	Overall Mean	+	Stress Difference	+	Task Difference	=	Expected Value
Group 1	18.75		+0.75		+1.25		20.75
Group 2	18.75		+0.75		−1.25		18.25
Group 3	18.75		−0.75		+1.25		19.25
Group 4	18.75		−0.75		−1.25		16.75

Now compare the actual group means with these expected group means:

Actual

	Moderate	High	
Simple	Group 1 $\bar{X} = 19$	Group 3 $\bar{X} = 21$	$\bar{X} = 20$
Difficult	Group 2 $\bar{X} = 20$	Group 4 $\bar{X} = 15$	$\bar{X} = 17.5$
	$\bar{X} = 19.5$	$\bar{X} = 18.0$	$\bar{X} = 18.75$

Expected

	Moderate	High	
Simple	Group 1 $\bar{X} = 20.75$	Group 3 $\bar{X} = 19.25$	$\bar{X} = 20$
Difficult	Group 2 $\bar{X} = 18.25$	Group 4 $\bar{X} = 16.75$	$\bar{X} = 17.5$
	$\bar{X} = 19.5$	$\bar{X} = 18.0$	$\bar{X} = 18.75$

(Note that we could use the differences between expected and observed values to compute the sum of squares for interaction directly. Each group differs from its expected mean by 1.75. Square this value and multiply by the number of cases to get $1.75^2 \times 20 = 61.25$.)

We see that Group 1 actually did less well than we would expect, knowing they were under moderate stress and doing a simple task. Group 2, doing a difficult task under moderate stress, did better than we would expect. Considering the groups under high stress, we find that Group 3, with the simple task, did better than expected, whereas Group 4, with the difficult task, did less well than expected. Since our *F*-test indicated that the interaction was significant, we conclude that moderate stress produces higher scores when combined with a difficult task than with a simple task, whereas high stress produces higher scores when combined with a simple task than when combined with a difficult task.

The use of multifactor analysis has been of great value in educational research since many of the questions that educators need to investigate are inherently complex in nature. These techniques enable us to analyze the combined effects of two or more independent variables in relation to a dependent variable. For example, a simple comparison of the dependent variable means of two groups of pupils taught by different methods might yield insignificant results. But if intelligence is incorporated into the experiment as a measured independent variable, we might find that one method works better with the less intelligent pupils while the other works better with the more intelligent pupils.

Multifactor analysis of variance is not limited to two independent variables as in our example. Any number of independent variables may be incorporated in this technique. Several intermediate statistics books, including Edwards',[5] explain the computation and interpretation of these procedures.

The Chi-Square Test of Significance

Sometimes we need to find the significance of differences among the *proportions* of subjects, objects, events, and so forth, that fall into different categories. A statistical test used in such cases is called the *chi-square* (χ^2) test.

In the chi-square test two sets of frequencies are compared: *observed frequencies* and *expected frequencies*. Observed frequencies, as the name implies, are the actual frequencies obtained by observation. Expected frequencies are theoretical frequencies, which are used for comparison.

Consider the hypothesis that the proportion of male to female students in statistics courses is different from that of male to female students in a school of education as a whole. If we know that 40 percent of the total enrollment in the school is male and that 300 students are enrolled in statistics courses, our expected frequencies will be

Male students   120 $\Big\}$ 300
Female students 180

Now suppose that our observed frequencies are found to be

Male students   140 $\Big\}$ 300
Female students 160

[5]Allen L. Edwards, *Experimental Designs in Psychological Research,* 3rd ed. (New York: Holt, Rinehart and Winston, 1968), chs. 11 and 12.

We want to determine whether the difference between our expected and observed frequencies is statistically significant. To determine this we apply the chi-square formula, which is

$$\chi^2 = \sum \left[\frac{(f_o - f_e)^2}{f_e} \right] \tag{6.16}$$

where
χ^2 = the value of chi-square
f_o = the observed frequency in each cell
f_e = the expected frequency in each cell

Applying this formula to our data, we obtain

$$\chi^2 = \frac{(140 - 120)^2}{120} + \frac{(160 - 180)^2}{180} = 5.55$$

To determine whether this chi-square value is significant we consult the table of χ^2 values in the Appendix (A.5). The first column in this table shows the number of degrees of freedom involved in any given chi-square problem. The remaining columns present the values needed for different levels of significance. The number of degrees of freedom, as we have discussed previously, is based on the number of observations that are free to vary once certain restrictions are placed upon the data. When we have a fixed number of observations divided into only two categories, as soon as the number falling into one category has been determined, the other is fixed. Thus, when we find that the number of male students is 140, the number of female students in the total of 300 must be 160. In this example there is only one degree of freedom. In problems such as this the number of degrees of freedom equals $K - 1$, where K is the number of categories used for classification. By consulting the Table of χ^2 we find that our observed value of 5.55 is statistically significant at the .05 level.

Interpreting this result we can now state that the proportion of males who take statistics courses within our school is significantly greater than that of females at the .05 level of confidence. The significance level of .05 means that there are less than five chances in a hundred of observing such a difference between the proportions of male and female students through chance alone. Thus the data lend support to our research hypothesis that the proportion of male students who tend to take statistics courses is greater than that of female students.

The use of the chi-square test is not limited to situations in which there are only two categories of classification; this test can also be used to test a null hypothesis that there is no significant difference between the proportion of the subjects falling into any number of different categories. Suppose, for example, we have asked a sample of 120 undergraduate students to indicate whether they prefer to live in a dormitory or in town, or whether they have no preference, with the results shown in Table 6.8.

Table 6.8   The Observed Frequencies of Responses of 120 Undergraduate Students as to Their Preferences with Respect to Living Accommodations

Subject	Dormitory	Town	No Preference	Total
Undergraduate students	40	50	30	120

If there were no difference between the three categories of response, we would have 40 responses in each category. These would be our expected frequencies, as shown in Table 6.9.

Table 6.9   The Expected Frequencies of Responses of 120 Undergraduate Students as to Their Preferences with Respect to Living Accommodations

Subject	Dormitory	Town	No Preference	Total
Undergraduate students	40	40	40	120

A comparison of the two sets of frequencies presented in Tables 6.8 and 6.9 shows that there are differences between our expected and observed data. To find whether or not they are significant, we apply the chi-square test. The value of χ^2 for these data, using formula (6.16), would be

$$\chi^2 = \frac{(40 - 40)^2}{40} + \frac{(50 - 40)^2}{40} + \frac{(30 - 40)^2}{40} = 5.00$$

The degrees of freedom, again, equal the number of categories minus one $(K - 1)$ or, in this case, $3 - 1 = 2$. Referring to the Table of χ^2 we see that with two degrees of freedom a X^2 value of 5.991 or greater is required for significance at the .05 level. However, our obtained χ^2 value is smaller than this value and therefore is not statistically significant. This means that the observed differences between categories could easily have happened by chance. Consequently, the null hypothesis that there is no significant difference between the frequencies of the three categories, cannot be rejected. In other words, if the proportions of preferences for the three categories in the entire undergraduate population were equal, we would expect to observe sample differences as great as those in our sample more often than five times in a hundred through chance.

THE CHI-SQUARE TEST OF INDEPENDENCE

So far we have only considered examples in which observations were classified along a single dimension. Sometimes, however, we wish to use more than one dimension for classification. Suppose, for example, we add another dimension to the previous problem and ask both graduate and undergraduate students to state their preferences as to their living accommodations. Assume the frequencies as shown in Table 6.10 were the result.

Table 6.10 The Observed Frequencies of Responses of 200 Undergraduate and Graduate Students as to Their Preferences with Respect to Living Accommodations

Subjects	Dormitory	Town	No Preference	Total
Undergraduate students	40	50	30	120
Graduate students	20	40	20	80
Total	60	90	50	200

In this case our null hypothesis might be that the preference for living accommodations is the same for graduates as it is for undergraduates—that is, the variables student status and preference for living accommodations are unrelated. Our observations show that 30 percent of all students prefer dormitories, 45 percent prefer town, and 25 percent state no preference. If the null hypothesis is true, we would expect to find identical proportions among both graduates and undergraduates, as shown in Table 6.11. We can compute expected cell frequencies by multiplying the row frequency associated with a cell by the column frequency associated with that cell, then dividing this product by the grand total. For example, the expected

Table 6.11 The Expected Frequencies of Responses of 200 Undergraduate and Graduate Students as to Their Preferences with Respect to Living Accommodations

Subjects	Dormitory	Town	No Preference	Total
Undergraduate students	36	54	30	120
Graduate students	24	36	20	80
Total	60	90	50	200

frequency of response for undergraduate students who want to live in a dormitory is $120 \times 60 \div 200 = 36$, for those undergraduate students who prefer to live in town it is $120 \times 90 \div 200 = 54$, and for graduate students who want to live in a dormitory it is $80 \times 60 \div 200 = 24$. Using this approach, we find the expected frequencies for each cell.

Note that all the row and column totals in Table 6.11 are exactly the same as those shown in Table 6.10. We now ask if the observed frequencies differ enough from the expected frequencies to enable us to reject the likelihood that these differences could have occurred merely by chance. Applying the formula, we obtain

$$\chi^2 = \frac{(40 - 36)^2}{36} + \frac{(50 - 54)^2}{54} + \frac{(30 - 30)^2}{30} + \frac{(20 - 24)^2}{24} + \frac{(40 - 36)^2}{36} + \frac{(20 - 20)^2}{20}$$

$$\chi^2 = 1.8518$$

The number of degrees of freedom for a two-way table is found by applying the formula

$$df = (C - 1)(R - 1) \tag{6.17}$$

where
df = the number of degrees of freedom
C = the number of columns
R = the number of rows

Applying this formula to the problem under consideration, we obtain

$$df = (3 - 1)(2 - 1) = 2$$

Referring to Table A.5 we see that with two degrees of freedom a χ^2 value of 5.991 is needed for significance at the .05 level. But our obtained χ^2 value of 1.8518 is smaller than this table value and is therefore not significant. This means that the differences between expected and observed frequencies are not beyond what would be expected by chance. In other words, we do not have reliable evidence that there is a relationship between the variables student status and living accommodation preference in the population from which our sample was drawn.

Summary

Investigators hope to form generalizations about populations by studying groups of individuals selected from the populations. These generalizations will be sound only if the selected groups—the samples—used in these studies are representative of the larger groups—the populations—from which they are chosen.

A sample is random if all the members of a population have an equal chance of being included within that sample. It is the preferred means of subject selection for behavioral research.

Sometimes it is important for the purpose of a specific study to choose independent samples from different subgroups or strata of a population and to obtain separate measures for each stratum. This is stratified sampling.

When the target population is unwieldy, an investigator may choose randomly a number of groups for study rather than individual subjects. This is called cluster sampling. A cluster sample is more subject to sampling errors than is simple random sample.

Inferential statistics provide tools by means of which researchers are able to estimate how confident they can be in inferring that phenomena observed in samples would also be observed in the populations from which the samples were drawn. In other words, inferential statistics enable us to estimate how reliable our observations may be.

A basic strategy in inferential statistics is to compute the extent of difference among observations that would be likely to arise by chance alone. The result of this computation is often called the error term. Then the observed differences among observations are compared with the error term. If the observed differences are similar to the differences that could arise by chance, the researcher cannot reject the likelihood that the observed differences were merely a function of chance. If the observed differences are greater than the error term, the researcher consults the tabled values of the statistic to determine whether the ratio of observation to error is great enough to reject the chance explanation at a predetermined level of confidence.

The indices most commonly used in inferential statistics are: the t-test, analysis of variance, and the chi-square test of significance. The t-test is used to find whether the difference between two sample means is statistically significant. There are two types of t-tests: (1) the t-test for independent groups, which is used to compare two sample means when the samples have been drawn independently from a population and (2) the t-test for nonindependent groups, which is employed with two samples in which the subjects are matched or with two repeated measures obtained from the same subjects.

Analysis of variance is used to compare the means of two or more samples and to test the null hypothesis that no significant differences exist between the means obtained from these samples. Multifactor analysis of variance enables us to test the effect of more than one independent variable and also the interaction effect of such variables.

The chi-square statistic is an index employed to find the significance of differences between proportions of subjects, objects, events, and so forth, that fall into different categories, by comparing observed frequencies and expected frequencies.

Exercises

1. Does the accuracy of a sample in representing the characteristics of the population from which it was drawn always increase with the size of the sample? Explain.

2. You have been asked to determine whether teachers in the Central School District favor the ''year around school'' concept. Because the district is rather large you are asked to contact only 500 teachers. Determine the number you would choose from each of the following levels to draw a proportioned stratified random sample:

Level	Total Number
Elementary	3,500
Middle School	2,100
High School	1,400
Total	7,000

3. You are asked to conduct an opinion survey on a college campus with a population of 15,000 students. How would you proceed to draw a representative sample of these students for your survey?

4. A national magazine has one million subscribers. The editorial staff wants to know which aspects of the magazine are liked and which are not. The staff decides that a personal interview is the best method to obtain the information. For practical and economic reasons only 500 people in five cities will be surveyed. In this situation, identify:
   a. the target population
   b. the accessible population
   c. the sample

5. Investigators wish to study the question, Do blondes have more fun?
   a. What is the null hypothesis in this question?
   b. What would be a Type I error in this case?
   c. What would be a Type II error in this case?
   d. If one investigator uses an .05 level of significance in investigating this question and another investigator uses an .001 level of significance, which would be more likely to make a Type I error?
   e. If one investigator uses an .05 level of significance in investigating this question and another investigator uses an .001 level of significance, which would be more likely to make a Type II error?

6. Inferential statistics enable researchers to:
   a. reach infallible conclusions
   b. reach reasonable conclusions with incomplete information
   c. add an aura of legitimacy to what is really sheer guesswork

7. What two conditions are necessary for a Type I error to occur?

8. Which of the following statements describes the role of the null hypothesis in research?
   a. It enables us to determine the probability of an event occurring through chance alone when there is no real relationship between variables.
   b. It enables us to prove there is a real relationship between variables.
   c. It enables us to prove there is no real relationship between variables.

9. A Type II error occurs when one:
   a. rejects a false null hypothesis
   b. rejects a true null hypothesis
   c. has already made a Type I error

    d. retains a false null hypothesis

    e. retains a true null hypothesis

10. The phrase *level of significance* refers to

    a. the probability of an event being due to chance alone, which is calculated after the data from an experiment are analyzed

    b. the probability of a Type I error that an investigator is willing to accept

    c. the actual probability of a Type II error

    d. the probability of a Type II error that an investigator is willing to accept

11. How does one determine the level of significance to use in an experiment?

12. A cigarette manufacturer has employed researchers to compare the rate of occurrence of lung cancer among smokers and nonsmokers. Considering the results of previous research on this question, the manufacturer would probably urge the researchers to be especially careful to avoid making a

    a. Type I error

    b. Type II error

13. What is indicated when the results of a study are not statistically significant?

14. You have a list of pupils in a high school who have been assigned the number 1 to 1,000. Use the table of random numbers in the Appendix to select a sample of 50 from the hypothetical list. List the numbers selected for the sample.

Answers

1. A larger *randomly* drawn sample is more likely to be representative of the population than is a smaller *random* sample. A large sample obtained with a method that permits systematic bias will not be any more representative than a small biased sample.

2. To obtain a proportional stratified sample, divide the 500 teachers in proportion to their representation in the population, as follows:

Elementary	$\frac{3500}{7000} \times 500 =$	250
Middle School	$\frac{2100}{7000} \times 500 =$	150
High School	$\frac{1400}{7000} \times 500 =$	100
Total Sample		500

3. Number a list of all students, then select a random sample of a given number by using a table of random numbers. Starting at a random point in the table, go up or down the column and include those students whose numbers are listed.

4. a. all subscribers to the magazine

    b. the subscribers in the five cities

    c. 500 individuals who are interviewed.

5. a. There is no relationship between hair color and fun.

    b. The investigators make a Type I error if they declare that blondes have more fun than nonblondes or that blondes have less fun than nonblondes, when in fact the two groups have an equal amount of fun.

    c. The investigators make a Type II error if they fail to conclude that blondes have more fun or less fun, when in fact they do.

    d. the investigator with the .05 level of significance.

    e. the investigator with the .001 level of significance.

6. b
7. The null hypothesis must be true and the investigator must reject it.
8. a
9. d
10. b
11. by weighing the consequences of Type I and Type II errors
12. a
13. The results could easily be a function of chance; the evidence is insufficient to justify a conclusion.

Part

4

Tools of Research

Fundamentals of Measurement

7

One of the aims of educational research is to obtain greater understanding of relationships among variables in populations. For example, one might ask, What is the relationship between intelligence and creativity among six-year-olds? We cannot directly observe either intelligence or creativity. Nor can we directly observe all six-year-olds. But this does not mean that we must remain in ignorance about this and similar questions. We have indicators that approximate the constructs of intelligence and of creativity; that is, there are observable behaviors that are accepted as being valid indices of these constructs. The use of indicators to approximate constructs is the measurement aspect of research.

Measuring Instruments

A major task is the selection of dependable measuring instruments for the purpose of quantifying the behaviors and attributes to be studied. In some cases this presents no problems. For example, if one wishes to ascertain the birth order of a group of subjects or the education level of their parents, one merely asks these questions of the subjects and records their answers. The task of quantifying the information is not always as easy as this. Many research questions require the development of dependable devices that can measure abstract and complicated qualities. One has to select or develop scales and instruments that can measure characteristics such as intelligence, achievement, personality, motivation, attitudes, aptitudes, interests, and so forth. Different devices are used for quantifying different qualities. In the following section we will discuss briefly some of the kinds of instruments that are used in educational research.

INTERVIEWS AND QUESTIONNAIRES

One way of obtaining data is simply to ask questions. The interview and the questionnaire both utilize this approach. These instruments can be used to obtain information concerning facts, beliefs, feelings, intentions, and so on. Although both the interview and the questionnaire make use of the question approach, there are important differences between the two methods.[1]

---

[1] A worthwhile general discussion of questionnaires and interviews as research instruments is included in J. W. Wrightstone, J. Justman, and I. Robbins, *Evaluation in Modern Education* (New York: American Book, 1956), ch. 8.

Interviews

Interviewing is a well-established method of data collection, which, because of some unique qualities, is still widely used. One of the most important aspects of interviewing is that it is flexible. The rapport established with the subjects provides for a cooperative atmosphere in which truthful information can be obtained. One can take into consideration the kind of person one is interviewing and the situation within which the interview is taking place. The interviewer can elaborate on questions and explain their meanings in case they are not clear to the subjects. None of these advantages is present when other types of data collection, such as questionnaires and tests, are used.

There are two types of interviews: *structured* and *unstructured*. In structured interviews the questions and the alternative answers permitted to the subject are predetermined and are rigidly followed with all respondents. The advantage of this approach is that it is standardized and therefore the answers can be easily classified and analyzed. Its disadvantage is that it is inflexible and may seem formal. Restrictions that are put on this type of interview increase their reliability but may decrease their depth.

Unstructured interviews are more informal. Free questioning of the subjects is possible regarding their views, attitudes, beliefs, and other information. Such interviews are flexible and are usually planned to suit the subjects and the conditions within which the interviews take place. The subjects are given freedom to go beyond simple responses to the questions asked and to reveal their views in any way they wish. The questions may deviate from the original plans and center around points that seem to be important. Unstructured interviews require expert, skillful, and alert interviewers. This kind of interview does not lend itself readily to quantification but it does help to generate and clarify the dimensions present in the topic under consideration. Unstructured interviews are commonly used in clinical psychology, in counseling and guidance, and in case studies. In research their use is usually limited to preliminary stages, in which the investigator is determining the variables that should be involved in the study. For example, to determine what skills potential employers want the schools to teach in an office skills program, one could begin with unstructured interviews to identify the skills that are frequently mentioned, then list these skills and ask employers, in structured interviews, to rate the importance of each skill.[2]

Questionnaires

The direct contact with subjects involved in interviewing is time-consuming and expensive. Much of the same information can be gathered by means of a written questionnaire presented to the subjects. As compared with interviewing, the written questionnaire is typically more efficient and practical and allows for the use of a larger sample. It is widely employed in educational research.

[2]For detailed directions on interviewing, the reader is referred to C. Cannell and R. Kahn, ''The Collection of Data by Interviewing,'' in L. Festinger and D. Katz, *Research Methods in the Behavioral Sciences* (New York: Holt, Rinehart and Winston, 1953), ch. 8.

Further advantages of this technique are that standard instructions are given to all subjects and the personal appearance, mood, or conduct of the investigator will not color the results.

Questionnaires are of two types: *structured,* or closed form, and *unstructured,* or open form. A structured questionnaire contains the questions and alternative answers to them. The answers provided for each question should be exhaustive of all possible responses and at the same time mutually exclusive. Unstructured questionnaires do not include suggested answers.

The administration and scoring of a structured questionnaire are straightforward and the results lend themselves readily to analysis. This type of questionnaire has the disadvantage of forcing subjects into choosing one of a number of preselected alternative answers to questions for which they might feel they do not have clear answers, or into choosing alternatives that do not really represent their attitudes. In contrast, the unstructured questionnaire has the advantage of giving the respondents freedom to reveal their opinions and attitudes. It has the disadvantage that the information generated is difficult to process and analyze. In responding to unstructured questionnaires, subjects may omit important points or emphasize things that are of no interest to the researcher and of no importance to the purpose of the research. For this reason most investigators avoid this type of questionnaire and prefer to use the structured type.

A disadvantage of both types of questionnaires is the possibility of misinterpretation of the questions by the respondents. It is extremely difficult to formulate a series of questions whose meanings are crystal clear to every reader. The investigator may know exactly what is meant by a question, but because of poor formulation or differential meaning of terms, an entirely different interpretation is made by the respondents. Pilot studies, in which the questionnaire is tried out with a few subjects typical of those on whom it will be used, may help to alleviate this disadvantage.

A disadvantage peculiar to mailed questionnaires is low return. Typically one can expect fewer than half to be returned, which not only reduces the size of one's sample but may also bias the results, so that valid generalizations cannot be made. It cannot be assumed that nonresponse is randomly distributed throughout a group. Studies have shown that there are usually systematic differences in the characteristics of respondents and nonrespondents to questionnaire studies.[3] Respondents may be more intelligent, better educated, more conscientious and interested, or generally more favorable to the issue involved in the questionnaire. Such an unrepresentative group may damage the generalizability of the results. The goal in a questionnaire study is typically 70–80 percent returns. If there are more than 30 percent nonreturns, one would question the worth of the results.

A well-constructed questionnaire is more likely to elicit a good response than is a poorly constructed one.

[3]C. M. Bennett and R. E. Hill, "Comparison of Selected Personality Characteristics of Responders and Non-responders to a Mailed Questionnaire Study," *Journal of Educational Research* 58 (December 1964): 178–80.

Constructing Questionnaires.   Constructing questionnaires is a difficult and time-consuming task. The following are suggestions for constructing items for a written questionnaire:

1. *Construct the instrument in such a way that it reflects quality.* A questionnaire that appears to have been thrown together quickly will not elicit high returns. During the process of constructing the questionnaire, numerous revisions may be necessary in order to eliminate ambiguous or unnecessary items.

2. *Keep the questionnaire as brief as possible so that it requires a minimum of the respondents' time.* Respondents are much more likely to complete and return a short questionnaire. The researcher must make an effort to eliminate all unnecessary items, especially those whose answers are available from other sources. All the items of a questionnaire should serve a research problem function; that is, they should elicit data needed to test the hypotheses or answer the questions of the research study. For example, a question that asks the respondent's age in a study where this information is not needed in the data analysis can be eliminated.

3. *Phrase questionnaire items so that they can be understood by every respondent.* The vocabulary used should be nontechnical and should be geared to the least-educated respondent. Construct sentences that are short and simple. It is a good idea to have some other people, preferably ones whose background is similar to those who will be included in the study, read and give their interpretation of the content of each question. For example, questions using terms like *deficit spending, balance of trade, gross national product,* might not be appropriate in a survey designed for the general public.

4. *Phrase questionnaire items so as to elicit unambiguous answers.* Whenever possible, responses should be quantified. For example, instead of having respondents check ''sometimes,'' ''often,'' or ''always,'' state the alternative ''number of times per week.'' Words like *often* and *sometimes* have different meanings for different people.

5. *Phrase questionnaire items so as to avoid bias or prejudice that might predetermine a respondent's answer.* That is, the wording of a question should not influence the respondent in a certain direction. For this reason, stereotyped, prestige-carrying, emotionally loaded, or superlative words should be avoided.

For example, the question, Have you registered to vote? would be preferable to, Have you exercised your American right and registered to vote? The question, Would you be in favor of the United States' developing nuclear energy as an alternative source of energy? might elicit different responses from, In light of the longest coal strike in history, would you recommend that the United States develop nuclear energy as an alternative source of energy?

6. *Questionnaire items should not mislead because of unstated assumptions.* The frame of reference for answering the questions should be clear and consistent for all respondents. If any assumptions have to be made before respondents give an answer, then questions designed to inquire into these assumptions should also be included.

For example, in a survey designed for high school seniors the question, Do you think your high school has adequately prepared you for college? assumes that the student is going to college and that he knows what is required in the way of preparation. The question, Have you registered to vote for the upcoming election? assumes that the high school student is 18 years of age, which may or may not be true.

7. *Alternatives to the various questionnaire items should be exhaustive; that is, all the possible alternatives on the issue should be expressed.* For example, What is your marital status? should include not only the alternatives *married* or *single,* but also *widowed, divorced, separated.*

In developing the alternatives for questionnaire items designed to identify attitudes or opinions on issues, it is a good idea first to present the questions in an open-ended form to a small sample of respondents. Their answers can then be used as alternatives in the final product. On questions for which there are a wide variety of possible responses, one should always include the alternative *other* along with a request that the respondent explain that choice. For example, the question, What is your position in the school system? might be followed by the alternatives *administrator, teacher, librarian, other (please specify).*

8. *Avoid questions that might elicit reactions of embarrassment, suspicion, or hostility in the respondent.* Questions should not put the respondent on the defensive. For example, people often resent questions about their age, income, religion, or educational status. It is preferable to phrase questions relating to age in terms of age ranges—rather than exact ages—allowing the respondent to check the appropriate category. The question, Do you have a high school diploma? might cause embarrassment to one who did not graduate from high school. The question might ask, What grade had you completed when you left school?

9. *Arrange questions in correct psychological order. If both general and specific questions are asked on a topic, ask the general questions first.* For example, one would first ascertain whether or not respondents were satisfied with working conditions before asking for changes that they would recommend. Objective questions on an issue or situation should precede more subjective questions. People are sometimes reluctant to answer questions about attitudes, preferences, personal feelings, motives, and the like. But if objective questions can be used first to clarify and specify the situation, it may be easier for respondents to formulate and express opinions on the issue.

10. *Arrange questions in such a way that responses can be tabulated and interpreted readily.* One must think ahead to what form of data is needed for the desired analysis and make sure the questionnaire will yield that data. If the data are to be key punched onto computer cards, the arrangement of the questionnaire should facilitate this process.

11. *A cover letter addressed to the respondent by name and title must accompany the questionnaire.* This letter explains the purpose and value of the study and the reason why the respondent was included in the sample. The cover letter should so promote the study that the respondent will be motivated to reply. Respondents should be made to feel that they can make an important contribution to the study.

The signature on the letter is also important in influencing the return of the questionnaire. It may be helpful for a person well known to the respondents, such as the head of a university department or the dean of a school, to sign the cover letter. This signature is likely to be more effective than that of an unknown graduate student. If there is a sponsor for the study, such as a foundation or some agency, this should be mentioned.

It may be possible for the respondents to remain anonymous. At any rate, they must be assured that their responses will be confidential. An offer should also be made to share the findings of the study with the respondents if they are interested. Always enclose a stamped, self-addressed envelope. If the respondents are to remain anonymous, it is wise to include a postcard, to be mailed separately to the investigator, indicating that the questionnaire has also been mailed. In this way, a record can be kept of returned questionnaires.

Urge immediate return of the questionnaire. If a time period such as a month is permitted, the respondents may lay the questionnaire aside and, in spite of good intentions, forget about it.

12. *A planned follow-up is necessary if one is to reach the maximum percent of returns*. If the questionnaire has not been returned soon after the initial mailing, a postcard reminder should be sent to the respondents. After that, a second mailing of the questionnaire along with a new cover letter is recommended. Perhaps a different approach could be taken in this letter to persuade them to complete and return the questionnaire. For further information on the construction of questionnaires, readers are referred to a text by Selltiz, Wrightsman, and Cook.[4]

Dealing with Nonresponse.   The usual approach is to try to interview a small random sample of the nonrespondents for the purpose of learning something of their characteristics and obtaining their responses. It may be that no significant differences are found when their responses to the questionnaire items are compared with those of the initial respondents. In this case one could assume that the respondents represent an unbiased sample of all who received the questionnaire. Or it is possible, after establishing the pattern of answers for the nonrespondents through the interviews, to weight their responses in the final analysis of data.[5]

If one finds that certain clearly identifiable subgroups did not return the questionnaire, it may be necessary to change the original research question to exclude these subgroups. For example, if secondary teachers showed a much lower rate of returns than did elementary teachers in a survey, the researcher might restrict the survey to elementary teachers and restate the question to indicate this.

Validity of Questionnaires.   All too often questionnaires in research are used without any prior consideration of their appropriateness for measuring what they are intended to measure. This question relates to the problem of validity, which is

[4]C. Selltiz, J. W. Wrightsman, and S. Cook, *Research Methods in Social Relations,* 3rd ed. (New York: Holt, Rinehart and Winston, 1976), Appendix B.

[5]This is a rather complicated procedure, the details of which may be found in M. H. Hansen and W. N. Hurwitz, ''The Problem of Non-response of Sample Surveys,'' *Journal of the American Statistical Association* 41 (December 1946): 517–29.

discussed in greater detail in chapter 8. It is important to note here that the validity of a questionnaire cannot be assumed but must be established.

A factor specifically affecting the validity of questionnaires is whether or not a signature is required. It may be reasonable to assume that greater truthfulness would be obtained if the respondents could remain anonymous. However, this probably depends on the nature of the specific questions included—that is, whether or not very personal information is sought. If identification of the subjects is not important in the analysis of results, it is wiser to let them remain anonymous.

Some studies have used direct observation of behavior as the criterion of the validity of questionnaire responses. That is, after responses were obtained by means of the questionnaire, observations were made to see whether the actual behavior of the subjects agreed with their expressed attitudes and opinions. In other instances validity considerations require studies of the interpretation subjects are making of the questions. Often such studies indicate ambiguities or imprecision in the questions.

TESTS

Tests are valuable measuring instruments for educational research. A test is a set of stimuli presented to an individual in order to elicit responses on the basis of which a numerical score can be assigned. This score, based on a representative sample of the individual's behavior, is an indicator of the extent to which the examinee possesses the characteristic being measured. Two essential requirements for tests are validity and reliability, characteristics which will be discussed in chapter 8.

Another essential requirement for a test is objectivity, shown by a maximum level of agreement among scorers. Once the scoring key is prepared for an objective test, the scoring can be accomplished by an untrained person or by a machine.

A wide variety of characteristics may be examined by the use of objective tests. Useful sources for identifying tests for one's research purposes are Buros's *Mental Measurements Yearbooks* and *Tests in Print II,* described in chapter 3. Instructions for administering, scoring, and interpreting tests are given in the manuals provided by test publishers.

Achievement Tests

In most research concerned with the effectiveness of instructional methods the dependent variable is achievement. Therefore achievement tests are widely used in educational research, as well as in school systems. They measure the mastery and proficiency of individuals in different areas of knowledge.

Achievement tests are generally classified as standardized and teacher- or researcher-made. Standardized tests are published tests that have resulted from careful and skillful preparation and cover broad academic objectives common to a large number of school systems. These are tests for which comparative norms have been derived; their validity and reliability, established; and directions for administering and scoring, prescribed.

In order to establish the norms for these tests, their originators administer them to a sample that they have chosen to represent the country as a whole. The mean for a particular grade level in the sample becomes the norm for that grade level. The skills measured are not necessarily what ''ought'' to be taught at any grade level, but the use of norms does give educators a basis for comparing their groups with an estimate of the mean for all children at that grade level.

Standardized tests are available for individual school subjects, such as mathematics and chemistry, and also in the form of comprehensive batteries measuring several areas of achievement. For example, the California Achievement Test (CAT) contains tests in the areas of reading, language, and arithmetic. The Sequential Tests of Educational Progress (STEP) cover tests in seven areas.

In selecting an achievement test, researchers must be careful to choose one that is reliable and is appropriate (valid) for measuring the aspect of achievement in which they are interested. Sometimes they will not be able to select the test, but will have to use what the school system has already selected. Buros presents a comprehensive listing, together with reviews of the different achievement tests available.

If an available test measures the desired behavior and if the reliability and the norms are adequate for the purpose, then there are advantages in the use of a standardized instrument. In addition to the time and effort saved, investigators will realize an advantage from the continuity of testing procedures. That is, the results of their studies can be compared and interpreted with respect to those of other studies using the same instrument.

When the use of standardized tests of achievement is not deemed suitable for the specific objectives of a research study, research workers may construct their own tests. It is much better to construct one's own test than to use an inadequate standardized one just because it is available. In this case, one should take great care in preparing the test, particularly with respect to determining the validity and reliability of that test before employing it. For suggestions on test construction one may refer to specialized texts in measurement such as those by Gronlund, Stanley, and Thorndike and Hagen.[6]

Sometimes grade-point averages of the subjects in their schools are used as indicators of success and academic achievement. Caution is in order when the GPAs of students of different school systems are being used. Letter grades in different schools do not necessarily mean the same thing and cannot be relied on to indicate the same degree of mastery and proficiency.

Intelligence Tests

Intelligence tests differ from achievement tests in that the former attempt to measure general performance, whereas the latter attempt to measure performance in specific areas. They attempt to measure the subject's ability to perceive relationships, solve problems, and apply knowledge in a variety of contexts.

---

[6]Norman E. Gronlund, *Measurement and Evaluation in Teaching*, 3rd ed. (New York: Macmillan, 1976); Julian C. Stanley, *Measurement in Today's Schools* (Englewood Cliffs, N.J.: Prentice-Hall, 1964), Robert L. Thorndike and Elizabeth Hagen, *Measurement and Evaluation in Psychology and Education*, 4th ed. (New York: Wiley, 1977).

Intelligence tests should *not* be considered as measures of innate or "pure" intelligence. Performance on such tests is partly dependent on the background and schooling of the subject. Because of the controversy over the meaning of the concept intelligence and because of peoples' tendency to associate intelligence with inherited ability, the use of the term *intelligence* to describe these tests has declined in recent years. *Intelligence* is being replaced by *scholastic aptitude*—a more descriptive term because it points out specifically the main function of these tests, which is to predict school performance.

Educators have found these tests useful and generally valid for the purpose of predicting school success. Researchers also use these tests extensively. Intelligence is an independent variable that must usually be controlled in educational experiments. To control this variable, the researcher uses the scores from some intelligence test. Of the many tests available, some have been designed for use with individuals and others for use with groups.

Individual Intelligence Tests.   The most widely used of this type are the Stanford-Binet and the three Wechsler tests. The Stanford-Binet presently in use is the outcome of several revisions of the device developed originally by Alfred Binet in France to measure the differences in the mental maturity of children. This test was originally used for measuring an individual's *mental age*. Later the concept of *intelligence quotient* was introduced. This quotient is derived by dividing mental age (MA) by chronological age (CA) and multiplying the result by 100. The present revision of the Stanford-Binet yields mental ages but does not employ the MA/CA ratio for determining IQ. Instead the IQ is found by comparing an individual's performance (score) with norms obtained from his or her age-group through the use of standard scores (see chapter 5). A major characteristic of the Stanford-Binet test is that it gives a general measure of intelligence. It does not attempt to measure separate abilities, as do some other tests.

The Wechsler tests are the outcome of an attempt by David Wechsler to develop a device for measuring adult intelligence. His first test was published in 1939 and was followed by three other tests: one in 1949, the Wechsler Intelligence Scale for Children (WISC), which was revised in 1974 and is known as the WISC-R; one in 1955, the Wechsler Adult Intelligence Scale (WAIS); and one in 1967, the Wechsler Preschool and Primary Scale of Intelligence (WPPSI), which was introduced for the 4–6½ age-group.

An important characteristic of the Wechsler tests is that they are divided into subtests, which enable the examiner to obtain two scores for each subject, one for verbal IQ and the other for nonverbal IQ. These subtests are further divided into subscales, which indicate the examinee's performance on specific tasks.

Group Tests of Intelligence.   A Stanford-Binet or Wechsler test must be given by a trained psychometrician to an individual subject, a procedure expensive in both time and money. They are impractical when intelligence measures for large groups of individuals are desired. In this situation group tests of intelligence are used. The first group test of mental capacity was developed during World War I for the purpose of measuring the intelligence of men in military service. One form of this test, the Army Alpha, was released for civilian use after the war and became the model for a number of group tests. Today there are many group tests of intelligence available.

PERSONALITY INVENTORIES

Obtaining measures of personality is another area of concern to educational research workers. There are several different types of personality measures, each reflecting a different theoretical point of view. Some reflect trait and type theories, whereas others have their origins in psychoanalytic and motivational theories. Researchers must know precisely what they wish to measure and then select the instrument, paying particular attention to the evidence of its validity. The three most widely used types of personality measures in research are (1) inventories, (2) rating scales, and (3) projective techniques.

Inventories

In an inventory, subjects are presented with an extensive collection of statements describing behavior patterns and are asked to indicate whether or not each statement is characteristic of their behavior, by checking *yes, no,* or *uncertain.* Their score is computed by counting the number of responses that agree with a trait the examiner is attempting to measure. For example, paranoids would be expected to answer yes to the statement, People are always talking behind my back, and no to the statement, I expect the police to be fair and reasonable. Of course, such responses to just two items would not indicate paranoid tendencies. However, such responses to a large proportion of such items could be considered an indicator of paranoia.

Some of the self-report inventories measure only one trait, such as the *California F-Scale,* which measures authoritarianism. Others, such as Cattell's *Sixteen Personality Factor Questionnaire,* measure a number of traits. Other well-known inventories in research are the *Minnesota Multiphasic Personality Inventory,* the *Guilford-Zimmerman Temperament Preference Survey,* the *Mooney Problem Check List,* and the *Edwards Personal Preference Schedule.*

Inventories have been used in educational research to obtain trait descriptions of certain defined groups, such as underachievers, dropouts, members of minority groups, and so forth. They have also been used in research concerned with interrelationships between personality traits and such variables as intelligence, achievement, and attitudes.

Inventories have the advantages of economy, simplicity, and objectivity. Most of the disadvantages are related to the problem of validity. Their validity depends in part upon the respondents' being able to read and understand the items, their understanding of themselves, and especially their willingness to give frank and honest answers. As a result, the information obtained from inventories may be superficial or biased. This possibility must be taken into account when using results obtained from such instruments.[7]

[7]Ibid., ch. 12.

Rating Scales

One of the most widely used measuring instruments is the rating scale. Rating scales involve assessments by one person of another's behavior or performance. Typically the rater is asked to place the person being rated at some point on a continuum or in a category that describes his or her characteristic behavior. A numerical value is attached to the point or category. It is assumed that the raters are familiar with the individual's typical behavior. Ratings have been used in research on children's development and on many other aspects of behavior.

There are several different types of rating scales. One of the most widely used is the *graphic scale*, in which the rater simply places a check at the appropriate point on a horizontal line that runs from one extreme of the behavior in question to the other. Figure 7.1 is a typical example of a graphic scale. The rater can check any

	Low	Medium	High
Personal Appearance			
Social Acceptability			
Speaking Skills			

Figure 7.1   Example of a graphic scale

point on the continuous line. On some graphic scales the test constructor assigns numerical values to the descriptive points; such scales are referred to as *numerical rating scales*. The speaking skills item in Figure 7.1 could look like this in a numerical scale:

1	2	3	4	5	6	7
one of the poorest speakers			an average speaker			one of the very best speakers

A second type of rating scale is the *category scale,* which consists of a number of categories that are arranged in an ordered series. Five to seven categories are most frequently used. The rater picks the one that best characterizes the behavior of the person being rated. Suppose a student's abilities are being rated and one of the characteristics being rated is creativity. A category item might be:

How creative is this person? (check one)

exceptionally creative
very creative
creative
not creative
not at all creative

Brief descriptive phrases sometimes make up the categories in this type of scale. For example:

How creative is this person? (check one)

always has creative ideas
has many creative ideas
sometimes has creative ideas
rarely has creative ideas

In using the graphic and category scales, raters make their judgments without directly comparing the person being rated to other individuals or groups. In *comparative rating scales,* on the other hand, raters are instructed to make their judgments with direct reference to the positions of others with whom the individual might be compared. The positions on the rating scale are defined in terms of a given population with known characteristics. A comparative rating scale is shown in Figure 7.2. Such a scale might be used in selecting applicants for admission to

Area of Competency (to be rated)	Unusually low	Poorer than most students	About average among students	Better than most	Really superior	Not able to judge
1. Does this person show evidence of clear-cut and worthy professional goals?						
2. Does this person attack problems in a constructive manner?						
3. Does he take well-meant criticism and use it constructively?						

Figure 7.2   Example of a category scale

graduate school. Raters are asked to judge the applicant's ability to do graduate work as compared with all the students the rater has known. If the rating is to be valid, the judge must have an understanding of the range and distribution of the abilities of the total group of graduate students.

All techniques of rating are subject to considerable error, which reduces their validity and reliability. Among the most frequent systematic errors in rating people is the *halo effect,* which occurs when raters allow a generalized impression of the subject to influence the rating given on very specific aspects of behavior. This general impression carries over from one item in the scale to the next. For example, a teacher might rate a student who does good academic work superior in intelligence, popularity, honesty, perseverance, and all other aspects of personality.

Another type of error is the *generosity error,* which refers to the tendency to give the subject the benefit of any doubt. That is, when raters are not sure, they are likely to speak favorably about the person they are rating. In contrast, there is the *error of severity,* which is a tendency to rate all individuals too low on all characteristics. Another source of error is the *error of central tendency,* which refers to the tendency to avoid either extreme and rate all individuals in the middle of the scale.

One way of reducing such errors is to train the raters thoroughly before they are asked to make ratings. They should be informed about the possibility of making these types of errors. It is absolutely essential that raters have adequate time to observe the individual and his or her behavior before making a rating. Another way to prevent error is to make certain that the behavior to be rated and the points on the rating scale are clearly defined. The points on the scale should be described in terms of overt behavior that can be observed rather than in terms of behaviors which require inference on the part of the rater. The reader is referred to Guilford for an excellent discussion of ways of dealing with rater error.[8]

The reliability of ratings is usually increased by having several raters make independent ratings of an individual. These independent ratings are pooled or averaged to obtain a final score.

PROJECTIVE TECHNIQUES

Projective techniques are measures in which an individual is asked to respond to an ambiguous or unstructured stimulus. They are called projective because a person is expected to project into the stimulus his or her own needs, wants, fears, anxieties, and so forth. On the basis of the subject's interpretation and responses, the examiner attempts to construct a comprehensive picture of the individual's personality structure.

Projective methods are used mainly by clinical psychologists for the study and diagnosis of persons with emotional problems. They are not frequently used in educational research because of the necessity of specialized training for administration and scoring, and the expense involved in individual administration. Furthermore, many researchers feel that their validity has not been satisfactorily established.

The two best-known projective techniques are the Rorschach and the Thematic Apperception Test (TAT). The Rorschach uses ink blots as the stimulus, and in the TAT the respondent is shown pictures and asked to tell a story about each one. Further discussion of these tests and the methods of interpreting them can be found in Anderson and Anderson's book.[9]

[8]J. P. Guilford, *Psychometric Methods* (New York: McGraw-Hill, 1954), ch. 11.

[9]For a discussion of projective techniques, see H. H. and G. L. Anderson, *Projective Techniques* (Englewood Cliffs, N.J.: Prentice-Hall, 1951).

SCALES

A scale is a set of numerical values assigned to subjects, objects, or behaviors for the purpose of quantifying and measuring qualities. Scales are used to measure attitudes, values, and interests. They differ from tests in that the results of these instruments, unlike those of tests, do not indicate success or failure, or strength or weakness. They measure the degree to which an individual possesses the characteristic of interest. For example, we may use a scale to measure the attitude of college students toward religion.

The development of scales for measuring attitudes, values, and interests can involve several different techniques. In the following discussion we will attempt to introduce some of these techniques.

Attitude Scales

There are four main types of attitude scales: (1) summated rating scales (Likert scales), (2) equal-appearing intervals (Thurstone scales), (3) cumulative scales (Guttman scales), and (4) semantic differential scales.

Likert Scales: Method of Summated Ratings   Scales of the Likert type present a number of positive and negative statements regarding an attitude object.[10] In responding to the items on these scales the subjects indicate whether they strongly agree, agree, are undecided, disagree, or strongly disagree with each statement. The numerical value assigned to each response depends on the degree of agreement or disagreement with individual statements. A subject's score is determined by summing the values assigned to individual responses. For example, one may score a Likert-type scale by assigning a value of two points to each response indicating strong agreement with favorable statements, a value of one for agreement with these statements, zero for indecision, minus one for disagreement, and minus two for strong disagreement. For unfavorable statements one reverses the scoring procedure, since disagreement with an unfavorable statement is assumed to be psychologically equivalent to agreement with a favorable statement.

It makes no difference whether 2 is high and −2 is low, or vice versa. The main consideration is that the responses be scored consistently in terms of the attitude they represent. Of course, whether *strongly approve* or *strongly disapprove* is the favorable attitude depends upon the content of the statement.

To construct a Likert-type scale, one usually follows these steps:

1. Collect a large number of favorable and unfavorable statements regarding the attitude object.
2. Select from these approximately equal numbers of favorable and unfavorable statements.
3. Administer these items to a number of individuals, asking them to indicate

[10]Rensis Likert, A Technique for the Measurement of Attitudes,'' *Archives of Psychology,* No. 140 (1932). (This is Likert's original monograph.)

their opinions regarding each statement by determining whether they strongly agree, agree, are undecided, disagree, or strongly disagree with each statement.

4. Compute the score of each individual using the scoring procedure discussed previously.
5. Carry out an item analysis to select those items that yield the best discrimination. Through item analysis one finds the correlation between the subjects' total scores and their response to each item.[11]

Consider these examples selected from the "attitudes toward the Negro" items in Likert's "A Survey of Opinions."

If the same preparation is required, the Negro teacher should receive the same salary as the white teacher.	SA (2)	A (1)	U (0)	D (−1)	SD (−2)
Negro homes should be segregated from those of white people.[12]	SA (−2)	A (−1)	U (0)	D (1)	SD (2)

Thurstone Scales: Method of Equal-Appearing Intervals.   Thurstone developed a method for assigning specific scale values to items representing different degrees of favorable attitude. To develop this type of scale one follows these steps:

1. Collect a large number of statements regarding the attitude object.
2. Give the statements to a number of people who will judge them. Fifty to a hundred judges are usually used for evaluating the statements. The judges work independently and are asked to sort all the statements into seven, nine, or eleven categories according to the degree of favorableness expressed in the statement. In the first pile the judge places the statements he considers most favorable to the object; in the second pile, those he considers next most favorable; and so on. The sixth pile represents the neutral position and the eleventh pile contains the statements considered most unfavorable. It is important to note that this classification has nothing to do with the judges' own attitudes toward the object but represent only their judgments as to the favorableness of the statements.
3. Find the scale that will be assigned to each statement value by determining the median of the weights or scale positions assigned to it by the judges. Items showing very large variability are eliminated.
4. Select twenty to thirty statements that are spread out evenly along the scale from one extreme to the other. These statements become the attitude scale. The following items with their scale values are taken from Thurstone's scale measuring attitudes toward the church.

[11]J. P. Guilford and Benjamin Fruchter, *Fundamental Statistics in Psychology and Education,* 5th ed. (New York: McGraw-Hill, 1973).

[12]Gardner Murphy and Rensis Likert, *Public Opinion and the Individual* (New York: Harper & Row, 1938), pp. 20–21.

Scale Value

0.2	I believe the church is the greatest institution in America today.
1.5	I believe church membership is almost essential to living life at its best.
2.3	I find the services of the church both restful and inspiring.
3.3	I enjoy my church because there is a spirit of friendliness there.
4.5	I believe in what the church teaches, but with mental reservations.
5.6	Sometimes I feel that the church and religion are necessary, and sometimes I doubt it.
6.7	I believe in sincerity and goodness without any church ceremonies.
7.4	I believe the church is losing ground as education advances.
8.3	I think the teaching of the church is altogether too superficial to have much social significance.
9.6	I think the church is a hindrance to religion, for it still depends upon magic, superstition, and myth.
11.0	I think the church is a parasite on society.[13]

To administer a Thurstone-type scale one either asks the subjects to select from the list those statements that represent their position or to select the three statements that are closest to their position. The scale values, of course, are not indicated on the attitude scale and the items are arranged in a random order rather than in the order of their scale value. The score of each subject would be the mean of the values of the statements he or she has selected.[14]

Guttman Scales: Cumulative Technique.   Critics of the Thurstone and Likert attitude scales pointed out that these scales contained heterogeneous statements concerning various dimensions of an attitude object. For example, in Thurstone's scale measuring attitudes toward war, no attempt was made to separate ethical statements from statements concerning the economic results of war or those reflecting other possible aspects of attitudes toward war. As a result of this combining of several dimensions on one scale, it may be difficult to make any clear interpretation of the scores obtained.

Guttman developed a technique to attempt to overcome this problem. His technique, characterized as a unidimensional scale, aims to determine if the attitude being studied actually involves only a single dimension. An attitude is considered unidimensional *only* if it yields a cumulative scale—one in which the items are related to one another in such a way that a subject who agrees with item 2 also agrees with item 1; one who agrees with item 3 also agrees with items 1 and 2, and so on. Thus individuals who approve of a particular item in this type of scale will have a higher score on the total scale than those who disapprove of that item. For example, consider the following items with which respondents are asked either to disagree or agree:

---

[13]L. Thurstone and E. Chave, *The Measurement of Attitude* (Chicago: University of Chicago Press, 1929), pp. 61–63.

[14]For a detailed comparison of the Thurstone and Likert methods, see Allen L. Edwards and K. C. Kenney, ''A Comparison of the Thurstone and Likert Techniques of Attitude Scale Construction,'' *Journal of Applied Psychology* 30 (1946): 72–83.

1. The PTA is worth the time spent on it.
2. The PTA is a strong influence for improving schools.
3. The PTA is the most important organization in the United States for improving schools.

If this is a cumulative scale, it should be possible to arrange all the responses of the respondents into the type of pattern shown in Table 7.1. Thus, if we know an individual's score, it should be possible to tell exactly which items he or she approved. For example, all individuals with a score of 2 believe that the PTA is worth the time spent on it and that it is a strong influence for improving schools, but do *not* believe that it is the most important organization in the United States for improving schools. Subjects can be ranked according to their scale responses.

Table 7.1   Example of Cumulative Technique*

Score	Agrees with Item			Disagrees with Item		
	3	2	1	3	2	1
3	X	X	X	0	0	0
2	0	X	X	X	0	0
1	0	0	X	X	X	0
0				X	X	X

*The respondent scores one for each agreement.

When constructing a cumulative scale one must determine first of all whether or not the items form a unidimensional scale.[15] To do this, one analyzes the *reproducibility* of the responses—that is, the proportion of responses that actually fall into a pattern as shown in Table 7.1. On the basis of the total score, a prediction is made of the pattern of responses to particular items. Then the actual pattern of responses is studied and a measure is made of the extent to which the responses were reproducible from the total score. One technique is to divide the total number of errors by the total number of responses and subtract from one. Guttman suggests .90 as the minimum reproducibility coefficient necessary for a series of items to be recognized as forming a unidimensional or cumulative scale.

Semantic Differential Scales.   Another approach to measuring attitudes toward objects, subjects, and events is the semantic differential. This technique was developed and used by Osgood, Suci, and Tannenbaum.[16] The semantic differential is based on the viewpoint that objects have two different types of meaning for individuals, *denotative* and *connotative,* which can be rated independently. One can

[15]For a detailed discussion, see Allen L. Edwards, *Techniques of Attitude Scale Construction* (New York: Appleton, 1957), chs. 7 and 9.

[16]C. E. Osgood, G. J. Suci, and P. H. Tannenbaum, *The Measurement of Meaning* (Urbana, Ill.: University of Illinois Press, 1957).

easily state the denotative meaning of an object but not its connotative meaning. It is possible and useful to measure the connotative meaning of objects indirectly by using a number of bipolar adjectives and asking individuals to rate the objects against these adjectives. Thus the meaning of an object for an individual would be the pattern of his or her ratings of that object on the bipolar adjective scales used. Osgood and his associates use seven-point scales, having a zero midpoint and going up to $+3$ and down to -3 for attitude ratings. For illustration consider the following examples:

Good	$+3$	$+2$	$+1$	0	-1	-2	-3	Bad
Clean	$+3$	$+2$	$+1$	0	-1	-2	-3	Dirty
Sweet	$+3$	$+2$	$+1$	0	-1	-2	-3	Sour
Strong	$+3$	$+2$	$+1$	0	-1	-2	-3	Weak
Large	$+3$	$+2$	$+1$	0	-1	-2	-3	Small
Heavy	$+3$	$+2$	$+1$	0	-1	-2	-3	Light
Active	$+3$	$+2$	$+1$	0	-1	-2	-3	Passive
Fast	$+3$	$+2$	$+1$	0	-1	-2	-3	Slow
Hot	$+3$	$+2$	$+1$	0	-1	-2	-3	Cold

By obtaining the subjects' ratings of an object, the researcher can determine whether each one's attitude toward that object is positive or negative. The attitude scores of an individual respondent can be compared with the typical attitude toward the object by a designated group. One can also arrive at an attitude score for the respondents by comparing the attitudes of a number of persons toward that object, and comparing the pattern of their ratings with that of the others.

Osgood, Suci, and Tannenbaum have found, through factor analytic studies, three clusters of adjectives: *evaluative,* consisting of adjectives such as good and bad, or clean and dirty; *potency,* consisting of adjectives such as strong and weak or large and small; and *activity,* consisting of adjectives such as active and passive or fast and slow. The evaluative cluster, among the three clusters, has been reported to be the most conspicuous one.

Reports on the validity and reliability of the semantic differential scales are generally satisfactory. The validity studies show correlation coefficients of approximately .80 between the semantic differential ratings and Thurstone, Likert, and Guttman scales. The test-retest reliability of the semantic differential is reported to be about .90, a result which is satisfactory. Although it seems that the semantic differential is not as widely used as the other three types of attitude scales, it is a useful technique for measuring attitudes toward objects.

SOCIOMETRIC TECHNIQUES

Sociometric techniques are used for studying the organization of social groups. The basic procedure, though it may be modified in several ways, involves requesting the members of a particular group to indicate their first, second, and subsequent choices for companions on the basis of a specific criterion, usually for some particular activity. For example, the members of a group are asked, Whom would you like to work with on this project, or sit next to, or eat lunch with, or play with after school? The sociometric method is essentially a study of the choices made by each person in a group. The choices obtained are plotted on what is called a sociogram, which shows the pattern of interpersonal relations in a group. Figure 7.3 shows a

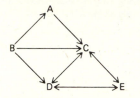

Figure 7.3   Sociogram of a group

sociogram, in which C is the most frequently chosen member, who might be referred to as the "star." Notice that D, C, and E choose one another. This represents a clique; that is, three or more individuals who mutually chose one another. B received no choices, although he did make choices within the group; he is an *isolate*. The choices revealed in a sociogram can be quantified and used for research purposes.

Sociometric methods have been widely used for research in social psychology and also in educational research, where sociometric status may be studied in its relationship to other variables, such as mental ability, achievement, and teachers' preferences for children.[17]

DIRECT OBSERVATION

In many cases systematic direct observation of behavior is the most desirable measurement method. An investigator identifies the behavior of interest and devises a systematic procedure for identifying, categorizing, and recording the behavior in either a natural or a "staged" situation.

Urban's study "Behavior Changes Resulting from a Study of Communicable Diseases" is an excellent example of the use of this procedure in a natural setting.[18] Observers recorded the number of instances of undesirable behavior, such as putting fingers or other objects in the mouth, and the number of desirable behaviors, such as using one's handkerchief when coughing or sneezing. Following this, an experimental group was selected and taught a six-week course on communicable diseases which was designed to change their overt behavior as well as to provide them with factual information and understanding. At the end of the course the undesirable behaviors were again recorded. It was found that they had been dramatically re-

[17]For further discussion, see G. Lindzey, *Handbook of Social Psychology,* vol. 1 (Reading, Mass.: Addison-Wesley, 1954), ch. 11; or M. Jahoda, M. Deutsch, and S. Cook, *Research Methods in Social Relations,* part 2 (New York: Holt, Rinehart and Winston, 1951), ch. 17.

[18]J. Urban, "Behavior Changes Resulting from a Study of Communicable Diseases," *Teachers College Contributions to Education,* No. 896 (1943).

duced and the desirable behaviors dramatically increased in the experimental group, while there was little change in the control group, which had not had the course. Observations twelve weeks later found these differences between the control and experimental groups persisting.

Hartshorne, May, and Shuttleworth used direct observation to measure such traits as self-control, cooperativeness, truthfulness, and honesty.[19] They made observations of children engaged in routine school activities and also staged situations to focus on specific behaviors. For example, they gave vocabulary and reading tests to the children, collected the tests, and without the children's knowledge made duplicate copies of their answers. Later the children were given answer keys and were asked to score their original papers. The difference between the scores the children reported and the actual scores obtained from scoring the duplicate papers provided a measure of cheating.

There are five important preliminary steps to be taken when using direct observation.

1. *The aspect of behavior to be observed must be selected.* Since it is not possible to observe everything that happens, the investigator must decide beforehand which behaviors to record and which to ignore.
2. *The behaviors falling within the chosen category must be clearly defined.* The observers must understand what actions will be classified as, for instance, cooperative behavior or selfish behavior.
3. *The people who will carry out the observations must be trained.* Training and opportunity for practice are necessary in order that the investigator can rely on the observers to follow an established procedure in observing, and in interpreting and reporting observations.
4. *A system for quantifying observations must be developed.* The investigator must decide on a standard method for counting the observed behaviors. For instance, it must be established beforehand whether an action and the reaction to it are to be counted as a single incident of the behavior observed or as two incidents. A suggested approach is to divide the observation period into brief time segments and to record for each period, say, thirty seconds, whether the subject showed the behavior or not.
5. *Detailed procedures for recording the behavior must be developed.* The memory of most observers is usually not reliable enough for meaningful research. The best solution is a coding system that allows the immediate recording of what is observed using a single letter or digit, rather than a narrative system, which takes too much of the observers' time and attention.

A widely used example of such a coding plan is the Flanders system for categorizing classroom verbal behavior. As can be seen in Figure 7.4, this system provides exhaustive and mutually exclusive categories, each of which can be re-

[19]H. Hartshorne, M. A. May, and F. K. Shuttleworth, *Studies in the Organization of Character* (New York: Macmillan, 1930).

corded as a single digit. Trained observers are able to record a digit every three seconds. The chain of digits produced can easily be analyzed to provide not only a record of the proportions of verbal behavior falling into each category but also a picture of which behaviors preceded or followed which other behaviors.

Figure 7.4   Flanders's Interaction Analysis Categories (FIAC)

TEACHER TALK:	
Response	1.* *Accepts feeling:* accepts and clarifies an attitude or the feeling tone of a pupil in a nonthreatening manner. Feelings may be positive or negative. Predicting and recalling feelings are included.
	2.* *Praises or encourages:* praises or encourages pupil action or behavior. Tells jokes that release tension, but not at the expense of another individual; nodding head or saying ''Um hm?'' or ''go on'' are included.
	3.* *Accepts or uses ideas of pupils:* clarifies, builds, or develops ideas suggested by a pupil. Teacher extensions of pupil ideas are included, but, as the teacher brings more of his own ideas into play, they shift to category 5.
	4.* *Asks questions:* asks a question about content or procedure, based on teacher ideas, with the intent that a pupil will answer.
Initiation	5.* *Lectures:* gives facts or opinions about content or procedures; expresses his own ideas, gives his own explanation, or cites an authority other than a pupil.
	6.* *Gives directions:* gives directions, commands, or orders to which a pupil is expected to comply.
	7.* *Criticizes or justifies authority:* makes statements intended to change pupil behavior from nonacceptable to acceptable pattern; bawls someone out; states why he is doing what he is doing; extreme self-reference.
PUPIL TALK:	
Response	8.* *Pupil-talk—response:* talk by pupils in response to teacher. Teacher initiates the contact, solicits pupil statement, or structures the situation. Freedom to express own ideas is limited.
Initiation	9.* *Pupil-talk—initiation:* talk by pupils that they initiate. They express their own ideas; initiate a new topic; have freedom to develop opinions and a line of thought, like asking thoughtful questions; go beyond the existing structure.
Silence	10.* *Silence or confusion:* Pauses, short periods of silence, and periods of confusion in which communication cannot be understood by the observer.

*There is NO scale implied by these numbers. Each number is classificatory; it designates a particular kind of communication event. To write these numbers down during observation is to enumerate, not to judge, a position on a scale.

SOURCE: From Ned A. Flanders, *Analyzing Teaching Behavior* (Boston: Addison-Wesley, 1970), p. 34.

Summary

An important task of researchers in the behavioral sciences is the selection of dependable measuring instruments for the purpose of quantifying research information. Subjects may be asked direct questions through interviews or through questionnaires. Either of these techniques may be unstructured or structured. In unstructured interviews and questionnaires the questions are presented to subjects and their free responses are recorded. In structured forms the questions are organized and a limited choice of answers is offered to the subjects.

In educational research tests are major means of data collection. A test is defined as a set of stimuli which elicit the individual's typical performance. Achievement tests are prime examples of this kind of instrument. There are a variety of achievement tests available that provide norms that can be used as a basis for comparison. Intelligence tests are tools for assessing an individual's verbal and nonverbal capacities. Personality inventories are designed to measure the subject's personal characteristics.

Attitude scales are tools for measuring individuals' beliefs, feelings, and reactions to certain objects. The major types of attitude scales are Likert-type scales, Thurstone scales, Guttman scales, and the semantic differential.

Sociometric techniques are means of assessing individuals' standings among their peers. Through these techniques it is possible to locate popular members of groups (stars), isolates, and cliques.

A number of methods for systematically observing the behavior of subjects have been developed as direct observation methods.

Exercises

1. What are the advantages and disadvantages of structured and unstructured interviews?
2. In what ways can the accuracy of answers to questionnaire items be increased?
3. What is the meaning of the term *standardized* when applied to measuring instruments?
4. What is the dfference between comparative rating scales and graphic and category scales?
5. List some of the common sources of bias in rating scales.
6. Why is a Guttman scale considered unidimensional as compared with the Thurstone and Likert scales?
7. What is the main measurement use of the semantic differential?
8. What are some procedures for increasing the accuracy of direct observation techniques?
9. Construct a five-item Likert scale for measuring teachers' attitudes toward foreign language instruction in the elementary school.
10. List two research problems for which the questionnaire would be the appropriate instrument for gathering the data.
11. Construct a five-item graphic rating scale that would be useful for evaluating a research problem.

Answers

1. Structured interviews have answers which can be readily analyzed, thus increasing reliability. Unstructured interviews are more informal and thus allow for more depth of coverage. However, their data are difficult to quantify and they require skilled interviewers for maximum effectiveness.
2. Questions written clearly, without technical terms or emotion-laden phrases, are less likely to be misinterpreted by respondents. Response choices should be unambiguous and quantified if possible. Questions that might arouse embarassment or hostility may be given unobjective answers by respondents.
3. *Standardized* refers to instruments for which comparative norms have been derived, their reliability and validity have been established, and directions for administration and scoring prescribed.
4. In judging an individual on graphic and category scales, raters do not make a direct comparison of the subject with other persons. In judging an individual on a comparative rating scale, the rater must have knowledge of the groups with which the individual is being compared.
5. Raters may be less than objective in judging individuals when influenced by such tendencies as the halo effect, the generosity error, the error of severity, or the error of central tendency.
6. The Thurstone and Likert scales may contain statements on various dimensions of the attitude object. A Guttman scale is considered unidimensional because it asks questions about degrees of reaction to a single topic. Therefore it is cumulative; that is, a person who agrees with a given item on the scale can be predicted to agree on all items below that item on the scale.
7. The semantic differential is used to measure the connotative meaning that a person attaches to an object.
8. The behaviors to be observed must be specified; behaviors falling within a category must be defined; a system for quantification must be developed; and the observers must be trained to carry out the observations according to this established procedure.

Validity and Reliability

Research is always dependent upon measurement. There are two important characteristics that every measuring instrument should possess: *validity* and *reliability*. Validity refers to the extent to which an instrument measures what it is intended to measure. Reliability, on the other hand, is the extent to which a measuring device is consistent in measuring whatever it measures. An educational researcher must inquire into the validity and reliability of the instruments used in a study and must include this information in the research report. If a researcher's data are not obtained with valid and reliable instruments, one would have little faith in the results obtained or in the conclusions based on the results.

Evidence of validity and reliability is especially important in educational research because most of the measurements attempted in this area are obtained indirectly. One needs to assess to what extent an educational or a psychological measuring instrument measures precisely and dependably what it is intended to measure.

Validity

The validity question is concerned with the extent to which an instrument measures what one thinks it is measuring. It is absolutely essential that the researcher ask this question. Educational and psychological testing instruments are designed for the purpose of appraising constructs such as achievement, intelligence, creativity, aptitude, attitudes, motivation, and the like. However, there are no direct means of measuring these constructs such as exist in the physical sciences for the measurement of characteristics like length, volume, and weight. Researchers must develop indirect means to measure complex attributes. These indirect means involve tests and scales consisting of a number of tasks that are selected to serve as indicators of the complex constructs. One is never sure that these indirect procedures measure what they are supposed to be measuring. Researchers must ask the following kinds of questions: Does this test really measure achievement motivation? Does this test measure other qualities as well? Can this creativity test really separate the highly creative persons from the less creative persons? Could one make useful predictions based on scores on this aptitude test? Is it an appropriate instrument for use with all pupils, or should it be used only with certain groups? These questions all concern aspects of a test's validity.

The question of an instrument's validity is always specific to the particular situation and to the particular purpose for which it is being used. A test that has validity in one situation may not be valid in a different situation. For example, a standardized history test that emphasizes understanding and interpretation may have validity for one history teacher, but would not be valid for another teacher who has stressed the learning of dates and factual knowledge. The purpose for which the test is being used is also a major factor in validity. A standardized chemistry test may be used to measure end-of-the-year achievement in chemistry. In this case one would have questions about just what the test measures and how well it does so. The same test might be used to predict achievement in college chemistry. In this case one would be interested in how well the test can predict future achievement. These different purposes of tests involve different types of validity.

Various aspects of validity have been delineated. The best known classification of the types of validity has been set forth by a joint committee of the American Psychological Association, the AERA, and the National Council on Measurements in Education.[1] This committee distinguished three types of validity: *content validity, criterion-related validity,* and *construct validity.* These three types of validity cover the basic purposes for which tests are used.

CONTENT VALIDITY

Classroom tests are generally used for the purpose of assessing students' knowledge and skills in a defined content area. The ideal way to accomplish this would be to use an examination that would include all the questions that could possibly be asked about that content. Obviously such a procedure is not feasible. The usual alternative is to prepare a sample of the total content area and then to use this sample as a basis for inferences about students' knowledge of the entire universe of content. Since inferences are to be made on the basis of only a sample, it is very important that that sample be representative of the total content universe, i.e., that it be a valid sample. This brings us to the question of *content validity.*

Content validity refers to the extent to which the instrument represents the content of interest. In assessing the content validity of a measuring instrument, one is concerned with the question: How well does the content of the instrument represent the entire universe of content which might be measured? In order to have content validity, a measure must adequately sample both the topics and the cognitive processes included in the content universe under consideration. Furthermore, the topics and cognitive processes must be sampled in proportion to their emphasis in the entire content universe.

Such a content universe is theoretical, of course. However, it is possible to prepare an outline of the topics, skills, and abilities that make up the content area being measured along with an indication of the importance of each. A large number of test items could be written using this outline as a guide. From each category of the outline test items could be randomly drawn with the number of items reflecting the proportionate weight of that category in the whole. Such a sample of items should be representative of the content universe and hence would have content validity. For example, the universe of content for a test on the Civil War might be

---

[1]American Psychological Association, *Standards for Educational and Psychological Tests and Manuals* (Washington, D.C., 1974).

defined as a knowledge and understanding of topics such as the causes, the military strategies and campaigns, important personalities, economic impact, effects on subsequent history, and so on. The test items written on each of these topics should measure not only knowledge of the topic, but also understanding, interpretation, analysis, and any other cognitive objectives emphasized in the course. The number of items covering each topic and each type of objective should reflect the emphasis given that topic and that objective in the total course. Assume a teacher of English literature has emphasized an understanding of the ideas of selected authors and the relevance of those ideas in the twentieth century. If this teacher's test contained mostly items asking students to match authors' names with their works and to recall their birth dates, the teacher has failed to obtain a representative sample of the content area and the test would not have content validity.

Content validity cannot be expressed in terms of a numerical index. Content validation is essentially and of necessity based on judgment and such judgment must be made separately for each situation. It involves a careful and critical examination of the test items as they relate to the specified content area. One must judge if the content and objectives measured by the test are representative of those that constitute the content domain. One should determine whether the items in the test represent the course and objectives as stated in curriculum guides, syllabuses, and texts. In order to obtain an external evaluation of content validity the test maker should ask a number of experts or other teachers to examine the test content systematically and evaluate its relevancy to the specified universe. If all agree that the test items represent the content domain adequately, the test can then be said to have content validity. It should also be established that the test is free from the influence of factors that are irrelevant to the purpose of the measurement. For example, performance on a mathematics test should not be influenced by reading speed and vocabulary. The presence of these factors in a mathematics test would lower its validity since the test would be measuring something other than what it was intended to measure.

The researcher must always evaluate the content validity of any self-constructed or standardized achievement test to be used in a study. Test publishers generally provide information on the content validity of standardized tests. However, it must be stressed again that an achievement test which has high content validity for the test constructor may not have content validity for another user who may define the content universe in a different way. Only the user of a test can ultimately judge its content validity for his/her own purpose.

CRITERION-RELATED VALIDITY

Criterion-related validity refers to the relationship between the scores on a measuring instrument and an independent external variable (criterion) believed to measure directly the behavior or characteristic in question. For example, when one investigates the relationship between the scores on a scholastic aptitude test and college grade-point average (GPA), one is investigating the criterion-related validity of the aptitude test. GPA is the criterion in this case. The extent to which scores on the aptitude test are related to success in college as measured by GPA is the extent to which the aptitude test has criterion-related validity for the purpose of predicting GPA.

As the name indicates, the emphasis in this type of validity is on the criterion rather than on the instrument itself. One is primarily interested in what the instrument can predict rather than in the test content. In contrast to content validity, criterion-related validity uses empirical techniques to study the relationship between scores on the instrument in question and the external criterion. Thus, the identification of the criterion or criteria is crucial to the investigation of this type of validity. There are several characteristics that a criterion measure should possess. Of these, the most important is *relevance*. One must judge whether the criterion chosen really represents successful performance on the behavior in question. If the criterion does not reflect the attribute under study, it would be meaningless to use it as a basis for validating another instrument. GPA is considered a relevant measure of success in college and is generally chosen as the criterion for validating aptitude tests constructed for the selection of college applicants. To validate a test designed to select salespersons, the relevant criterion might be dollar value of sales made in a specified time. In some cases it may be difficult to find relevant criteria. For example, it has been difficult to locate criteria for use in validating measures to be used for predicting teacher effectiveness. With neither an agreed-upon description of teacher effectiveness nor an effective method of measuring that variable, it is practically impossible to establish the validity of any instrument designed to identify promising teacher candidates.

A second characteristic is that a criterion must be *reliable*. This means that the criterion must be a consistent measure of the attribute over time or from situation to situation. If the criterion itself is not consistent, one would not expect it to relate consistently to any predictors.

A criterion should be *free from bias*. That is, the scoring of a criterion measure should not be influenced by any factors other than actual performance on the criterion. Assume that a supervisor's rating is the criterion used to validate a test to select applicants for a certain job. If the supervisor lets a general opinion of the individual or any factor other than actual performance influence the rating, then the criterion score will be biased. In order to avoid bias when the criterion is a rating, one should give explicit instructions on the characteristics to be rated and how the rating is to be done. The more objective the rating procedure, the less bias there will be in the criterion. Another possible source of bias in a criterion is *contamination*. Contamination occurs when an individual's score on the criterion is influenced by the scorer's knowledge of the subject's predictor score. For example, assume that one has an art aptitude test that is to be validated by using grades in art class as the criterion. If the teachers who grade the students' works are aware of the students' scores on the aptitude test, such awareness may influence the teachers' evaluation of the students. Contamination of the criterion can be prevented by not permitting the person who grades or rates the criterion to see the predictor scores.

Once the external criterion has been defined, empirical data are gathered in order to assess the relationship between scores on the measuring instrument (X) and on the criterion (Y). The instrument to be validated is administered to a group of individuals representative of those on whom the measure will be used. The scores made by these subjects on the predictor (X) are put aside and are not used to make any decisions that might influence subsequent events for this particular group in order to avoid contamination of the criterion scores. When the criterion data (Y) become available at a later time, the original tests are retrieved and the scores on the tests are then correlated with the scores on the criterion. The resulting coefficient of correlation between the two sets of measures is called a *validity coefficient* (r_{xy}) and indicates how accurately the test scores (X) can predict the criterion (Y). The larger the r_{xy}, the more accurately the test predicts.

An example of this procedure occurred in the validation of the Scholastic Aptitude Test (SAT). The SAT was given to a large number of high school seniors and the tests were filed away until the students completed the freshman year of college. At that time the SAT scores were correlated with the first year GPA (the criterion) in order to obtain the validity coefficient of the test. Because the SAT was found to have useful criterion-related validity, it is now routinely used to predict performance in college. High school students usually take the SAT during their senior year and submit the scores to colleges. College admissions officers, aware of the predictive validity of the SAT, examine the scores and make admissions decisions based, at least in part, on the SAT scores. The higher the score on the SAT, the greater the probability of success in college.

Tests with high criterion-related validity are typically used for selection and classification purposes. However, before a test can be used for these purposes, it must be demonstrated through a validity study, such as that used in the example above, that the test can in fact predict performance on the specified criterion. One often asks what size correlation coefficient is required for a test to have criterion-related validity. There is, unfortunately, no clear and universal answer to this question. A correlation coefficient of .40 could be very helpful in cases for which no predictive instrument has previously been available. In other cases a correlation of .65 might be considered low and unsatisfactory if other predictors are available that have a higher relationship with the criterion. In general an instrument has "good" criterion-related validity if it has a higher correlation with the criterion than do competing instruments. Determining the criterion-related validity of a test requires time and patience. In some cases it is necessary to wait for several years to determine whether or not performance on a measure is useful for predicting success on a criterion.

Some writers make a distinction between two types of criterion-related validity: *predictive validity* and *concurrent validity*. Both are concerned with the empirical relationship between test scores and a criterion, but a distinction is made on the basis of the time when the criterion data are collected.

Concurrent validity is concerned with the correlation between test scores and a criterion measure available at the same or a very close point in time. Predictive validity is concerned with the correlation between test scores and a criterion that occurs at a later point in time. For example, if we administer a reading test when students are completing the fourth grade, we could assess concurrent validity by correlating scores with the grades the subjects received during the year in fourth grade reading and later assess predictive validity by correlating the test scores with the grades the students subsequently received in fifth grade reading.

Because a validity coefficient is a correlation coefficient, its size will be influenced by the same factors that influence any correlation coefficient, namely, the linearity of the relationship between test and criterion and the range of individual differences in the group (see pp. 120–21).

CONSTRUCT VALIDITY

When researchers ask the question, What does this test really measure? they are inquiring into the construct validity of the test. Construct validity is concerned with the extent to which a test measures a specific trait or construct. It is the type of validity that is essential for tests that are used to assess individuals on certain psychological traits and abilities. Some common examples of constructs are anxiety, intelligence, motivation, reasoning ability, attitudes, critical thinking, aptitude in various areas, reading comprehension, and self-concept. The construct validity of a test refers to the extent to which performance on the test can be interpreted in terms of constructs such as these.

The term *construct* is used to refer to something that is not itself directly measurable but which explains observable effects. The construct ''social maturity'' was ''constructed'' to account for observed behavior patterns. Social maturity cannot itself be measured directly but many of the behaviors that we believe to be aspects of this construct can be described and measured and the sum of these measures can give us an indirect measure of the abstract construct ''social maturity.''

Throughout history people have put together, or constructed, more complex abstractions from their concepts. Just as a child puts together tinker toy pieces and labels them ''horse'' or ''house'' or ''man,'' so people create constructs by combining concepts and less complex constructs in purposeful patterns. The impetus for construct validation came from personality theory and the researchers' need for a method of validating the instruments used in theory development. Neither content nor criterion-related validity directly focuses on the construct being measured by a test. In the construct approach to validity the object is to determine what psychological construct is being measured by a test and how well it is being measured.

Construct validation combines both a logical and an empirical approach. One aspect of the logical approach is to ask if the elements the test measures are the elements that make up the construct. For example, when Doll originated the Vineland Social Maturity Scale in 1935[2] he defined the construct social maturity as a

[2]Edgar A. Doll, *Vineland Social Maturity Scale* (Circle Pines, Minn.: American Guidance Service, Inc.). The scale was revised in 1949, and again in 1965.

combination of interrelated elements of self-help, self-direction, locomotion, occupation, communication, and social relations. Those who reviewed the first revised version of the test in Buros's *Mental Measurements Yearbook*[3] tended to agree that these elements are aspects of the construct that should be incorporated in a test of social maturity. Sometimes there is disagreement on what the elements of a construct are. For example, if one thinks of the construct intelligence as primarily a combination of skills that enable an individual to cope with an academic environment, one will expect such skills to be measured in an intelligence test. If one defines intelligence as a set of skills that are no more related to school environments than to other environments, one will not want school specific skills incorporated into the test.

Another aspect of the logical approach is to inspect the items to determine if they seem appropriate for assessing the elements in the construct. In the Vineland scale, for example, the parent of a six-year-old is asked if the subject . . . uses skates, sled, wagon (occupation), . . . goes to bed unassisted (self-help), . . . prints simple words (communication), . . . plays simple table games (locomotion), and . . . is trusted with money (self-direction). These questions seem appropriate for measuring elements of social maturity. If the original test had included questions concerning the child's preference for certain foods or whether he or she is left-handed or right-handed, these items would have been deleted as they are not directly related to the elements in the construct.

There are also empirical aspects to construct validity: (1) Internally, relationships within the test should be as predicted by the construct. (2) Externally, relationships between scores on the test and other observations should be consistent with the construct. Doll was able to show that Vineland scores for occupation, self-help, and so forth were positively correlated with one another. These observations provided internal support for the theory that the construct social maturity consists of interrelated elements and provided evidence that the Vineland scale was successful in measuring these interrelated elements.

If the relationships of elements within a test are not what were predicted by the construct, then either the construct itself is inappropriate or the test is failing to measure the elements within the construct.

For example, one might propose to measure the construct sociobiological instinct by first positing that the construct consisted of interrelated elements: (1) will to survive, (2) will to reproduce, (3) desire to select healthy mates, (4) willingness to sacrifice in order to promote the survival only of one's own children and near relatives. If, when the test is constructed and administered, one finds that these elements are not positively related, one would conclude that the measure lacked construct validity and that either the test or the construct itself should be revised.

Scores on a test should be related to external measures in a manner consistent with the construct. Doll and others have shown that scores on the Vineland scale do correlate with chronological age, mental age, and with independent assessments of

[3]O. K. Buros, *Mental Measurements Yearbook,* Vol. 4 (Highland Park, N.J.: Gryphon Press, 1949).

social maturity. Therefore, it can be said that scores on the Vineland scale show the relationships with external measures that should be expected in a scale of social maturity that has construct validity.

A measure of a particular construct should be as independent as possible of measures of other constructs. For example, if we develop a test designed to measure arithmetic problem-solving skills and find scores on this test are very highly correlated with scores on reading tests, we would conclude that we have developed another test of reading rather than an arithmetic problem-solving test *per se*. It is probably not possible to develop a test of arithmetic problem solving that is completely unrelated to reading. However, if we have two competing arithmetic problem-solving tests that are both correlated with an arithmetic computation test ($r = .7$), but one correlates with a reading test ($r = .8$) and the other correlates with the reading test ($r = .6$), we would judge the latter to have greater construct validity since it is more independent of reading.

Methods Used in Gathering Evidence for Construct Validity

There is no single method used to establish construct validity. Evidence is gathered from a variety of sources, including content and criterion-related validity data. Any data that would help interpret the meaning of test scores are relevant. Some of the most common procedures used to investigate construct validity are presented below.

Correlation with Other Measures.   One may attempt to show that a test correlates highly with another measure that is considered to be a valid measure of the construct. For example, a newly developed intelligence test would be correlated with a well-established test of intelligence such as the Stanford-Binet or the Wechsler. If the correlation is high, one assumes that the new test is measuring the same construct (intelligence) as the established test. As was mentioned in the example above, a scholastic aptitude test should correlate highly with grades in school, achievement test scores, or teachers' ratings of aptitude. As evidence of construct validity, Campbell writes of the need for a *convergence* of indicators of the construct as well as *discriminability* from other constructs.[4] Convergence means that the measure is related to other measures presumed to be valid indicators of the same construct. One looks for convergence of indicators of the construct. That is, one points out the other measures with which the construct is correlated and how they are correlated. Convergence also implies that the results from administrations of the instrument to different groups in different places and at different times would be as predicted by the theory behind the construct. Campbell and Fiske stressed, however, that convergence of indicators is not sufficient evidence of construct validity.[5] They pointed to the need for evidence that the construct could be empiri-

[4]Donald T. Campbell, "Recommendations for APA Test Standards Regarding Construct, Trait, and Discriminant Validity," *American Psychologist* 15 (1960):546–53.

[5]Donald T. Campbell and D. W. Fiske, "Convergence and Discriminant Validation by the Multitrait-Multimethod Matrix," *Psychological Bulletin* 56 (1959):81–105.

cally distinguished from other constructs. To establish descriminablity one seeks evidence that the construct is not substantially correlated with instruments known to measure different constructs. That is, one identifies measures with which the construct is not or should not be substantially correlated.

Another aspect of the correlational approach to construct validity is factor analysis. Factor analysis is a statistical method for studying the intercorrelations among a set of test scores and determining the number of factors (constructs) needed to account for the intercorrelations. One starts with a large number of different measures; but by examining the intercorrelations among them and finding which measures seem to go together (correlate), one may reduce the large number to a smaller number of factors or constructs that are actually measured. The intercorrelations indicate not only what tests measure the same factor but also the extent to which they measure the factor. The reader is referred to advanced statistics books for a complete discussion of factor analysis.[6]

Experimental Studies.   It may be hypothesized that test scores would change when certain types of experimental treatments are introduced. For example, in establishing the construct validity of an anxiety scale, one might hypothesize that scores on the scale would change when individuals are put into an anxiety-provoking situation. If anxiety is manipulated in a controlled experiment and the resulting scores on the anxiety scale do change in the predicted way, one would have some evidence that the scale does measure anxiety.

Comparison of Scores of Defined Groups.   One can use groups already known to be different and hypothesize that scores on the instrument in question would discriminate one group from another. One would expect that scores on a musical aptitude test would discriminate between students currently enrolled in music school and an unselected group of college students. Similarly, if mechanics and non-mechanics could be discriminated on the basis of their scores on a mechanical aptitude test, this would provide support for the validity of the test. If an inventory measures psychological adjustment, then scores on the inventory could be expected to discriminate between groups previously identified as adjusted and those previously identified as neurotic. The different groups used for comparison in validity studies may be age-groups, sex groups, groups with different amounts of training in some area related to the construct, groups known to be normal and those known to be maladjusted, and so on. If the predicted differences in test scores are confirmed, one has support for the construct validity of the test.

The Intratest Analysis.   The intratest analysis method examines the test itself and gathers information about the content of the test, the processes used in responding to the items of the test, and correlations among items of the test. Data from content validity studies may provide relevant information about the construct validity of a test. When the behavioral universe being sampled by a test is specified, one

[6]See, for example, Wilson H. Guertin and John P. Bailey, *Introduction to Modern Factor Analysis* (Ann Abor, Mich.: Edwards Brothers, Inc., 1970).

has some insight into the nature of the construct being measured by the test. For example, if one were to define the behavioral universe of a reasoning test by describing the abilities that are being sampled by the test (such as the ability to reason with quantitative and verbal analogies), one would gain some insight about the construct validity of the test.

One might also investigate the mental processes and skills that individuals use when responding to the items of a test. For example, students might be asked to "think aloud" as they work through a verbal reasoning test. Such a procedure may reveal that the test is measuring this reasoning ability as it claims, or it may reveal that other factors, such as vocabulary or reading comprehension, are being measured.

Another procedure investigates the homogeneity of the test content in order to ascertain if the test measures a single trait or quality. A statistical formula developed by Kuder and Richardson provides a measure of the internal consistency of a test.[7]

Evaluation of Construct Validity

Construct validity has been the subject of an exciting debate between authorities in the field of testing and measuring. Some authors, such as Cronbach and Meehl, regard the concept of construct validity as a major advance in modern measurement and practice.[8] These authors think it is the most useful of the validity concepts because it goes beyond looking just for correlation between test performance and an external criterion, because it probes for operations which form a predictor, and because it concerns itself with the meaning of the traits and behaviors to be measured. Loevinger believes that construct validity is the essence of validity and that all other types of validity can be subsumed under it.[9] Other authors, however, are not as convinced about the value of construct validity. Bechtoldt and Ebel, for example, criticize construct validity for lack of logical precision and charge that it is an attempt to bring in vaguely defined variables instead of operationally defined concepts.[10] They and a number of other authors are concerned that overemphasis on this type of validity may result in an underrating of the practical side of testing and evaluation.

COMPARISON OF THE TYPES OF VALIDITY

Each of the major types of validity has a place in contemporary testing and measurement and each one is used extensively. Assume that a teacher wants to construct a test to be used with a sixth grade reading class. What procedures should be followed if the teacher wants to gather evidence about the three types of validity?

[7]M. W. Richardson and G. F. Kuder, "The Calculation of Test Reliability Coefficients Based on the Method of Rationale Equivalence," *Journal of Educational Psychology* 30 (1939):681–87.

[8]L. J. Cronbach and P. E. Meehl, "Construct Validity in Psychological Tests," *Psychological Bulletin* 52 (July 1955):281–302.

[9]J. Loevinger, "Objective Tests as Instruments of Psychological Theory," *Psychological Reports, Monograph Supplement,* 3 (1957):635–93.

[10]Harold P. Bechtoldt, "Construct Validity: A Critique," *American Psychologist* 14 (October 1959):619–30; and R. L. Ebel, "Must All Tests Be Valid," *American Psychologist* 16 (1961):640–47.

First, the teacher would decide on the universe of content to be included, specifically, the textbooks, outside reading materials, class exercises, and so forth. Samples from this universe would be selected in such a way that the test comprises a representative sample of all the content and the objectives of the course. Other teachers would be asked to make a judgment concerning the adequacy of the content.

For criterion-related validity, scores on the test would be correlated with the performance of these students on some criterion. That is, a follow-up study would be carried out to see whether there is a correlation between these test scores and reading achievement in seventh grade. If there is a high correlation, then the reading test would have validity for predicting seventh grade reading achievement. The scores on the test could also be correlated with scores on a standardized reading test and with the students' grades in reading class.

For construct validity, the teacher would decide on a rationale for the test content. The content should reflect certain hypotheses about the nature of reading proficiency and an attempt would be made to determine whether these hypotheses are supported by the test performance of the students. Differences in the performance of high scorers versus low scorers would be studied, and an attempt would be made to determine whether test performance is related to a theory of instruction in reading, and so on. Another method would involve a study of the convergence of reading scores with other variables.

APPLICATION OF THE VALIDITY CONCEPT

Although we define validity in a general way as the extent to which a test measures what it is intended to measure, validity is *not* some general characteristic that a test has. Validity is specific to the particular job that one wants a test to do. A test is valid for a specific purpose. One must know the setting in which the test will be used and then ascertain the test's validity for those particular circumstances. A test may be highly valid for one teacher and one situation and entirely lacking in validity for another teacher in a different situation and with different objectives.

Reliability

The reliability of a measuring instrument is the degree of consistency with which it measures whatever it is measuring. This quality is essential in any kind of measurement. A post office will soon take action to repair a scale if it is found that the scale sometimes underestimates and sometimes overestimates the weight of packages. Psychologists and educators are equally concerned about the consistency of their measuring devices when they attempt to measure such complex traits as intelligence, achievement, motivation, anxiety, and the like. They would not consider an intelligence test worthwhile if it yields markedly different results each time it is used on the same subject. People who use such measuring instruments must identify and utilize techniques that will help them to determine to what extent their measuring instruments are consistent or reliable.

THEORY OF RELIABILITY

As a way of distinguishing the reliability concept from the validity concept it is useful to identify *random errors of measurement* and *systematic errors of measurement*. Random error refers to error that is a result of pure chance. Random errors of measurement may inflate or depress any subject's score in an unpredictable manner. For example, one element in the President's Physical Fitness Test for elementary students is the baseball throw. Subjects are instructed to throw a baseball as far as they can and the distance of the throw is measured. Although the object of the test is to get a score that is typical of a subject's performance, certainly if we have a single subject throw a baseball on several occasions, we would find that the child does not throw it the same distance every time.

Assume we have each student make a throw on two consecutive days. If we then compare the two scores (distance thrown) for each student, we would find that they are almost never exactly the same. Most of the differences would be small, but some would be moderately large and a few, quite large. The results are inconsistent from one day's throw to the next. One throw is not completely reliable as a measure of a student's throwing ability.

There are three types of chance or random influences that lead to inconsistency between scores achieved on the two days:

1. *The student may actually change from one day to the next.* On one day he or she may feel better than on the other. On one day the student may be more motivated or less fatigued. Perhaps the student's father, hearing about the task, begins coaching the child in throwing a baseball.
2. *The task itself may change* for the two measurements. For example, the ball used one day may be firm, whereas on the second day it may be wet and soggy. One day perhaps the examiner permits the students to take a running start up to the throwing line, whereas on the second day he permits them only a couple of steps. These changes may help some students more than others.
3. *The limited sample* of behavior results in an unstable score. A small sample of behavior is subject to many kinds of chance influences. Maybe there is a gust of wind as the ball is thrown. Maybe the student loses his or her balance when starting to throw the ball, or maybe his or her fingers slip while gripping the ball.

Reliability is concerned with the effect of such random errors of measurement on the consistency of scores.

On the other hand, some errors involved in measurement are predictable or systematic. Using the example of the baseball throw, imagine a situation in which the instructions for the throw are given in English but not all the subjects understand

English. The scores of the non-English-speaking subjects could be systematically depressed because the subjects do not comprehend what they are expected to do. Such systematic errors of measurement are a validity problem. The validity of a test is lowered whenever scores are systematically changed by the influence of anything other than what we are attempting to measure. In this instance we are measuring not only baseball throwing ability but also, in part, English comprehension.

To decide whether we are dealing with reliability or validity, we determine whether we are considering random errors or systematic errors. If a class is being given the baseball throw test and two balls are being employed, one firm and one soggy, and it is purely a matter of chance who gets which ball, the variation due to the ball used is a reliability problem. The variation due to the ball represents random error that affects the consistency of the measurements. If class members are called to take the test in alphabetical order and it is a rainy day and the one baseball provided gets wetter with each successive throw, the variation due to the increasing wetness of the ball is a validity problem. Scores in this case are increased for those near the beginning of the alphabet and decreased for those near the end. The validity of the baseball throw scores is lessened because the scores reflect not only baseball throwing prowess but alphabetical order as well. This is an instance of systematic error that affects the validity of the measurement.

Reliability is concerned with how consistently we are measuring whatever we are measuring. It is not concerned with whether we are measuring what we intend to measure: that is the validity question. It is possible for a measuring instrument to be reliable without being valid. However, it cannot be valid unless it is first reliable. For example, someone could decide to measure intelligence by determining the circumference of the head. The measures might be very consistent from time to time (reliable), but this method would not be considered a valid measure of intelligence since circumference of the head does not correlate with any other criteria of intelligence nor is it predicted by any theory of intelligence.

Reliability is affected by random errors, which are any factors that will result in discrepancies between scores in repeated administrations of a measuring instrument.

Random errors arise from a number of sources. Errors may be inherent in the instrument itself. For example, if a test is very short, those subjects who happen to know the few answers required will get higher scores than they deserve, whereas those who do not know those few answers get lower scores than they deserve. For example, if a test is given to assess how well students know the capitals of the fifty states, but only five questions are asked, it is possible that a student who knows only ten capitals could get all five correct, whereas a student who knows forty could get none correct. In a short test luck is more of a factor than it is in a long test. If a test is so easy that everyone knows most of the answers, the subjects' relative scores again depend upon only a few questions and luck is a major factor. If questions are ambiguous, "lucky" subjects respond in the way the examiner intended, whereas "unlucky" subjects respond in another equally correct manner, but their answers are scored as incorrect. The scoring procedure also affects reliability. Precise scoring procedures enhance reliability, whereas vague scoring procedures depress it.

Errors may be inherent in the administration of the instrument. An inexperienced person may depart from standardized procedures in administering or scoring the test. Testing conditions such as light, heat, and ventilation may affect performance. Instructions for taking the test may be ambiguous.

There is also pupil error. That is, fluctuations in motivation, interest, fatigue, physical condition, anxiety, and other mental and emotional factors may seriously affect the test results. A pupil breaking a pencil point on a timed test would increase the error component in the results.

EQUATIONS FOR RELIABILITY

It is generally accepted that all measurements of human qualities contain some error. Reliability procedures are concerned with determining the degree of inconsistency in scores due to random error.

When one administers a test to a student, one secures a score, which can be called the *observed score*. If one had tested this student on some other occasion with the same instrument, one probably would not have obtained exactly the same observed score. The observed score contains an error of measurement. Therefore, one concludes that every test score consists of two components, the *true score* plus some error of measurement. As noted above, this error component may be due to any one, or a combination, of a number of factors associated with variations within the subject from time to time or with the administration of the test to that subject.

The reliability of a test is expressed mathematically as the best estimate of what proportion of the total variance of scores on the test is true variance. As explained in chapter 5, variance is an index of the spread of a set of scores. If we administer a test to a group of students, some of the spread (variance) is due to true differences among the group and some of the spread (variance) is due to errors of measurement.

The idea of error component and true component in a single test score may be represented mathematically by formula (8.1).

$$X = t + e \qquad\qquad (8.1)$$

where
X = the observed score
t = the true component
e = the error component

The true component may be defined as the score an individual would make under conditions in which a perfect measuring device is used. The error component can be either positive or negative. If it is positive, the individual's true score will be overestimated by the observed score; if it is negative, the person's true score will be underestimated. Since it is assumed that an error of measurement is just as likely to be positive as it is to be negative, then it can be concluded that the sum of the errors and the mean of the errors would both be zero if the same measuring instrument or an equivalent form of the instrument were administered an infinite number of times to a subject. Under these conditions, the true component would be defined as the individual's mean score on an infinite number of measurements. The true score is a theoretical concept, since an infinite number of administrations of a test to the same subject is not feasible.

In the usual research situation the investigator has one measure on each of a group of subjects. In other words, the researcher has a single set of test scores to consider. Each observed score has a true score component and an error score component. It has been shown mathematically that the variance of the observed scores of a large group of subjects (σ_x^2) is equal to the variance of their true scores (σ_t^2) plus the variance of their errors of measurement (σ_e^2) or

$$\sigma_x^2 = \sigma_t^2 + \sigma_e^2 \tag{8.2}$$

Reliability may be defined theoretically as the ratio of the true-score variance to the observed-score variance in a set of scores. That is, reliability is equal to

$$r_{xx} = \frac{\sigma_t^2}{\sigma_x^2} \tag{8.3}$$

where
r_{xx} = the reliability of the test
σ_t^2 = the variance of the true scores
σ_x^2 = the variance of the observed scores

Reliability is the proportion of the variance in the observed scores that is free of error. This notion can be expressed in the following formula derived from formulas (8.2) and (8.3).

$$r_{xx} = 1 - \frac{\sigma_e^2}{\sigma_x^2} \tag{8.4}$$

The *coefficient of reliability* (r_{xx}) can range from 1, when there is no error in the measurement, to 0, when the measurement is all error. (When there is no error in the measurement, σ_e^2 in the preceding equation is zero and $r_{xx} = 1$. If measurement is all error, $\sigma_e^2 = \sigma_x^2$ and $r_{xx} = 0$) This degree of error is indicated by the degree of departure of the correlation coefficient from 1.00. Thus, to the extent that the reliability coefficient is depressed below 1.00, a measuring instrument has error and low reliability. Conversely, if the reliability coefficient is near 1.00, the instrument has high reliability.

APPROACHES TO RELIABILITY

A test is reliable to the extent that the scores made by an individual remain nearly the same in repeated measurements. There are two approaches to expressing the reliability of a set of measurements.

1. One approach indicates the amount of variation to be expected within a set of repeated measurements of a *single* individual. If it were possible to weigh an individual 200 times, we would get a frequency distribution of scores to represent his or her weight. This frequency distribution would have an average value, which we could consider the "true" weight. It would also have a standard deviation, indicating the spread. This standard deviation is called the *standard error of measurement* since it is the standard deviation of the "errors" of measuring the weight for one person. With psychological or educational data, we do not often make repeated measurements on an individual. But if we have a pair of measurements for each individual, we can estimate what the variation of scores would have been if we had made repeated measurements.

2. Reliability of measurement also tells the extent to which each individual maintains the same relative position in the group. The person who scores highest on a test today should also be one of the highest scorers the next time the test is given. Each person in the group should stay in the same position. We can compute a coefficient of correlation between two adminstrations of the same test to determine the extent to which individuals maintain the same relative position. This coefficient is called a reliability coefficient (r_{xx}). Thus, reliability of a measure is indicated by a low standard error of measurement or by a high reliability coefficient.

THE RELIABILITY INDICES

Reliability can be estimated by correlating the scores obtained by the same individuals on different occasions or with different sets of equivalent items. These procedures require two administrations of a test. Other procedures either artificially split one test into two parts or determine the internal consistency of the test.

Test-Retest Reliability

An obvious way to estimate the reliability of a test is to administer it to the same group of individuals on two occasions and correlate the paired scores. The correlation coefficient obtained by this procedure is called a *test-retest reliability coefficient*. For example, a physical fitness test may be given to a class during one week and the same test given again the following week. If the test is reliable, each individual's relative position on the second administration of the test will be near his or her relative position on the first administration of the test. The reliability coefficient (r_{xx}) will be near +1.00. Any change in relative position from one occasion to the next is considered as error. If the test contains considerable error, the r_{xx} will be nearer zero. As explained earlier, a reliability coefficient is an estimate of the proportion of observed variance in test scores that is true variance. The difference between the value of the reliability coefficient and +1.00 is an unbiased estimate of the proportion of error variance in a test. For example, a test-retest reliability of .80 on the physical fitness test indicates that our best estimate is that 80 percent of the observed variance is true variance and 20 percent is error variance.

The test-retest reliability coefficient, because it is indicative of the consistency of subjects' scores over time, is sometimes referred to as a coefficient of stability. It tells us whether we can generalize from the score a person receives on one occasion to a score that person would receive if the test had been given at a different time.

A test-retest coefficient assumes that the characteristic being measured by the test is stable over time, so any change in scores from one time to another is due to random error. The error may be due to the condition of the subjects themselves or to testing conditions. The test-retest coefficient also assumes that there is no practice effect or memory effect. For example, students may learn something just from taking a test and thus will react differently on the second taking of the test. These practice effects from the first testing will not likely be the same across all students, thus lowering the reliability estimate. If the interval of time is short, there may also be a memory effect. That is, students may mark a question the same way they had previously just because they remember marking it that way the first time. This memory effect tends to inflate the reliability estimate. The memory effect can be controlled somewhat by increasing the time between the first test and the retest. On the other hand, if the time between testings is too long, differential learning may be a problem. That is, students will learn different amounts during the interval, which would affect the reliability coefficient.

Because of the problems discussed above, the test-retest procedure is not usually appropriate for tests in the cognitive domain. The use of this procedure in schools is largely restricted to measures of physical fitness and athletic prowess.

Equivalent-Forms Reliability

The equivalent-forms technique of estimating reliability, which is also referred to as the alternate- or parallel-forms technique, is used when it is probable that subjects will recall their responses to the test items. Here, rather than correlating the results of two administrations of the same test to the same group, one correlates the results of equivalent forms of the test administered to the same individuals. If the two forms are administered at essentially the same time (in immediate succession), the resulting reliability coefficient is called the *coefficient of equivalence*. This measure reflects variations in performance from one specific set of items to another. It indicates whether we can generalize a student's score to what the student would receive if another form of the same test had been given. The question is: To what extent does the student's performance depend upon the particular set of items used in the test?

If subjects are tested with one form on one occasion and with another form on a second occasion and their scores on the two forms are correlated, the resulting coefficient is called the *coefficient of stability and equivalence*. This coefficient reflects two aspects of test reliability: variations in performance from one time to another as well as variations from one form of the test to another. This is the most demanding and the most rigorous measure available for determining the reliability of a test.

Designing alternate forms of a test that are truly equivalent is the major problem with this technique of estimating reliability. If this is not successfully achieved, then the variation in scores from one form to another could not be considered as error variance. Equivalent forms of a test are independently constructed tests that must meet the same specifications; that is, they must have the same number of items, form, instructions, time limits, format, content, range, and level of difficulty, but the actual questions are not the same. Ideally one should have pairs of equivalent items and assign one of each pair to each form. The distribution of the test scores must also be similar.

The equivalent-forms technique is recommended when one wishes to avoid the problem of recall or practice effect and in cases when one has available a large number of test items from which to select equivalent samples. It is generally considered that the equivalent-forms procedure provides the best estimate of the reliability of academic and psychological measures.

Split-Half Reliability

It is possible to get a measure of reliability from a single administration of one form of a test by using split-half procedures. The test is administered to a group of subjects and later the items are divided into two comparable halves. Scores are obtained for each individual on the comparable halves and a coefficient of correlation calculated for the two scores. If each subject has a very similar position on the two sections, the test has high reliability. If there is little consistency in positions, the reliability is low. This method requires only one form of a test, there is no time lag involved, and the same physical and mental influences will be operating on the subjects as they take the two sections.

A problem with this method is in splitting the test to obtain two comparable halves. If, through item analysis, one establishes the difficulty level of each item, one can place each item into one of the two halves on the basis of equivalent difficulty and similarity of content. The most common procedure, however, is to correlate the scores on the odd-numbered items of the test with the scores on the even-numbered items.

The correlation coefficient computed between the two halves will systematically underestimate the reliability of the entire test. Longer tests are more reliable than shorter tests if everything else is equal. Therefore, the correlation between the odd 50 and even 50 items on a 100-item test is a reliability estimate for a 50-item test, not a 100-item test. To transform the split-half correlation into an appropriate reliability estimate for the entire test, the Spearman-Brown prophecy formula is employed:

$$r_{xx} = \frac{2r_{\frac{1}{2}\frac{1}{2}}}{1 + r_{\frac{1}{2}\frac{1}{2}}} \tag{8.5}$$

where
r_{xx} = the estimated reliability of the entire test
$r_{\frac{1}{2}\frac{1}{2}}$ = the Pearson r correlation between the two halves

For example, if we find a correlation coefficient of .65 between two halves of a test, the estimated reliability of the entire test, using the Spearman-Brown formula, would be

$$r_{xx} = \frac{(2)(.65)}{1 + .65} = .79$$

The Spearman-Brown procedure is based on the assumption that the two halves are parallel. As this assumption is seldom correct, in practice the split-half technique with the Spearman-Brown correction tends to overestimate the reliability that would be obtained if test-retest or equivalent-forms procedures are used. This should be borne in mind when evaluating the reliabilities of competing tests.

Split-half reliability is an appropriate technique to use when time-to-time fluctuation in estimating reliability is to be avoided and when the test is relatively long. For short tests the other techniques, such as test-retest or equivalent forms, are more appropriate.

The split-half procedure is not appropriate to use with speed tests since it yields spuriously high coefficients of equivalence in such tests. A speed test is one that purposefully includes easy items so that the scores are mainly dependent upon the speed with which subjects can respond. Errors are minor; most of the items are correct up to the point where time is called. If a student responds to 50 items, his split-half score is likely to be 25–25; if another student marks 60 items, his split-half score is likely to be 30–30, and so on. Since individuals' scores on odd- and even-numbered items are very nearly identical, within-individual variation is minimized and the correlation between the halves would be nearly perfect. Thus other procedures are recommended for use with speed tests.

A split-half reliability coefficient is interpreted like a coefficient of equivalence since it reflects fluctuations from one item sample to another. However, the split-half coefficient is also referred to as a *coefficient of internal consistency* since the two equivalent forms are contained within a single test.

Rationale Equivalence

Several formulas have been developed for estimating the reliability of a test without splitting the test and employing correlational procedures. From the theoretical definition of reliability (σ_t^2/σ_x^2) these procedures estimate reliability through determining how all items on a single test relate to all other items and to the test as a whole. Among these procedures are the Cronbach Alpha, the Hoyt analysis of variance technique, and the Kuder-Richardson formulas 20 and 21.[11] The most convenient of these is the Kuder-Richardson formula 21:

$$r_{xx} = \frac{K\sigma_x^2 - \bar{X}(K - \bar{X})}{\sigma_x^2(K - 1)} \tag{8.6}$$

where

r_{xx} = the reliability of the whole test
K = the number of items in the test
σ_x^2 = the variance of the scores
$\bar{X}$ = the mean of the scores

[11]See Julian C. Stanley, ''Reliability,'' in Robert L. Thorndike, ed., *Educational Measurement,* 2nd ed. (Washington D.C.: American Council on Education, 1971), pp. 356–442.

This method is by far the least time-consuming of all the reliability estimation procedures. It involves only one administration of a test and employs only easily available information. As such, it can be recommended to teachers for classroom use.

For example, suppose a teacher has administered a 50-item test to a class and has computed the mean as 40 and the standard deviation as 6. Applying formula (8.4) the reliability could be estimated as follows:

$$r_{xx} = \frac{(50)6^2 - 40(50 - 40)}{6^2(50 - 1)} = \frac{1800 - 400}{1764} = .79$$

Since the Kuder-Richardson procedures stress the equivalence of all the items in a test, they are especially appropriate when the intention of the test is to measure a single trait. For a test designed to measure several traits, the Kuder-Richardson reliability estimate will usually be lower than reliability estimates based on a correlational procedure.

It has been shown through deductive reasoning that the Kuder-Richardson reliability for any test is mathematically equivalent to the mean of the split-half reliability estimates computed for every possible way of splitting the test in half. This fact helps explain the relationship between the two procedures. If a test is of uniform difficulty and is measuring a single trait, any one way of splitting that test in half is as likely as any other to yield similar half scores. Therefore the Spearman-Brown and Kuder-Richardson methods will yield similar estimates. If a test has items of varying difficulty and is measuring various traits, the Kuder-Richardson estimate is expected to be lower than the split-half estimate. For example, suppose a secretarial skills test samples typing, shorthand, spelling, and English grammar skills. In applying the split-half method the test maker would assign equal numbers of items from each subtest to each half of the test. If the test is doing a good job of measuring this combination of skills, the split-half reliability will be high. The Kuder-Richardson method, which assesses the extent to which all the items are equivalent to one another, would yield a considerably lower reliability estimate.

Interpretation of Reliability Coefficient

The interpretation of a reliability coefficient should be based on a number of considerations. There are certain factors that affect reliability coefficients and unless these factors are taken into account, any interpretation of reliability will be superficial.

The reliability of a test is in part a function of the length of the test. The longer the test, the greater its reliability. A test usually consists of a number of sample items, which are, theoretically, drawn from a universe of test items. We know from what we have studied about sampling that the greater the sample size, the more representative it is expected to be of the population from which it is drawn. This is true also of tests. If it were possible to use the entire universe of items, the score of a person who takes the test would be his true score. A theoretical universe of items consists of an infinite number of questions and is not a practical possibility. One therefore constructs a test that is a sample from such a theoretical universe. The greater the length of this test (that is, the greater the number of items included in the test), the more representative it should be of the true scores of the persons who take it. Since reliability is the extent to which a test represents the true scores of individuals, the longer the test, the greater its reliability, provided that all the items in the test belong in the universe of items.

Reliability is in part a function of group heterogeneity. The reliability coefficient increases as the spread or heterogeneity of the subjects who take the test increases. Conversely, the more homogeneous the group is with respect to the trait being measured, the lower will be the reliability coefficient. One explanation of reliability is that it is the extent to which we can place individuals, relative to others in their groups, according to certain traits and qualities. Such placement is easier when one is dealing with measures that fall in a large range rather than those that fall in a small range. It does not take a sensitive device to determine the placement of children in a distribution according to their weights when the age range of these children is from 5 to 15. In fact, this placement is possible with some degree of accuracy even without using any measuring device. It does take a sensitive device, however, to carry out the same placement if all those who are to be compared and placed in the distribution are five years old. Thus the heterogeneity of the group with whom a measuring instrument is used is a factor that affects the reliability of that instrument. The more heterogeneous the group used in the reliability study, the higher the reliability coefficient.

This fact should be kept in mind when you are selecting a standardized test. The publisher may report a high reliability coefficient based on a sample with a wide range of ability. However, when the test is used with a group having a much narrower range of ability, the reliability will be lower.

The reliability of a test is in part a function of the ability of the individuals who take that test. A test may be reliable at one level of ability but unreliable at another level. The questions in a test might be difficult and beyond the ability level of those who take it or the questions might, on the other hand, be easy for the majority of the subjects. This difficulty level affects the reliability of the test. When a test is difficult, the subjects are guessing on most of the questions and a low reliability coefficient will result. When it is easy, all subjects have correct responses on most of the items, and only a few more difficult items are discriminating among subjects. Again we would expect a low reliability.

There is no simple rule by which one can determine how difficult, or how easy, a test should be. It depends on the type of test, the purpose, and the population for which it is being constructed.

Reliability is in part a function of the specific technique used for its estimation. Different procedures for estimating the reliability of tests result in different coefficients of reliability. The equivalent-forms technique gives a lower estimation of reliability than either test-retest or split-half procedures because in the equivalent-forms technique form-to-form as well as time-to-time fluctuation is present. The split-half method, on the other hand, results in higher reliability coefficients than do its alternatives because in most tests some degree of speed is involved and to

that extent the reliability coefficient is overestimated. Thus, in evaluating the reliability of a test, one would give preference to a test whose reliability coefficient has
been estimated by the equivalent-forms technique, rather than other techniques,
when the reported reliabilities are similar. The same generalization would be true
when comparing test-retest reliability with split-half. The same coefficient is more
satisfactory if it results from the test-retest procedure rather than from the split-half
method.

Reliability is in part a function of the nature of the variable being measured.
Some variables of interest to researchers yield consistent measures more often than
do other variables. For instance, most established tests of academic achievement
have quite high reliabilities, whereas tests of personality variables have only moderate reliabilities.

What is the minimum reliability that is acceptable for an instrument? Perhaps the
best response to this question is that a good reliability is one that is as good as or
better than the reliability of competing measures. A spelling achievement test with a
reliability of .80 is unsatisfactory if competing tests have reliability coefficients of
.90 or better. A coefficient of .80 for a test of creativity would be judged excellent if
other tests of the same construct have reliabilities of .60 or less.

STANDARD ERROR OF MEASUREMENT

As explained earlier in this chapter, the reliability, stability, or dependability of a
test may also be expressed in terms of the standard error of measurement. The
standard error of measurement provides an estimate of the range of variation in a set
of repeated measurements of the same thing. Returning to our example of the
baseball throw, we would expect with repeated administration, by chance, to obtain
a number of different scores for the same individual. We would have a frequency
distribution of scores. This frequency distribution has a mean, which is the best
approximation of the true score. The distribution also has a standard deviation,
indicating the extent of the variation in the scores. Since this standard deviation is
the standard deviation of the errors of measurement, it is called the standard error of
measurement. If one were to construct a frequency polygon showing this distribution of scores, its shape would approximate that of the normal curve. Measurement
errors are normally distributed; there may be many small errors but few large ones.
The standard deviation of this distribution of error (standard error of measurement,
σ_M) would give us an estimate of how frequently errors of a given size might be
expected to occur when the test is used.

In many situations, one does not have repeated measures, but one can get an
estimate of the standard error of measurement by using the reliability coefficient:

$$\sigma_M = \sigma_x \sqrt{1 - r_{xx}} \tag{8.7}$$

where
σ_M = the standard error of measurement
σ_X = the standard deviation of test scores
r_{xx} = the reliability coefficient

If an intelligence test has a reliability coefficient of .96 and a standard deviation of 15, then $\sigma_M = 15\sqrt{1 - .96} = 15\sqrt{.04} = 3$.

The standard error of measurement can be interpreted like any other measure of standard deviation. That is, if it can be assumed that the errors of measurement are normally distributed about a given score and equally distributed throughout the score range, one can say that there are about two chances in three that an individual's true score lies in the range of his observed score $\pm 1\sigma_M$. For example, if a subject has an observed score of 110 on the intelligence test where the standard error of measurement is 3, one could infer at the 68 percent confidence level that the subject's true score lies somewhere between 107 and 113. Or to state it differently, if the subject could be retested on this intelligence test a number of times, one could expect in about two-thirds of the retests a score between 107 and 113, and a score higher than 116 or lower than 104 only about five times in a hundred.

Thus one looks for a low standard error of measurement or a high reliability coefficient as indications of a test's reliability.

Summary

The multiplicity of measuring instruments available to the researcher require the use of criteria for the evaluation of these instruments. The two most important criteria for measuring devices are validity and reliability.

Validity is more significant, and also more difficult to determine, than reliability. To measure a given trait, one must define that trait operationally—that is, in terms of observable phenomena. One then measures the observable phenomena and draws conclusions about the unobservable trait. There is always the possibility that one is not measuring what one intends to measure at all. This is the problem of validity: To what extent are we measuring what we intend to measure? Both logical and empirical approaches are employed in determining validity. Validity can be analyzed into content, criterion-related, and construct components, each of which is applicable to certain types of tests.

It can be seen that each of the three types of validity is concerned with a different aspect of the general question: Does the test measure what it is supposed to measure?

The content-validity question is, How well does the content of the test sample the subject matter domain about which conclusions are to be drawn?

The criterion-related question is, With what criteria do scores on the test correlate and how well do they correlate? What kind of performance can be predicted from this test?

The construct-validity questions are, What psychological or educational constructs does the test measure? and What is the relationship between the content and the rationale of the test?

It is important to know what use is to be made of test scores. A test may be valid for one use but invalid for other uses. An IQ test may be a valid measure of scholastic aptitude but not valid as a measure of art aptitude.

We must also ask, How consistently does the test measure whatever it does measure? This is the problem of reliability. No test can have validity unless it measures accurately and consistently—that is, unless it is reliable. Reliability refers to the extent to which the test is consistent in measuring whatever it does measure. Specifically, reliability refers to the extent to which an individual remains nearly the same in repeated measurements as indicated by a high reliability coefficient or by a low standard error of measurement. Reliability coefficients can be computed in various ways, depending upon the source of error being considered. The reliability coefficient shows the extent to which random errors of measurement influence scores on the test. The standard error of measurement enables us to employ the normal curve to estimate the limits within which a subject's true score can be expected to lie.

Exercises

1. Compare *validity* and *reliability* with respect to:
   a. the meaning of each concept
   b. the relative importance of each concept
   c. the extent to which one depends on the other
2. Explain the statement: A measuring device may be reliable without being valid, but it cannot be valid without being reliable.
3. How would you propose to validate a new scholastic aptitude test that had been developed for use with high school seniors?
4. You have been asked to validate an instrument designed to measure a student's academic self-concept, that is, the way he sees himself as a student. How would you go about establishing the validity of this instrument?
5. Which of the three types of validity is indicated in each situation?
   a. The high school language proficiency test scores of college dropouts and college persisters are compared in order to determine whether the test data correlate with the subjects' college status.
   b. A new scholastic aptitude test is found to have a correlation of .93 with the SAT that has been used to predict college success.
   c. A new intelligence test has been developed. The author argues that the mental processes required by the test are congruent with the Z theory of intelligence. Furthermore, he shows that the average score on the test increases with each year of age.
   d. A teacher carefully examines a standardized achievement test to see if it covers the knowledge and skills that are emphasized in the class.
   e. The mean difference between the rankings of members of the Ku Klux Klan and members of the Americans for Democratic Action on the liberalism scale was found to be highly significant.
   f. A mathematics test is judged by a group of teachers to be an adequate and representative sample of the universe of test items.

6. Identify the type of procedure for estimating reliability that is illustrated in each of the following:
   a. The same test was given twice to a certain group. The correlation between the scores on the two administrations of the test was .90.
   b. The group's scores on the odd items of a test were correlated with their scores on the even items of the same test: $r_{xx} = .95$.
   c. Parallel forms of the test were administered after one month and results of the two administrations were correlated: $r_{xx} = .85$.
   d. The variance, the mean, and the number of items are used to estimate reliability.
7. How would you account for the differences in the reliability coefficients in question 6 assuming that the groups tested were the same?
8. How would you validate a reading readiness test?
9. What can one do to increase reliability when constructing a test?
10. Indicate the type of validity that would be most important for the following types of tests:
    a. a classroom spelling test
    b. an instrument to measure achievement motivation
    c. a measure designed to identify potential dropouts
11. Explain how a mathematics test could have high content validity in one mathematics class and low content validity in another mathematics class.
12. Criticize the following statement: The reliability of the intelligence test is .90. Therefore one can assume that the test is really measuring intelligence.
13. Determine the standard error of measurement for a test with a standard deviation of 16 and a reliability coefficient of $r_{xx} = .84$. How would you interpret this standard error of measurement?
14. Select a standardized achievement test that you might use in a research study and obtain the necessary validity data on this test. (You may use Buros and the manual that accompanies the test you select.)
15. Check the test manual for the achievement test being used in your school. What type of reliability data is reported there?

Answers

1. Validity refers to the extent to which an instrument measures what it is designed to measure. Reliability is the extent to which an instrument is consistent in measuring. Validity is considered a more important aspect than reliability because lack of validity implies lack of meaning. However, an instrument cannot be valid without first being reliable.
2. A measure may give consistent scores when made repeatedly on a given group of subjects, yet may bear no relationship to other accepted measures of the construct or not be able to predict behavior associated with the construct. Scores on a test with zero reliability are entirely random and therefore cannot correlate with any criterion.
3. To determine the construct validity, one first must define what is meant by *aptitude*. If one wishes to measure general academic ability, then content validity could be determined by examining the test items for representativeness. Do they assess the basic academic skills of reading, spelling, math, etc.? Criterion-related validity would be assessed by the correlation coefficients between the test scores and senior-year GPA, freshman-college GPA, and other criteria. Correlation with other validated aptitude test scores could also be done.

4. The items of the scale or questionnaire would need to cover aspects of the student behavior that would logically be a part of the construct, academic self-construct (e.g., I intend to go to college). Criterion measures could be personal interviews with students or independent assessment by teachers. Assuming academic self-concept is related to achievement, self-concept scores could be correlated with GPA and/or achievement test scores.

5. a. criterion-related
    b. criterion-related
    c. construct
    d. content
    e. construct
    f. content

6. a. test-retest reliability
    b. split-half reliability
    c. equivalent-forms reliability
    d. rational equivalence (Kuder-Richardson formula 21)

7. Split-half reliabilities tend to be higher than test-retest reliabilities because subject variability due to maturation, increase in testing skill, and other random factors are less. Equivalent-forms reliability is lower than same-test reliability because (a) it is impossible to construct exactly equivalent forms and (b) there is an added source of variability when nonidentical forms are used. The rational equivalence reliability will be depressed if the test is not homogeneous.

8. One would first identify which specific skills (e.g., letter recognition, left-to-right orientation) comprise reading readiness and then determine if the test incorporated these skills in appropriate proportions. When subjects who have taken the test have begun their reading programs, one would determine how scores on the test and on subtests correlate with reading test scores, teachers' ratings, and other criteria.

9. Rewriting ambiguous items and clarifying instructions will increase reliability. Making a test longer by including additional items drawn from the same universe increases reliability, as does testing on a more heterogeneous group.

10. a. content
    b. construct
    c. criterion-related

11. A mathematics test that covered only computation would have little validity in a class that stressed concepts and reasoning. If content and emphasis of a different class do match the content and emphasis of the test, the test will have high validity in that class.

12. A test can be reliable without measuring what it intends to measure. To determine validity, one needs to look at content, constructs, and relations with other measures of the same construct as well as relations with measures of behavior assumed to be correlated with the construct.

13. By the formula (8.5):

$$\sigma_M = \sigma_x \sqrt{1 - r_{xx}}$$
$$= 16\sqrt{1 - .84} = (16)(.4) = 6.4$$

One interprets the standard error of measurement as a standard deviation. Thus one can say that there are two chances in three that the individual's true score will fall in the range of the actual score ± 6.4 score points from the observed score.

Part

5

Research
Methods

Experimental Research in Education

It is now appropriate to focus on the structure of research studies designed for hypothesis testing. The experiment is generally regarded as the most sophisticated research method for testing hypotheses. This method begins with a question concerning the relationship between two or more variables. At the same time, the researcher advances one or more hypotheses stating the nature of the expected relationship. The experiment is the event planned and carried out by the researcher to gather evidence relevant to the hypotheses. The experimenter deliberately and systematically introduces changes into natural phenomena and then observes the consequences of those changes. The hypotheses express expectations as to the findings that will result from the changes that are introduced. In conducting an experiment, the researcher devotes great care to the manipulation and control of variables and to the observation and measurement of results. It is through such a research method that the researcher can obtain the most convincing evidence of the effect that one variable has on another.

Early scientists learned the value of observation in the study of our environment but soon realized that nature's complexity could not be understood through simple observation of its many events. They found that events occurring in their "natural" state were often so complicated by irrelevant factors that the operation of the factor they wished to study was obscured. The difficulty was solved by bringing the event into the laboratory and controlling the conditions under which it occurred so that the irrelevant factors were eliminated. There scientists could vary the specific factors in which they were interested and gather data under conditions created specifically for that purpose. In other words, they began to perform experiments.

Because the application of experimental methods was fruitful in the investigation of the physical world, these methods were applied to other fields. The nineteenth century saw these methods introduced into the biological sciences, and great advances were made in zoology, physiology, and medicine. Toward the end of the nineteenth century, scholars began to apply the same methods to psychological problems, thus beginning experimental psychology. In the 1890s the experimental method was first used to study an educational problem. Rice's investigation of spelling achievement in the schools marks the first attempt at educational field experimentation.[1] Thorndike and other early investigators extended the experimental method to education.[2]

In its simplest form an experiment has three characteristics: (1) an independent variable is manipulated; (2) all other variables except the independent variable are

---

[1]Joseph M. Rice, "The Futility of the Spelling Grind," *Forum,* 23 (April and June 1897):163–72, 409–19.

[2]Edward L. Thorndike, "Mental Discipline in High School Subjects," *Journal of Educational Psychology* 15 (1924):1–22, 83–98.

held constant; (3) the effect of the manipulation of the independent variable on the dependent variable is observed. Thus in an experiment the two variables of major interest are the independent variable and the dependent variable. The independent variable is manipulated or changed by the experimenter. The variable upon which the effects of the changes are observed is called the dependent variable, which is observed but not manipulated by the experimenter. The dependent variable is so named because its value is hypothesized to depend upon, and vary with, the value of the independent variable. For example, to examine the effect of different teaching methods upon achievement in reading, an investigator would manipulate method, the independent variable, by using different teaching methods in order to ascertain their effect upon achievement, the dependent variable.

We will illustrate an experiment in education by describing an investigation conducted at the college level. Note carefully the italicized terms that appear in the outline since these terms will be used throughout our discussion of experimental research.

Lane reported a study that investigated the effect of the type of supplemental materials used in a college mathematics class taught by closed-circuit television. The experiment compared the use of a programmed booklet with two other techniques for presenting supplemental material in the television-taught class.[3]

Hypothesis. The achievement of students who use programmed supplemental materials will be superior to the achievement of students who use nonprogrammed supplemental materials.

Or, stated in a null form: The achievement of students who use programmed supplemental materials will not differ from the achievement of students using non-programmed supplemental materials.

Sample. All students enrolled in the course, Fundamental Principles of Mathematics, at George Peabody College for Teachers were used.

Independent variable. The independent variable was the type of supplemental material used in the mathematics class.

Dependent variable. The dependent variable was the score on a mathematics achievement test administered at the end of the study.

Controls. Subjects were *randomly* assigned to three groups, which differed only in the type of supplemental material used. To eliminate teacher differences, the experimenter was responsible for all three of the supplementary methods. To insure a uniform presentation of material, the assigned homework problems were selected prior to the experiment and a complete set of solutions was prepared. These notes were used in the presentation to each of the three experimental groups. An analysis of covariance was used to analyze the achievement test scores.

Procedure. The experiment used a simple randomized design with three treatment groups. Each group in a separate room viewed the same televised lecture during the first half of each class period. This lecture was developmental in nature and based on a common reading assignment from the required textbook. During the

[3]Bennie R. Lane, ''An Experiment with Programmed Instruction as a Supplement to Teaching College Mathematics by Closed-Circuit Television,'' *Mathematics Teacher* 57 (October 1964):395–97.

second half of the period, each group received instruction based on assigned homework problems.

Group I viewed a kinescope film of the solutions of the homework exercises. The students were instructed to compare their homework with the television explanation to verify their solutions or to obtain necessary assistance. Some review topics were discussed but no new developmental material was presented.

Group II participated in a classroom help session in which the experimenter answered questions pertaining to the assigned exercises. The students assisted the teacher in the solution of problems as he worked at the chalkboard. Other pertinent questions were answered, but there was no presentation of new material.

Group III studied a programmed booklet prepared by the experimenter and based on the assigned exercises. It was suggested that the students compare their solutions of the problems with those in the programmed material. The last section of each lesson summarized concepts presented in the lecture, but included no new material.

After twelve class meetings of experimental instruction, the students were given an achievement test. The design of the study is summarized as follows:

	Group	Independent Variable	Dependent Variable
(R)	I	kinescope film	achievement test
(R)	II	classroom discussion	achievement test
(R)	III	programmed booklet	achievement test

Results. Analysis of covariance was used to test the significance of the differences in the means of the achievement test scores. The results indicated significant differences in the mean achievement of the three groups. In a comparison of Group III with Group I and with Group II, the mean achievement of Group III was significantly higher at the .05 level in each case. The mean achievement of Group I and Group II did not differ significantly.

Conclusions. (1) The programmed material provided a supplement to televised instruction that was more effective than either of the other two supplementary methods. (2) the classroom discussion and the televised problem session methods appeared to be equally effective.

From the description one can see the major aspects of an experiment: (a) a question for which the experimenter seeks an answer—a question concerned with the relationship between two variables; (b) hypotheses as to the nature of the relationship between the two variables; (c) introduction of the experimental conditions and measurement; (d) analysis of data so that the researcher can decide whether or not there is a relationship between the variables.

Experiments in education may be conducted in either a laboratory or in a field situation. The control of extraneous variables, which is so crucial to the experimental method, can usually be handled most adequately in the laboratory. In a laboratory experimenters can control the environment in such a way that the independent variables of interest can be isolated. They can thus be very specific in the operational definition of variables. For these reasons laboratory experiments can be replicated with a high degree of precision.

Field experiments can be conducted in classrooms, playgrounds, interest club meetings, or other natural settings. The experimenter controls the extraneous variables as much as possible while manipulating the independent variable or variables, but in a field experiment control is inevitably less complete. However, field experiments have certain advantages. First, experimental variables can be much stronger in field experiments than in laboratory experiments. It is difficult to implement a treatment in a laboratory situation for more than a short period of time, whereas a field experiment can encompass daily sessions for an entire school year. Second, because field experiments are conducted in a more realistic setting, their results are more likely to provide solutions to the actual daily problems of educators.

Laboratory experiments are generally preferred for theoretical problems and field experiments for pragmatic problems. There are two general types of experimentation conducted under classroom conditions: (1) the *methods study,* in which two or more ways of doing something are compared in an unbiased fashion, and (2) *fundamental research,* the purpose of which is to derive general principles applicable beyond the immediate situation. Both types of classroom research are greatly needed.

Characteristics of Experimental Research

There are three essential ingredients with which the scientist is actively involved in the conduct of an experiment: control, manipulation, and observation.

CONTROL

Control is the essence of the experimental method. Without control it is impossible to evaluate unambiguously the effects of an independent variable. Let us examine briefly this concept of control in experimentation.

Basically the experimental method of science rests upon two assumptions regarding variables: (1) If two situations are equal in every respect except for a factor that is added to or deleted from one of the situations, any difference appearing between the two situations can be attributed to that factor. This statement is called the *law of the single variable.*[4] (2) If two situations are not equal but it can be demonstrated that none of the variables is significant in producing the phenomenon under investigation, or if significant variables are made equal, any difference occurring between the two situations after the introducton of a new variable to one of the systems can be attributed to the new variable. This statement is called the *law of the only significant variable.*

[4]John Stuart Mill, *A System of Logic* (New York: Harper & Brothers, 1846), p. 224.

The purpose of control in an experiment is to arrange a situation in which the effect of variables can be investigated. The conditions underlying the law of the single variable are more likely to be fulfilled in the physical sciences than in education. Since educational research is concerned with human beings, there are always many variables present. To attempt to reduce educational problems to the operation of a single variable is not only unrealistic but perhaps even impossible. Fortunately such rigorous control is not absolutely essential since many aspects in which situations differ are irrelevant to the purpose of the study and thus can be ignored. It is sufficient to apply the law of the single *significant* independent variable. For example, in a study of the differential effects of two methods of teaching arithmetic, one would wish to have two groups of children who are identical in every respect except the way in which they are taught arithmetic. Since it is impossible to have two absolutely identical groups of children, the experimenter seeks to establish two groups that are as similar as possible in respect to those variables that are related to arithmetic achievement, such as reading ability, motivation, general intelligence, and the like. Other variables that are highly unlikely to be related to arithmetic, such as athletic ability, height, or color of hair, are ignored. Although the law of the single variable cannot be followed absolutely, the experimenter endeavors to approximate it as closely as possible in all relevant variables. Therefore in experimental studies in education we need procedures that permit us to compare groups on the basis of significant variables. A number of methods of control have been devised to make such comparisons possible.

Let us assume that we wish to test the hypothesis that children taught by the inductive method (Group A) show greater gains in learning scientific concepts than children taught by the deductive method (Group B). In other words, we wish to study the relationship between teaching method (independent variable) and the learning of scientific concepts (dependent variable). In order for us to draw a conclusion concerning the relationship of the independent variable and the dependent variable, we must control for the effects of any extraneous variables. An extraneous variable is a variable that is not related to the purpose of the study but may affect the dependent variable. *Control* is the term used to indicate an experimenter's procedures for eliminating the differential effects of all variables extraneous to the purpose of the study. The experimenter controls, for instance, when the groups are made comparable on extraneous variables that are related to the dependent variable. If a variable is known to be unrelated to the dependent variable, then it could not influence the dependent variable and we do not need to control for its effects.

In the experiment mentioned above, intelligence is a factor that certainly affects the learning of scientific concepts; therefore it would be considered an extraneous variable and must be controlled. Otherwise, if the children in Group A were more intelligent than those in Group B, the greater gains in learning by Group A could be attributed to intelligence and therefore we could not properly evaluate the effects of the teaching method on learning. In other words, intelligence has confounded the relationship between the variables in which we are interested. The term *confounding* refers to the "mixing" of the variables extraneous to the research problem with the independent variable(s) of the research study in such a way that their effects cannot be separated. It could not be clearly stated whether the relation found is (1) between the independent variable and the dependent variable of the study, or (2) between the extraneous variables and the dependent variable, or (3) a combination of (1) and (2). Confounding is eliminated by controlling for the effect of relevant extraneous variables.

Where there is no known relationship, as between the size of a student's shoes and his or her ability to learn science concepts, there would be no need for the experimenter to control for shoe size.

Our first efforts must be directed toward controlling for any relevant preexisting differences between the subjects used in an experiment. Only in this way can one be fairly confident that any postexperimental differences can be attributed to the conditions of the experiment rather than to preexisting subject differences. There are five basic procedures that are commonly used to increase equivalence among the groups that are to be exposed to the various experimental situations. These five procedures for controlling intersubject differences are (1) random assignment, (2) randomized matching, (3) homogeneous selection, (4) analysis of covariance, (5) use of subjects as their own controls.

CONTROLLING INTERSUBJECT DIFFERENCES

Random Assignment

Let us consider the experimenter's task. There is an available supply of subjects who for experimentation must be divided into two groups that will be treated differently and then compared. In assigning subjects to groups for the experiment, the experimenter needs a system that operates independently of personal judgment and of the characteristics of the subjects themselves. For example, the known high scorers must not all be assigned to Group A and the low scorers, to Group B. A system that satisfies these requirements is *random assignment*. Random assignment is the assignment of subjects to groups in such a way that, for any given placement, every member of the population has an equal probability of being assigned to any of the groups. The term *randomization* is often used as a synonym for random assignment.

To obtain randomized groups, the experimenter could number all the available subjects and then from a table of random numbers draw the needed number for the experimental group and the control group. A coin flip could then determine which of the two groups drawn is to be the experimental group and which is to be the control group.

When subjects have been randomly assigned to groups, the groups can be considered *statistically equivalent*. Statistically equivalent does not mean that the groups are absolutely equal, but it does mean that any difference between the groups is a function of chance alone and not a function of experimenter bias, subjects' choices, or any other factor. A subject with high intelligence is as likely to be assigned to the experimental group as to the control group. The same is true for a subject with low intelligence. For the entire sample, the effects of intelligence on the dependent variable will tend to balance or randomize out. In the same manner subjects' differences in political viewpoints, temperament, motivation, and other characteristics will tend to be approximately equally distributed between the experimental and control groups.

When random assignment has been employed, any pretreatment differences between groups are a function of chance alone. When this is the case, inferential statistics can be employed to determine how likely it is that posttreatment differences are due to chance alone.

Note that not only known extraneous variables, but also other relevant extraneous variables unknown to or unimagined by the experimenter, can be expected to randomize out.

Randomized Matching

An alternative procedure for assigning subjects to groups is to match individual subjects on as many extraneous variables as one thinks might affect the dependent variable and then to use some random procedure to assign the members of the matched pairs to the experimental conditions. If the groups are adequately matched on these variables, then there is reasonable assurance that any postexperimental differences can be attributed to the experimental treatment.

Although matching is a method for providing partial control of intersubject differences, there are several difficulties one may encounter. The first of these is to determine what variable or variables to use for matching. Variables such as IQ, MA, socioeconomic status (SES), age, sex, reading score, or pretest score may be used. The variables on which subjects are matched must be substantially correlated to the dependent variable or else the matching is useless. As a general rule, we suggest that unless the variable correlates .50 or higher with the dependent variable, it should not be employed for the matching procedure since it would do little to increase the precision of the study. Ideally we would like to match on two or more variables that correlate well with the dependent variable and do *not* correlate significantly with each other. However, when we try to match on more than two variables, it becomes almost impossible to find subjects who are well matched on these several variables. Subjects are lost because no match can be found for them.

Another question that arises is how closely to match the subjects on the variable(s). Matching closely increases the precision of the method but, at the same time, it also increases the number of subjects who cannot be matched. This, of course, reduces the sample size and introduces sampling bias into the study.

Procedures for Matching

The researcher must decide what matching procedure is feasible in each particular situation.

1. The usual method is to use a person-to-person procedure, in which an effort is

made to locate two persons from among the available subjects who score within the limits decided upon. For example, if the matching variable is IQ, then the researcher locates two subjects who are within, say, 5 points of each other on the IQ scale, and then randomly assigns one subject to the experimental group and the matching subject to the control group. It would not be too difficult to match subjects on just the IQ variable. But if sex and social class were also relevant variables, then it would become extremely difficult to find pairs who match on all three variables. Those subjects for whom no match can be found are lost to the experimenter.

2. Another matching procedure that is sometimes used is to match groups rather than individuals on the relevant variable. An effort is made to show that the two groups do not differ significantly, in terms of mean and standard deviation, on the matching variable. This method is often employed in a school situation where previously established groups must be used. For example, the experimenter may analyze intelligence test scores, reading scores, or pretest scores of the two groups and report that there is no significant difference in the means and standard deviations. The experimenter then randomly decides which is the experimental group and which is the control group. Matching groups is much less precise than individual matching. Furthermore, there is the problem of trying to locate groups that match on all the variables that may be correlated with the dependent variable of the study.

3. A third method of matching is to place all subjects in rank order on the basis of their scores on the matching variable. The first two subjects are selected from the rank order list (regardless of the actual difference in their scores) to constitute the first pair. One subject of this pair is then randomly assigned to the experimental group and the other, to the control group. The next two subjects on the list are selected, and again one is randomly assigned to the experimental group and the other, to the control group. This process is continued until all subjects have been assigned. It is somewhat simpler to match according to this procedure, but it is less precise than the person-to-person method. Note that randomized matching requires that the subjects be matched first and then randomly assigned to treatments. A study where subjects who are already experiencing one treatment are matched with subjects who are already experiencing another treatment cannot be classified as an experimental study. Such studies (discussed in chapter 10) where matching is present, but random assignment to groups is not present, can lead researchers to erroneous conclusions.

Homogeneous Selection

Another method that can be used to make groups comparable on an extraneous variable involves selecting samples that are as homogeneous as possible on that variable. If the experimenter suspects that age is a variable that might affect the dependent variable, only children of a particular age would be selected. By selecting only six-year-old children, for instance, the experimenter would control for the effects of age as an extraneous independent variable. Similarly, if intelligence is likely to be a variable affecting the dependent variable of the study, then subjects would be selected from children within a restricted range of IQ, say, 100–110. By this procedure the effects of IQ have been controlled. Then the experimenter randomly assigns individuals to groups from the resulting homogeneous population and can be confident that they were comparable on IQ. Beginning with a group that is homogeneous on the relevant variable eliminates the difficulty of trying to match subjects on that variable.

Although homogeneous selection is an effective way of controlling extraneous variables, it has the disadvantage of decreasing the extent to which the findings can be generalized to other situations. If a researcher investigates the effectiveness of a particular method with such a homogeneous sample, say, of children with average IQs the results could not be generalized to children of other IQ ranges. The effectiveness of the method with children of low intelligence or very high intelligence would not be known and the experiment would have to be repeated with subjects from different IQ strata.

As is the case with matching, a true experiment requires that the subjects be selected first and then assigned randomly to treatments.

Analysis of Covariance

Another form of control is the statistical method called analysis of covariance. Analysis of covariance is a method for analyzing differences between experimental groups on the dependent variable after taking into account any initial differences between the groups on pretest measures or on any other measures of relevant independent variables. Such a measure used for control is called a *covariate*.

Analysis of covariance is especially useful for educational research conducted in a school setting, where the researcher must use intact class groups. Let us assume that a researcher is interested in the effectiveness of a new method of teaching reading upon achievement in second grade reading. Subjects cannot be assigned to groups at random since the two second grade classes are already organized. Intelligence and previous reading ability are two extraneous variables that should be controlled in this experiment. Since the classes are not random samples, the researcher cannot assume that intelligence or reading ability are randomly distributed among the groups. In this case analysis of covariance makes it possible to provide partial control of these extraneous variables.

The experiment could proceed as planned and the dependent-variable measures, reading achievement scores at the end of the study, obtained. In the analysis of covariance, the dependent-variable scores are analyzed for significant differences, but the scores are adjusted for any initial differences in IQ or prior reading scores between the groups.

Analysis of covariance is a statistical method that partially controls extraneous variables that confound the relationship between the independent variable and the dependent variable. Analysis of covariance does have limitations and cannot be thought of as a substitute for random assignment. A discussion of these limitations is included in chapter 10. The actual computation involved in analysis of covariance is rather complex and is beyond the scope of this text. However, computer programs are now available for analysis of covariance, thus eliminating computational effort on the part of the researcher.

Use of Subjects as Their Own Controls

Still another procedure involves assigning the same subjects to all experimental conditions and then obtaining measurements of the subjects first under one experimental treatment and then under the other. The experimental treatment generally consists of selected values of an independent variable. For instance, the same subjects might be required to learn two different lists of nonsense syllables, one list with high association value and the other with low association value. The difference in learning time between the two lists is found for each subject and the average difference in learning time for all subjects then can be tested for significance.

This is an efficient method of control when feasible, but there are circumstances in which it cannot be used. In some types of studies, exposure to one experimental condition would make it impossible to use the subjects for the other experimental condition. We cannot teach children a spelling list one way and then erase their memory and teach it another way.

In the foregoing experiment, where one group of subjects was used to investigate the relative ease of learning high-association and low-association nonsense syllables, there could be a "learning to learn" effect, and thus whichever list appeared second would have an advantage over the first. Conversely, fatigue or interference effects might result in poorer performance on the second list. In this case, we would have a confounding-of-order effect and no reliable conclusions could be drawn. A more efficient procedure would involve a random division of the subjects into two groups; one group of the subjects would then be given one order and the second group, the other order.

CONTROLLING SITUATIONAL DIFFERENCES

In addition to intersubject differences, it is also necessary to control any extraneous variables that might operate in the experimental situation itself. If situational variables are not controlled in an experiment, one cannot be sure whether it is the independent variable or these incidental differences operating in the groups that is producing the difference in the dependent variable.

For instance, let us assume that an experimenter is interested in the effectiveness of a film in producing changes in attitude toward some issue. One group of children is selected at random from a classroom and sent off to see the film, leaving a comparable group in the classroom. Unknowingly, the experimenter may have set in motion a large number of forces. The children in the control group may be resentful, or feel rejected or inferior to the others. Any of these factors could have an effect on the outcome of the study. The difference that the experimenter wants to attribute to the use of the film could really be due to one of these incidental features. In this case steps must be taken to ensure that the control subjects also see a film of some sort and that both groups, or neither of the groups, know that they are taking part in an experiment. This precaution is necessary in order to control what is known as the Hawthorne effect, which refers to the observation, first made at the Hawthorne plant of the Western Electric Company, that almost any change, any extra attention, any experimental manipulation, or even the absence of manipulation but the knowledge that an experiment is being done, is enough to cause subjects to change. In short, any type of attention may lead subjects to respond.

In an experiment to study the effect of a drug on the performance of a manipulative skill, all groups must think that they are taking the drug. Therefore the experimenter must give every subject the same kind of substance as far as quantity, taste, and color are concerned. For some subjects this will be the drug under investigation and for the remainder, an inert chemical known as a *placebo*. Otherwise just the knowledge that they had been given a drug might act by suggestion on the experimental subjects and lead them to be either extra cautious or quite reckless, and the experimenter would not know whether it was the effect of the drug or the subjects' attitude or both which produced the result.

There are three methods commonly used to control potentially contaminating situational variables. One can (1) hold them constant, (2) randomize them, or (3) manipulate them systematically and separately from the main independent variable.

Holding extraneous variables constant means that all subjects in the various groups are treated exactly alike except for their exposure to the independent variable. For instance, in a reading experiment it would be necessary to control for the size of the groups since size of group is known to be a factor affecting reading achievement. One must see that the experimental and control groups have the same number of subjects. The teacher variable must be controlled since teacher efficiency and enthusiasm are factors that may affect the outcome of any learning experiment. Thus the same teacher should be used with two teaching methods that are to be compared.

In an experiment the various assistants must follow the same procedures; use the same instructions, apparatus, and tests; and try to assume the same attitudes with all groups. All groups should meet at the same time of day and in the same room. One would not want the experimental group to meet during the first period in the morning of a school day and the control group during the last period of the day. Environmental conditions such as temperature, light intensity, humidity, and furniture in the room, and the presence or absence of distracting noises should be the same for all groups.

If conditions cannot be held constant, the experimenter must attempt to randomize or balance out certain situational variables. For instance, if it is not possible to have the same teacher for both treatments, an experimenter may divide the two major groups into two smaller groups and randomly assign half of the experimental subjects and half of the control subjects to each teacher. The same could be done with other experimental conditions, such as apparatus. In this way situational variables are randomized; a variety of extraneous conditions is represented but is not allowed to affect the dependent variable systematically.

It is possible to control extraneous situational variables by manipulating them systematically. In many educational experiments it is necessary to use a sequence of experimental and control conditions in order to control progressive effects, like those of practice and fatigue. This is done by controlling the order in which experimental conditions are presented through a counterbalancing; half the subjects may receive an AB order and the other half a BA order. In this case an extraneous variable is being systematically manipulated. This procedure not only controls the potentially contaminating effect of order, but it can also provide an estimate of the size of the order effect by determining whether the average A and B values obtained in the two sequences are different.

It should be mentioned here that other types of variables, such as those associated with the subjects themselves, can be built into an experimental design and thus controlled. For example, if sex is to be controlled in an experiment and it is not possible to use any of the methods for controlling intersubject differences, then one could add sex as another independent variable. This not only controls the extraneous variable, but also yields information about the effect of this variable on the dependent variable as well as its possible interaction with the other independent variables.

This method for controlling extraneous variables amounts to the same thing as adding more independent variables to the experiment. Although it increases the complexity of the study, it has the advantage of furnishing additional information about the effect of relevant variables on the dependent variable and their interaction with the main independent variables. The use of this method of control has been increasing since the introduction of electronic computers to handle the analysis of data in complex studies.

At this point we need to make a distinction between the concept of controlling for extraneous variables and the concept of the control group. Both are necessary in order to add definitiveness to a scientific study. In an experiment where subjects are selected randomly and then randomly assigned to two groups, randomization is a means of controlling extraneous variables. Random assignment of individuals to two groups makes them comparable on any extraneous independent variable related to the dependent variable. We may do this with one or more experimental groups. However, we need a control group in order to make a comparison so that the effect of the independent variable can be unambiguously assessed. Comparisons are essential in all scientific investigations and the control group makes the comparison possible. Traditionally the experimental group receives the experimental treatment (the independent variable), which is withheld from a comparable group (the control group).

MANIPULATION

The manipulation of a variable refers to a deliberate operation performed by the experimenter. In educational research and other behavioral sciences, the manipulation of a variable takes a characteristic form in which the experimenter imposes a predetermined set of varied conditions on the subjects. The set of varied conditions is referred to as the independent variable, the experimental variable, or the treatment variable. The different conditions are designed to represent two or more values of the independent variable; these may be differences in degree or differences in kind. We may manipulate a single variable or a number of variables simultaneously. Multivariate analysis saves time and effort in that it permits the simultaneous investigation of a number of variables considered singly and in interaction—the latter often being the most significant aspect of the study.

OBSERVATION

In experimentation we are interested in the effect of the manipulation of the independent variable on a response variable. Observations are made with respect to some characteristic of the behavior of the subjects employed in the research. These observations, which are quantitative in nature if possible, are the dependent variable.

The dependent variable in educational research is often achievement of some type, such as learning. We are often interested in explaining or predicting achievement. Note that we cannot measure learning directly. We can only estimate learning through such measures as scores on a test. Therefore, strictly speaking, the dependent variable is scores or observations rather than achievement per se.

Experimental Comparison

For the simplest experiment two groups of subjects are required: the experimental group and the control group. Each group is subjected to a different treatment. Frequently one of the treatments is the usual set of conditions and the group receiving this treatment is referred to as the control group. The group given the more unusual or novel treatment is referred to as the experimental group. In an experiment investigating the effect of a new teaching method, the group of students taught by the usual method would serve as the control group. The experimental and control groups must be equivalent in all factors that may affect the dependent variable; they differ only in exposure to the independent variable. After the experimenter has imposed the different conditions on the subjects, each subject is measured on the dependent variable.

Measurement is followed by evaluation. Is there a difference between the two groups? Is the effect of treatment A different from that of treatment B? This question implies and requires a comparison of the measures of the dependent variable in the one group with the measures of response in the other group. The comparison should tell the experimenter whether or not differences on the dependent variable are associated with differences on the independent variable as represented by the two conditions, A and B.

Experimental Design

Experimental design refers to the conceptual framework within which the experiment is conducted. An experimental design serves two functions: (1) It establishes the conditions for the comparisons required by the hypotheses of the experiment and (2) it enables the experimenter through statistical analysis of the data to make a meaningful interpretation of the results of the study. If a design is to accomplish these functions, the experimenter, when selecting it, must keep in mind certain general criteria. Detailed descriptions of the various types of experimental design follow the discussion of these general criteria.

The most important criterion is that the *design be appropriate* for testing the particular hypotheses of the study. The mark of a sophisticated experiment is not complexity or simplicity but rather appropriateness. A design that will do the job it is supposed to do is the right design. Thus the first task for the experimenter is to select the design that best arranges the experimental conditions to meet the needs of the particular experimental problem.

If the research hypothesis is an interaction hypothesis, then it can be tested adequately only by means of a factorial type of design. Unfortunately, one often finds that educational researchers have tried to test an interaction hypothesis by performing two or more separate experiments. The latter type of design would be incapable of testing the hypothesis. Let us assume that a researcher is interested in the effects of programmed instruction on the learning of basic scientific concepts in elementary school science, believing that there may be a differential effect of this method based on class size and the intelligence level of the students. This problem calls for a factorial type of design. The researcher could not answer the question by performing two or three separate experiments, each with a single independent variable.

Another example of an inadequate design is the attempt to use a matched-subjects design in cases when it is impossible for the experimenter to match the subjects on all the relevant extraneous variables. Even though matching may be successful on one or two variables, it cannot be assumed that the groups are equivalent on all relevant variables. A randomized-subjects design would be superior in these circumstances.

A second criterion is that the design must provide *adequate control* so that the effects of the independent variable can be evaluated. Unless the design controls extraneous variables, one can never be confident of the relationship between the variables of the study. As we have mentioned earlier, *randomization* is the single best way to achieve the necessary control. Therefore the best advice is to select a design that utilizes randomization in as many aspects as possible. If it is not possible to select subjects at random, then try to *assign subjects to groups randomly*. If neither of these is feasible, then at least an attempt should be made to assign experimental treatments to the groups at random.

VALIDITY OF RESEARCH DESIGNS

A very significant contribution to the evaluation of research designs has been made by Campbell and Stanley who suggest that there are two general criteria of research designs: *internal validity* and *external validity*.[5]

[5]Donald T. Campbell and Julian C. Stanley, "Experimental and Quasi-Experimental Designs for Research on Teaching," in N. L. Gage ed., *Handbook of Research on Teaching* (Washington, D.C.: American Educational Research Association, 1963). Copyright by American Educational Research Association, Washington, D.C. This material also appears in Campbell and Stanley, *Experimental and Quasi-Experimental Designs for Research* (Skokie, Ill.: Rand McNally, 1966), p. 5. (The authors are indebted to the work of Campbell and Stanley for the terminology and designs used in this section of the chapter.)

Internal Validity

Internal validity is concerned with such questions as: Did the experimental treatment really bring about a change in the dependent variable? Did the independent variable really make a significant difference? These questions of internal validity cannot be answered positively by the experimenter unless the design provides adequate control of extraneous variables. That is, if the design provides control of variables, one is able to eliminate alternative explanations of the empirical outcome and interpret it as showing some kind of intrinsic relationship between variables. Internal validity is essentially a problem of control. The design of appropriate controls is a matter of finding ways to eliminate extraneous variables—that is, variables that could lead to alternative interpretations. Anything that contributes to the control of a design contributes to its internal validity.

Campbell and Stanley have identified eight extraneous variables that frequently represent threats to the internal validity of a research design. These variables must be controlled or else they might very well produce an effect that could be mistaken for the effect of the experimental treatment.[6]

1. *History*. Specific events, other than the experimental treatment, may occur between the first and second measurements of the subjects to produce changes in the dependent variable.

2. *Maturation*. Processes that operate within the subjects simply as a function of the passage of time may produce effects that could mistakenly be attributed to the experimental variable. Subjects may perform differently on the dependent-variable measure simply because they are older, hungrier, more fatigued, or less motivated than they were at the time of the first measurements.

3. *Pretesting*. Exposure to the pretest may affect the subjects' performance on a second test, regardless of the experimental treatment.

4. *Measuring instruments*. Changes in the measuring instruments, the scorers, or the observers used may produce changes in the obtained measures. If the posttest is more difficult or if different observers are used for pre- and postmeasures, these factors may account for observed differences in the two scores.

5. *Statistical regression*. If groups are selected on the basis of extreme scores, statistical regression may operate to produce an effect that could be mistakenly interpreted as an experimental effect. This regression effect refers to the tendency for extreme scores to regress or move toward the common mean on subsequent measures. For example, let us assume that the lowest fourth of the scorers on an English proficiency test are selected for a special experimental program in English. The mean of this group will tend to move toward the mean of the population on a second test whether or not an experimental treatment is applied. Similarly, high initial means would tend to go down toward the population mean on a second testing.

Let us illustrate regression with a scattergram (Figure 9.1) that shows the pattern we would get if the correlation of fourth grade reading test scores and fifth grade reading test scores is $r = .7$. Each dot represents both z-scores for an individual. If we select individuals with a particular z-score (X) on the fourth grade reading test

---

[6]Campbell and Stanley, *Experimental and Quasi-Experimental Designs*, p. 5.

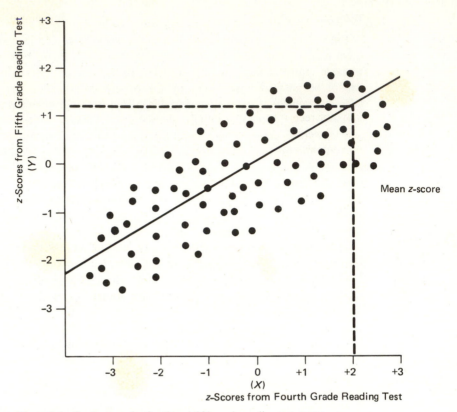

Figure 9.1   Scattergram for fourth and fifth grade reading test scores

and look at their scores on the fifth grade reading test, we find that not all have the same score on the fifth grade reading test. If the fourth grade z-score for this subgroup is above the mean, we find that a minority of the students score further above the mean in fifth grade than they did in fourth grade, but the majority of them have z-scores closer to the mean, and some even fall below the mean.

For the subgroup with a z-score one standard deviation above the mean on X, the mean on Y is $+.7$; for the subgroup with z-scores two standard deviations below the mean on X, the mean on Y is -1.4; the group with a z-score of $+2$ on X has a mean z-score of $+1.4$ on Y, and so forth. The slanted line on the scattergram connects these means on Y for various scores on X. Note that for each group with scores above the mean on the fourth grade reading test, the mean score on Y is *lower* on the fifth grade reading test. For each group with scores below the mean on the fourth grade reading test, the mean score is *higher* on the fifth grade reading test. In other words, all scores move closer to the mean—which is the result of regression.

Regression inevitably occurs when the correlation between two variables is less than perfect. Since practically none of the variables of interest in education are perfectly correlated, we must always be aware of effect of regression in the design of our experiments. An aspect of regression is captured in the old adages, ''When you are at the bottom you have nowhere to go but up'' and ''When you are on top you have nowhere to go but down.''

6. *Differential selection of subjects*. There may be important differences between the groups even before the application of the experimental treatment. If the experimental group in a learning experiment is more intelligent than the control group, the former may perform better on the dependent-variable measure even if this group does not receive an experimental treatment.

7. *Experimental mortality*. There may be differential loss of respondents from the comparison groups. If a particular type of subject drops out of one group during the course of the experiment, this differential loss may affect the outcome of the study. If, for example, several of the lowest scorers on a pretest gradually drop out of the experimental group, this group will have a higher mean performance on the final measure, not because of the experimental treatment but because the low scoring subjects are absent.

8. *Selection-maturation interaction*. This type of interaction may occur in a quasi-experimental design where the experimental and control groups are not randomly selected but instead are preexisting intact groups such as classrooms. Even though a pretest may show that the groups are equivalent, the experimental group may happen to have a higher rate of maturation than the control group and it is the increased rate of maturation that accounts for the observed effect. More rapidly maturing students are ''selected'' into the experimental group and it is the selection-maturation interaction that may be mistaken for the effect of the experimental variable.

For example, a group who elected to take an honors freshman English class might show more vocabulary growth than a group in a regular freshman English class because their vocabulary growth was at a higher rate both before and during their freshman year. A comparison of pretest and posttest differences of the honors and the regular classes might lead one to conclude erroneously that the independent variable was responsible for a difference in gain which is due only to selection-maturation interaction. This problem also frequently arises when volunteers are compared with nonvolunteers. The volunteers may be more motivated to make gains on the dependent variable than are the nonvolunteers, and this difference in gains may be mistakenly attributed to the independent variable—as can happen even when the groups are equivalent on a pretest.

All the methods of control discussed earlier in this chapter are designed to control those extraneous variables that pose a threat to the internal validity of a design.

External Validity

External validity refers to the generalizability or representativeness of the findings. The experimenter asks the question, To what populations, settings, experimental variables, and measurement variables can these findings be generalized?

Any single study is necessarily performed on a particular group of subjects, with selected measuring instruments and under conditions that are, in some respects, unique. Yet the researcher wants the results of the study to furnish information about a larger realm of subjects, conditions, and operations than were actually investigated. In order to make generalizations from the observed to the unobserved, the researcher needs some kind of assurance that the sample of events actually studied represents the larger population to which results are to be generalized. To the extent that the results of an experiment can be generalized to different subjects, settings, and measuring instruments, the experiment possesses external validity.

Bracht and Glass have identified two types of external validity: *population validity* and *ecological validity*.[7] Population validity is concerned with the identification of the population to which the results of an experiment are generalizable. It asks the question, What population of subjects can be expected to behave in the same way as did the sample experimental subjects? Ecological validity is concerned with generalizing experimental effects to other environmental conditions. It asks the question, Under what conditions (that is, settings, treatments, experimenters, dependent variables, and so on) can the same results be expected?

Population Validity.   It is the researcher's hope that findings can be generalized from the experimental group of subjects to a much larger population, as yet unstudied. For example, let us assume that a researcher, having discovered an effective new method of teaching reading to a sample of first graders, would like to conclude that this method is superior for other groups of first graders, perhaps all first graders in the United States. In order to be able to make valid inferences from the experimental results to larger populations, the researcher must correctly identify the populations to which the results would be generalizable. Relevant to this problem is Kempthorne's distinction between the *experimentally accessible population* and the *target population* referred to in chapter 6.[8] The experimentally accessible population refers to the population of subjects that is accessible or available to the researcher for his study. The target population is the total group of subjects to whom the researcher wants to apply the conclusions from the findings. In the foregoing example, the experimentally accessible population would likely be all the first graders in the local school district. The target population would be all first grade students in the United States. The researcher's generalizations would occur in two stages: (1) from the sample to the experimentally accessible population, and (2) from the accessible population to the target population.

If the researcher has randomly selected the sample from the experimentally accessible population (all first graders in the school district), then the findings can be generalized to this larger group with no difficulty. Note that such generalizing is defensible only if the principle of randomization has been followed in the selection of the sample. You may recall that this procedure requires that the experimenter specify the accessible population and that every member of the accessible popula-

---

[7]Glenn Bracht and Gene V. Glass, "The External Validity of Experiments," *American Educational Research Journal* 5 (November 1968):437–74.

[8]Oscar Kempthorne, "The Design and Analysis of Experiments with Some Reference to Educational Research," in Raymond O. Collier, Jr., and Stanley M. Elam, eds., *Research Design and Analysis: Second Annual Phi Delta Kappa Symposium on Educational Research* (Bloomington, Ind.: Phi Delta Kappa, 1961), pp. 97–126.

tion be listed and numbered so that a sample can be taken through the use of a table of random numbers.

In the second stage the researcher wants to generalize from the accessible population to the target population (all first graders in the United States). This type of generalizing is somewhat risky and cannot be made with the same degree of confidence as the former type. To make such an inference requires a thorough knowledge of the characteristics of both populations. The more nearly similar the accessible and target populations are, the more confidence one has in generalizing from the one to the other. For example, if the researcher has randomly sampled from all first graders in the state (the experimentally accessible population) instead of using just the local district, then the accessible population would be more like the target population and generalizations could be made to the target population with much more confidence. Of course, extending the accessible population to include the whole state presents problems in managing the conduct of the experiment. Kempthorne suggests that it is better to have reliable knowledge about a more restricted population and to have the resulting uncertainty of extending this knowledge to the target population than to define the experimentally accessible population so broadly as to be uncertain about inferring from the sample to the accessible population. When one attempts to generalize from the accessible population to the target population, it is important to know whether the one is similar to the other with respect to certain relevant characteristics. For example, an externally invalid result might be obtained if an experimenter samples from one age-group (the accessible population) and then tries to generalize the findings across age-groups (the target population).

There may be a "selection by treatment" interaction, which acts as a source of external invalidity when one attempts to generalize from population to population. When two experimentally accessible populations are not representative of the same target population, seemingly similar studies can lead to entirely different results. That is, an interaction may occur between the treatment and the characteristics of the one group that would not occur in another group with different characteristics. Thus it would not be possible to generalize the findings from one group to another. This type of interaction may occur when volunteers are used in a study. For example, if only volunteer instructors are used in an experiment on a new teaching method, it could appear effective simply because all the instructors happen to believe in it rather than because the method is inherently superior. The findings could not be generalized to a population whose instructors are not keen on the new method.

Ecological Validity. Experimenters must also be concerned with ecological external validity; that is, they want to be able to say that the same findings will be obtained under other experimental environmental conditions. To have ecological validity, a design must provide assurance that the experimental effect is independent of the particular experimental environment.

Obviously the first requirement for ecological validity is that the experimenter furnish a complete description of the operations and the experimental setting involved in the study. Only then could a reader judge to what extent the results can be generalized to other situations. The representativeness of the setting is a factor that influences the extent to which the findings can be generalized. For instance, one would ask if the findings on the effectiveness of a teaching method in one curricular area are applicable in other areas. Perhaps they would not be, unless a variety of teaching situations is included in the study or unless there is an adequate sample of relevant conditions. Would the findings of the study be the same if a rural school is used instead of an urban school in a replication of the study? Would the findings hold if a private school is used? a parochial school?

There may be a reactive effect due to the experimental arrangements. Subjects' knowledge that they are participating in an experiment may alter their responses to the treatment. The presence of observers or equipment during an experiment may so alter the normal responses of subjects participating in the experiment that one could not generalize about the effect of the experimental variable upon persons exposed to it in a nonexperimental setting.

Certain interaction effects may threaten the generalizability of experimental findings. For instance, a pretest may increase or decrease the experimental subjects' sensitivity or responsiveness to the experimental variable and thus make the results that are obtained for this pretested population unrepresentative of the effects of the experimental variable for the unpretested population from which the experimental subjects are selected. In this case one could generalize only to pretested groups but not to unpretested ones.

A somewhat less obvious concern in ecological validity is the question of the representativeness of the variables, both experimental and measured, used in the study. Variable representativeness influences the generalizability of the findings and hence is a factor in the external validity of the design. Can one be sure that the particular task used is a fair sample of the function one is measuring? Can one assume that the creativity measured by tests is the same as the creativity that the English teacher or the art teacher would discuss? When one speaks of aggression, what kind of aggression does one mean? Is the aggression induced by barring children from desirable toys the same as the aggression stimulated by verbal attacks?

Many psychological experiments have been concerned with the variable of anxiety. In some it is induced by electric shock; in others, by verbal instructions to the subjects. Are these the same kind of anxiety? Can one generalize the findings from one type of situation to another?

The measures used for the dependent variable may also influence the ecological validity of a design. If an objective test is used to measure the dependent variable, can the experimenter say that the same effect would be observed if an essay test is used as the measuring instrument?

Researchers must give thoughtful attention to the external validity of their designs; the tendency to overgeneralize experimental findings has been a problem in much of educational research.

Bracht and Glass have categorized the threats to external validity into two classes, which correspond to the two types of external validity: (1) those threats dealing with generalizations to populations of persons (population validity) and (2) those threats dealing with the "environment" of the experiment (ecological validity).[9]

1. *Population Validity*
    A. Experimentally Accessible Population vs. Target Population: Generalizing from the population of subjects that is available to the experimenter (the accessible population) to the total population of subjects about whom he is interested (the target population) requires a thorough knowledge of the characteristics of both populations. The results of an experiment might apply only for those special sorts of persons from whom the experimental subjects were selected and not for some larger population of persons.
    B. Interaction of Personological Variables and Treatment Effects: If the superiority of one experimental treatment over another would be reversed when subjects at a different level of some variable descriptive of persons are exposed to the treatments, there exists an interaction of treatment effects and personological variables.
2. *Ecological Validity*
    A. Describing the Independent Variable Explicitly: Generalization and replication of the experimental results presuppose a complete knowledge of all aspects of the treatment and experimental setting.
    B. Multiple-Treatment Interference: When two or more treatments are administered consecutively to the same persons within the same or different studies, it is difficult and sometimes impossible to ascertain the cause of the experimental results or to generalize the results to settings in which only one treatment is present.
    C. Hawthorne Effect: A subject's behavior may be influenced partly by his perception of the experiment and how he should respond to the experimental stimuli. His awareness of participating in an experiment may precipitate behavior which would not occur in a setting which is not perceived as experimental.
    D. Novelty and Disruption Effects: The experimental results may be due partly to the enthusiasm or disruption generated by the newness of the treatment. The effect of some new program in a setting where change is common may be quite different from the effect in a setting where very few changes have been experienced.
    E. Experimenter Effect: The behavior of the subjects may be unintentionally influenced by certain characteristics or behaviors of the experimenter. The expectations of the experimenter may also bias the administration of the treatment and the observation of the subjects' behavior.
    F. Pretest Sensitization: When a pretest has been administered, the experimental results may partly be a result of the sensitization to the content of the treatment. The results of the experiment might not apply to a second group of persons who were not pretested.
    G. Posttest Sensitization: Treatment effects may be latent or incomplete and appear only when a postexperimental test is administered.
    H. Interaction of History and Treatment Effects: The results may be unique because of "extraneous" events occurring at the time of the experiment.

[9]Bracht and Glass, "External Validity of Experiments, p. 438. Copyright by American Educational Research Association, Washington, D.C. The reader is referred to this source for a more extended discussion of the threats to external validity.

I. Measurement of the Dependent Variable: Generalization of results depends on the identification of the dependent variables and the selection of instruments to measure these variables.

J. Interaction of Time of Measurement and Treatment Effects: Measurement of the dependent variable at two different times may produce different results. A treatment effect which is observed immediately after the administration of the treatment may not be observed at some later time and vice versa.

Although internal validity is the *sine qua non,* the experimenter wants to select a design that is strong in both internal and external validity. However, in some cases, obtaining one type of validity tends to threaten the other types. For instance, as we arrange for more rigorous control in an educational experiment, we may increase its artificiality and cut down on the applicability of the findings to an actual classroom setting. In practice we try to reach a compromise between internal and external validity, which amounts to choosing a design that provides sufficient control to make the results interpretable, while preserving some realism, so that the findings will generalize to the intended settings.

In the discussion of experimental designs that follows, designs are classified as preexperimental, true experimental, or quasiexperimental depending upon the degree of control provided. Comments are made about the internal and external validity of the designs as they are presented. Before we begin the discussion of the experimental designs, it is necessary to introduce the reader to the terms and symbols that will be used.

1. X represents the independent variable, which is manipulated by the experimenter; it will also be referred to as the experimental variable or the treatment.
2. Y represents the measure of the dependent variable. Y_1 represents the dependent variable *before* the manipulation of the independent variable X; it is usually a pretest of some type administered before the experimental treatment. Y_2 represents the dependent variable *after* the manipulation of the independent variable X; it is usually a posttest administered to subjects after the experimental treatment.
3. S represents the subject or respondent used in the experiment; the plural is Ss.
4. E group refers to the experimental group—the group that is given the independent-variable treatment.
5. C group refers to the control group—the group that does not receive the experimental treatment.
6. R indicates random assignment of subjects to the experimental groups and the random assignment of treatments to the groups.
7. M_r indicates that the subjects are matched and then members of each pair assigned to the comparison groups at random.

In the paradigms for the various designs, the Xs and Ys across a given row are applied to the same persons. The left-to-right dimension indicates the temporal order, and the Xs and Ys vertical to one another are given simultaneously. A dash (—) indicates that the control group does *not* receive the X treatment.

PREEXPERIMENTAL DESIGNS

This section presents two designs that have been classified as preexperimental because they provide little or no control of extraneous variables. Unfortunately one finds that these designs are still being used in educational research. It will be helpful to begin our discussion with these poor designs because they illustrate quite well the way that extraneous variables may operate to jeopardize the internal validity of a design. If readers become aware of these sources of weakness in a design, they should be able to avoid them.

Design 1. One-Group Pretest-Posttest Design

The one-group design usually involves three steps: (1) administering a pretest measuring the dependent variable; (2) applying the experimental treatment X to the subjects; and (3) administering a posttest again measuring the dependent variable. Differences attributed to application of the experimental treatment are then determined by comparing the pretest and posttest scores.

Design 1   One-Group Pretest-Posttest Design

Pretest	Independent Variable	Posttest
Y_1	X	Y_2

To illustrate the use of this design, let us assume that an elementary teacher wants to evaluate the effectiveness of a new technique for teaching fourth grade social studies. At the beginning of the school year the students are given a standardized test that appears to be a good measure of the achievement of the objectives of fourth grade social studies. The teacher then introduces the new teaching technique, and at the end of the year administers the standardized test a second time and compares scores from the first and second administrations of the test in order to determine what difference the exposure to the new teaching method, X, has made.

Since Design 1 involves only one group and one teacher, it would seem to control intersubject differences and situational variables. The control is only superficial, however.

The major limitation of the one-group design is that, since no control group is used, the experimenter cannot assume that the change between the pretest and posttest is brought about by the experimental treatment. There is always the possibility that some extraneous variables account for all or part of the change. Thus this design is lacking in internal validity.

What are some of the extraneous variables that could operate to produce the change noted between the pretest and posttest scores? Two extraneous variables that are not controlled in this design are *history* and *maturation*. History as a source of extraneous variance refers to the specific events that can occur between the pretest and the posttest, other than the experimental treatment. In the social studies example widespread community interest in an election, increased emphasis on social studies in the school, or the introduction of a particularly effective teacher could increase student achievement in this area. An epidemic causing increased absences could decrease achievement. Maturation refers to changes in the subjects themselves that occur with the passage of time. Between pretest and posttest, children are growing mentally and physically and they may have learning experiences that could affect the dependent variable. History and maturation become increasingly influential sources of extraneous variance when the time interval between Y_1 and Y_2 is long.

Another shortcoming of Design 1 is that it affords no way of assessing the effect of the pretest Y_1 itself. We know that there is a practice effect when subjects take a test a second time or even take an alternate form of the test. That is, subjects do better the second time even without any instruction or discussion during the interval. This is true not only for achievement and intelligence tests but also for personality tests. In the case of personality tests, a trend toward better adjustment is generally observed.

This test-retest gain is an aspect of the larger problem of the *reactivity* of measuring instruments. Reactivity refers to the fact that there is often a reaction between the subject and the pretest measure and it is this reaction rather than the manipulation of X that produces the change in the Y_2 measure. Measures that cause the subject to react are called *reactive* measures. For example, in a study of attitude change, scales may themselves function as a stimulus; that is, the subject may react to the content of the scale and it is this reaction that brings about the observed change in attitudes even without any experimental treatment. This effect is most obvious when the pretest has novel or controversial content or when it has a particular motivating effect on the subjects.

Design 1 has little to recommend it. Without a control group to make a comparison possible, the results obtained in a one-group design are basically uninterpretable.

Design 2. Two Groups, Static Design

Design 2 utilizes two groups, only one of which is exposed to the experimental treatment. These two groups are assumed to be equivalent in all relevant aspects and differing only in their exposure to X. The dependent-variable measures for the two groups are compared to determine the effect of the X treatment.

This design has been used in much of the methods research in education. The achievement of students taught by a new method is compared with that of a similar class taught by the traditional method.

Design 2 has a control group, which permits the comparison that is required for scientific respectability. If the experimental group is superior on the Y_2 measure, the researcher then has more confidence in his conclusion that the difference is due to the experimental treatment.

However, there is a basic flaw in this design. Since neither randomization nor even matching is used to assign subjects to the experimental and control groups, we cannot assume that the groups are equivalent prior to the experimental treatment.

They may differ on certain relevant variables, and it may be these differences rather than X that are responsible for the observed change. Because we cannot be sure that the groups are equal in respect to all factors that may influence the dependent variable, this design is considered to be lacking in the necessary control and must be classified as preexperimental.

Design 2   Two Groups, Static Design

Group	Independent Variable	Posttest
E	X	Y_2
C	—	Y_2

TRUE EXPERIMENTAL DESIGNS

The designs in this category are the most highly recommended designs for experimentation in education because of the control that they provide.

Design 3. Two Groups, Randomized Subjects, Posttest-Only Design

Design 3 is one of the simplest yet one of the most powerful of all experimental designs. It requires two randomly assigned groups of subjects, each assigned to a different condition. No pretest is used; the randomization controls for all possible extraneous variables and assures that any initial differences between the groups are attributable only to chance and therefore will follow the laws of probability.

After the subjects are assigned to groups, only the experimental group is exposed to the experimental treatment. In all other respects the two groups are treated alike. Members of both groups are then measured on the dependent variable Y_2. Scores are compared to determine the effect of X. If the obtained means of the two groups are significantly different (that is, more different than would be expected on the basis of chance alone), the experimenter can be reasonably confident that the experimental conditions are responsible for the observed result.

The main advantage of Design 3 is randomization, which assures statistical equivalence of the groups prior to the introduction of the independent variable. Recall that as the number of subjects is increased, the likelihood that randomization will produce equivalent groups is increased. Design 3 controls for the main effects of history, maturation, and pretesting; because no pretest is used, there can be no interaction effect of pretest and X. This design is especially recommended for situations in which pretest reactivity is likely to occur. It is also useful in studies in which a pretest is either not available or not appropriate—as, for example, in studies with kindergarten or primary grades, where it is impossible to administer a pretest since the learning is not yet manifest. Another advantage of this design is that it can be extended to include more than two groups if necessary.

Design 3   Two Groups, Randomized Subjects, Posttest-Only Design

	Group	Independent Variable	Posttest
(R)	E	X	Y_2
(R)	C	—	Y_2

Design 3 does not permit the investigator to assess change. If such an assessment is desired, then a design, such as Design 5, that utilizes both a pre- and posttest should be used.

Design 4. Two Groups, Randomized Matched Subjects, Posttest-Only Design

This design is similar to Design 3 except that it uses a matching technique, rather than random assignment, to obtain equivalent groups. Subjects are matched on one or more variables that can be measured conveniently, such as IQ or reading scores. Of course, the matching variables used are those that presumably have a significant correlation with the dependent variable. Although a pretest is not included in Design 4, if pretest scores on the dependent variable are available, they could be used very effectively for the matching procedure. The measures are paired so that opposite members' scores are as close together as possible; one member of each pair is randomly assigned to one treatment and the other, to the second treatment. A flip of the coin can be used to achieve this random assignment.

Design 4   Two Groups, Randomized Matched Subjects, Posttest-Only Design

	Group	Independent Variable	Posttest
(M_r)	E	X	Y_2
	C	—	Y_2

Matching is most useful in studies where small samples are to be used and where Design 3 is not appropriate. Design 3 depends completely upon random assignment to obtain equivalent groups. With small samples the influence of chance alone may result in a situation in which random groups are initially very different from each other. Design 3 provides no assurance that small groups are really comparable before the treatments are applied. The matched-subjects design, however, serves to reduce the extent to which experimental differences can be accounted for by initial differences between the groups; that is, it controls preexisting intersubject differences on variables highly related to the dependent variable that the experiment is designed to affect. The random assignment of the matched pairs to groups adds to the strength of this design.

Design 4 is subject to the difficulties that we mentioned earlier in connection with matching as a means of control. The matching of all potential subjects must be complete, and the assignment of the members of each pair to the groups must be determined randomly. If one or more subjects should be excluded because an appropriate match could not be found, this would bias the sample. When using Design 4, it is essential to match every subject, even if only approximately, before random assignment.

Design 5. Randomized Groups, Pretest-Posttest Design

In Design 5 subjects are assigned to the experimental and control groups by random methods and are given a pretest on the dependent variable Y. The treatment is introduced only to the experimental subjects for a specified time, after which the two groups are measured on the dependent variable. The average difference between the pretest and posttest $(Y_2 - Y_1)$ is found for each group and then these average difference scores are compared in order to ascertain whether the experimental treatment produced a greater change than the control situation. The significance of the difference in average changes (found when the average change for the control group is subtracted from the average change for the experimental group) is determined by an appropriate statistical test, such as the t-test or F-test. Another, more precise, statistical procedure is to do an analysis of covariance with posttest scores as the dependent variable and pretest scores as the covariate.

Design 5   Randomized Groups, Pretest-Posttest Design

	Group	Pretest	Independent Variable	Posttest
(R)	E	Y_1	X	Y_2
(R)	C	Y_1	—	Y_2

The fact that the control group does not receive the experimental treatment does not mean that control subjects receive no experience at all. In research on teaching methods the control group is generally taught by the traditional or usual procedure. In certain learning experiments it is common practice to give the control group some kind of irrelevant activity between pre- and posttests while the experimental group is receiving specific training for the task. In an experiment on the effects of a particular drug, one would administer a placebo (such as aspirin or a sugar pill) to the control group without letting them know that they were being treated differently from the experimental group.

The before-and-after measures in Design 5 permit the investigator to study change and it is often referred to as the classical design for change experiments. The main strength of this design is the initial randomization, which assures statistical equivalence between the groups prior to experimentation; also the fact that the experimenter has control of the pretest can provide an additional check on the equality of the two groups on the dependent variable Y. Design 5, with its randomization, thus controls most of the extraneous variables that pose a threat to internal validity. For example, the effects of history, maturation, and pretesting are experienced in both groups; therefore any difference between the groups on the Y measure could probably not be attributed to these factors. Differential selection of subjects and statistical regression are also controlled through the randomization procedure.

The main concern in using Design 5 is external validity. Ironically, the problem stems from the use of the pretest, an essential feature of the design. As was mentioned earlier, there may be an interaction between the pretest and the subjects that can change them or sensitize them in certain ways. Although both E and C groups take the pretest and may experience the sensitizing effect, it can cause the experimental subjects to respond to the X treatment in a particular way just because of their increased sensitivity. The crucial question is, Would the effect of X on the experimental subjects be the same without the exposure to the pretest? This problem has been particularly evident in studies of attitude change. When the first attitude scale is administered as the pretest in a study, it can arouse interest or sensitize subjects to the issues or material included in the scale. Then when the experimental treatment (a lecture, film, or the like) is administered, the subjects may be responding not so much to the X treatment as to a combination of their aroused sensitivity to the issues and the experimental treatment.

Or let us consider another example. Suppose that one criterion for the success of a new teaching method in high school social studies is the number of students who report that they get their news from a source like the *Wall Street Journal*. During the course itself no special emphasis is placed on this particular source; but it, along with several other papers of somewhat lower repute, is made available to students. If the study uses a pretest-posttest design, the pretest questionnaire might include such an item as, "Do you read the *Wall Street Journal* for daily news?" This question alone may be enough to sensitize the experimental students to that newspaper, so when it becomes available during the course they will be more likely to pick it out from the others. But the control group is not exposed to the various news sources; hence the pretest question does not have an opportunity to exert its sensitizing effect on them. What might happen in such a study, as a result, is that the experimental group shows greater use of the *Wall Street Journal* on the posttest than does the control group, not because of the course content only but because of the combined effect of course content and pretest. A new class taught by the same method, but not pretested, hence not sensitized, may show no greater attentiveness to the *Journal* than the control group.

Such an effect represents an interaction between the pretest and the experimental treatment. Because a pretest might increase (or decrease) the subject's sensitivity or responsiveness to the X manipulation, the results obtained for a pretested sample may be unrepresentative of the effects of the experimental variable for the unpretested population from which the experimental subjects are taken. Thus we have a problem in generalizability; we may only be able to generalize the experimental findings to pretested groups and not to unpretested ones. This interaction between pretest and treatment is a threat to external validity.

In spite of this shortcoming, Design 5 is widely used because the interaction effect is not a serious problem in most educational research. The pretests used are generally achievement tests of some type and therefore do not have significant sensitizing effect on subjects who are accustomed to such testing. However, if the testing procedures are somewhat novel or motivating in their effect, then it is recommended that the experimenter choose a design not involving a pretest. Alternatively, whenever one suspects that the effect of the pretest might be interactive, it is possible to add a new group or groups to the study—a group that is *not* pretested. Solomon has suggested two designs that overcome the weakness of Design 5 by adding an unpretested group or groups.[10]

Design 6. Solomon Three-Group Design

The first of the Solomon designs uses three groups with random assignment of subjects to groups.

It can be seen that the first two lines of this design are identical to Design 5. However, this Solomon design has the advantage that it employs a second control group and thereby overcomes the difficulty inherent in Design 5—namely, the interactive effect of pretesting and the experimental manipulation. This second control group, labeled C_2, is *not* pretested but is exposed to the X treatment. Their Y_2 measures are then used to assess the interaction effect.

Design 6   Solomon Three-Group Design

	Group	Pretest	Independent Variable	Posttest
(R)	E	Y_1	X	Y_2
(R)	C_1	Y_1	—	Y_2
(R)	C_2		X	Y_2

An assessment of the interaction effect is achieved through a comparison of the Y_2 scores for the three groups. Only the posttest scores are entered into the analysis. Even though the experimental group has a significantly higher mean on Y_2 than does the first control group, we cannot be confident that this difference is due to X. It might have occurred because of the subjects' increased sensitization after the pretest and the interaction of their sensitization and X. However, if the Y_2 mean of the second control group is also significantly higher than that of the first control group, then we can assume that the experimental treatment, rather than the pretest-X interaction effect, has produced the difference since the second control group is not pretested. This group, though receiving the X treatment, is functioning as a control and is thus labeled C_2.

Design 7. Solomon Four-Group Design

Design 7 provides still more rigorous control by extending Design 6 to include one more control group. This fourth group receives neither pretest nor treatment. Again the third group, though receiving the X treatment, is functioning as a control group.

Design 7 has strength because it incorporates within it the advantages of several other designs along with its own unique contribution. The first two lines (Design 5)

[10]R. L. Solomon, "On Extension of Control Group Design," *Psychological Bulletin* 46 (1949):137–50.

Design 7   Solomon Four-Group Design

	Group	Pretest	Independent Variable	Posttest
(R)	E	Y^1	X	Y_2
(R)	C_1	Y_1	—	Y_2
(R)	C_2	—	X	Y_2
(R)	C_3	—	—	Y_2

control extraneous factors such as history and maturation, and the third line (Design 6) provides control over the pretest-X interaction effect. When the fourth line is added to make Design 7, we have control over any possible contemporary effects that may occur between Y_1 and Y_2. The last two lines represent Design 3, so actually we have a combination of the pretest-posttest experimental-control design with the simple randomized-subjects design. In addition to the strengths of each design taken separately, we also have the replication feature provided by the two experiments. This combination takes advantage of the information provided by the pretest-posttest procedure and at the same time shows how the experimental condition affects an unpretested group of Ss.

In Design 7 one can make several comparisons to determine the effect of the experimental X treatment. If the posttest mean of the E group is significantly greater than the mean of the first control group, C_1, and if the C_2 posttest mean is significantly greater than that of C_3, we have evidence for the effectiveness of the experimental treatment. The influence of the experimental conditions on a pretested group can be determined by comparing the posttests of E and C_1 or the pre-post changes of E and C_1; the effect of the experiment on an unpretested group is found by comparing C_2 and C_3. If the average differences between posttest scores, $E - C_1$ and $C_2 - C_3$, are about the same, then the experiment must have had a comparable effect on pretested and unpretested groups.

Design 7 actually involves conducting the experiment twice, once with pretests and once without pretests. If the results of these two experiments are in agreement as indicated above, the investigator can have much greater confidence in the findings.

The main disadvantage of this design is the difficulty involved in carrying it out in a practical situation. More time and effort are required to conduct two experiments simultaneously and there is the problem of locating the increased number of subjects of the same kind that would be needed.

Another difficulty is with the statistical analysis. There are not four complete sets of measures for the four groups. As noted above, we can make comparisons between E and C_1 and between C_2 and C_3, but there is no single statistical procedure that would make use of the six available measures simultaneously. Campbell and Stanley suggest working only with posttest scores in an analysis of variance design. The pretest is considered as a second independent variable, along with X. The design is as follows:

	No X	X
Pretested	Y_2, control 1	Y_2, experimental
Unpretested	Y_2, control 3	Y_2, control 2

From the column means, one can determine the main effect of X; from row means, the main effect of pretesting; and from cell means, the interaction of testing with X.

Design 7 is not a design that the graduate student is likely to use routinely in research. It is generally restricted to a more advanced level of hypothesis testing and research.

FACTORIAL DESIGNS

The designs presented thus far have been the classical single-variable designs in which the experimenter manipulates one independent variable to produce an effect on the dependent variable. Educational research has been criticized in the past because of an overreliance on the one-variable design. Critics have pointed out that in the case of complex social phenomena there are generally several variables interacting simultaneously, and to attempt to restrict a study to one variable is to impose an artificial simplicity on a complex situation. The X variable alone may not produce the same effect as it might in interaction with another X, so the findings from a one-variable design may be meaningless. For instance, the effectiveness of a particular method of teaching may well depend upon a number of variables, such as the intelligence level of the students, the personality of the teacher, the general atmosphere of the classroom, and so on. Programmed instruction, for example, may be more effective with slower students than with brighter ones. A classical one-variable design would not reveal this interactive effect of method and intelligence level. The information yield of an experiment can be increased markedly by ascertaining the simultaneous effects of two or more independent variables in a factorial design. In fact, it has been said that the real breakthrough in educational research came with Fisher's development of factorial designs.

A factorial design is one in which two or more variables are manipulated simultaneously in order to study the independent effect of each variable on the dependent variable as well as the effects due to interactions among the several variables.

Factorial designs are of two types. In the first type of design, one of the independent variables may be experimentally manipulated. In this case the experimenter is primarily interested in the effect of a single independent variable but must take into consideration other variables which may influence the dependent variable. Typically, these other variables are attribute variables, such as sex, intelligence, race, socioeconomic status, achievement, and the like. Their influence can be investigated (and at the same time controlled) by building the attribute variable directly into a factorial design. The experimenter assesses the effect of the main independent variable at each of several "levels" of the one or more attribute independent variables. The different levels of the attribute variable typically represent naturally occurring selected groups of subjects, as when a study uses bright and slow students to determine the effectiveness of an instructional technique. Building the attribute variables into a factorial design not only increases the precision of the experiment but also its generalizability. Since one is able to determine whether the treatment has comparable effects over all levels, the generalizability of the experimental findings is increased.

In the second type of design, all of the independent variables may be experimentally manipulated. Here the experimenter is interested in several independent variables and wishes to assess both their separate and their combined effects. Both independent variables are experimentally manipulated. For instance, an experiment might compare the effects of class size as well as the introduction of programmed instruction on the learning of science concepts. In this study both variables would be manipulated; there would be two treatments of the variable method of instruction, namely, programmed versus traditional, and two treatments of the second variable, size of class, namely, large versus small. Such a design permits an analysis of the main effects for both experimental variables as well as an analysis of the interaction between the treatments.

Design 8.   Simple Factorial Design

Factorial designs have been developed at varying levels of complexity. The simplest factorial design is the 2 by 2 (2×2). In this design each of two independent variables has two values.

In Design 8 the independent variable, which is manipulated, is called the experimental variable; the second independent variable, which has been divided into levels, is the attribute variable. The effect on the dependent variable of the main experimental treatment is assessed at each of the two levels of the other variable. Thus in Design 8 some Level 1 subjects receive Treatment A (Cell 1) and others, Treatment B (Cell 3). Some Level 2 subjects receive Treatment A (Cell 2) and others, Treatment B (Cell 4).

Design 8   Simple Factorial Design

Attribute Variable (X_2)	Experimental Variable (X_1)	
	Treatment A	*Treatment B*
Level 1	Cell 1	Cell 3
Level 2	Cell 2	Cell 4

To illustrate, let us assume that an experimenter is interested in comparing the effectiveness of two types of programmed textbooks—Methods A and B—on the achievement of ninth grade science students, believing that there may be a differential effect of these methods based on the level of intelligence of the students. The experimenter stratifies the population into high and low IQ scores and randomly selects 60 Ss from the high group and assigns 30 Ss to Method A and 30 Ss to Method B. This process is repeated for the low-IQ group. Teachers are also randomly assigned to the groups.

In our hypothetical experiment we have two experimental treatments and two levels of intelligence. Table 9.1 shows the 2 × 2 factorial design for measuring the effects of the two methods of instruction on the learning of students. Note that a 2 × 2 design requires four groups of subjects; subjects within each of two levels of intelligence are randomly assigned to the two treatments.

The scores in the four cells represent the mean scores of the four groups on the dependent variable, the science achievement test. In addition to the four cell scores representing the various combinations of treatments and levels, we notice that there are four marginal mean scores: two for the columns and two for the rows. The marginal column means are for the two methods, or treatments, and the marginal row means are for the two levels of intelligence.

From the data given we can first determine the *main effects* for the two independent variables. The treatment mean scores without regard to IQ level indicate the main effect for treatments. If we compare the mean score of the two Method A groups, 67.5, with that of the two Method B groups, 68.5, we find that the difference between these means is only one point. Therefore we could not conclude that one method is more effective than the other; the method used has little effect on the dependent variable.

Now let us examine the mean scores for the levels in order to determine the main effect of X_2, intelligence level, on achievement scores. The main effect for levels does not take into account any differential effect due to treatments. The mean score for the two high-IQ groups is 74, and the mean score for the two low-IQ groups is 62; since this difference is 12 points, we would assume that there is an effect attributable to intelligence level. The high-IQ group has a markedly higher mean score; thus, regardless of treatment, the high-IQ groups perform better than the low-IQ groups.

Table 9.1   Example of a Factorial Design

(X_2) IQ	Programmed Instruction (X_1)		
	Method A	*Method B*	*Mean*
High	75.0	73.0	74
Low	60.0	64.0	62
Mean	67.5	68.5	

In addition a factorial design permits the investigator to assess the interaction between the two independent variables—that is, the differential effects of one of them at different levels of the other. If there is an interaction, the effect that the treatment has on learning will differ for the two IQ levels. If there is no interaction, the effect of the treatment will be the same for both levels of intelligence. From an examination of the mean scores in Table 9.1, we can see that Method A is more effective than Method B for the high-IQ group, and Method B is more effective for the low-IQ group. Thus a particular combination of treatment and level of IQ interacts to produce greater gains than do some other combinations. This interaction effect between method and intelligence levels is shown graphically in Figure 9.2. This figure shows clearly that the effectiveness of the method depends upon the IQ level. One method is more effective at one level of intelligence, and the reverse is true for the other level.

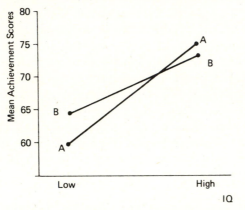

Figure 9.2   Illustration of interaction between method and IQ level

Let us examine another set of data obtained in a hypothetical 2×2 factorial study.

Table 9.2   Example of a Factorial Design

	Treatment (X_1)		
(X_2) IQ	*Method A*	*Method B*	*Mean*
High	50	58	54
Low	40	48	44
Mean	45	53	

Table 9.2 shows the results of a study designed to investigate the effect of two methods of instruction on achievement. Again, since the investigator anticipates that the method may be differentially effective depending on the intelligence level of the subject, the first step is to distinguish two levels of intelligence. Subjects within each level are randomly assigned to the two methods. Following the experimentation period, achievement tests are administered and the scores are recorded for every subject. The mean scores for the four groups are shown in Table 9.2. If we compare the mean score of the two groups taught by Method B, 53, with that of the two

groups taught by Method A, 45, we see that the former is somewhat higher. Therefore Method B appears to be more effective than Method A. The difference between the means for the two IQ levels, on the main effects for intelligence, is 10; that is, 54 versus 44. Regardless of treatment, the high-IQ group performs better than the low-IQ group. The data reveal no interaction between treatment and levels. Method B appears to be more effective regardless of the IQ level. In other words, treatments and levels are independent of each other. The lack of interaction is illustrated graphically in Figure 9.3. It is not possible to demonstrate either the presence or absence of such interaction without using a factorial design.

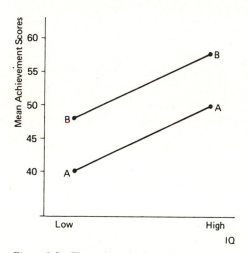

Figure 9.3   Illustration of a lack of interaction between method and IQ level

The factorial design can be extended to more complex experiments, in which there are a number of independent variables; the numerical values of the digits indicate the number of levels for the specific independent variables. For instance, in a $2 \times 3 \times 4$ factorial design there are three independent variables with two, three, and four levels, respectively. Such an experiment might use two teaching methods, three ability levels, and four grades. Theoretically a factorial design may include any number of independent variables with any number of levels of each. However, when too many factors are manipulated or controlled simultaneously, the study and the statistical analysis become unwieldy and some of the combinations may be artificial. In the $2 \times 3 \times 4$ design 24 groups would be required in order to represent all combinations of the different levels of the multiple independent variables. The number of groups required for a factorial design is the product of the digits that indicate the factorial design: $2 \times 3 \times 4 = 24$. The mere thought of the complexities involved in arranging for large numbers of subjects under large numbers of conditions will perhaps help the reader to understand why most educational researchers attempt to answer their questions with the simplest possible designs, even though the statistical analysis can now usually be handled by electronic computers.

The advantages of the factorial design are that it (1) accomplishes in one experiment what otherwise might require two or more separate studies and (2) provides an opportunity to study interactions that are often so important in educational research. (3) provides a more powerful test of hypotheses.

QUASI-EXPERIMENTAL DESIGNS

The goal of the experimenter is to use designs that provide full experimental control through the use of randomization procedures. These are the true experimental designs as presented in the previous section (Designs 3 through 8). There are many situations in educational research in which it is not possible to conduct a true experiment. Neither full control over the scheduling of experimental conditions nor the ability to randomize can always be realized. For instance, in research conducted in a classroom setting, it may not be possible for the experimenter to assign subjects randomly to groups. In this case, one must use designs that will provide as much control as possible under the existing situation. These designs are known as quasi-experimental designs and are used where true experimental designs are not feasible.[11] Since the quasiexperimental design does not provide full control, it is extremely important that the researcher know which of the variables may be inadequately controlled, be aware of the sources of both internal and external invalidity, and consider these sources in the interpretation.

Design 9. Nonrandomized Control-Group, Pretest-Posttest Design

Although randomized assignment of subjects to groups is the ideal, it often is not possible in practice. In a school situation, schedules cannot be disrupted or classes reorganized in order to accommodate the experimenter's study. In this case it is necessary to use groups as they are already organized into classes.

Design 9   Nonrandomized Control-Group, Pretest-Posttest Design

Group	Pretest	Independent Variable	Posttest
E	Y_1	X	Y_2
C	Y_1	—	Y_2

Since randomization is not possible, every effort must be made to employ groups that are as equivalent as possible at the beginning of the study. Pretest scores should be analyzed to determine whether the means and standard deviations of the two groups differ significantly. If the scores for the two groups on the pretest are not equivalent, it is possible to proceed with the study and then use the analysis of covariance technique to compensate partially for this lack of equivalency between

---

[11]Campbell and Stanley, *Experimental and Quasi-Experimental Designs*, p. 34.

the groups. Similarity on other relevant extraneous factors, such as sex, age, intelligence tests, and so on, should also be checked. If possible, the experimental treatments should be assigned at random. Flip a coin to determine which is to be the experimental group.

As mentioned earlier, it is especially important that one check for sources of internal and external invalidity when a quasi-experimental design is used. If the equivalency of the groups is confirmed by the scores on the pretest, then we can assume that the main effects of maturation, testing, and instrumentation have been controlled and will not be mistaken for the effect of X.

The main source of trouble for this design is with the specific *selection* differences that may distinguish the E and C groups. Selection becomes a factor whenever Ss are not randomly selected and assigned but are selected into groups on bases extraneous to the purpose of the study, as is the case in Design 9. These selection differences may result in an interaction effect between selection and certain extraneous variables that could be mistakenly attributed to the effect of X. The most commonly occurring interactions are those involving selection and maturation. Such an interaction may occur if one of the groups has a higher rate of maturation than the other. The more rapidly maturing group will show greater change on the dependent variable even without the introduction of the experimental variable. That is, it is the selection by maturation interaction, rather than the experimental treatment, that results in the observed effect.

Self-selection may occur when experimental Ss volunteer for exposure to the X treatment and there is no comparable group of volunteers to serve as a control group. If classes know in advance that two methods, experimental and traditional, are to be used in a study and are permitted to volunteer for one method or the other, then any subsequent difference between the classes cannot be attributed to the teaching method since preexisting characteristics of the subjects may have disposed them to volunteer for a particular method of instruction. Consequently it might have been these preexisting characteristics that accounted for their response to the method or even for their postcourse achievement regardless of teaching method.

Statistical regression is the other major internal validity problem for Design 9. This term refers to the tendency for extreme scores to regress or move toward the common mean on subsequent measurements. Such a regression effect could be introduced into this design if the groups used in the study were drawn from populations having different means. Even though the groups are equivalent on a pretest, the regression effect that occurs could result in a shift or change from pre- to posttest that is incorrectly interpreted as an experimental effect.

Let us assume that the E group in a study has a mean of 75 on a pretest, which is below the mean of its parent population, whereas the control group with a pretest mean of 75 is somewhat above the mean of its population. Since each group will regress toward the mean of the parent population when retested, the E group will reach a higher mean on the posttest, whether or not X is introduced; on the other hand, the mean of the C group will regress downward. The E group would appear to have made greater progress during the course of the study than the C group, which would most likely be erroneously attributed to the effect of X. Regression is a source of invalidity that can be avoided through careful selection of samples for study. Randomization, of course, is the best way to control for possible regression effects.

The threats to external validity in Design 9 are similar to those encountered with Design 5. An advantage of Design 9, however, is that the reactive effects of experimentation are more easily controlled than they are in Design 5. When intact classes are used, subjects are probably less aware of an experiment being conducted than when Ss are drawn from classes and put into experimental sessions. This contributes to the generalizability of the findings, Incidentally, it might also be noted that an experimenter in a school situation is much more likely to obtain administrative approval to conduct an experiment if intact classes are used, as in Design 9.

Another problem in Design 9 is the measurement of the change from pretest to posttest. In nonrandomized designs serious problems with change or ''gain'' scores arise. Some measurement experts have even recommended that change scores not be used at all.

Although it is not possible to go into the problems of change scores in detail in this text, let us point out some of the difficulties. A negative correlation is usually found between pretest scores and the gain made from pretest to posttest. Does this mean that students with low initial scores learn more (as measured by the change scores) than students with high initial scores? Probably not. The negative correlation is most likely due to the peculiar psychometric characteristics of change scores. For one thing, most educational tests have a ceiling, which means that the range of achievement on the test items is limited. If a student answers 92 items correctly on a 100-item pretest, it is only possible for this student to gain 8 points on the posttest. On the other hand, a student with a score of 42 on the pretest could make a gain of 58 points. Because of this ceiling effect, students in the high achievement group on the pretest are restricted to a low change score on the posttest.

Regression toward the mean presents another confounding factor in the interpretation of change scores. The regression effect means that students who have high scores on the pretest will be expected to have somewhat lower scores on the posttest, whereas students with low pretest scores will be expected to have somewhat higher scores on the posttest.

An additional problem with gain scores is that they assume equal intervals at all points on a test. But a gain in score from 92 to 98 may not be equivalent to a gain from 42 to 48. It is probably harder to make a gain of 6 points over a high pretest score than it is to make the same gain over an average pretest score. Another difficulty is that change scores are usually less reliable than the scores of the pretest and posttest themselves.

Although the limitations of change scores cannot be overcome completely, there are certain statistical procedures that can be used to overcome the problem partially. The most common procedure is to use residualized change scores, which are scores calculated by predicting the posttest scores from the pretest scores and then subtracting the predicted score from the actual posttest score to obtain what is called a "residual gain" score. This procedure removes the effect of the pretest score from the posttest score. Analysis of covariance is a procedure for testing the significance of the difference between the means of the residuals.[12]

Design 10. Counterbalanced Design

Design 10, another design that can be used with intact class groups, rotates the groups at intervals during the experimentation. For example, the E group and C group might use Methods A and B, respectively, for the first half of the experiment and then exchange methods for the second half. The distinctive feature of Design 10 is that all subjects receive all experimental treatments at some time during the experiment. In effect this design involves a series of replications; in each replication the E groups are shifted so that at the end of the experiment each group has been exposed to each X. The order of exposure to the experimental situation differs for each group. The counterbalanced design is usually employed when several treatments are to be tested, but also may be used with only two treatments.

Design 10   A Sample Counterbalanced Design

| Replication | Experimental Treatments | | | |
	X_1	X_2	X_3	X_4
1	Group A	B	C	D
2	Group C	A	D	B
3	Group B	D	A	C
4	Group D	C	B	A
	column mean	column mean	column mean	column mean

Each row in Design 10 represents one replication. For each replication the groups are shifted so that Group A first experiences X_1, then X_2, X_3, and finally X_4. Each cell in the design would contain the mean scores on the dependent variable for the group, treatment, and replication indicated. The mean score for each column would indicate the performance of all four groups on the dependent variable under the treatment represented by the column.

A classroom teacher could use a counterbalanced study to compare the effectiveness of two methods of instruction on learning in science. The teacher could choose two classes and two units of science comparable in difficulty, length, and so on. It is essential that the units be equivalent in the complexity and difficulty of the concepts involved. During the first replication of the design, Class 1 is taught Unit 1 by Method A, and Class 2 is taught by Method B. An achievement test over Unit 1 is administered to both groups. Then Class 1 is taught Unit 2 by Method B, and Class 2 is taught by Method A; both are then tested over Unit 2. The arrangement is shown in Table 9.3.

[12]See Allen L. Edwards, *Experimental Design in Psychological Research,* 3rd ed. (New York: Holt, Rinehart and Winston, 1968), ch. 16.

Table 9.3   Example of a Counterbalanced Design

Replication	Experimental Treatments	
	Method A	*Method B*
(Unit) 1	Class 1	Class 2
(Unit) 2	Class 2	Class 1
	column mean	column mean

After the study the column means are computed to indicate the mean achievement for both groups (classes) when taught by the method indicated by the column heading. A comparison of these column mean scores through an analysis of variance indicates the effectiveness of the methods upon achievement in science.

Design 10 overcomes some of the weaknesses of Design 9. This is, when intact classes must be used, counterbalancing provides an opportunity to rotate out any differences that might exist between the groups. Since the treatments are administered to all groups, the results obtained for each X cannot be attributed to preexisting differences in the subjects. If one group should be more intelligent on the average than the other, each X treatment would benefit from this superior intelligence.

The main shortcoming of Design 10 is that there may be a carry-over effect from one X to the next. Therefore it should be used only when the experimental treatments are such that exposure to one treatment will have no effect on subsequent treatments. This requirement may be hard to satisfy in much of educational research. Furthermore, there is the necessity for establishing the equivalence of the learning material used in the various replications. It may not always be possible to locate equivalent units of material. Another weakness of the counterbalanced design is the possibility of boring students with the repeated testings required by this method.

TIME-SERIES DESIGNS

Design 11. One-Group Time-Series Design

Design 11 involves periodic measurement on one group and the introduction of an experimental treatment into this time series of measurements. As the design indicates, a number of measurements on a dependent variable, Y, are taken, X is introduced, and additional measurements of Y are made. By comparing the measurements before and after X, it is possible to ascertain the effect of X on the performance of the group on Y. A time-series design might be used in a school setting to study the effects of a major change in administrative policy upon disciplinary incidents. Or a study might involve repeated measurement of students' attitudes and the effect produced by the introduction of a documentary film designed to change attitudes.

Design 11   One-Group Time-Series Design

Y_1	Y_2	Y_3	Y_4	X	Y_5	Y_6	Y_7	Y_8

Figure 9.4 illustrates some possible patterns from time-series studies into which an experimental treatment is introduced. It shows the series of measurements Y_1 through Y_8 with the introduction of the experimental treatment at point X. We can assess the effect of the X by examining the stability of the repeated measurements.

From an examination of the difference between Y_4 and Y_5 in pattern A, perhaps one would be justified in assuming that X has an effect on the dependent variable. Pattern B also indicates the possibility of an experimental effect of X. However, one could not assume that X produces the change in either patterns C or D. Pattern C appears to result from maturation or a similar influence. The erratic nature of pattern D suggests the operation of extraneous factors.

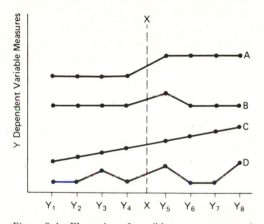

Figure 9.4   Illustration of possible outcome patterns in a time design

Design 11 is similar to Design 1 in that it uses before-and-after measures and lacks a control group. However, it has certain advantages over Design 1 that make it a more useful design in educational research. The multitesting provides a check on some of the common threats to internal validity. Maturation, testing, and regression could be ruled out as plausible explanations of the shift occurring between Y_4 and Y_5, since such shifts do not occur in the previous time periods under observation. It is recommended that no change in measuring instruments be made during the course of the time study. In this way one eliminates changes in instrumentation as a possible explanation of the Y_4–Y_5 difference.

The major weakness of Design 11 is its failure to control history; that is, one has to rule out the possibility that it is not X but some simultaneous event that produces the observed change. Perhaps such factors as seasonal or weather changes or such school agents as examinations could account for the change. In a study designed to assess the effect of a lecture-film situation on student attitudes toward school integration, to what extent would the attitude measurements be affected by a nationally publicized black riot in a distant city? The extent to which history (uncontrolled contemporary events) is a plausible explanatory factor must be ascertained by the experimenters as they attempt to interpret their findings.

One must also consider the external validity of the time design. Since there are repeated tests, perhaps there is a kind of interaction effect of testing that would restrict the findings to those populations subject to repeated testing. However, as long as the measurements are of a typical, routine type used in school situations, this is not likely to be a serious limitation. Further, a selection-X interaction may occur, especially if one selects some particular group that may not be typical.

Statistical interpretation can be a particular problem with time data. Since individual and mean scores are so variable over the time period, it is tempting to attribute these changes to the X treatment when they may in fact result from other variables. The usual tests of significance may not be appropriate with a time design. The reader is referred to Campbell and Stanley for a discussion of the statistical tests that may be used with this design.

Design 12. Control-Group Time-Series Design

Design 12 is an extension of Design 11 to include a control group. The control group, again representing an intact class group, would be measured at the same time as the E group but would not experience the X treatment. This design overcomes the weakness of Design 11—that is, failure to control history as a source of extraneous variance. The control group permits the necessary comparison. If the E group shows a gain from Y_4 to Y_5, but the C group does not show a gain, then the effect must be due to X rather than any contemporaneous events, which would have affected both groups.

Design 12   Control-Group Time-Series Design

Group									
E	Y_1	Y_2	Y_3	Y_4	X	Y_5	Y_6	Y_7	Y_8
C	Y_1	Y_2	Y_3	Y_4	—	Y_5	Y_6	Y_7	Y_8

Other variations of the time-series design include adding more control groups, more observations, or more experimental treatments.

VALIDITY PROBLEMS WITH EXPERIMENTAL DESIGNS

Some of the sources of invalidity in the one-variable experimental designs are summarized in Table 9.4. This brief summary must not be depended upon as the sole guide in selecting a design. It must be accompanied by a thorough consideration of the qualified presentation appearing in the text in order that the reader understand the particular strengths and weaknesses that characterize each design.

Table 9.4   Factors Jeopardizing the Validity of Experimental Designs

Sources of Invalidity	Preexperimental		True experimental					Quasi-experimental			
	1	2	3	4	5	6	7	9	10	11	12
Internal Validity											
Contemporary history†	−	+	+	+	+	+	+	+	+	−	+
Maturation processes	−	?	+	+	+	+	+	+	+	+	+
Pretesting procedures	−	+	+	+	+	+	+	+	+	+	+
Measuring instruments	−	+	+	+	+	+	+	+	+	?	+
Statistical regression	?	+	+	+	+	+	+	?	+	+	+
Differential selection of Ss	+	−	+	+	+	+	+	+	+	+	+
Experimental mortality	+	−	+	+	+	+	+	+	+	+	+
Interaction of selection and maturation, and the like	−	−	+	+	+	+	+	−	?	+	+
External Validity											
Interaction of selection and experimental variable	−	−	?	?	?	?	?	?	?	?	−
Interaction of pretesting and experimental variable	−		+	+	−	+	+	−	?	−	−
Reactive experimental procedures	?		?	?	?	?	?	?	?	?	?
Multiple-treatment interference									−		

*Designs are as follows:
1. One group, pretest-posttest
2. Two groups, static
3. Two groups, randomized Ss, posttest only
4. Two groups, randomized matched Ss, posttest only
5. Randomized groups, pretest-posttest
6. Solomon, three groups

7. Solomon, four groups
9. Nonrandomized control group, pretest-posttest
10. Counterbalanced
11. One group, time series
12. Control group, time series

†A plus sign indicates that the factor is controlled, a minus sign indicates lack of control, a question mark indicates a possible source of concern, and a blank indicates that the factor is not relevant.

Summary

Experimentation is the most rigorous and the most desirable form of scientific inquiry. The controlled conditions that characterize the experiment make it possible to identify verified functional relationships among the phenomena of interest to educators. Experimenters who control the conditions under which an event occurs have distinct advantages over observers who simply watch or study an event without control: (1) They can manipulate or vary the conditions systematically and note the variation in results. (2) They can make the event occur at a time when they are prepared to make accurate observations and measurements. (3) They can repeat their observations under the same conditions, for verification, and can describe these conditions so that other experimenters can duplicate them and make an independent check on the results.

Although experimentation is the ideal approach to the solution of educational problems, one must remember that there are many important questions in education that cannot be solved by experimentation. Other types of research are also needed.

Exercises

1. From a group of students enrolled in social studies in a high school, a researcher randomly selected 60 students. The students were then divided into two groups by random assignment of 30 to Group A, the traditional social studies curriculum, and 30 to Group B, a new program designed to deal with the history of certain ethnic groups. The two groups were compared at the end of the semester on a scale designed to measure attitudes toward ethnic groups. In this study, identify
   a. the independent variable
   b. the dependent variable
   c. the control group
   d. the experimental group
   e. the method(s) used to control for differences between the groups
   f. the research design used

2. Consider the following research question: Does teaching the first year of French through an oral-aural approach, rather than the grammar-transformational method, alter pupil performance on a standardized year-end test in grammar, reading, and vocabulary?
   a. Design the *ideal* experiment to answer this question, assuming that there are no administrative or other restrictions.
   b. Design the experiment that would most likely be required in the typical high school setting.
   c. State the relative advantages of the ideal experimental design (a) as compared with the design in question b.

3. Evaluate the following research designs with respect to methods used and the control provided. Make suggestions for improvements if needed.
   a. A researcher wanted to ascertain if homogeneous grouping improves learning in a first course in biology. The researcher designated one of two high schools in a small town to serve as the experimental school and the other, as the control. Both schools had about the same number of students in each of four sections of science. In the experimental school pupils were grouped homogeneously on the basis of IQ and scores on achievement tests in science. In the control school pupils were placed in sections at random. At the end of the year all pupils were given a standardized test in biology. Statistical tests showed the experimental group to be superior on the test. The researcher concluded that homogeneous grouping results in greater learning in biology.
   b. A history teacher was concerned about her students' lack of knowledge of their state and national governments and of current events. She decided to experiment with some new materials and methods to see if she could obtain improvement. In Classes A and B she introduced the

new materials and methods. In Classes C and D she used the traditional methods. Classes A and B were administered both the pretest and posttest; Classes C and D were administered only the posttest. When comparisons were made on the posttest, Classes A and B were found to be superior. Their superior performance was attributed to the new materials and methods.

4. Design the *ideal* experiment to test the following hypothesis: Children who view films of harmonious racial interaction will show a more positive attitude toward racial minorities than will children shown films that depict racial conflict.

5. Returning to the research problem in question 2, suppose you also want to know if the two methods of teaching French have differential effects for boys and girls? Outline the experimental design that would permit you to answer this question at the same time.

6. Assume an investigator had used two methods of instruction (A_1 and A_2) with two groups of students (B_1 and B_2) having varying levels of achievement motivation. The groups were compared on an achievement test at the end of the study. The means are presented below. What interpretation would you make of these results?

	A_1	A_2
B_1	35	15
B_2	15	35

Answers

1. a. type of social studies curriculum
   b. scores on an ethnic attitude scale
   c. Group A, the present curriculum
   d. Group B, curriculum with ethnic history
   e. random selection of the sample from the population and random assignment of the sample to the experimental and control groups
   f. Design 3, the two groups, randomized subjects, posttest-only design

2. a. Use Design 3, that is, randomly assign first-year French students to either the grammar-transformational (control) or oral-aural (experimental) group. Maintain the same conditions, time spent, teachers, classroom facilities for both groups so that only the teaching method is different. Administer test at the end of the year and compare group achievement.
   b. Randomly assign intact classes of first-year French students to the two teaching methods. Each teacher has an equal number of the two types of classes.
   c. In the ideal design threats to external and internal validity are better controlled through randomization of individual students. The design in question b could have problems with nonequivalence of subjects before treatment is given, so that test score differences could be due to factors other than difference in treatment.

3. a. Because the researcher could not assign students randomly to the high schools, there are several threats to internal validity. Students in the experimental school may have been brighter or have had more background in science than students in the control school. Differences in the quality of teaching biology in the schools have not been controlled. Because the researcher used only schools in a small town, the results of the study could not be generalized to other high schools in different settings.

The researcher could compare initial science achievement and IQ scores for the schools to see if the groups were equivalent before treatment. Using several high schools, with classes within each high school being randomly assigned to experimental conditions, would control for factors specific to a given school.

b. Classes not randomly assigned may not be equivalent. Pretesting could have been used to determine equivalence, but was given to only two of the groups. The pretesting of the experimental groups alone may have sensitized the groups and influenced the differences found. Classes should be randomly assigned to treatments, even if individual students cannot be randomly assigned.

4. The ideal experiment would randomly assign students to groups. The results of a posttreatment measure of attitudes toward racial minorities would be used to compare the experimental and control groups.

5. This question requires a factorial design with two groups of boys and two groups of girls assigned randomly to the control and experimental conditions.

6. It appears that there is an interaction between achievement motivation and type of instruction. Students with achievement motivation at level B_1 did better with method A_1, while those at level B_2 did better with method A_2. The significance of this interaction could be tested with an F-test. There is no overall effect of motivation or instructional method, as the means for A_1 and A_2, and B_1 and B_2, are the same.

Ex Post Facto Research

As we probe educational questions such as, Why are some children better readers than others? Why do some youths become delinquent while others do not? we find that only some of our questions can be investigated through experimental research. If we wish to investigate the influence of such variables as home environment, motivation, intelligence, parental reading habits, and so forth, we cannot randomly assign students to different categories of these variables. Independent variables such as these are called *attribute variables*. An attribute variable is a characteristic that a subject possesses before a study begins.

In contrast, an independent variable that an investigator can directly manipulate is an *active variable*. An investigator can determine which students will have access to a shorthand laboratory and which will not, which will use Program A to study a unit in algebra and which will use Program B. When active independent variables are involved, we can employ experimental or quasi-experimental research. When we have attribute independent variables, we must turn to *ex post facto research*.

The designation *ex post facto,* Latin for "from after the fact," serves to indicate that the research in question is conducted after variations in the independent variable have already been determined in the natural course of events. Kerlinger has defined ex post facto research quite succinctly as

> systematic empirical inquiry in which the scientist does not have direct control of independent variables because their manifestations have already occurred or because they are inherently not manipulable. Inferences about relations among variables are made, without direct intervention, from concomitant variation of independent and dependent variables.[1]

Researchers achieve the variation they want, not by direct manipulation of the variable itself but by selection of individuals in whom the variable is present or absent, strong or weak, and so on. They present brain-damaged and nonbrain-damaged children with the same perceptual task; or they compare the performance of high-IQ and low-IQ children on the same measure of anxiety.

Ex Post Facto and Experimental Approaches Compared

In both types of research, interest is focused upon discovery or establishment of relationships among the variables in one's data. Ex post facto research, as well as experimental research, can test hypotheses concerning the relationship between an

---

[1]Fred N. Kerlinger, *Foundations of Behavioral Research,* 2nd ed. (New York: Holt, Rinehart and Winston, 1973), p. 379.

independent variable, X, and a dependent variable, Y. In basic logic experimental and ex post facto approaches are similar. The aim of both is to compare two groups, similar on all relevant characteristics but one, in order to measure the effects of that characteristic. Thus much of the same kind of information that an experiment provides can also be obtained through an ex post facto analysis.

However, with an experiment it is possible to obtain much more convincing evidence for causal or functional relationships among variables than can be obtained with ex post facto studies. The effects of extraneous variables in an experiment are controlled by the experimental conditions, and the presumably antecedent independent variable is directly manipulated in order to ascertain its effect on the dependent variable. If Y is observed to vary concomitantly with the variation in X in this controlled situation, then one has obtained evidence for the validity of the hypothesized antecedent-consequence relationship between X and Y. In an ex post facto situation, on the other hand, the researcher cannot control the independent variables by manipulation or by randomization. The term *ex post facto* indicates that changes in the independent variable have already taken place; the researcher is faced with the problem of trying to determine the antecedents of the observed consequence. Because of the lack of control, it is more hazardous to infer that there is a genuine relationship between X and Y in an ex post facto study.

Let us illustrate the difference between an ex post facto and an experimental approach by examining these two approaches to the same research question. Consider the question of the effect that students' anxiety in an achievement-testing situation has on their examination performance. The ex post facto approach to this problem would involve measuring the already existing anxiety level at the time of the examination, then comparing the performance of "high anxious" and "low anxious" students. The weakness of such an approach is that one could not necessarily conclude that it was the students' anxiety that produced the observed difference in achievement examination performance. Both sets of scores may have been influenced by a third factor, such as general intelligence. General intelligence may be the major cause of both the level of anxiety and the achievement test results.

An experimental approach to the same problem would involve the administration of the examination under two conditions that are identical in every respect except that one is anxiety-arousing and the other, neutral. The experimenter can induce anxiety by telling the subjects that their final grade is dependent upon their performance, that the test is extremely difficult, or that the test will be used to identify the incompetent. The neutral group would merely be told that their cooperation is needed for the experiment. The investigator could randomly assign subjects to the two conditions. Then if the anxious group performed better than the neutral, it could be concluded that the anxiety had a facilitating effect on test performance. Such a conclusion could be legitimately drawn because of the control provided by the random assignment of groups to treatments and by the direct manipulation of the independent variable by the experimenter. Anxiety is one of the few variables that can be either an active or an attribute independent variable. That is, one can manipulate it actively, as described (experimental approach), or one can take subjects and classify them on the basis of their scores on an anxiety measure (ex post facto approach).

In a sense the ex post facto study can be viewed as a reverse approach to experimentation. Instead of taking groups that are equivalent and exposing them to different treatments, the ex post facto study starts with groups that are different and tries to determine the antecedents of these differences. An ex post facto study begins with a description of a present situation, which is assumed to be an effect of some previously acting factors, and attempts a retrospective search to determine the assumed antecedent factors, which began operating at an earlier time. Such a procedure does not provide the safeguards, typical in experimentation, that are necessary for making inferences about causal relationships. An investigator who finds a relationship between the variables in an ex post facto study, has secured evidence only of some concomitant variation. Because the investigator has not controlled X or other possible variables that may have determined Y, there is no basis for inferring a causal relationship between X and Y. In order to be able to make a type of antecedent-consequent relationship between the variables, one must gather evidence to show that Y did not precede X or that the Y effect has not been produced by some other factor that is related to the presumed antecedent factor. For example, if we give children with brain damage and children without damage a perceptual test, the differences in their performance might reflect the effects of brain damage or they might reflect such other factors as differences in anxiety associated with certain types of illness. Or let us consider an early study by Rogerson and Rogerson that reported the finding that a group of children who had been breast-fed during infancy subsequently exhibited a higher level of performance in elementary school than did a group of children who had been bottle-fed.[2] It cannot be concluded from such a finding that performance in school may be improved by breast feeding during infancy. Most likely the relationship observed by these investigators was an outcome of variations in one or more variables that influenced both the type of feeding received by the children studied and the level of performance they subsequently achieved in school. The authors report that the study was conducted at a clinic where breast feeding was encouraged and that failures to do so were often the result of poor health of the infant or the mother, or both. Thus the most reasonable interpretation would probably be that both the type of feeding received by the infants and their subsequent performance in school were influenced by health, good health tending to result more often in successful breast feeding *and* in superior school performance. So despite the observed relationship between these two factors, we certainly would not want to conclude that level of school performance was a direct consequence of type of feeding.

Ex post facto research, though not a satisfactory substitute for experimentation, does provide a method that can be used in the circumstances under which much of educational research must be conducted. It remains a useful method that can supply much information of value in educational decision making.

[2]B. C. F. Rogerson and C. H. Rogerson, "Feeding in Infancy and Subsequent Psychological Difficulties," *Journal of Mental Science* 85 (1939):1163–82.

Conditions Necessary for Inferring Causal Relationships

If one wishes to reach a conclusion that one variable (X) is the cause of another variable (Y), *three* kinds of evidence are necessary:

1. that a statistical relationship between X and Y has been established
2. that X preceded Y in time
3. that other factors did not determine Y

Because of the safeguards built into an experimental design, experimental studies provide evidence on all of these, so that causal inferences can be made. In ex post facto studies, however, the safeguards of the experimental situation are lacking and interpretation of causal relationship is much more hazardous.

If one does establish a relationship between two variables in an ex post facto study, one must proceed to look for evidence on the other two points. The investigator must establish the time sequence; that is, one must consider whether Y might have occurred before X and hence could not be an effect of X. Decisions about the time relationship between X and Y can be made either on a logical basis or as a result of measurements that show the groups did not differ on Y before exposure to X.

It is also extremely important that the investigator consider whether or not factors other than X might have determined Y. One proceeds to check this possibility by introducing other relevant variables into the analysis and observing how the relationship between X and Y is affected by these additional variables.

One may find that the relationship between X and Y holds up even when the other variables are introduced. In this case one has some evidence to support a causal inference. On the other hand, one may find that the presence of the other variables may change the relationship between X and Y, or even eliminate it. In this case one concludes either that X does not determine Y or that the relationship between X and Y is *spurious*.

POSSIBILITIES FOR SPURIOUS RESULTS IN EX POST FACTO RESEARCH

The difference between an active independent variable and an attribute independent variable is exceedingly important. When investigators can control the treatment (X) and then observe the dependent variable (Y), they have reasonable evidence that X influences Y. If they cannot control X, they may be led to inappropriate conclusions because the observed relationship may be a *spurious* one, that is, a relationship that is due to other causes, not to X influencing Y. Among the possible origins of spurious relationships are common cause, reverse causality, and the presence of other independent variables.

Common Cause

In an ex post facto investigation, one must consider the possibility that both the independent and dependent variables of the study are merely two separate results of a third variable. For example, if we use average teachers' salary as an independent variable and sales of distilled spirits as a dependent variable for each year since the repeal of Prohibition in the United States, we find a high positive correlation between the two variables. Does this mean that whenever teachers' salaries are raised they spend their money on alcohol? A more plausible explanation is that both teachers' salaries and sales of distilled spirits are the result of increasing affluence and inflation since 1933.

It is well established that the average income of private high school graduates is much higher than the average income of public and parochial high school graduates. Does this mean that private schools better prepare students for financial success? Or is the difference due to the fact that those families with enough money to send their children to private schools are also able to finance their children's professional training, set them up in business, or buy them ambassadorships or seats in the United States Senate?

In city X we find that over the last twenty years an increase in the consumption of electricity has been accompanied by a corresponding increase in cases of mental illness. Does this mean that increase in the use of electricity leads to increase in mental illness? A check of census figures shows that the population of city X has increased through the years and that the consumption of electricity and cases of mental illness are both functions of population growth.

An ex post facto researcher must always consider the possibilities of common cause or causes accounting for an observed relationship. In our examples fairly obvious common causes could be identified. However, in ex post facto research there is always a nagging doubt that there may be common causes that no one has thought of which explain a relationship. It has been shown that the injury rate of drivers who use seat belts is lower than the injury rate of drivers who do not. Is this because the use of seat belts reduces injury or is it that cautious drivers (a) use seat belts and (b) have fewer injury-causing accidents?

Reverse Causality

In interpreting an observed relationship in an ex post facto study, one must consider the possibility that the reverse of the suggested hypothesis could also account for the finding. That is, instead of saying that X causes Y, perhaps it is the case that Y causes X. For instance, it is a fact that the proportion of Episcopalians who are listed in *Who's Who in America* is much greater than the proportion of Episcopalians in the general population. Does this mean that Episcopalianism leads to the kind of success that results in being listed in *Who's Who?* It is just as plausible, or perhaps more so, to hypothesize that successful people tend to gravitate to the Episcopal church.

If we find that college students who drink have a lower GPA than nondrinkers we cannot automatically conclude that alcohol consumption depresses academic performance. Perhaps bad grades drive students to drink. (Or, of course, there may be any number of common causes that could lead to both drinking and poor grades.)

Investigations on the effects of child-rearing practices have revealed that there is more aggressive behavior on the part of children who are frequently punished. Does this mean that one can conclude that parental punishment leads to aggressive children, or is it that aggressive children are more likely to be punished?

The hypothesis of reverse causality is easier to deal with than the hypothesis of common cause. With the latter there may be numerous common causes in each case that could produce a spurious relationship. With reverse causality there is only one possibility in each case; Y caused X instead of X caused Y.

In any situation when X always precedes Y in time, the very nature of our data rules out the possibility of reverse causality. For example, numerous studies have shown that the average annual income of college graduates is higher than the average annual income of nongraduates. We can rule out the hypothesis of reverse causality since graduation or nongraduation precedes the subsequent annual income. We cannot rule out a variety of possible common causes.

A method of establishing the time order of variables is to obtain measurements of the same subjects at different times. Let us assume that one is interested in the relationship between acceptance of the philosophy of a corporation and promotion within that corporation. If one merely interviewed a sample of the employees and found that those in higher positions held attitudes and opinions more in line with the company's value system, one would not know whether acceptance of company values and objectives was conducive to promotion or whether promotion increased acceptance of the company value system. To rule out reverse causality as an explanation, one could interview a group of new trainees and obtain by means of a questionnaire, rating scale, or the like, a measure of their acceptance of the corporation philosophy. Then after a period of time, perhaps 18 months, the investigator could determine from company records which of the employees had been promoted. If the findings showed that a significantly higher proportion of those who had expressed attitudes and opinions consistent with corporation philosophy had been promoted, as compared with those who had not, one would have better evidence that conformity with company philosophy was conducive to promotion. (One is still left with the possibility that some common cause or causes account for differences in both philosophy and promotion.)

Other Possible Independent Variables

There may be independent variables other than the one under consideration in the ex post facto study that could bring about the observed effect on the Y variable. That is, in addition to X_1, other variables, X_2 and X_3, might also be antecedent factors for the variation in the dependent variable.

It is known that the recorded suicide rate in Sweden is the highest in the world. Does this mean that the Swedish environment causes more people to commit suicide? Does it mean that the Swedish people are more suicide prone than others? Perhaps there is truth in one or both of these hypotheses. It is equally possible, however, that the actual independent variable is the honesty of coroners in Sweden compared with the honesty of coroners in other countries. In a country where great social stigma falls on the families of those who commit suicide, coroners may well use every conceivable means to record a death as accidental rather than suicide. Therefore the difference between reported suicide rates may be a function of coroner behavior and nothing else.

At a governors' conference, Governor X points with pride to the low crime rate in his state. Another governor points out that the police forces in Governor X's state are seriously undermanned and the low crime rate may indicate only that very few crimes there are ever reported. An industrialist asks his personnel manager why he does not hire more Old Siwash graduates, asserting that since so many of them are rapidly moving up the promotion ladder, they are obviously more competent than other graduates. The personnel manager tactfully points out that the phenomenon might not be explained by competence but rather by the fact that the industralist is himself an Old Siwash graduate and may be subconsciously favoring his fellow alumni in promotion decisions.

An obvious first task for investigators is to make an attempt to list all the possible alternative independent variables. Then by holding the others constant, we can test in turn each of the variables to determine if it is related to Y. If we can eliminate the alternative independent variables by showing that they are not related to Y, we gain support for the original hypothesis of a relationship between X and Y.

In the following report the data show a relationship between automobile use and academic achievement.

DO AUTOMOBILES AND SCHOLARSHIP MIX?

No, says Madison HS, Rexburg, Idaho. A study made of the 4-year grade averages of a typical Madison senior class and car drivers showed the following:

No straight A student had the use of a car.

Only 15% of the B students drove a car to school.

Of C students, 41% brought cars to school.

Of D students, 71% drove to school

Of E students, 83% drove to school.

Action Program

As a result of the study, Rexburg's Board of Education adopted a resolution on August 11, 1958, which specified that—

1. Junior and senior high-school students who drive cars to school must make written application to the School Board showing the reason or need to drive their cars to school. Those granted permission will receive student permits.
2. Students driving cars to school on the student permits must park them in designated areas.
3. Students failing to comply with established rules and regulations will have their student permits revoked. If students persist in non-compliance, they will be subject to expulsion from school by action of the School Board.

Community Cooperation

The entire community has organized to support the Board of Education's regulations. The Citizen's Law Enforcement Council and the Rexburg Youth Conference have enlisted the participation of the Civic Club, Rotary Club, American Legion, newspapers, police department, and parents in their drive for high-school traffic safety. Hundreds of citizens have signed a pledge to back the drive and have received membership cards issued by the Council and Conference. Madison's principal, W. G. Nelson, strongly supports the community-wide action against unrestricted car use by high-school students. "We believe that restriction on automobile use will make for better attendance and closer attention to studies. We haven't 'arrived' but we certainly are on the way."

A Texas Principal

Commenting on the Rexburg program, [a Texas principal] said, "It has long been my opinion that there is a high correlation between rate of failure, scholarship, and ownership and operation of automobiles freely by high-school youth. We are finding it difficult to obtain much interest from able-bodied boys in major athletics. So many of the boys are paying for automobiles or for their maintenance and operation by holding down part-time jobs after school hours that they don't go out for athletics. If they have money to operate their cars, they prefer to ride in them around town after school. There are a few parents who have sufficient control of and influence with their youngsters to prevent them unwise use of their own cars, but they are very scarce."

(Note: The University of Virginia has recently banned all student-owned automobiles from the campus because of their adverse effect on scholarship. Princeton University has forbidden car privileges for students since before 1945.)[3]

Is the conclusion that automobile use causes lower academic achievement justified? Let us consider the possible alternative hypotheses.

1. *Common cause*. Are there variables that may influence both auto use and scholarship? We know social class is related to scholarship. If social class also influences auto use, the apparent relationship between grades and auto use would be not a cause-effect relationship but two aspects of social class differences. Differences in student life-style or values could also account for the apparent relationship. If some students value driving highly and have little interest in scholarship, denying them access to cars would not necessarily increase their scholarship. We could propose a number of credible common cause hypotheses.

2. *Reverse causality*. Is it possible that poor grades are a cause of car use? We could reasonably hypothesize that students who do poorly in school look for other paths to social acceptance and that car use is one of the possibilities.

3. *Other possible independent variables*. Could it be that teachers perceive car users as disinterested students and assign them lower grades than they deserve? Perhaps the knowledge that the school is investigating the relationship between grades and car use has influenced the attitude of car users in a way that in turn influences their grades. Perhaps the fact of the investigation itself affects teacher attitudes toward car users. There are so many credible alternate hypotheses that one should hesitate to interpret the data as indicating a cause-effect relationship.

[3]Do Automobiles and Scholarship Mix?" *NASSP Spotlight on Junior and Senior High Schools* 36 (1959):3.

Asher and Schusler investigated the same issue with a design that incorporated more control than had previous studies.[4] Instead of considering only present grades and auto use, they recorded grades of seniors at the end of the first semester and the grades of the same subjects when they were freshmen. If auto use affects scholarship, then the grades of drivers would be expected to drop between the time they were freshmen, and therefore ineligible for driver's licenses, and the time they were seniors. Asher and Schusler used the difference between freshman and senior GPA as their dependent variable. They also co-varied (see p. 283) on IQ. They found no significant relation between auto use and change in grades. They concluded, "access to an automobile seems not to cause an established pattern of grades to decline, or for that matter, to go up."

Partial Control in Ex Post Facto Research

There are strategies for improving the credibility of ex post facto research although none of them can adequately compensate for the inherent weakness of such research, namely, lack of control of the independent variable. Among these strategies are change scores, matching, analysis of covariance, partial correlation, homogeneous groups, and building extraneous variables into the design.

CHANGE SCORES

In the car-use examples we found that the conclusion reached when the difference between subjects' senior grades and freshman grades were used did not agree with the conclusion reached when only grades *per se* were used. Certainly the former has more credibility than the latter since the latter completely fails to take into account the possibility that car users were poorer students than nonusers before any of them might have had access to cars.

With change scores one takes into account previous scores on the Y variable rather than just present scores on Y. When one compares how much a treatment group changes in comparison with a control group, one may be somewhat less likely to be misled than when only present scores are used. However, the use of change scores is only a partial solution and the results of such studies must be treated with caution. For example, Principal A has introduced a new reading program in the fifth grade and after it has been in use for a year he wants to compare its effectiveness with the effectiveness of the reading program it replaced. In the same district Principal B's school is still using the old program. Both schools give the same standardized reading test at the end of each school year. Principal A compares the mean grade equivalent reading scores for fifth graders in the two schools. He finds the mean grade level equivalent for his fifth graders is 6.0, while the mean for

---

[4]William Asher and Marian M. Schusler, "Students' Grades and Access to Cars," *Journal of Educational Research* 60 (July–August 1967):10.

Principal B's fifth graders is 4.0. Is this dramatic evidence of the effectiveness of the new method? Principal A realizes that the difference between means could be due to differences between the pupils when they began the fifth grade in the two schools. He obtains scores for the reading test administered when the pupils were finishing fourth grade. He finds that his students had a mean grade level equivalent of 4.8, while Principal B's students had a mean grade level equivalent of only 3.2. Therefore he must make an adjustment for the fact that the two groups were not at the same point when they began fifth grade. For each pupil for whom both scores are available, Principal A subtracts the fourth grade score from the fifth grade score. He finds a mean difference of +1.2 for his pupils and +.8 for Principal B's pupils. The difference of .4 between the two groups' mean change scores is less dramatic but more convincing than the difference of 2.0 obtained when only fifth grade scores were used and no adjustment was made for previous performance.

Can Principal A now conclude that the new method is more effective than the old one? Given the nature of change scores, he cannot. Differences in change scores may be due to the continuation of previous patterns. In order to find the pattern in this case, Principal A divides the final mean grade level equivalent, obtained at the end of the fourth grade year, by four (the number of years in school). Principal A's pupils with a mean score of 4.8 at the end of their fourth year have had an average grade equivalent gain in reading performance of 1.2 per year, while Principal B's students have averaged a reading grade equivalent gain of .8. In both cases the gains in reading scores during the fifth grade are just what one would expect given the previous gain patterns, and therefore there is no support for the hypothesis that the new method is more effective than the old method. An inherent weakness in change scores is that an apparent greater gain in one group compared with another group may well be a continuation of a previous pattern and not due to the treatment at all.

Consider another example. It is hypothesized that the study of Latin improves high school students' English vocabulary. The investigators have freshman and senior vocabulary scores for both those who took and those who did not take Latin. If we look at Figure 10.1, we see that the gain in the vocabulary scores from grade 9 to grade 12 for the Latin group (from 80 to 95 points) is greater than the gain for the non-Latin group (from 54 to 63 points). However, we see in Figure 10.1 that those who elected to take Latin are merely continuing a previous pattern of accelerated vocabulary growth, and those who did not elect to take Latin are continuing their previous pattern. The gain for both groups in the three years from grades 9 to 12 is the same as their gain from grades 6 to 9. A very naive investigator, looking at only the senior scores of the two groups and not taking into account their different starting places, might conclude that the difference of 32 points (95–63) is due to the Latin experience. A less naive investigator, using change scores from grade 9 to grade 12 for the two groups, attributes only 6 points (15–9) to the Latin experience. However, this investigator has also reached the wrong conclusion. Who is the most likely to mislead the unaware? The conclusion of the first investigator is less likely to be accepted because the idea that the two groups may well differ on previous English vocabulary proficiency is a fairly obvious one, and readers are likely to be skeptical of a conclusion based on only senior scores. The use of change

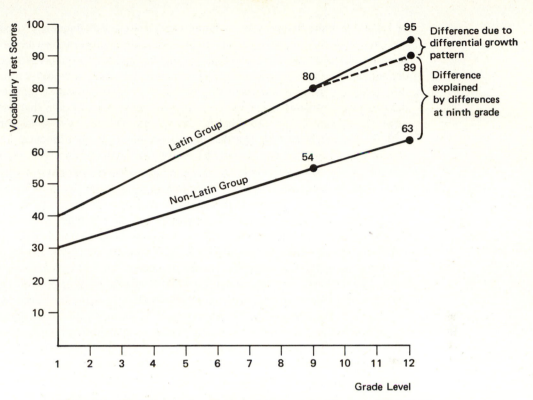

Figure 10.1 The influence of previous vocabulary growth patterns on change scores

scores *seems* to solve the problem of preexisting differences and the second investigator's conclusion seems more credible. However, the use of change scores is only a partial solution.

Change scores adjust for (*a*) groups beginning at different points. They do *not* adjust for (*b*) preexisting differences in growth rates. Whenever preexisting differences in growth rate do exist, differences in posttreatment scores are due to both (*a*) and (*b*). The use of change scores removes the spurious effect of (*a*) but not the spurious effect of (*b*). Therefore the change scores are only a partial solution. We can be misled by the underadjustment.

MATCHING

A common method of providing partial control in ex post facto investigations has been to match the subjects in the experimental and control groups on as many extraneous variables as possible. The matching is usually done on a subject-to-subject basis to form matched pairs. For example, if one is interested in the relationship between scouting experiences and delinquency, one could locate two groups of boys classified as delinquent and nondelinquent according to specified criteria. It would be wise in such a study to select pairs from these groups matched on the basis of socioeconomic status, family structure, and other variables known to be related to both choosing the scouting experience and delinquency. Analysis of the data from the matched samples could be made, to determine whether or not scouting characterizes the nondelinquent and is absent in the background of the delinquent. The matching procedure in ex post facto research presents some of the difficulties described in our discussion of its use in experimentation (chapter 9). In the first place, utilizing matching in an ex post facto study assumes that one knows what the relevant factors are—that is, the factors that may have some correlation with the dependent variable. Furthermore, matching is likely to reduce greatly the number of subjects that can actually be used in the final analysis. The loss of cases inherent in the matching process is an even more serious problem in ex post facto research than in experimentation, where matching precedes the introduction of the independent variable. At least in the experimental approach there may be a possibility (although it is not recommended) of adding new cases to replace the ones that do not match. This cannot be done in ex post facto research.

One of Chapin's studies shows the loss of subjects that occurs as a result of matching.[5] Chapin was interested in the influence of high school graduation on an individual's success and community adjustment after a ten-year period. The initial data revealed that those who had completed high school were more successful than those who had not. However, an examination of the high school files revealed that those who had graduated also had higher marks in elementary school, younger ages, higher parental occupations; lived in better neighborhoods, and so on. These factors could have been the causative factors for both completion of high school and later success. To partially control these common causes, Chapin examined subgroups of students matched on all these background factors and differing only in completion of high school. Matching reduced the number of cases from 1,194 to 46, or 23 graduates and 23 nongraduates—fewer than 4 percent of the number interviewed.

A more serious problem than loss of subjects is the role regression plays in an ex post facto matched pairs design. Let us use our reading example to illustrate the point. In order to use matched pairs instead of unmatched change scores, Principal A would take a student from his school with a fourth grade reading score of 3.1 and match that student with a student from Principal B's school with a fourth grade reading score of 3.1, a student from his school with a score of 4.8 with a student from B's school with a score of 4.8, and so on. However, since the mean of the B population is lower than the mean of the A population, there will be many low-scoring B students for whom there is no match in A and many high-scoring A students for whom there is no match in the B group. The scores of all the unmatchable students will be excluded from the data analysis. For those who could be matched the mean score for the fourth grade reading test for group A and group B will be identical. Therefore it appears that we have successfully created a group from school B who are the same as the group from school A in reading achievement.

This all sounds very good. Can we now attribute differences in fifth grade reading scores to a difference in the effectiveness of the old and new methods? Alas, no! Our matched pairs are basically those students with poorer fourth grade reading

---

[5]F. S. Chapin, *Experimental Designs in Sociological Research* (New York: Harper & Row, 1947).

scores from population A and those students with higher scores from population B. The matched A students' scores will regress *up* toward the total A mean and the matched B students' scores will regress *down* toward the total B mean. Thus, when we compare the fifth grade reading scores of the matched groups, we would expect the A mean to be higher than the B mean even if the new method is no more effective than the old method.

Matching looks good since it provides experimental and control groups that are equal on a pretreatment variable or variables. However, when two matched groups are drawn from different populations, regression toward the original population means will be expected to create spurious results whenever the two populations are not equal. Matching pairs from within a *single* population is often a useful strategy. Matching subjects from one population with subjects from another population is a *bad* strategy. As is the case with change scores, matching only partly adjusts for preexisting differences between groups. This underadjustment can mislead us in the same manner that the underadjustment in change scores can mislead us.

ANALYSIS OF COVARIANCE AND PARTIAL CORRELATION

Analysis of covariance and partial correlation are statistical procedures that, like matching, partially adjust for preexisting differences between groups.[6] Partial correlation deals with the residual relationship between two variables where common influence of one or more other variables has been removed. For example, we could find the correlation between creativity and achievement with the effect of chronological age removed. Neither procedure requires matching, so the data from all subjects can be used rather than only data on matched pairs. However, although analysis of covariance and partial correlation are, in general, better methods than matching, they also underadjust for initial differences and can yield spurious results.

A well-known example of the dangers of matching and analysis of covariance is the Westinghouse/Ohio University ex post facto study of the effects of the Head Start program.[7] This study compared the academic achievement of students who had been in the Head Start program with the achievement of those who had not been in the Head Start program. Children who had been in the Head Start program were matched with non-Head Start children from the same neighborhoods on sex, racial-ethnic groups, and kindergarten attendance. Analysis of covariance was used to adjust for differences in income per capita, educational level of father, and occupational level of father. The results indicated that the achievement of the non-Head Start group was greater than that of the Head Start group even when scores were adjusted for initial differences, suggesting that the effect of the Head Start program was a harmful one.

[6]A number of statistics books describe these techniques. We recommend Glass and Stanley, *Statistical Methods in Education and Psychology*.

[7]V. Cicirelli et al., *The Impact of Head Start: An Evaluation of the Effects of Head Start on Children's Cognitive and Affective Development*. A report presented to the Office of Economic Opportunity pursuant to Contract B89–4536, June 1969. Westinghouse Learning Corporation, Ohio University. (Distributed by Clearinghouse for Federal Scientific and Technical Information, U.S. Department of Commerce, National Bureau of Standards, Institute for Applied Technology, PB 184 328.)

Campbell and Erlebacher pointed out that since both matching and analysis of covariance underadjust for initial differences between groups, we would expect adjusted posttreatment scores of a disadvantaged group to be less than adjusted posttreatment scores of a less disadvantaged group.[8] Since the extent of the underadjustment is unknown, we cannot safely conclude that the Head Start experience was harmful or beneficial, or had no effect.

HOMOGENEOUS GROUPS

You may recall from the discussion of control in experimentation that it is possible to control for the effects of a variable by selecting samples that are as homogeneous as possible on that variable. A similar procedure can be followed in ex post facto research. Instead of taking a heterogeneous sample and comparing matched subgroups within it, an investigator may control a variable by including in the sample only subjects who are homogeneous on that variable. If intelligence is a relevant extraneous variable, the investigator could control its effect by using subjects from only one intelligence level. This procedure serves the purpose of disentangling the independent variable in which the investigator may be interested from other variables with which it is commonly associated so that any effects that are found can more justifiably be associated with the independent variable.

Suppose one wishes to investigate whether having a quiet room at home, with desk, books, and so on, in which to study affects the grades of high school students. If one simply selects a cross section of high school students, asks them whether or not they have a quiet room in which to study, and then compares the grades of those who have a room and those who do not, one may erroneously conclude that having a quiet room in which to study leads to good grades. An alternative explanation is that there are other factors associated with social class that may influence both one's study arrangements and grades received in school. Low-income families, for instance, are more likely to be overcrowded and are less likely to put emphasis on scholastic achievement than are middle- and upper-class families. If one wants to control for the effects of social class, one can limit the study to subjects of only one socioeconomic level. If one finds a relationship between study arrangements and grades within the one social class, one would have somewhat more confidence in the conclusion that the difference in grades is due to study arrangements and not to socioeconomic differences. Of course, this procedure limits the generalizability of the findings to the one social class used in the study; one would not know whether the relationship exists in other social classes.

The use of homogeneous samples is only a partial solution to the problems inherent in ex post facto research. We can control for some common cause variables by selecting samples who are alike on a suspected common cause variable. We

[8]Donald T. Campbell and Albert Erlebacher, ''How Regression Artifacts in Quasi-Experimental Evaluations Can Mistakenly Make Compensatory Education Look Harmful,'' in *Compensatory Education: A National Debate,* vol. 3, *Disadvantaged Child,* J. Hellmuth, ed. (New York: Brunner/Mazel, 1970).

cannot be sure we have subjects who are homogeneous on all suspected or unsuspected common cause variables. In our example it is quite possible that *within* middle-class families both having or not having a quiet room and academic achievement are a function of family size or other variables. Regression can also be a problem with homogeneous samples. For example, if Principal A in our earlier example had used only children in the two schools who scored exactly 4.0 on the fourth grade reading test, regression would cause the A group to regress up and the B group to regress down, as they did when subjects were matched.

BUILDING EXTRANEOUS VARIABLES INTO THE DESIGN

It may be possible to build relevant extraneous independent variables into the ex post facto design and use a factorial analysis-of-variance technique. For example, assume that intelligence is a relevant extraneous variable and it is not feasible to control it through any other means. In such a case intelligence could be added to the design as another independent variable and the subjects of the study classified in terms of intelligence levels. The dependent variable measures would then be analyzed through the analysis of variance, and the main and interaction effects of intelligence might be determined. Such a procedure would reveal any significant differences among the groups on the dependent variable, but no causal relationship between intelligence and the dependent variable could be assumed. Other extraneous variables could be operating to produce both the main effect and any interaction effect.

For example, many studies have reported a relationship between birth order and intellectual attainment and occupational achievement: first born doing better than second born, second born doing better than third born, and so forth. After a thorough review of the literature, Schooler concluded: "The most frequently reported differences between birth ranks—the greater occurrence of first borns among groups marked by unusual intellectual attainment or occupational achievement— seems to be most parsimoniously explained in terms of differences among social class trends in family size."[9] Since there is an inverse relationship between social class and family size, the average social-class standing of fifth children would be lower than the average social-class standing of fourth children, and so forth. As social class is related to achievement, the apparent relationship between birth order and achievement might be due solely to differences in average social-class standing and not to birth order *per se*.

Later Belmont and Marolla studied birth order and scores on the Raven Progressive Matrices test (a nonverbal intelligence test) for nearly 400,000 young men in the Netherlands.[10] They found that *within* each family size intelligence declined

[9]C. Schooler, "Birth Order Effects: Not Here, Not Now!" *Psychological Bulletin* 72 (1972):161–75.
[10]L. Belmont and F. A. Marolla, "Birth Order, Family Size, and Intelligence," *Science* 182 (1973):1096–101.

with birth order. Since they were comparing scores only within five-child families, within four-child families, and so forth, differences in social class could not account for their results.

Do the Belmont and Marolla results now enable us to say that birth order *per se* is related to intelligence? We would be wise to treat this as only a tentative conclusion. One reason for our reservation is that there may be variables other than social class that account for the apparent relationship. Certainly the average age of the parents of fourth children is older than the average age of parents of third children and this may have something to do with the phenomenon. Perhaps it is accounted for by something we cannot even imagine.

Building other variables into an ex post facto design is a partial solution, but we can never be sure that we have selected the right variables or that we have employed *all* the variables that should have been considered.

It has been emphasized throughout this chapter that the major weakness of ex post facto designs is the lack of control. Since it is not feasible to utilize randomization to assign subjects to groups or to have direct manipulation of the independent variable in a controlled situation, there is always the possibility that there are uncontrolled variables that are responsible for the variation in the dependent variable. Because of this, one cannot assume that the groups are similar at the beginning of a study. Since the researcher has no control over who has been exposed to the experience and who has not, it is quite possible that something else about the people or their environment determines exposure in the first place. Therefore it may be that it is the "something else" rather than the experience itself that constitutes the critical independent variable.

As a result of the inadequate control in an ex post facto study, interpretation of the findings may be particularly hazardous. The risk of incorrect interpretation is great. When a relationship between two variables has been established in the course of an ex post facto study, the analysis has, in a sense, taken only its first step. The investigator must consider and test any plausible alternative hypotheses, and, even after doing so, must realize that an apparent relationship may be due to some other unfathomable cause. Procedures such as the use of change scores, matching, analysis of covariance, partial correlation, homogeneous groups, and building extraneous variables into a study, can help avoid gross errors in ex post facto studies, but they all underadjust for pretreatment differences among groups. Listing alternative hypotheses (common cause, reverse causality, and alternate independent variables) can help one assess more realistically ex post facto results.

Designing the Ex Post Facto Investigation

When attempting to answer such questions as, What was the contributing factor in a given situation? or What effect has a certain social situation or practice had? or What are the characteristics that distinguish this group from another? the researcher may set up an ex post facto investigation in which two or more groups are compared: One group has been exposed to the experience in question and the other has not. Or the researcher may study two groups that are different in some respects in order to discover the reasons for this difference. The basic design for ex post facto investigations is a modification of experimental design (see chapter 9) in which the investigator compares two groups on a dependent variable Y. The arrangement is schematized in Table 10.1.

Table 10.1   Ex Post Facto Design

Group	Independent Variable	Dependent Variable
E	(X)	Y_1
C	—	Y_2

The supposed effect of treatment occurs in the experimental but not in the control group, or in the control group to a different extent, shown by the Y_1 and Y_2 measures. That is, Y_1 and Y_2 indicate that the two groups differ on the dependent variable measure. The researcher attempts to relate the dependent variable Y to a previously occurring independent variable, a nonmanipulable variable indicated by (X), which occurred in the experimental group but not in the control group. Note that the nonmanipulable independent variable is indicated by (X) in contrast to a manipulable independent variable X. For example, an investigator may study underachievement, Y, by looking into underachieving students' backgrounds for possible contributing factors (X) that might have led to their poor scholastic achievement. The performance of a group of normal achievers would be compared on a number of standardized measures with that of the underachievers. The investigator would try to accomplish a pre-(X) equation of the groups on relevant pre-(X) attributes—that is, relevant extraneous variables—by matching or by statistical means, such as analysis of covariance, partial correlation, or change scores.

Although, as explained earlier, one variable in an ex post facto investigation cannot with confidence be said to depend upon the other in the same sense as in an experimental study, it is nevertheless customary in an ex post facto study to designate one of the variables as independent and the other as dependent. The independent variable is the one on the basis of which the individuals are grouped (in an earlier example, the anxiety level); the dependent variable is the one observed or measured following grouping (in the same example, examination performance). The terms help to denote the direction of the prediction—from subjects' status on the independent variable to their status on the dependent variable.

Procedure in an Ex Post Facto Investigation

Let us consider the steps involved in planning an investigation to ascertain the relationship of creativity to the problem-solving performance of college students. The ex post facto study would compare the problem-solving performance of creative and noncreative college students. The hypothesis would read: Creative college students will exhibit greater speed and accuracy on a problem-solving task than will noncreative college students. This hypothesis clearly indicates the need for an ex post facto design since the investigators can neither manipulate creativity nor assign students randomly to groups. They must start with two groups who already differ on the independent variable, creativity, and compare them on the dependent variable, problem-solving performance.

The investigators must define *creative college student* and *noncreative student* in precise operational terms. The creative college student might be defined as those undergraduates in the school of education scoring above the upper quartile on both the Guilford Test of Alternate Uses and Consequences and an anagram test. Those students scoring below the first quartile on the tests would be defined as noncreative.

The investigators should try to identify variables other than creativity that could affect the dependent variable of problem-solving performance and take steps to equate the experimental and control groups on these variables by matching or by statistical means. For example, in this study other independent variables that should be controlled are intelligence, sex, and perhaps college major or college year. A bright male sophomore in the creative group might be matched with his counterpart in the noncreative group.

After the formation of the matched groups, both groups would be given a measure of the dependent variable, a problem-solving task. Further analysis of the data by means of a *t*-test would reveal any significant differences in the problem-solving performance of the two groups and perhaps show a relationship between creativity and problem-solving performance. Although one may conclude from such a study that there is a relationship, one cannot assume a causal connection between creativity and problem-solving performance. There may be other uncontrolled variables that singly or in combination could influence problem solving. The alert investigator is aware of the need to examine other plausible alternative explanations of an ex post facto finding.

Another type of ex post facto study is one in which one makes a comparison of groups who have been exposed to contrasting experiences. Many studies were done in the 1950s on the effect of increased contact with the object of an attitude on changing that attitude. For example, Deutsch and Collins studied the changes in the attitudes of white tenants toward blacks during residence in an integrated housing project.[11] In this study the independent variable was the occupancy pattern of the housing project and the dependent variable was the change in attitudes.

The first step taken by these investigators was to select public housing projects that differed in their occupancy patterns. Some projects in the city were integrated and others were segregated; the investigators used only public housing projects, however, in order to control extraneous variables, such as socioeconomic level of the subjects and the experience of living in a housing project. The investigators selected, on a random basis, white housewives within these projects.

Thus this study used the two-group design described earlier. There was an ex-

[11]M. Deutsch and M. E. Collins, *Interracial Housing: A Psychological Evaluation of a Social Experiment* (Minneapolis: University of Minnesota Press, 1951).

perimental group, which had been exposed to the experience of living with blacks as neighbors in an integrated housing occupancy pattern, and a control group, which had not had this experience. The control group was selected from residents of biracial housing projects within which whites and blacks were segregated.

Steps had to be taken to investigate whether the two groups were initially similar in their positions on the dependent variable or in certain characteristics believed to be relevant to it. A questionnaire was administered to gather data from which the researchers could infer whether the two groups were or were not initially similar in their attitudes toward blacks. The questionnaire asked such questions as: Before you moved here, how did you feel about coming to live where there were blacks? Do you like it here now better, worse, about the same? Have you changed your attitudes about blacks since coming here?

It is usually necessary to check on the likelihood of self-selection in an ex post facto study of this type. There is always a possibility that people who have undergone different experiences *chose* them. Such self-selection means that the groups being compared are *not* initially equivalent. They may differ in ways that would definitely influence their status on the dependent variable. Therefore, in this study, Deutsch and Collins asked the white housewives whether, at the time they applied for admission to the projects, they knew that black tenants were there. They also questioned the groups on their education, religion, political attitudes, and other characteristics that other studies had found to be related to whites' attitudes toward blacks. In order to control for the effects of these differences, they compared matched subgroups within the two larger groups. For example, groups were matched on political attitudes to determine whether those in integrated projects still showed more friendly attitudes toward blacks. Deutsch and Collins report that their data support the conclusion that the experience of living in an integrated housing project and having closer contact with blacks resulted in a change toward more favorable attitudes.

Although the methodology of this study is too involved to describe completely here, perhaps enough of the steps were described to give the reader some understanding of the procedure involved in designing this type of ex post facto study.

The Role of Ex Post Facto Research

Given the hazards involved in interpreting ex post facto research, there are many in our profession who say we should not engage in this type of research at all. Basically their contention is that it is better to admit that we are ignorant than to risk reaching conclusions that are incorrect.

On the other hand, there are those who contend that many of the variables that are of great interest to us are not amenable to experimental research. We cannot randomly assign children to broken or intact homes, to high or low social class, to achievement-oriented or nonachievement-oriented peer groups, and so forth.

Therefore, if we want to learn anything about relationships between such attribute variables and other variables, the ex post facto method is our only recourse. If we use appropriate methods of partial control and if we consider alternative hypotheses, perhaps we can be right more often than we are wrong. Kerlinger expresses this view well:

> Despite its weaknesses, much ex post facto research must be done in psychology, sociology, and education simply because many research problems in the social sciences and education do not lend themselves to experimental inquiry. A little reflection on some of the important variables in educational research—intelligence, aptitude, home background, parental upbringing, teacher personality, school atmosphere—will show that they are not manipulable. Controlled inquiry is possible, of course, but true experimentation is not. Sociological problems of education, such as extreme deviation in group behavior and its effect on educational achievement, and board of education decisions and their effects on teacher and administrator performance and morale, are mostly ex post facto in nature. Even if we would avoid ex post facto research, we cannot.
>
> It can even be said that ex post facto research is more important than experimental research. This is, of course, not a methodological observation. It means, rather, that the most important social scientific and educational research problems do not lend themselves to experimentation, although many of them do lend themselves to controlled inquiry of the ex post facto kind. Consider Piaget's studies of children's thinking, Gross' study of boards of education and superintendents, the authoritarianism studies of Adorno et al., the enormously important study, *Equality of Educational Opportunity*. If a tally of sound and important studies in the behavioral sciences and education were made, it is possible that ex post facto studies would outnumber and outrank experimental studies.[12]

Certainly there have been many highly credible ex post facto studies. The surgeon general's study of the relationship between smoking and lung cancer is a well-known example. It is not possible to designate randomly a group of human subjects who are to smoke and a group who are not to smoke for years, so the study had to be done ex post facto. The reversed causality hypothesis that lung cancer causes people to smoke, is not plausible. None of the common cause hypotheses offered seem very likely: nervous people are prone to both smoking and lung cancer, some genetic predisposition leads to both, and so forth. The surgeon general controlled for many alternative independent variables by, for example, analyzing separately samples from areas of high air pollution and low air pollution. Experimental evidence with animals who were made to inhale or not inhale cigarette smoke has produced evidence of a cause-to-effect relationship. Given all this, despite the dangers inherent in ex post facto research, most of us would conclude that it is better to bet that there is a cause-to-effect relationship between smoking and lung cancer among humans than to bet that there is not such a relationship.

We all can deplore the many instances when ex post facto research has been employed in situations where true experimental or, at least, quasi-experimental designs could have been used. It is dismaying how often local or state agencies or

---

[12]Kerlinger, *Foundations of Behavioral Research*, pp. 391–92.

the federal government have ''tested'' new programs by entering all eligible subjects into the program, and then attempted to evaluate the effects of the program ex post facto. Too often governmental agencies, including schools, have responded to pressure to ''do something'' about a problem by instituting a new program for all eligible subjects. Evans (of the U.S. Office of Education) and Schiller (of the Office of Economic Opportunity) describe the way government agencies have responded to this pressure:

> Attempts to implement the required condition of random assignment will continue to face the objections of program clients on the grounds that such procedures involve an arbitrary deprivation of the program to those designated as controls. Among the dissatisfied, the vocal ones will complain to officials and congressmen. Program directors consequently will want to avoid this procedure and will be on the side of those opposing it.
>
> Our experience leads us to conclude, though reluctantly, that in the actual time-pressured and politically loaded circumstances in which social action programs inevitably arise, the instances when random assignment is practical are rare; and the nature of political and governmental processes makes it likely that this will continue to be the case. Unfortunately, the political process is not orderly, scheduled, or rational. Crests of public and congressional support for social action programs often swell quickly and with little anticipation. Once legislation is enacted, the pressures on administrators for swift program implementation are intense. In these circumstances—which are the rule rather than the exception—pleas that the program should be implemented carefully, along the lines of a true experiment with random assignment of subjects so we can confidently evaluate the program's effectiveness, are bound to be ignored.[13]

We contend that any dissatisfaction encountered among clients ''deprived'' of a new program is a drop compared with the flood of dissatisfaction from taxpayers who discover that millions have been spent on programs that lacked a well-planned method for determining whether these programs actually accomplished anything or not. There must be ways of handling the public relations problems in random assignment. Could not the government offer to several schools a fully funded program for a random half of their pupils? If the program is attractive, we would think many communities would be willing to participate in such an experiment, figuring that a random half a loaf is better than no loaf at all. Then when the evidence is in, the government would offer all pupils those programs that have shown their worth, and quietly drop those that have not.

Summary

The ex post facto design is used when investigators are not in a position to test a hypothesis by assigning subjects to different conditions in which they directly

[13]John W. Evans and Jeffry Schiller, ''How Preoccupation with Possible Regression Artifacts Can Lead to a Faulty Strategy for the Evaluation of Social Action Programs: A Reply to Campbell and Erlebacher,'' in Hellmuth, *Compensatory Education*, pp. 217–18.

manipulate the independent variable. In ex post facto studies the changes in the independent variable have already taken place and the researchers must study them in retrospect for their possible effects on an observed dependent variable.

Although there are many disadvantages of the ex post facto approach, it nevertheless is frequently the only method by which educational researchers can obtain necessary information about characteristics of defined groups of students or information needed for the intelligent formulation of programs in the school. It permits researchers to investigate situations in which it is impossible to introduce controlled variation. Attributes such as intelligence, creativity, socioeconomic status, and teacher personality cannot be manipulated and hence must be investigated through ex post facto research rather than through the more rigorous experimental approach.

Many ex post facto investigations have been notable in their influence on education. Variables such as home background, genetic endowment, brain damage, and early experiences are very important educational variables even though they are beyond the control of educators.

The possibility of spurious relationships is always present in ex post facto research. Considering the possibilities of common cause, reversed causality, and possible alternate independent variables can help us evaluate such research more realistically. Several partial control strategies can help us avoid gross errors in ex post facto designs, but none can entirely solve the problems inherent in those designs. We must always exercise caution in interpreting ex post facto results.

Exercises

1. How do attribute variables and active variables differ from each other?
2. Under what conditions does one use ex post facto research? What is the major weakness of ex post facto designs?
3. Which of the following research hypotheses call for *experimental research* and which call for *ex post facto research?*
   a. Young children who are read a story by a stranger will not retain it as long as those who are read the same story by their own mothers.
   b. Creative fifth grade students have higher achievement motivation than do noncreative fifth grade students.
   c. Adolescents from single-parent homes more frequently have police records than do adolescents from homes where both parents reside.
   d. First grade students who learn to spell phonetically will score higher on a spelling test than will those who learn to spell using the ''whole-word'' method.
   e. Students at Learning University who score above 1200 on the Graduate Record Examination will receive higher grades in the College of Education than will students who do not score above 1200.
   f. Handicapped children have lower self-concepts than do nonhandicapped children.

4. Define, and give an example of, each of the following terms:
   common cause
   reverse causality
   other independent variables
5. What do change scores adjust for and what do they not adjust for?
6. What are the advantages and disadvantages of matching?
7. How can a researcher deal with a relevant extraneous variable that cannot be controlled through matching or other means?

Answers

1. An attribute variable is a characteristic that a subject possesses before the study begins; therefore it cannot be directly manipulated. An active variable is also an independent variable, but it can be directly manipulated by the researcher.
2. Ex post facto research is used when there are attribute independent variables, that is, when the subjects possess the independent variables before the study begins and therefore those variables are not manipulable. The major weakness of ex post facto designs is control. Since randomization and manipulation of the independent variables are impossible, uncontrolled variables may be responsible for the variation in the dependent variable.
3. a. experimental
   b. ex post facto
   c. ex post facto
   d. experimental
   e. ex post facto
   f. ex post racto
4. *Common cause* means that if variables A and B are related, it is possible that neither one caused the other, but both were caused by a third variable, C. For example, if it is shown that high scores on an achievement test and high grades in academic work are related, it is possible that both are caused by a third factor, general intelligence.

   Reverse causality means that the reverse of the suggested hypothesis could account for a relationship. For example, one may observe that there is a relationship between unemployment and excessive drinking, and hypothesize that drinking to excess causes a worker to lose his or her job, when in reality it may be that those who lose their jobs tend to drink to excess.

   Other independent variables are variables, other than those observed, that may be responsible for relationships. For example it, is known that the proportion of the population confined to mental hospitals for schizophrenia is greater in the United States than it is in Great Britain while the proportion of the population in Great Britain confined for depression is greater than the proportion in the United States. This does not necessarily mean that the American environment is more conducive to schizophrenia and the British enviornment is more likely to produce depression. It may be that the British are more tolerant of schizophrenic symptoms and less likely to hospitalize those with such symptoms while Americans are more tolerant of the manifestation of the symptoms of depression.

5. Change scores adjust for initial differences between groups. They do not adjust for differential change patterns.
6. Matching provides groups that are equivalent on a particular variable or set of variables before treatment. Statistical regression can be expected to distort results when the matched groups are from different populations. Matching also reduces the number of subjects available.
7. The researcher may build the relevant extraneous variable into the ex post facto design and use an analysis-of-variance technique. This procedure requires an analysis of the main and interaction effects.

Descriptive and Historical Research

Descriptive Research

Descriptive research studies are designed to obtain information concerning the current status of phenomena. They are directed toward determining the nature of a situation as it exists at the time of the study. There is no administration or control of a treatment as is found in experimental research. The aim is to describe "what exists" with respect to variables or conditions in a situation.

Descriptive research is not generally directed toward hypothesis testing. For example, a school administrator wishes to know how many first graders are likely to be enrolled in school next year in order to plan the most effective use of school facilities and staff in accommodating the total school population. There is no need to study first grade enrollment as a variable related to some other variable. In other words, the administrator is not testing a hypothesis but is seeking information to assist in decision making.

There are several types of studies that may be classified as descriptive research. These are (1) case studies, (2) surveys, (3) developmental studies, (4) follow-up studies, (5) documentary analyses, (6) trend analyses, and (7) correlation studies. Although these methods may sometimes be used for hypothesis testing, they are generally classified as descriptive methods.

CASE STUDIES

The typical case study is an intensive investigation of one individual. However, case studies are sometimes concerned with single small social units such as a family, a club, a school, or a teenage gang.

In a case study the investigator attempts to examine an individual or unit in depth. The investigator tries to discover all the variables that are important in the history or development of the subject. The emphasis is on understanding why the individual does what he or she does and how behavior changes as the individual responds to the environment. This requires detailed study for a considerable period of time. The investigator gathers data about the subject's present state, past experiences, environment, and how these factors relate to one another.

Most case studies arise from endeavors to solve problems. The well-known case studies of Freud began with his attempt to assist his subjects in solving their personality problems. As he attempted to probe deeply into the dynamics of his patients' personalities, he reasoned that the relationships that he observed between them and their environments might also be characteristic of other individuals with similar problems. He published detailed accounts of his interviews with patients and his interpretations of their thoughts, dreams, and actions, on the assumption that far-reaching generalizations could be made from these studies.

The greatest advantage of a case study is the possibility of depth; it attempts to understand the whole child or the whole adult in the totality of that individual's environment. Not only the present actions of an individual but his or her past, environment, emotions, and thoughts can be probed. The researcher attempts to determine *why* an individual behaves as he or she does and not merely to record behavior.

Case studies often provide an opportunity for an investigator to develop insight into basic aspects of human behavior. The intensive probing characteristic of this technique may lead to the discovery of previously unsuspected relationships.

On the other hand, the advantages of the case study are also its weaknesses. Although it can have depth, it will inevitably lack breadth. The dynamics of one individual or social unit may bear little relationship to the dynamics of others. In practice most case studies arise out of counseling or remedial efforts and therefore will provide information on exceptional rather than representative individuals.

The opportunities for insight in a case study are also opportunities for subjectivity or even prejudice. The preconceptions of an investigator can determine which behaviors are observed and which are ignored as well as the way in which the observations are interpreted.

The reputation of the case study approach has suffered because some investigators in the past have explained their observations in constructs that are impossible either to confirm or refute through empirical study.

Since the extent to which case studies can produce valid generalizations is extremely limited, their major usefulness is not as tools for testing hypotheses but rather in the production of hypotheses, which can then be tested through more rigorous investigation. For example, the insights Jean Piaget gained in his famous case studies on the maturation of intellect provided useful hypotheses that have since been investigated through other methods.

In those instances when case studies result from attempts to learn about individuals in order to help them, the research aspect of the study takes second place. However, case studies are also frequently conducted with the primary aim of gaining knowledge. Itard's classic case study on the Wild Boy of Aveyron[1] was an effort to learn about the effects of civilization through studying a boy who had grown up in isolation from civilization in eighteenth-century France. Piaget's case studies were conducted in order to learn about mental growth in children rather than to benefit the subjects involved.

Case studies have sometimes been conducted for the purpose of hypothesis testing. Researchers concerned with investigating the effects of operant conditioning on human behavior have produced many case studies. In a typical study the inves-

---

[1] Jean-Marc Gaspard Itard, *The Wild Boy of Aveyron,* trans. George and Muriel Humphrey (New York: Appleton, 1962).

tigator identifies a specific behavior in the subject and systematically records the frequency of this behavior, and then introduces an operant-conditioning treatment and records the frequency of the specified behavior during treatment. After the investigator is satisfied that the behavior has changed as a result of operant conditioning, reversal conditioning is begun; that is, operant conditioning is used to change the behavior back to what it was before the original conditioning was instituted. The reversal is included to add to the credibility of operant conditioning—rather than maturation or other extraneous variables—as the cause of the behavior.

Case studies of this particular type would of course be classified as experimental research since the researcher is manipulating the independent variable. However, case studies in general are classified as descriptive research techniques.

SURVEYS

A survey gathers relatively limited data from a relatively large number of cases. The purpose is to gather information about variables rather than information about individuals. Some typical survey questions are: What proportion of American youth graduate from high school? How many books per pupil do high school libraries contain? What proportion of American adults condone corporal punishment in the schools?

Most surveys are basically inquiries into the status quo. Typically they attempt to measure what exists without questioning why it exists. Survey questions are usually designed to provide information about variables rather than to relate variables to one another, although information gathered in surveys may point out relationships between variables. The questions asked in a survey are information-gathering questions such as those seen in the U.S. census. Originally this census was undertaken to determine the correct apportionment of seats in the House of Representatives. The U.S. census remains primarily an information-gathering rather than a hypothesis-testing endeavor, although the data collected are of great value to scholars who analyze and interpret them and use them to test hypotheses. In brief, surveys usually seek information to be used for problem solving rather than for hypothesis testing.

A survey that covers the entire population of interest is referred to as a census. One that studies only a portion of the population is known as a sample survey.

Schools engage in surveys to answer a variety of questions, such as: How many children ride the school buses? What is the average class enrollment? How many teachers have permanent certificates? Such surveys arise from obvious needs for planning and problem solving.

However, surveys are not necessarily confined to simple tabulations of tangible objects but may also be conducted to measure opinion, achievement, or other psychological or sociological constructs. Public opinion surveys measure constructs rather than tangibles, whereas the counting of ballots in an election measures tangibles.

If we classify surveys on the basis of their scope (census or sample survey) and their subject matter (tangibles or intangibles), we arrive at four categories: (1) a census of tangibles, (2) a census of intangibles, (3) a sample survey of tangibles, (4) a sample survey of intangibles. Each type has its own contributions to make and its own inherent problems.

A Census of Tangibles

When one seeks information about a small population, such as a single school, and when the variables involved are concrete, there is little challenge in finding the required answers. If a school principal wants to know how many desks are in the school, how many children ride the school bus, or how many teachers have master's degrees, a simple count will provide the information. Since the study covers the entire population, the principal can have all the confidence characteristic of perfect induction. Well-defined and unambiguous variables are being measured, and as long as the enumeration is accurate and honest, the principal can say without much fear of contradiction, "On the first of September there were 647 children's desks in our school," or "Sixty-five percent of the present faculty have master's degrees." The strength of a census of this type lies in its irrefutability. Its weakness lies in its confinement to a single limited population at a single point in time. The information provided by such a census may be of immediate importance to a limited group, but typically such surveys add little to the general body of knowledge in education.

A Census of Intangibles

Suppose the school principal now seeks information about pupil achievement or aspirations, teacher morale, or parents' attitude toward school. The task will be more difficult since this census deals with constructs that are not directly observable but must be inferred from indirect measures.

An example of this type of census is the achievement-testing program carried out by most schools. All children are tested and the test scores are used to compare their performance with national norms, their own previous performance, and so on. The principal must be knowledgeable about the nature of the measuring instruments used and their appropriateness for measuring pupil achievement in the school, and so must ask how reliable the tests are, whether they measure the same construct of achievement as that defined by the goals of the school, and how well they measure that construct.

The value of a census of intangibles is largely a question of the extent to which the instruments used actually measure the construct of interest. Reasonably good instruments are available for measuring aptitude and achievement in a variety of academic areas. Many other variables remain very difficult to measure. Those who undertake censuses or sample surveys of intangibles usually find the most difficult part of their task is the selection or development of instruments that will successfully approximate the constructs involved. Because we lack instruments that can meaningfully measure the constructs involved, many important questions in education have not been dealt with successfully. Such variables as teacher success, student motivation, psychological adjustment, and leadership have been difficult to define and measure operationally.

A Sample Survey of Tangibles

When investigators seek information about large groups, the expense involved in carrying out a census is often prohibitive. Therefore sampling techniques are used and the information collected from the sample is used to make inferences about the population as a whole. We have seen that, when sampling is well done, the inferences made concerning the population can be quite reliable.

A well-known example of a sample survey is the Coleman report.[2] This study was conducted in response to Section 402 of the Civil Rights Act of 1964, which directed the Commissioner of Education to conduct a survey of inequalities in educational opportunities among various groups in the United States. The sample studied included over 600,000 children in grades one, three, six, nine, and twelve of approximately 4,000 schools. The schools were considered generally representative of all American public schools, although there was some intentional overrepresentation of schools with minority group populations.

From the data generated by the survey it was concluded that 65 percent of blacks attended schools in which over 90 percent of students were black, and 80 percent of whites attended schools enrolling over 90 percent white. When comparisons were made concerning class size, physical facilities, and teacher qualifications, relatively little difference was found among schools serving different racial and ethnic groups. However, these variables did differ between metropolitan and rural areas and between geographical regions. Those disadvantaged in regard to these variables appeared to be rural children and those in the South, regardless of race.

As the Coleman report illustrates, survey research can provide not only data on what exists but also information on relationships between variables, in this case a relationship between geographical location and other tangible aspects of schools.

The value of a sample survey of tangibles depends on the appropriateness of its sampling procedure, the accuracy of its data-collecting method, and the relevance of the information obtained for throwing light on important questions in the area.

A Sample Survey of Intangibles

The most challenging type of survey is one that seeks to measure psychological or sociological constructs for a large population. In such a study one must bring to bear not only the skills involved in proper sampling but also the skills involved in identifying or constructing appropriate measures and employing the scores on these measures to make meaningful statements about the constructs involved.

The public opinion polls are examples of this type of study. Opinion is not directly observable but must be inferred from responses made by the subjects to questionnaires or interviews. For example, where respondents have been willing to reveal their preferences freely before elections, the pollsters have been quite accurate in inferring public opinion from which they have predicted subsequent election results. These polls have provided excellent examples of the usefulness of sample

[2]James S. Coleman, Ernest Q. Campbell, Carol J. Hobson, James McPartland, Alexander M. Mood, Frederic D. Weinfield, and Robert L. York, *Equality of Educational Opportunity* (Washington, D.C.: Government Printing Office, 1966).

statistics in estimating population parameters. When those who support one candidate are reluctant to reveal their preference, while those who support the other candidate feel free to say so, considerable error is introduced into the results of the poll. In the 1969 campaign for mayor of Los Angeles the opinion polls found more people who stated an intention to vote for Bradley than people who declared an intention to vote for Yorty, but a large proportion declared themselves undecided. The pollsters surmised that many who would vote for Yorty were reluctant to say so. However, the pollsters had no way of determining the extent of this phenomenon. When the ballots were counted, the total for Yorty equaled the percent of the pollsters' sample who had declared their intention to vote for Yorty plus all those who had declared themselves undecided.

How someone is going to vote is an intangible, but what is marked on a ballot is a tangible. The television network news services have done very well in predicting how states will vote when only a few precincts have reported, but they are able to use tangible measures of a sample (that is, how some ballots have been marked) to predict the vote of a population. Therefore the risks are only those involved in estimating population parameters from sample statistics. However, pollsters who estimate how a population will vote on the basis of how people say they will vote have the additional handicap of measuring what is intangible at the time the measurements are made. Surveys of intangibles are limited by the fact that the data we collect are only indirectly measuring the variables we are concerned about. The seriousness of this limitation is an inverse function of how well the observations measure the intangible variable.

The same survey may study tangibles and intangibles at the same time. The authors of the Coleman report asked the students to answer questionnaires and administered intelligence and achievement tests in order to make inferences about social class, ability, and achievement, and the relationship of these variables to each other and to tangible variables in the study.

In assessing the reliability of a census of tangibles, we need only be concerned with routine clerical matters. Were the measurements done honestly and accurately? Were all members of the population included? In assessing a sample survey, we must also ask how well the sample represents the population. The rigor desired in a sampling procedure and the inferences that can be made from samples to population apply in survey research in the same way that they apply to experimental research. In a census or sample survey of intangibles we must also be concerned with how well the instruments we use measure the constructs involved.

Uses of Surveys

Surveys have suffered a bad reputation among educators for the past forty years or more. Perhaps this has been partly a result of the many poor survey studies that have been done in the past. Many school officials are tired of being asked to complete questionnaires that appear to have been thrown together hastily with little thought as to what information is sought or what purpose the information will serve. Perhaps the profession on the whole has concentrated on improving skills in experimental research, while neglecting the skills involved in survey research. Seiber and Lazarsfeld found that only about one-third of the projects supported by the Cooperative Research Program, of the USOE, from 1956 to 1963 involved surveys. Even more interesting was the fact that 40 percent of noneducators used surveys in these projects, while 24 percent of educators used them.[3] Sociologists have not shared our feelings against surveys and have used them widely to study relationships between variables as well as for purely descriptive purposes. Educators who plan to do survey research would do well to study the methods of sociologists such as Coleman, Barton and Lazarsfeld, and Blaloch.[4]

Surveys can be used not only for describing existing conditions but also for comparing these conditions with predetermined criteria or for evaluating the effectiveness of programs. Surveys can also be used to study relationships or test hypotheses.

DEVELOPMENTAL STUDIES

It is important for the profession of education to have reliable information about what children are like at various ages, how they vary from one another within age levels, and how they grow and develop. Knowledge of physiological, intellectual, and emotional growth is important for numerous practical as well as theoretical questions. Physical plant, curriculum, and teaching methods must take into consideration the relevant characteristics of the learner, as must any comprehensive theory of learning or instruction. Two complementary techniques have emerged for investigating the characteristics of children and the ways in which these characteristics change with growth. These are generally referred to as the longitudinal method and the cross-sectional method.

The Longitudinal Method

In the longitudinal method the same sample of subjects is studied over an extended period of time. Researchers studying the development of quantitative concepts in elementary school pupils, for example, would start by measuring the quantitative skills of a group of first graders and would continue by making annual measurements of their skills at each successive grade level. Thus the researchers could assess how these skills develop over a period of time for this group. Since they are dealing with the same individuals, such factors as initial ability will remain constant and the differences observed between two grade levels can be interpreted as changes in quantitative skills related to the growth of the subjects.

[3]Sam D. Seiber and P. F. Lazarsfeld, *The Organization of Educational Research,* Cooperative Research Project 1974, Bureau of Applied Social Research (New York: Columbia University Press, 1966), p. 113.

[4]James S. Coleman, *Introduction to Mathematical Sociology* (New York: Free Press of Glencoe, 1964), pp. 28–36. Allen H. Barton and P. F. Lazarsfeld, ''Methodology of Quantitative Social Research,'' in B. N. Varma, ed., *A New Survey of the Social Sciences* (New York: Asia Publishing House, 1962); Hubert M. Blaloch, *Social Statistics* (New York: McGraw-Hill, 1960).

Using the longitudinal method, Honzik, Macfarland, and Allen studied the fluctuations of IQ scores of children from age 2 to age 18.[5] They found that the IQ scores of over half the group changed 15 or more points, the scores of 9 percent of the group changed 30 or more points, and scores separated by a short time period correlated more highly than scores separated by a long time period. When they studied individuals who showed consistent upward or downward trends, it was found that such changes tended to be in the direction of the family's socioeconomic status; that is, those children whose IQ scores showed consistent downward trends came predominantly from lower socioeconomic groups and those whose scores exhibited consistent upward trends were largely from higher socioeconomic groups.

The longitudinal method allows for intensive studies of individuals because the investigator accumulates data for the same subjects at various levels. However, longitudinal studies have inherent practical difficulties. To begin with, they demand an extended commitment from an individual or institution willing to spend time, money, and other resources for several years before completing the project. If the sample selected should prove to be a poor one, there is nothing that can be done to remedy it, nor can new longitudinal variables for investigation be introduced after the study has matured. Keeping up with subjects who move may become extremely difficult. In some cases, also, it proves difficult to maintain the cooperation of subjects for an extended period.

The Cross-Sectional Method

Many of the practical difficulties of the longitudinal method are not characteristic of the cross-sectional method. This approach studies subjects of various age levels at the same point in time. For example, a cross-sectional study of the development of quantitative skills would employ a different sample from each of the grade levels. It would compare the statistics derived from the samples and draw conclusions about the growth of children with respect to these skills.

A major disadvantage of the cross-sectional method is that chance differences between samples may seriously bias the results. One may by chance draw a sample of first graders who are more mature than average and a sample of second graders who are less mature than average, with the result that the difference between the groups appears to be much smaller than it really is. However, it is usually possible to obtain larger samples for cross-sectional studies than can be obtained for longitudinal studies, and the advantages of these large samples may in many cases outweigh the disadvantages of the cross-sectional approach.

A further disadvantage of the cross-sectional approach lies in the possibility of extraneous variables creating differences between the populations sampled. For example, suppose investigators are studying the vocabulary development of high school students. The seniors will probably be a less diverse group than the freshmen, inasmuch as the less capable students tend to drop out during the high

---

[5]Marjorie P. Honzik, Jean W. Macfarland, and Lucile Allen, "The Stability of Mental Test Performance between Two and Eighteen Years," *Journal of Experimental Education* 17 (December 1949):309–24.

school years in greater proportion than do the more capable students. Consequently, comparisons of vocabulary will tend to reflect this selection factor as well as students' vocabulary growth during high school. Of course, subjects can be lost from longitudinal studies for various reasons, with a corresponding lessening of comparability between data from various levels. However, the investigator with longitudinal data will know which subjects have been lost and how they differ from the remaining sample and can then take these differences into account in interpreting the results.

When we want to learn the characteristics of *typical* children at various stages, the cross-sectional method is preferred because of the greater possibility of obtaining large samples with this technique. It would also be preferred if we want to know how contemporary first graders differ from contemporary sixth graders, since a longitudinal study would be comparing first graders of five years ago with sixth graders of today.

If we want to study *change per se,* the longitudinal method is preferred since it follows the same subjects through their development. Spurts and plateaus of growth, which cannot be observed in a cross-sectional study, can be seen in a longitudinal study. For example, consider the following hypothetical mental age scores of three boys tested annually:

Bob	Joe	Paul	$\bar{X}$
6.0	6.0	6.0	6.0
6.5	8.0	6.5	7.0
7.0	8.5	8.5	8.0
9.0	9.0	9.0	9.0

Each has a growth spurt at a different stage, but the mean score for the three shows a steady increase.

FOLLOW-UP STUDIES

The follow-up study somewhat resembles the longitudinal method. Studies of this type are concerned with investigating the subsequent development of subjects after a specified treatment or condition. Among the best known are the studies by Terman and his associates of subjects who had been part of an original sample of gifted children in 1921–22.[6] The subjects were studied six years later and again in 1936, 1940, and 1945. Among other things, it was found that as adults these subjects had better physical and mental health than the general population. Only four of the

[6]Barbara S. Burks, Dortha W. Jensen, and Lewis M. Terman, *The Promise of Youth: Follow-up Studies of a Thousand Gifted Children,* vol. 3 (Stanford, Calif.: Stanford University Press, 1930); and Lewis M. Terman and Melita H. Oden, *The Gifted Child Grows Up: Twenty-Five Years' Follow-up Studies of a Superior Group,* vol. 4 (Stanford, Calif.: Stanford University Press, 1947).

1,467 subjects served terms in penal institutions. Approximately 90 percent of the males entered college and 70 percent of these graduated, 40 percent with honors. About 80 percent of the women entered college and 67 percent of these graduated, 32 percent with honors. In general, the gifted children matured into gifted and successful adults. Follow-up studies are frequently conducted to evaluate the success of particular programs.

DOCUMENTARY ANALYSES

Although the discipline of education is primarily concerned with people, many interesting and useful research projects in the field have been concerned with information obtained by examining records and documents. For example, Wilson and Dalrymple used business records to investigate the uses of fractions in the commercial world.[7] Of 102,000 instances where fractions were used, 90 percent were confined to halves, thirds, and fourths. This information has been useful for those who plan arithmetic curricula. Thorndike used documentary analysis to identify the most commonly used words in the English language.[8] His work has been a very valuable tool for developers of elementary language arts texts.

Documentary analysis, often referred to as content analysis, is not confined to simple counts but can also be used to study sociological and psychological variables. In comparing McGuffey readers of the 1870s with elementary reading texts of the 1930s, Estensen found many interesting differences in cultural and ethical values.[9] A thorough treatment of the conduct of documentary analysis and its uses will be found in a book by Berelson.[10]

TREND ANALYSES

In order to plan as effectively as possible, schools (as well as governmental agencies, businesses, and other institutions) need to project the demands that will be made on their services in the future. Through documentary analysis or surveys repeated at intervals, they are able to study the rate and direction of changes and use these trends to predict future status. For example, a large school district will attempt to locate new schools in the areas where the home building rates and population growth indicate there will be the greatest need. Projections made from the findings of studies made in the 1950s warned colleges and universities to expect an extremely increased demand for their services during the 1960s. This prediction was based on such factors as the increasing birthrate, the increasing proportion of stu-

[7]G. M. Wilson and C. O. Dalrymple, ''Useful Fractions,'' *Journal of Educational Research* 30 (January 1937):341.

[8]Edward L. Thorndike, *A Teacher's World Book of the Twenty Thousand Words Found Most Frequently and Widely in General Reading for Children and Young People,* rev. ed. (New York: Teachers College, Columbia University, 1932).

[9]R. B. Estensen, ''McGuffey—A Statistical Analysis,'' *Journal of Educational Research* 39 (1946):445–57.

[10]Bernard Berelson, *Content Analysis in Communication Research* (Glencoe, Ill.: Free Press, 1952).

dents completing high school, and the increasing need for a college-trained labor force.

Short-term predictions are often very reliable. A very reasonable forecast for first grade enrollment in the United States five years hence can be made on the basis of census figures for children less than one year old today, adjusted for immigration, emigration, and deaths. But to predict first grade enrollment ten years hence, one must first predict birthrate five years hence. Birthrate is difficult to predict since it is subject to many economic, technological, and social changes. Because of unforeseen contingencies, long-range prediction is in practice a matter of estimating as well as possible.

CORRELATIONAL STUDIES

Correlational studies are a frequently used type of descriptive research that is concerned with determining the extent of relationship existing between variables. They enable one to ascertain the extent to which variations in one variable are associated with variations in another. The magnitude of the relationship is determined through the use of the coefficient of correlation.[11] For instance, on the basis of personal experiences a researcher may hypothesize that there is a relationship between performance in mathematics and performance in chemistry at the high school level. The correlational procedure will enable this researcher to test the hypothesis about the relationship between these two variables as well as to assess the magnitude of the relationship.

The correlational study has been a popular type of research in education. It is relatively easy to design and conduct. It involves the collection of two or more sets of scores on a sample of subjects and the computation of the coefficient of correlation between these sets of scores. To test the hypothesis concerning a relationship between mathematics and chemistry, one would obtain the mathematics marks and the chemistry marks for a sample of twelfth grade students and then compute the coefficient of correlation between these sets of scores.

Correlational techniques may be employed in either hypothesis-generating or hypothesis-testing studies. In the hypothesis-generating study an investigator takes measures on a number of variables and computes correlation coefficients between them in order to see which variables appear to be related. The purpose of such studies is exploration rather than theory testing. For example, Krippner conducted an exploratory study to investigate variables that might be related to the degree of reading improvement manifested in a remedial program.[12] He hoped to identify the variables that would have predictive value in the selection and grouping of poor readers for remedial programs. Krippner correlated each subject's degree of improvement (the difference between pre- and posttest scores on the California Reading Test) with ten other variables: chronological age, grade placement, degree of

---

[11]The mathematical processes involved in these procedures are discussed in chapter 5.
[12]Stanley Krippner, "Correlates of Reading Improvement," *Education,* September 1963.

reading retardation, father's occupational level, social maturity, vocabulary, verbal IQ, performance IQ, total IQ, and a mental health measure. He tested the null hypothesis that no significant positive relationships would emerge from the ten correlations. Statistically significant correlation coefficients were found only between reading improvement and the four variables of mental health, verbal IQ, total IQ, and grade placement. It was concluded that these four variables would have the highest efficiency for predictive purposes.

In a hypothesis-testing study investigators have an a priori basis for expecting to observe a correlation between variables. They base their selection of variables for investigation on previously developed theory and can hypothesize the direction of the expected relationships. For example, from phenomenological theory one might hypothesize that there is a positive relationship between first grade children's perceptions of themselves and their achievement in reading.

Typically, correlational studies do not require large samples. It can be assumed that if a relationship exists, it will be evident in a sample of moderate size, for instance 50 to 100. If one is interested in making an inference about the relationship in a population, then the sample selected should be a representative sample of that population. It is well to recall at this point that the variability in the scores that are being correlated affects the size of the coefficient of correlation. A restricted range of the scores on one or both variables will result in a smaller coefficient than would be obtained with a wide range of scores on the variables.

It is important to select or develop measures that are appropriate indicators of the variables to be correlated. It is especially important that these instruments have reliability and are valid for measuring the variables under consideration. The size of a coefficient of correlation is influenced by the adequacy of the measuring instrument for its intended purpose. An instrument, for instance, that is too easy or too difficult for the subjects of a study would not discriminate among them and would result in a small correlation coefficient. Studies using instruments with low reliability and questionable validity are unlikely to produce evidence of any significant relationship.

Types of Correlational Analyses

A number of correlational techniques have been developed for use with various types of data. The most frequently used technique is the Pearson product moment coefficient of correlation. It is the most sensitive measure of correlation for situations that meet the assumptions necessary for its use. The assumptions underlying the use of the Pearson coefficient are discussed in chapter 5. Erroneous conclusions are likely to be reached in situations using a correlational technique for which the underlying assumptions are not met. Table 11.1 summarizes the types of correlation coefficients used when two variables are being correlated and the types of scales for which they are appropriate. Only the computation of the Pearson and the Spearman coefficients have been discussed in this text. The reader is referred to statistics books for the computations involved in the other types of correlation.

Table 11.1   Types of Correlation Coefficients and Corresponding Types of Scales

Correlation Coefficient	Type of Scale
1. Pearson product moment	1. Interval or ratio scale characteristic of both variables
2. Spearman rank	2. Ordinal scale characteristic of both variables
3. Point biserial	3. One variable on interval scale; the other a genuine dichotomous variable on a nominal scale
4. Biserial	4. One variable on interval or ratio scale; the other an artificial dichotomy*
5. Tetrachoric	5. Artificial dichotomy (nominal scale) used with both variables; both have underlying continuous distributions
6. Phi coefficient	6. Genuine dichotomy (nominal scale) characteristic of both variables

*An artificial dichotomy arbitrarily divides a continuous variable into two classes—for example, test scores divided into pass and fail categories—through the use of a cutoff point. Examples of genuine dichotomies are male-female and alive-dead.

Multiple Correlation

The correlational studies discussed in the previous section were concerned with the relationship between only two variables: an independent variable, X, and a dependent variable, Y. In many educational research situations, particularly those involving prediction, it is more useful to determine the correlation between a dependent variable and a combination of independent variables, each of which correlates to a certain extent with the dependent variables. The form of correlational analysis which uses two or more independent variables, X_1, X_2, . . . X_n, to predict a dependent variable, Y, is known as *multiple correlation*. In multiple correlation the independent or predictor variables are combined in such a way as to obtain the maximum possible correlation with the dependent variable. The result is that the accuracy of prediction is maximized. For example, a law school admissions officer may find that undergraduate grade point average correlates with law school grades +.44 and Law School Aptitude Test (LSAT) scores correlate with law school grades +.40. When the two predictor variables are combined with appropriate weightings, the combined predictor correlates with law school grades +.49. Thus the prediction obtained with both predictors is more accurate than either taken singly.[13]

Evaluation and Interpretation

The end result of the correlational study is a coefficient of correlation, a decimal number representing the degree of the observed relationship between the variables.

[13]A complete discussion of multiple correlation can be found in Fred N. Kerlinger and Elazar J. Pedhazur, *Multiple Regression in Behavioral Research* (New York: Holt, Rinehart and Winston, 1973).

Students often are not sure how to interpret this coefficient once it is available. It is often asked how large the coefficient should be before it is meaningful. This question may be approached in two ways: (1) by considering the strength of a relationship and (2) by considering the statistical significance of the relationship.

The strength of the relationship can be inferred from the numerical value of the correlation coefficient. Values near zero imply a weak relationship, whereas values closer to either $+1$ or -1 indicate a stronger relationship. For example, suppose a teacher correlates pupils' academic grades with their scores on a measure of popularity and finds $r = +.20$. However, when their scores on athletic ability are correlated with popularity, $r = +.60$. The teacher would conclude that for this group there is a stronger relationship between popularity scores and athletic scores than between popularity scores and grades.

When one wishes to use correlation coefficients derived from a sample to make inferences about the population from which it was taken, one must consider the statistical significance of the correlation one has obtained. Statistical significance indicates whether or not the coefficient obtained is *different from zero* at a given level of confidence. A statistically significant correlation represents evidence of an actual relationship rather than one due simply to chance. Table A.7 in the Appendix gives the minimum values of Pearson correlation coefficients needed to reach a given level of statistical significance.

The null hypothesis is that the correlation in the population is equal to zero and that any correlation observed in the sample is a function of chance. Statistical significance is related both to the strength of the observed correlation and to the number of paired scores in the sample. We use Table A.7 by first finding the degrees of freedom (the number of paired scores in our sample minus 2) in the first column and the value of r needed to reject the null hypothesis for various levels of significance in the other columns. For example, we can see from the table that when the correlation of 30 paired scores ($df = 28$) is equal to or greater than $+.361$ or equal to or less than $-.361$, the null hypothesis, that the correlation in the population is zero, will be rejected at the .05 level of confidence. When only 20 paired scores are involved, the observed correlation coefficient must be equal to or greater than $+.444$ or equal to or less than $-.444$ before the null hypothesis can be rejected at the .05 level.

With a reasonably large number of cases, a coefficient of correlation may be low in value and yet be statistically significant. Since it is the value of the correlation that indicates the degree of relationship between the variables, a low correlation always indicates a low relationship even when the correlation is statistically significant. For example, Jackson and Lahaderne, with a sample of 144 sixth grade girls, found a correlation of $+.25$ between the students' responses on a questionnaire measuring students' satisfaction with school and their teachers' predictions of how the girls would respond to the questionnaire.[14] Since the sample size was large,

---

[14]Philip W. Jackson and Henriette M. Lahaderne, "Scholastic Success and Attitude toward School in a Population of Sixth Graders," *Journal of Educational Psychology* 58 (1967):15–18.

the correlation, though low, was statistically significant at the .01 level. The findings indicate that in the population that was represented by the sample, the correlation is not likely to be zero. However, the low observed correlation suggests that, although teachers can predict student satisfaction at greater than chance level, the teachers' predictions of satisfaction have only a weak relationship with actual student satisfaction.

Many statistics texts include tables that indicate the value of the correlation coefficient required for rejecting the null hypothesis at various levels of confidence for given sample sizes for other correlation coefficients. In addition, most of these texts describe procedures for testing hypotheses concerning the significance of observed difference between correlations.

Another useful basis for interpretation of a coefficient is provided by the square of the coefficient of correlation. The square of the correlation coefficient, r^2, shows the proportion of variance in one variable that can be attributed to its linear relationship with the other variable. That is, it indicates how much of their variance the two distributions have in common. For example, if two variables, X and Y, show a correlation coefficient of .60, then $(.60)^2$ or .36 of the variation shown by Y scores can be attributed to the tendency of Y to vary linearly with X. If the correlation is $-.50$, then 25 percent $(-.50)^2$ of the variation in Y can be attributed to variation in X. Of course, when r is zero, then none of the variation in Y can be attributed to a linear relation with the X variable.

There are certain cautions that one must be aware of when interpreting a coefficient of correlation. In the first place, a coefficient is a simple number and is not to be interpreted as a percentage. An r of zero indicates no linear relationship between the variables; but an r of .50 does *not* mean 50 percent relationship between the variables. Furthermore, it is not correct to say that an r of .50 indicates twice as much relationship as that shown by an r of .25. An r of .50 actually indicates more than twice the relationship shown by an r of .25. As coefficients approach $+1$ or -1, a difference in the absolute value of the coefficients becomes more important than the same numerical difference between lower correlations. For example, a difference between $r = .92$ and $r = .98$ is much more important than the difference between $r = .42$ and $r = .48$.

Another caution is that a correlation does not necessarily indicate a cause-and-effect relationship between the two variables. Correlation must not be interpreted to mean that one variable is causing the scores in the other variable to be what they are. Frequently there are other factors that influence both of the variables under consideration. For example, it may be found that there is a negative correlation between measures of anxiety and measures of intelligence. It should not be interpreted that there is a causative relationship between anxiety and intelligence; that is, that pupils are anxious because they are unintelligent or that pupils appear unintelligent because they are anxious. It might be that there are other underlying characteristics of individuals that tend to make some appear unintelligent and anxious, and others, intelligent and not anxious. Interpretation of such a correlation is difficult without experimental confirmation. It is recommended in many instances that a relationship study be supplemented by an experimental study in which the alternative interpretations can become hypotheses for experimentation. For example, the relationship between anxiety measures and intelligence measures could be investigated experimentally by deliberately inducing anxiety in a testing situation and determining the effect on intelligence test scores.

The last word of caution is that a coefficient of correlation is not to be interpreted as an absolute fact. One must remember that the values of r are found for samples of cases and the extent of relationship found in one sample need not necessarily be the same as that found in another sample from the same population. There are many factors, such as the way the variables are measured or the range of measured values in the sample, that influence the size of a correlation coefficient in specific investigations. What a researcher finds in one study is a measure of the extent of relationship between the variables in one sample. If there is a question concerning the extent of relationship between the variables in the population from which the sample came, then inferential statistics must be used to test the significance of the correlation coefficient. To do this, the researcher must establish first of all that the sample of cases used was drawn at random from the population. Then the null hypothesis, that there is no linear relationship between the variables X and Y in the population, can be tested.

The Value of Correlational Studies

The possibility of the existence of relationships between variables is a reasonable question to investigate in educational research since there are numerous situations where such information is valuable in decision making. This is especially true in exploratory studies in an area. In the sampling aspect of a study one of the problems is securing representativeness in terms of the variables that are known to be related to the phenomena under investigation. But what are the factors ''known to be related''? Unfortunately one does not always know the characteristics that are related to the phenomena that one wishes to study. Fox writes:

> What we need is a massive series of studies whose primary function is to learn the nature and extent of the relationship between matrices of educational characteristics on the one hand and psychosocial characteristics on the other. If such studies were conducted, the researcher on any particular educational problem would then be able to know what characteristics were critical for him as he prepared to establish a sampling plan.[15]

In planning the control in experimental and ex post facto studies, the researcher must be able to identify the critical variables, that is, those variables that have a substantial correlation with the dependent variable of the study. For example, if one were investigating the effect of certain experiences on creativity scores, then it would be necessary to know what other variables are substantially correlated with the dependent variable of creativity in order that these variables might be controlled.

---

[15]David J. Fox, *The Research Process in Education* (New York: Holt, Rinehart and Winston, 1969), p. 323.

Information on such correlations can be obtained through exploratory relationship studies.

Correlation techniques are particularly useful in making predictions. If we know that there is a correlation between two variables, then we can predict from one variable to the other. For example, since we know that IQ and GPA are positively correlated, we can predict with some degree of accuracy that an individual with a high IQ will probably have a high GPA. To be valuable for prediction, the extent of correlation between two variables must be substantial and, of course, the higher the correlation, the more accurate the prediction.

A related use of the coefficient of correlation (discussed in chapter 8) is in determining the validity and reliability of measuring instruments.

Computation of the correlation coefficient gives a most useful tool for describing the strength of the relationship between two variables. However, care must be exercised in conducting and interpreting this type of research if any meaningful conclusions are to be reached.

STEPS IN DESCRIPTIVE RESEARCH

The process of descriptive research may be summarized in the following steps:

1. *Statement of the problem.* As in the case of experimental research, the researcher must start with a clear statement of the problem. This statement identifies the variables to be involved in the study and specifies whether the study is merely seeking to determine the status of these variables or whether it will also investigate relationships between the variables.

2. *Identification of information needed to solve the problem.* The researcher lists the information to be collected, states whether this information is of a qualitative or a quantitative nature, and identifies the form the information will take (counts, test scores, responses to questionnaires or interviews, and so on).

3. *Selection or development of instruments for gathering data.* Questionnaires, interviews, tests, and scales of various types are the most frequently used instruments for descriptive research. If the researcher will be using existing instruments, the reliability of these instruments, their validity for measuring the variables of concern, and their suitability for the population of interest must be investigated. Further insight into their qualities can be gained by reading previous studies in which the same instruments were used.

If the researcher must design his or her own instruments, it would be wise to try them out with a small group in order to evaluate them and make improvements if needed.

As you will recall, the instruments operationally define the variables in the study. Therefore, before proceeding, the researcher must be satisfied that the data that will be obtained with the instruments selected for the study are in fact the information needed to solve the problem.

4. *Identification of the target population and determination of any necessary sampling procedure.* The researcher determines the group about which information

is being sought. In a census this is typically a well-defined local group such as the children in a particular school or the voters in a certain district. Sample surveys usually deal with groups identified by specific characteristics, such as retarded readers, the culturally disadvantaged, beginning Spanish students, and so forth. In a sample survey the researcher attempts to select a sample that will adequately represent the population.

5. *Design of the procedure for data collection*. The researcher lays out the practical schedule for obtaining the sample and using the instruments.

6. *Collection of data*.

7. *Analysis of data*.

8. *Preparation of the report*.

Historical Research

Historical research is the attempt to establish facts and arrive at conclusions concerning the past. The historian systematically and objectively locates, evaluates, and interprets evidence from which we can learn about the past. Based on the evidence gathered the historian draws conclusions regarding the past so as to increase our knowledge of how and why past events occurred and the process by which the past became the present. The hoped-for result is increased understanding of the present and a more rational basis for making present choices.

The historian operates under different handicaps from those of researchers in other fields. Control over treatment, measurement, and sampling is limited and there is no opportunity for replication. As in descriptive and post facto research, the independent or treatment variables are not controlled by the researcher. All the cautions in interpreting those studies also apply to historical research. However, in descriptive and ex post facto research, measurement can usually be controlled through deciding what measures will be administered as the dependent variable. While historians have no choice concerning what documents, relics, records, and artifacts survive the passage of time, they do have some limited control over what questions they will ask of these sources and what measures they will apply to them. When interviewing witnesses of past events and when searching the historical record, researchers can decide what questions to ask and what is to be measured. But they can measure only those things that witnesses remember or the record contains.

In descriptive and experimental research investigators can attempt to control sampling; that is, they can decide for themselves whom they are going to study. Historians can study only those people for whom records and artifacts survive. If newspapers ignore a particular segment of a community, and no other sources for that community exist, then historians are unable to assess directly the contribution that particular segment of a population made to the life of that community. Another caveat impinging upon historical researchers is that no assumption about the past can be made merely because no record can be found, nor can it be assumed that a conspiracy of silence has distorted the historical record.

PRIMARY AND SECONDARY SOURCES

The historian classifies his materials as *primary* and *secondary sources*. Primary sources are original documents, relics, remains, or artifacts. These are the direct outcomes of events or the records of eyewitnesses. Examples would be the minutes of a school board meeting, an unedited videotape of a basketball game, a collection of artwork completed by a third grade class. In primary sources only the mind of the observer intrudes between original event and the investigator. Note that the mind of the observer *does* come between the event and the record in each of our examples: Someone has decided what will and will not be recorded in the proceedings of the school board; when the camera is to be on or off and where it is to be focused during the basketball game; which artwork is to be kept.

In secondary sources the mind of a nonobserver also comes between the event and the user of the record. If a newspaper reporter has been present at a school board meeting, the published report is a primary source. If the reporter relies on the minutes of the meeting or an interview with a participant to prepare the report, then this report is a secondary source. Common examples of secondary sources are history books, articles in encyclopedias, and reviews of research. Historians seek to employ primary sources whenever possible.

EXTERNAL AND INTERNAL CRITICISM

Two ideas that have proved useful in evaluating historical sources are the concepts of *external* (or lower) *criticism* and *internal* (or higher) *criticism*.

Basically external criticism asks if the evidence under consideration is authentic and, depending on the nature of the study, might involve such techniques as authentication of signatures, chemical analysis of paint, or carbon dating of artifacts. Suppose a historian has a letter describing Massachusetts schools that is believed to have been written by Horace Mann. Using external criticism, the investigator would ask, Is the paper of the right age? Is the handwriting Mann's? Are the point of view and the writing style consistent with Mann's other writings?

After the authenticity of a piece of evidence has been established, the historical investigator proceeds to internal criticism, which requires an evaluation of the worth of the evidence—for instance, whether a document provides a true report of an event. Such a question can best be answered by substantiating one piece of evidence by comparing it with others that throw light on an event or provide further information about an event and the people or circumstances surrounding it. In the example the investigator would ask, Is Mann's description of the schools unbiased? Does it agree with other contemporary descriptions of the schools?

Since historical research does have limitations, one could very well ask why it should be attempted. The fundamental reason is that there is no other way to investigate many questions. How else might one attempt to assess the effect of the Kent State shootings and other campus disorders in the spring of 1970?

An advantage of historical research, and sometimes a reason for using this approach, is that it is unobtrusive. The researcher is not physically involved in the situation studied. There is no danger of experimenter-subject interaction, nor is there any need to get the permission of school authorities for the research. The historian locates appropriate documents, gathers suitable data, and draws conclusions at a distance from the situation being studied.

In addition historical research may provide new perspectives to a crisis situation. The uninvolved nature of historical research may make it acceptable in an emotionally charged situation where other types of research would be impossible.

Because of its limitations, caution must be exercised in generalizing the results of historical research. Students who plan to do a historical study should consult appropriate bibliographies and sources on historical methodology.[16]

Summary

Descriptive research methods are used to obtain information about existing conditions and have been widely used in educational research. These methods range from the survey, which describes the status quo of educational variables, to the correlational study, which investigates the relationship between variables. Other descriptive methods include the case study, developmental study, follow-up study, documentary analysis, and trend analysis.

Descriptive methods are not restricted to data-gathering purposes. They can also be used in studies involving hypothesis testing.

Noncurrent records and remains are used in historical research to generate and test hypotheses. Primary sources are employed as much as possible. The historical researcher attempts to establish the authenticity of sources through external criticism and their veracity through internal criticism. Because of the inherent weaknesses, extreme caution should be exercised in generalizing conclusions reached through historical research.

Exercises

1. Identify the type of descriptive research—namely, the *case study, the survey, the developmental study,* the *follow-up study,* or *trend analysis*—indicated in each item:

[16]Jacques Barzun and Henry F. Graff, *The Modern Researcher,* rev. ed. (New York: Harcourt, Brace and World, 1970); William W. Brickman, *Guide to Research in Educational History* (Norwood, Pa.: Norwood Editions, 1973); William Brickman and Francesco Cordasco, *A Bibliography of American Educational History* (New York: AMS Press, 1975), and Jurgen Herbst, *The History of American Education: A bibliography* (Northbrook, Ill.: AHM Publishing, 1973).

    a. Terman's study of adults who were intellectually gifted as children

    b. a study in depth of a single unit

    c. analysis of data from the past and present in order to "predict" the future

    d. frequently used to generate hypotheses about human behavior

    e. employed in the Coleman report

    f. most frequently associated with the use of questionnaires

2. In developmental studies, when one wants to study how individual children change rather than what is typical at each stage of development, one would prefer the:

    a. cross-sectional method

    b. longitudinal method

3. An investigator gave a reading test to a sample of 1,000 children in order to assess the reading skills of children in his state. This study would be classified as a:

    a. census of tangibles

    b. sample survey of tangibles

    c. census of intangibles

    d. sample survey of intangibles

4. In a correlational study the investigator:

    a. compares the differences within a group on one variable with differences within the same group on another variable

    b. starts with a group that is initially homogeneous on a variable being studied

    c. compares the performance of one group on a variable with the performance of a comparable group on that variable

    d. creates, and then measures, a difference between two groups

5. The longitudinal technique in developmental studies has the advantage of:

    a. more intensive individual study

    b. providing data for different age-groups at the same point in time

    c. prompt data gathering

    d. no sampling errors

6. In order to compute a correlation coefficient between traits A and B, one must have:

    a. one group of subjects, some of whom possess characteristics of trait A and the remainder of whom possess those of trait B

    b. measures of trait A on one group of subjects and measures of trait B on another

    c. one group of subjects, some who have both traits A and B, some who have neither trait, and some who have one trait but not the other

    d. two groups of subjects, one of which could be classified as A or not A, the other as B or not B

    e. measure of traits A and B on each subject in one group

7. An investigation finds a positive correlation between IQ scores and length of attention span among ten-year-olds. From this finding one would state that:

    a. a long attention span is a cause of intelligence

    b. a high IQ is a cause of long attention span

    c. there is a high probability that a large sample of high-IQ ten-year-olds will have a shorter mean attention span than a large sample of low-IQ ten-year-olds

    d. one would predict longer attention spans for high-IQ ten-year-olds than for low-IQ ten-year-olds

8. Examine the following research titles and decide whether *experimental research*, *ex post facto research*, or *survey research* is the appropriate research design for each one:
   a. the effect of parents' divorce on the achievement motivation of the children
   b. the effect of a specific program of vocabulary instruction on social studies achievement
   c. the opinions of graduate students in education on the effect of Head Start on the reading achievement of culturally disadvantaged children
   d. the effect of phonics instruction upon the reading grade level of fourth grade students
   e. the relationship between school absence and school achievement
9. An investigator has a letter describing education in Uganda in 1977. It is supposed to have been written by President Idi Amin. What question would be asked in:
   a. external criticism
   b. internal criticism
10. When is a historical document considered to be secondary?
11. What are the advantages and disadvantages of historical research as compared with other types of research?

Answers

1. a. follow-up study
   b. case study
   c. trend analysis
   d. case study
   e. survey
   f. survey
2. b
3. d
4. a
5. a
6. e
7. d
8. a. ex post facto research
   b. experimental research
   c. survey research
   d. experimental research
   e. ex post facto research
9. a. Was the letter really written by Idi Amin?
   b. Does it accurately describe education in Uganda in 1977?
10. A document is secondary if the mind of a nonobserver comes between the event and the document.
11. One advantage of historical research is the unlikelihood of researcher or experimental interaction effects confounding interpretation of findings. A historical perspective can deal with issues and past situations that cannot be handled experimentally. The main disadvantage is the lack of experimental control, which makes unequivocal interpretation of data and generalization difficult. There is also the possibility of gathering inadequate or inaccurate information that is not verifiable.

Part

6

Communicating Research

Guidelines for Writing Research Proposals

In most cases researchers will need to present their projects in organized written form at two stages: (1) the initial stage which requires preparation of a research proposal and (2) the final stage, a finished report of the results of the research.

Writing a Research Proposal

Writing the research proposal can be the most crucial and exciting step in the research process. At this stage the whole project crystallizes into concrete form. In the proposal researchers demonstrate that they know what they are seeking and how they will recognize it, and explain why the search is worthwhile. The researchers' inspirations and insights are translated into step-by-step plans for discovering new knowledge. The format may be the relatively informal outline offered by a student to satisfy the requirements of a research course, a formal thesis or dissertation proposal presented to a committee, or a funding request to a foundation or governmental agency.

The following is a suggested outline for writing a research proposal and contains the steps essential to formulating and proposing a research study:

   I. Introduction
     A. Statement of the problem
     B. Review of the literature
     C. Questions and/or hypotheses

  II. Methodology
     A. Subjects
     B. Instruments
     C. Procedures

 III. Analysis of data
     A. Presentation of data
     B. Statistical procedures

 IV. Significance of the study
     A. Implications
     B. Applications

  V. Budget and Time Schedule
     A. Budget
     B. Time schedule

Although it is not necessary to follow this outline rigidly, it should provide a useful guide for the writing of any proposal since all the aspects listed here must be considered.

INTRODUCTION

A critical part of a research proposal is the introduction to the proposed study. The author should first state the research problem clearly and unambiguously, then link the problem to the body of information available in the field, and establish the importance of and the need for carrying out the research. Regardless of how tightly the design of the study is formulated and how well the statistical procedures are selected, unless the introduction is written carefully and intelligently, other parts of the proposal will probably not receive serious consideration. It is not unusual for proposals to be turned down solely on the basis of a poor introduction, without much consideration being given to the proposed methodology and statistical design. It is recommended that this section be prepared with care, caution, and the aim of promoting the reader's interest in the problem.

The introduction to a research proposal should include (a) a statement of the problem, (b) a review of the literature, and (c) questions and/or hypotheses.

Statement of the Problem

A clear and direct statement of the problem should be made very early in the introduction, ideally at the beginning of the first paragraph, and followed by a description of the background of the question. This section of the introduction should also include a brief indication of the potential significance of the study, although it is important to avoid the temptation to sell the importance of the topic before stating it. Two common errors to watch for are (1) beginning the introduction with an elaborate presentation of the background of a problem before the problem itself has been clearly stated and (2) concentrating on a justification for the study at this point with the statement of the problem buried in the discussion or only vaguely brought in near the end.

It is also unwise to assume that the reader knows as much about the content of the question and its significance as does the author. Guba writes:

> I want to emphasize especially the necessity for stating the problem distinctly and precisely in terms which are intelligible to someone who is generally sophisticated but who is relatively uninformed in the area of the problem. This seems to be the biggest single error that people make in writing proposals. They assume that the reader to whom the proposal is addressed is just as informed about the content as the proposer, just as keenly aware of the significance of the particular problem being proposed. Nothing could be further from the truth. The keynote then is good, clean, concise organization, accomplished early in the proposal.[1]

Usually the background of the problem will be developed in the section on related literature. However, it is sometimes appropriate to mention in the statement of the

---

[1]Egon Guba, ''Guides for the Writing of Proposals,'' in Jack A. Culbertson and Stephen P. Hencly, eds., *Educational Research: New Perspectives* (Danville, Ill.: Interstate Printers & Publishers, 1963), ch. 18.

problem those studies that have led directly to it. If the problem has arisen from the author's experience, this may be explained briefly in this section.

At an appropriate point in this section, any terms that may not be familiar to the reader or those to which the author is ascribing specific meanings should be defined in the way they will be used in the study. The specific limitations of the scope of the study and a foreshadowing of the hypothesis should close this section.

Review of the Literature

In the section on related literature the author presents what is so far known about the problem under consideration, thus providing the setting for the questions or hypotheses of the proposed study. The USOE advises that proposal writers "tie the relevant literature to the objectives of the proposed study. The literature does not have to be exhaustive, but should contain the most pertinent related studies and show an awareness of promising current practices."[2]

In this section the author of the proposal demonstrates not only how he or she proposes to proceed from the known to the unknown but also how firm the author's grasp of the field and awareness of recent developments are. This does not mean that the review should be a tour de force of the author's erudition. Only literature that clearly relates to the objectives of the study should be included.

The literature should be organized by topic. Topical organization serves to point out to the reader what is known about various aspects of the study. Thus a complete picture of the background of the study is put together step by step.

A pitfall to be avoided in a related literature section is the presentation of a series of abstracts, one per paragraph. By doing this, the author presents the audience with tedious reading and misses the opportunity for laying meaningful groundwork for the study. It is much better to organize by topic and to point out how the studies presented relate to the question or questions.

Not all related studies need to be discussed in detail. In reviewing several similar studies, the author may describe the most important one, then simply state that the results were confirmed in similar studies that are listed but not described in detail. Enthusiastic beginning researchers often imagine their proposed study is unique and that there is no related research available. This is very rarely the case. A thorough search will almost always turn up several research papers related to at least some aspect of a proposed study. Even if there should chance to be no research in the field, there is usually literature of a theoretical or speculative nature that should be included as part of the background of a study.

Of course the author should include theories and research results contrary to the stated hypothesis as well as those in agreement with it.

The related literature section should conclude with a discussion of the findings and their implications. Here the author shares the insights gained from the review of

---

[2]U.S. Department of Health, Education, and Welfare, *Small Project Research* (Washington, D.C.: Bureau of Research, U.S. Office of Education, 1966).

the literature and points out the gaps presently existing in what is known about the topic, and thus leads directly to the question he or she proposes to investigate.

Questions and/or Hypotheses

The problem, which has already been stated in a general way, should now be made specific. If the project is a survey, the problem will be stated in question form: for example, What percentage of teachers in the state of Iowa have tenure?

If the project is designed to test a theory, however, the problem will be stated in hypothesis form: for example, The chemistry achievement of students who have used the Chemical Bond Approach[3] materials in a chemistry course will be superior to the achievement of those students who have taken a more traditional course in chemistry.

Although the answer to a survey question may take any number of values, the answer to a hypothesis-testing experiment is always either yes or no.

The statement of the research hypothesis is typically determined by the implications of the related literature and the deductive logic of the study. In the chemistry example above one would assume that previous research or theory led the researcher to expect that students using the Chemical Bond Approach would learn more than those using another method. Therefore the researcher states in the hypothesis the expectation that the scores of the experimental group will exceed those of the control group.

Some authorities suggest that the hypothesis should be stated in null form since it is the null hypothesis that will be involved in the statistical test. However, we suggest that in this section of the proposal a research hypothesis be stated in terms of anticipated relationships between variables. In this way the author gives the readers a clearer indication of the intent of the study than would be conveyed if the null hypothesis were stated at this point. The use of the research hypothesis at this stage also allows the researcher to build the deductive logic underlying the study.

Although the hypothesis may be introduced in a general form, it is necessary that the operational definition of each element within the hypothesis be included at this point in the proposal. In the present example the proposer would need to define chemistry achievement operationally and to stipulate what is meant by student, Chemical Bond Approach, and traditional chemistry courses. Thus the hypothesis in operational form might read: *The ACS-NSTA Cooperative Examination: High School Chemistry* test scores of beginning high school chemistry students who have been instructed for one year from the Chemical Bond Approach course outline in the manner described in *Chemical Systems* will exceed the scores of an equivalent class taught for the same period of time according to the procedures described in the *Teacher's Guide to the Modern Chemistry Program.*[4]

It is a good thing if a hypothesis can be stated concisely in operational form. If

[3]Chemical Bond Approach Project, *Chemical Systems* (New York: McGraw-Hill, 1964).

[4]H. C. Metcalfe et al., *Teacher's Guide to the Modern Chemistry Program* (New York: Holt, Rinehart and Winston, 1966).

this is not possible, a hypothesis stated in general terms should be followed by the definitions and stipulations necessary to define it in operational form.

METHODOLOGY

In this part of the proposal the author shows how the study will be set up in order that the research question will be answered or the hypothesized relationships will be observed, if in fact these relationships do exist. In previous chapters appropriate research designs for different types of research have been introduced. The researcher should select from among these research designs, experimental or otherwise, the one that best suits the question and/or hypothesis under consideration. For example, if one is to compare two methods of teaching chemistry, one is in fact raising an experimental question. This research problem requires at least two groups of subjects: experimental and control. If one also wishes to investigate the interaction effect between methods of teaching chemistry and another variable—intelligence, for instance—the question, while still experimental, asks for a more sophisticated design than that of a two-group design. One needs, in this case, to set up a factorial design with at least four groups for such a study.

In the methodology part of the proposal the author includes all steps that will be taken to investigate the question under consideration. The proposed sampling procedures, methods of data collection, and instruments to be used are described.

A convenient way of presenting the research methodology is to categorize all information regarding the design as (a) subjects, (b) instruments, (c) procedures, as appropriate.

Subjects

The first step in identifying the subjects in a study is to describe the population of interest: Is the study concerned with college freshmen, dyslectic six-year-olds, principals of elementary schools, and so forth? Then the author/researcher describes the procedure for drawing the sample from the population. If random selection is not possible, it should be explained why a particular procedure for sample selection has been adopted and how the sample used does or does not resemble the population of interest. A careful description of the subjects can help the reader of the proposal to determine if, in the reader's view, the results of the study can be generalized to the extent intended.

Instruments

The goal of a research project is to investigate relationships between constructs. However, since constructs are usually impossible to measure directly, we must select or develop indicators that will approximate them as well as possible. In our earlier example the constructs of interest are method of teaching and chemistry achievement. We actively manipulate the independent variable, method of teaching, and measure the dependent variable, chemistry achievement. Since we cannot measure chemistry achievement directly, the *ACS-NSTA Cooperative Examination: High School Chemistry* could be chosen as the indicator of this construct. The methods of teaching are operationally defined by the procedures given in the teacher's guides.

Inasmuch as the instruments used will provide the operational definition of the variables, their use must be justified as being appropriate for that purpose. In the example the criterion is not, strictly speaking, achievement in chemistry but rather scores on the ACS-NSTA test. In this section of the proposal the author should explain why the instrument used was selected as the most appropriate definition of the variable under consideration.

If an instrument is one already established, the proposal should include reported evidence of its reliability and also its validity for the purpose of the study. In cases where the instruments are to be developed by the researcher, it is necessary to outline the procedure to be followed in developing them. This outline should include the steps that will be taken to obtain validity and reliability data on these instruments. If the description of the reliability and validity procedures results in so much detail that it interrupts the continuity of the proposal, it is preferable to include this material in an appendix rather than in the text.

Procedures

In the procedures section the author describes the way in which the experiment will be set up so that the hypothesized relationships can be observed if these relationships do in fact exist. In effect the researcher is saying, "*If* this hypothesis is true, *then* these results will be observed." In our example, *if* a relationship exists between method of teaching chemistry and student proficiency in chemistry, *then* when groups of students of equivalent ability are taught by different methods under conditions that are otherwise identical, one should observe different mean chemistry proficiency scores for the groups at the conclusion of the experiment. By designing the study explicitly as an operation to permit the observation of the hypothesized relationships, the researcher lays the foundation for the study.

A careful description of the procedures of a study is a basic requirement of any research proposal. In survey research the writing of this section is relatively simple since the procedure merely involves sending out a questionnaire to be filled out and returned or conducting an interview. However, all the steps—that is, preparing the questionnaire or interview schedule, training the interviewers, giving them directions as to how to approach the subjects and how to perform the interview—should be listed and explained.

In experimental research the procedures may be more complex. In this section, the author should list the groups, specify step by step the manipulations planned for each one, and link each treatment to the proposed questions and hypotheses. These steps should be completely designated in operational form. By basing the procedures of the experiment on the hypotheses, the author facilitates direct and unambiguous interpretation of results. The possibility of confounding variables, those variables that could account for criterion score differences that are not part of the independent variable, should also be considered here. In our example student ability, motivation, previous experience, teacher's ability, time spent in chemistry class, physical setting, and laboratory facilities of the groups would be among the possible confounding variables. It should be specified in the procedures section how the author/researcher proposes to control for these variables. For example, one might control for student and teacher differences by random assignment of students and teachers to the control and experimental groups. The time spent, physical setting, and laboratory facilities could also be made equivalent. This section should include all the steps that operationally define the experimental and control treatments.

Documents such as teaching or reading materials planned for an experiment need not be included in the main text of the proposal since discussion of such details usually interrupts the continuity of the proposal. It is recommended that the author place these documents in an appendix, describing them briefly but clearly in the procedures section. It is, however, essential to explain in this section any differences in the presentation of these materials to the different groups involved in the experiment.

After the section on procedures has been drafted, it should be read to verify that all the steps necessary to answer every question and test every hypothesis have been described. The completeness of this section can be checked with the question, Could the reader carry out this research by following the steps as described? If this question can be answered in the affirmative, this section is complete.

ANALYSIS OF DATA

The next part of the research proposal describes the methods of handling and presenting data and the statistical procedures to be used under the sections (a) presentation of data and (b) statistical procedures.

Presentation of Data

The presentation of the results of a research study can take different forms depending on the way the findings are organized. It is necessary to plan in advance for the arrangement of research results into an organized form. This is best done by reference to questions or hypotheses of the study. Planning in advance for the organization and presentation of data enables a researcher to determine whether the information being collected is relevant to the research questions. Those who bypass this step often find they have wasted considerable time and money in collecting irrelevant pieces of information.

Tables, figures, and charts are essential means for organizing and summarizing a whole set of data. While the research is in the planning stage, the researcher should be able to picture how the data will be organized and presented in tabular form.

Statistical Procedures

The design of the study determines what statistical techniques should be employed, not vice versa. In other words, the researcher decides what design will permit observation of the hypothesized relationships, then selects the statistical procedure that fits the questions asked and the nature of the data involved. The researcher does not first select an appealing statistic and then design the study to fit that statistic.

The most commonly used statistical procedures have been described in earlier chapters. They are summarized for convenience in Table 12.1 (Descriptive Statistics) and Table 12.2 (Inferential Statistics). Table 12.1 is designed to help identify the indices that may be used to describe in summary form the data of a study. The appropriate statistical procedure is determined partly by the type of measurement scale characterizing the dependent variable. Therefore the rows in the table are identified as interval, ordinal, and nominal. Columns (1), (2), and (3) list the various purposes descriptive statistics may serve. The most common uses of these statistics are:

1. to provide an index to describe a group or the difference between groups (measures of central tendency)
2. to provide an index to describe the variability of a group or differences in the variability of groups (measures of variability)
3. to locate an individual in a group (indices of location)
4. to provide an index to describe the relationship of variables within a population (measures of correlation)
5. to describe how a set is divided into subsets
6. to describe the interaction among two or more variables in relation to a criteron (measures of interaction)

The required cell can be located by identifying the row and column heading appropriate to one's study. Each cell is divided and the section to use is determined by whether the study is concerned with one group or with more than one group. (Recall that one *may* choose a procedure for a lower scale of measurement but not the reverse; for example, one may use a median or a mode to describe interval data but may not use a mean to describe ordinal or nominal data.)

In determining what type of scale to use in expressing the data, the researcher should consider the advantages of all three scales on the descriptive level. Interval data typically provide more information than ordinal data, and ordinal data provide more information than nominal data. In making inferences, statistical tests of interval data are more ''powerful'' than tests of ordinal data; that is, one has a greater chance of rejecting a null hypothesis when interval measures are used than when ordinal measures are used. In the same manner, ordinal tests are more powerful than nominal measures. Therefore, when a choice is possible, a researcher will prefer interval data to ordinal and ordinal to nominal.

For example, if we have interval data for the dependent variable and want an index to describe the difference between groups, the table identifies the difference between two means as an appropriate statistic. (We could, if we choose, use difference between medians or difference between modes, but these would be less powerful than the difference between means.)

Table 12.1 Descriptive Statistics

Type of Scale of Dependent Variable	PURPOSE OF THE STATISTIC					
	(1) Central Tendency		*(2) Variability*		*(3) Location*	
	One Group	More Than One Group	One Group	More Than One Group	One Group	More Than One Group
Interval	mean	difference between means	standard deviation or variance	difference between standard deviations or variances	z-score, t-score, or other standard score	difference between an individual's standard score is more than one distribution
Ordinal	median	difference between medians	quartile deviation	difference between quartile deviations	percentile rank*	difference between an individual's percentile rank in more than one distribution
Nominal	mode	difference between modes	range	difference between ranges	label or categorization	label or categorization

TABLE 12.1 (cont.)

Type of Scale of Dependent Variable	PURPOSE OF THE STATISTIC					
	(4) Correlation		(5) Subsets		(6) Interaction	
	One Group	More Than One Group	One Group	More Than One Group	One Group	More Than One Group
Interval	Pearson r	difference in Pearson rs for same variables in two groups			difference between observed cell means and expected cell means in factorial ANOVA (observed interaction)	differences in observed interaction among groups
Ordinal	Spearman rho or Kendall's W*	difference in Spearman rhos for same variables in two groups				
Nominal	point biserial correlation*	difference in point biserial correlations for same variables in two groups	proportion or percentage	differences in proportions or percentages	differences between observed cell frequencies and expected cell frequencies	differences in observed interaction among groups

*This statistic is not described in this text but may be found in any number of statistics texts.

TABLE 12.2 Inferential Statistics

Type of Scale of Dependent Variable	Central Tendency (1)		Variability (2)		Location (3)	
	One Group	More Than One Group	One Group	More Than One Group	One Group	More Than One Group
Interval	standard error of the mean	t-test or one-way ANOVA		Bartlett's test* or t-test for homogeneity of variance;* F-max* statistics	standard error of measurement*	standard error of difference scores*
Ordinal	standard error of median*	median test, sign test,* Kruskal-Wallis one-way ANOVA,* or Friedman's test*				
Nominal						

PURPOSE OF THE STATISTIC

TABLE 12.2 (cont.)

PURPOSE OF THE STATISTIC

Type of Scale of Dependent Variable	(4) Correlation		(5) Subsets		(6) Interaction	
	One Group	More Than One Group	One Group	More Than One Group	One Group	More Than One Group
Interval	t-test for Fisher's z transformation or F-test for linearity*	t-test for Fisher's z transformation*			F-test for multi-factor ANOVA	F-test for multi-factor ANOVA
Ordinal	test for Spearman's Rho or Kendall's W*					
Nominal	chi-square or test for significance of point biserial*	Cochran's Q*	chi-square or Fisher's exact test*	chi-square or Fisher's exact test*	information theory A*	chi-square test for information theory A*

*This statistic is not described in this text but may be found in any number of statistics texts.

If the study is inferential in nature, the researcher will proceed to test the statistical significance of the index selected. Appropriate statistics for this purpose are listed in Table 12.2. In our example the t-test or one-way ANOVA would be appropriate.

Remember that a statistical procedure is selected on the basis of its appropriateness for answering the question involved in the study. Nothing is gained by using a complicated procedure when a simple one will do just as well. Statistics are to serve research, not to dominate it.

In this section of the proposal a specific description of the plans for administering the instruments and collecting the data should be given. These plans should include the time schedule, procedures for replacing subjects lost during the course of the experiment, plans for counterbalancing for order effects if needed, and other necessary details. We often tell our students, "Imagine you have gotten a fantastic grant for doing your study, but you are run over by a truck the very next day. Could a colleague pick up your proposal and actually conduct the study?" If this question can be honestly answered in the affirmative, the data analysis part of the study is complete.

SIGNIFICANCE OF THE STUDY

Some researchers prefer to state the significance of the problem in the introduction to the proposal. Leaving this topic for a later section, however, provides the opportunity to relate it to both the background and the design of the study. This section is best handled in two stages: (a) implications and (b) applications.

Implications

Since the aim of research is to increase knowledge, the author of the proposal should show how his or her particular study will do this by discussing what the results will mean to theory and information in the specific area to which the research question is related, and to what extent these results will be useful in solving problems and answering questions in the general field. Finally the author should show how the results of the study will provide grounds for further research in the area. In addition it may be explained how the author/researcher's own experience and expertise, coupled with the facilities and goals of the institution where the study is being carried out, place him or her in a favorable position to solve the problem in question.

Applications

The author should be able to convince readers of the potential application of the findings to educational practice. This discussion should show how, and to what extent, educational practitioners could use the results in order to improve their work. To find the extent to which the study has application to educational practice, the researcher may ask: Will the results of my study change anything in the field of education? Would my results help teachers, school counselors, principals, or educational planners to improve their work?

This aspect carries considerable weight in attracting research funds for carrying out the study. Many foundations evaluate research proposals on the basis of whether or not they will have any application to practice.

BUDGET AND TIME SCHEDULE

All research should be planned with regard to the feasibility of carrying out the work. A proposal should conclude with a presentation of (a) budget and (b) time schedule.

Budget

Reviewing the previous sections of the proposal, the researcher now lists the personnel, equipment, space, and time that will be required for the project. Most universities and school systems have an office responsible for assisting in the preparation of research budgets. This office gives advice concerning the local and agency regulations and procedures and can assist in translating the needs of the proposal into dollars-and-cents figures.

Time Schedule

The researcher should also prepare a realistic schedule for completing the research within the time available. This information helps the reviewer of the proposal and the researcher to see how much time would be needed to complete the research, and should provide opportunities for periodically evaluating the development of the project.

Critiquing the Proposal

After completing the draft of a proposal, the author/researcher should go through it again carefully with a critical eye. It is also profitable to have colleagues read the proposal. Often someone else can identify weaknesses or omissions that are not evident to the author.

In his work with the Research Advisory Committee of the USOE Cooperative Research Program, Smith identified six common weaknesses that the committee found in proposals submitted for funding.[5]

1. The Problem Is Trivial

Problems that are of only peripheral interest to educators or show little likelihood of adding to knowledge in education are not considered to be deserving of support. Smith gives as an example a plan to study an adult education program for library trustees and comments, ''Not only is it of peripheral value to education and oriented

---

[5]Gerald R. Smith, ''A Critique of Proposals Submitted to the Cooperative Research Program,'' in Jack A. Culbertson and Stephen P. Hencly, eds., *Educational Research: New Perspectives* (Danville, Ill.: Interstate Printers and Publishers, 1963), ch. 17.

toward action rather than research, but it is, to put it bluntly, a problem of little significance.''

2. The Problem Is Not Delimited

The classic illustration by Good and Skates is a splendid example of this weakness.[6] A letter written by a graduate student to the Commissioner of Education for Alaska indicated that the student had selected for his thesis the topic ''The Teaching of English as Revealed in the Courses of Study of the English-Speaking Nations of the World.'' In the second paragraph, he asks the commissioner, ''Do you know some interesting books on Alaska: her history, her economic problems, commerce, imports, exports, human relations, religion, etc.''

In order to produce a feasible proposal, the researcher must focus the study. This is not to say that a study should never include a number of related variables. The researcher should attack those aspects of a problem that can reasonably be handled in a single study. A cluster of related variables can, and often should, be included in a study, but unwieldy overinclusive efforts should be avoided.

3. The Objectives, Hypotheses, or Questions Are Too Broadly Stated

Proposal writers are often tempted to state their objectives, hypotheses, or questions in broad, sweeping generalizations. In such cases one finds when reading the procedures section that the actual planned study is not capable of meeting the grand objectives set forth. Sometimes the objectives or hypotheses are stated in such broad, general terms that one must go to the procedures to discover what the study is really about. It seems obvious that the objectives and procedures should match; yet the Research Advisory Committee found that many proposals failed to meet this basic requirement.

4. The Procedures Are Lacking in Detail

Smith points out that ''an investigator who omits more than he includes should not expect the committee to read procedural details between the lines. The committee lacks both the desire and the clairvoyance to do so.'' Remember, the procedures should be complete enough to allow for replication.

5. A Simple Design Is Used to Investigate a Complex Problem

The design of a study should fit the problem. A simple comparison of the means of two groups is appropriate when a single variable is involved. More complex studies require more complex designs.

6. Relevant Variables Are Not Considered or Are Lightly Dismissed

Failure to consider relevant extraneous variables is a serious error in a research proposal. The researcher should demonstrate that he or she is aware of such variables and explain how they will be handled in the design of the study.

[6]Carter V. Good and Douglas E. Skates, *Methods of Research* (New York: Appleton, 1954), pp. 82–83.

The Importance of Completing the Proposal before Collecting Data

A clear, well-stated, complete proposal indicates that the prospective researcher is actually ready to set the study in motion. It shows that the researcher knows what to do, why to do it, and how to do it. A prospective researcher who cannot produce a complete and coherent proposal is clearly not yet ready to proceed to the data-collecting stage of the project. Novice researchers are ofttimes inclined to say, "Let me collect my data now and decide what to do with it later." Simultaneously collecting data and writing the proposal may seem to be a time-saving procedure, but such is seldom the case. Countless man-hours and thousands of dollars have been wasted in just that way. Until the proposal is formulated, one cannot be sure exactly what data will be needed, nor what will be the best way to handle this information in the light of the purpose of the study. Those working under deadlines should set for themselves a date for the completion of the proposal well in advance of the target date for completing the entire project.

This is not to say that data collection must *never* precede the proposal. A pilot study may be useful in planning a project, trying the instruments, determining the feasibility of the procedures, and so on. However, such pilots do not contribute substantive data to the study itself. They should be regarded as preliminary skirmishes and no more.

Research Ethics

Strict adherence to ethical standards in planning and conducting research is most important. Researchers have obligations both to their subjects and to their profession.

OBLIGATION TO SUBJECTS

When studying human subjects one must respect their integrity and humanity. Three major areas of concern are (1) protection of human subjects from harm, (2) respect for their right to know the nature and purpose of a study and their right to give or not give consent to participate (the right of informed consent), and (3) respect for subjects' privacy.

1. *Subjects must be protected not only from physical harm but from potential harm of any nature.* The present guidelines of the U.S. Department of Health, Education, and Welfare (DHEW) follow the established ethical standards of research by defining a "subject at risk" as one who might suffer physical, psychological, or social injury as a consequence of participation in any research.

In order to protect subjects and to guide those planning research, DHEW stipulates that "no grant or contract for an activity involving human subjects shall be made unless the application for such support has been reviewed and approved by an appropriate institutional committee.''[7]

After this requirement was made, those universities and other agencies that did not already have such committees established what are now generally known as institutional review boards. These boards determine if subjects are at risk under the guidelines provided by DHEW. The boards do not automatically disallow a study where subjects are at risk. They may approve studies where the subjects' risks are outweighed by ''the potential benefits to [them] or by the importance of the knowledge to be gained'' if the subjects have been informed concerning the risks and have voluntarily agreed to participate.

2. *The right of informed consent is due every potential research subject.* DHEW guidelines state that ''informed consent'' means the knowing consent of an individual or his or her legally authorized representative (usually a parent or guardian) so situated as to be able to exercise free power of choice without undue inducement or any element of force, fraud, deceit, duress, or other form of constraint or coercion. The basic elements of information necessary to such consent include:

a. a fair explanation of the procedures to be followed and their purposes, including identification of any procedures that are experimental
b. a description of any attendant discomforts and risks reasonably to be expected
c. a description of any benefits reasonably to be expected
d. a disclosure of any appropriate alternative procedures that might be advantageous for the subjects
e. an offer to answer any inquiries concerning the procedures
f. an instruction that the subjects are free to withdraw their consent and to discontinue participation in the project or activity at any time without prejudice to them

DHEW guidelines stipulate that if subjects are to be in any way at risk, their consent must be in the form of a signed statement. Normally the subjects themselves sign the consent if they are 18 years of age or beyond secondary school level. In other cases a parental signature is required.

In ordinary circumstances researchers must inform their subjects in advance of the purpose of the study. In exceptional cases, when the subjects' knowledge of the purpose of the research could influence the results of the study, researchers may withhold this information until the data have been collected. In these cases the subjects are told that they will be informed of the purpose of the study after it has been completed and this promise must be kept. One of the responsibilities of an institutional review board is to determine those cases in which the purpose of the investigation must be withheld from the subjects until after the study is complete.

Forcing individuals to participate as subjects of a study is unethical. One must avoid planning research studies in which a person's freedom of choice would be

---

[7]*The Institutional Guide to DHEW Policy on Protection of Human Subjects,* DHEW Publication No. (NIH) 72–102 (Washington, D.C., December 1, 1971).

violated. One should not compel one's students or employees to perform as subjects in one's research if they do not wish to participate. These individuals should have the same freedom not to participate in a research study as anyone else.

3. *The researcher should make sure that the subjects' privacy will not be invaded*. It is highly recommended that the subjects not be required to identify themselves when anonymous responses could serve the purpose. In situations where the nature of the research requires that the identity of the subjects be known to the researcher, one should first secure the consent of the subjects involved and then take necessary precautions to protect the confidentiality of the responses.

It is at present not clear how recent legislation concerning individual privacy should be interpreted in regard to educational research. DHEW is working to prepare clear guidelines on this matter. In many cases in educational research such as field studies, field experiments, and observational research, people often serve as subjects without awareness of their participation. Because of the nature of these kinds of research, it is not always possible to ask the participants for their consent. It is highly unlikely that DHEW guidelines will require subjects' consent in such cases unless individual subjects can be identified in the public report of the study. In the matter of subjects' right to privacy it is expected that DHEW guidelines will confirm the traditional ethical standard in this matter, which holds that subjects' informed consent is required whenever data about individuals are to become public. Whenever group statistics only are to be made public, consent is not required. In this matter, as in others, a researcher's institutional review board can assist in planning research that conforms to ethical and legal standards.

OBLIGATION TO THE PROFESSION

The researcher is also responsible to the consumers of research. Most research studies, in education as well as in other fields, are published in journals, monographs, books, and other media, and are referred to and consumed by professionals in the field. The researcher is morally obligated to plan a study in such a way that the findings obtained would not result in offering misleading information. Even more the researcher is obligated to report exactly and honestly what the findings were. Research must not be reported in such a way as to mislead. Reporting that misleads is a serious abuse of the researcher's responsibility to the profession.

Summary

A research proposal is a step-by-step plan for discovering new knowledge. It is at this stage that the researcher's inspiration and insights crystallize into concrete form. Several categories of information should be included in a research proposal.

A clear statement of the problem, accompanied by unambiguous definitions of terms, should be made early in the proposal. A review of pertinent literature should follow. A good review of literature shows what is so far known about the problem and lays the foundation for stating hypotheses regarding relationships between variables under consideration. In addition this part should be written with the aim of providing a foundation for the interpretation of results.

In the discussion of methodology that follows the introductory section, methods for subject selection, methods of data collection, observational procedures, and measurement techniques are all described with sufficient detail so that a reader could carry out the research by following the proposed steps exactly as the original writer of the proposal would.

The next part of the research proposal describes the procedures to be used for data presentation, such as tables, figures, and charts, and introduces the statistical techniques that will be used for data analysis.

A discussion of the potential significance of the study should follow. Here the researcher should attempt to show how the findings will increase knowledge and what the results will mean to theory and research in the field of interest. A discussion of the applications of the findings to practice would be helpful to readers who wish to assess the significance of the proposed research.

The final section of the proposal contains the time schedule and estimated budget of the study. This information is useful to readers in making an overall evaluation of the proposal.

A matter of considerable importance in planning research is the observation of ethical standards. Subjects must have the right of informed consent, they must be protected from harm, and their privacy must be respected.

Exercises

1. What are the basic components of a research proposal?
2. Why is it so important that the introduction be written carefully and intelligently?
3. At what point in the proposal should a clear statement of the problem be made?
4. Rewrite the following hypotheses, operationalizing all variables.
   a. Children who learn reading by the i/t/a method read better than those taught by a traditional approach.
   b. High school students who score above the top quartile of the XYZ Mechanical Aptitude Test make better mechanics.
   c. Scores on the math subtest of the SRA Achievement Test for smart seventh grade students who have been instructed with the new math approach for one year will exceed scores of smart seventh grade students who have been instructed with a traditional approach.
5. What are some confounding variables that may affect differences of mean achievement scores between classes of the same grade level? How could you control for these variables in your proposed procedures?
6. What is the appropriate statistic for measuring correlation if the scale of the dependent variable is nominal?
7. What measure of central tendency is appropriate for interval data?

8. For what types of data is ANOVA appropriate?
9. What is the function of an institutional board of review?
10. How might some research results be affected by subjects' knowledge of participation? How is the requirement of informed consent met in these circumstances?
11. What precautions should be taken to insure confidentiality of responses and subjects' privacy in research projects?

Answers

1. introduction, methodology, analysis of data, significance of the study, and budget and time schedule
2. If the introduction is not well done, the reader will not be inclined to read the rest of the proposal.
3. in the first paragraph of the introduction
4. a. Third graders who learned reading in first and second grade by the i/t/a method will score higher on the California Reading Test than third graders who learned to read using a basal reading approach.
   b. Juniors and seniors who scored above the top quartile of the XYZ Mechanical Aptitude Test before becoming apprentices will be rated more highly by supervisors after one year in a mechanics apprenticeship program than those scoring below the top quartile.
   c. Scores on the math subtest of the SRA Achievement Test of seventh graders with IQs above 115 on the WISC who have been instructed with the new math approach for one year will exceed scores of similar students who have been instructed with the traditional approach.
5. Different average ability levels, physical class environments, teachers, types and amount of materials are some factors. One can control for these variables by pretesting for ability level, selecting classes with similar environments, and pretraining teachers to certain levels of competence. Using large numbers of classes randomly assigned to conditions offers a different type of control.
6. point biserial
7. the mean
8. nominal independent variable and interval dependent variable
9. The institutional board of review determines if the subjects in a proposed experiment are at risk under DHEW guidelines and then determines if benefits outweigh the risks.
10. Knowledge that an unusual or experimental treatment is being used can influence subjects' psychological state and/or expectancy, which may influence or detract from the actual treatment effects. The subjects in such circumstances should be told that they will be informed of the purpose of the study when it is completed.
11. Subjects should not have to identify themselves unless necessary and should not be identified as individuals in the public report of the study unless they have given their consent.

Analyzing, Interpreting, and Reporting Results

Once the research data have been collected, the researcher should first analyze the results, then carefully interpret the findings, and, finally, write the report of the study. A brief discussion of each of these tasks is presented in this chapter.

Analysis of Data

For the researcher the first step in analyzing the data collected is to refer to the proposal to check the original plans for presenting data and performing the statistical analysis. Having done this, the researcher then develops the strategy for organizing the raw data and performing the necessary computations.

Today research projects in education and other behavioral sciences are often characterized by complexity and involved computational work. To achieve precision and to save time and energy, a majority of researchers choose to take advantage of electronic computing facilities for their data analysis. It is appropriate, therefore, to include here a brief discussion of computers and their use in data processing.

THE USE OF COMPUTERS IN DATA PROCESSING

The most important event in the history of research has been the invention of the computer. This phenomenon has changed the scope of research and has made it possible to conduct research studies that one would not otherwise think of undertaking. Because computers make it possible to analyze large quantities of data quickly and efficiently, researchers are able to design studies without concern for the number of variables or the complexity of the analysis that may be required. Before the days of computers, researchers avoided studies involving several variables and large numbers of subjects because of the time and labor involved in tabulating and analyzing the data. Sophisticated statistical tests and multivariate analysis were not often undertaken. The computer can process large amounts of data and perform complex statistical analyses with phenomenal speed and efficiency.

A computer is composed of four essential parts: an input device, a central processing unit, a storage unit, and an output device.

Preparing Data for the Computer

For the input device to accept data, they must be put into a form that permits statistical tabulation, analysis, and storage. Data processing may involve conversion of data from one form to another or reduction of information into a more manageable form. This processing of data for computer analysis involves a number of steps.

The first step is to code data into a form that is appropriate for computer analysis. Data coding involves the transformation of the data on variables from a verbal form into the numerical form that is required by the computer. For example, a subject's sex cannot be put into a computer through the use of words. Instead one uses a numerical code for the variable in which 1 represents a male subject and 2, a female subject. Codes are used for nominal data such as sex, race, socioeconomic status, class level, years of education completed, marital status, religious preference, political preference, state of residence. Numerical codes may also be used for ordinal or interval data when one wishes to have discrete categories for analysis purposes. For example, instead of using the actual ages of the teachers included in a study, one could code the ages with a 1 for those teachers under 25, 2 for those 26–30, 3 for teachers 31–35, and so on. Figure 13.1 is a data roster in which the first three items have been coded and the remaining ones are actual data. In a data roster the subjects are assigned a row and the variables for each subject are listed in columns.

Subject I.D.	Group	Sex	Class	Age	SAT Verbal	SAT Mathematical
01	1	1	3	16	450	495
02	1	2	4	17	560	460
03	2	1	3	15	570	530
04	2	2	4	18	620	640

Figure 13.1   Data roster for an experimental study

Possible ways of feeding these data into computers involve the use of electronic typewriters, magnetic discs or tape, electronic scanners, or punch cards. At present, punch cards are the most commonly used method for presenting data to the computer. Data are usually transferred onto punch cards by the keypunch machine. Learning to use this device is relatively easy and requires no more training than simple instructions given by a person who is familiar with its operation. Punch cards are rectangular cards with locations for digits from 0 to 9 for 80 columns. Thus 80 single digit numbers can be recorded on each card. It is also possible to use the letters of the alphabet for punching and recording on these cards. Prior to transferring a set of data to punch cards, one must decide which columns on the cards are to receive specific pieces of information, and then follow the same format on all the cards to be punched.

An alternative method of transferring data to punch cards is provided by the optical scanner. This machine scans especially prepared sheets with a photoelectric cell that records the fields in which responses have been marked, and then punches a hole in an appropriate column of an IBM card. The use of a scanner saves the researcher the time, effort, and expense of keypunching data onto cards. The optical scanner can punch approximately 1,000–1,200 cards per hour.

After the data are punched onto the cards, the next step is to inform the computer what is to be done with the data. This is done by means of the program. A computer program is a series of instructions that inform the computer what tasks to perform and in what sequence they are to be done. It gives instructions such as DO, READ, IF, PRINT. With the appropriate instructions the computer can perform statistical analyses ranging from measures of central tendency to multiple correlations.

Those who are knowledgeable in programming techniques may write their own programs. Fortunately, however, there are numerous prepared programs that are available for use at most computing centers. These are known as package or canned programs and are recommended for those with little or no programming experience. There are a number of different series of canned programs. One well-known series is the Biomedical Series developed originally for use in the biological and medical fields.[1] A great number of BIMED programs are available for various statistical analyses. Another, and one of the most popular series for the educational researcher, is the Statistical Package for the Social Sciences.[2] SPSS contains many of the most common statistical procedures employed by social scientists. SPSS uses a simple language that is easy to learn and requires no knowledge of how computers work. SPSS programs for statistical analyses include, among others:

Condescriptive Measures of Central Tendency and Dispersion
One-Way Frequency Distributions
Chi-Square
Bivariate Correlation Analysis and Scatterplots
Comparison of Sample Means: t-tests
One-Way to n-Way ANOVA and ANCOVA
Multiple Correlation and Regression
Partial Correlation
Guttman Scaling
Factor Analysis

Of course, the use of a package program does not spare the researcher the responsibility of understanding the statistical principles behind the program. The researcher must be able to interpret the output of the computer program or have a statistician explain it.

The final step in the processing of data for computer analysis is the preparation of control cards that permit the researcher to communicate with the computer program. These control cards represent specific instructions or commands to the computer so that it uses the appropriate program and reads in the data correctly. The exact format of the control cards needed for each program is specified in the users' manual, which also indicates the order in which control cards, data cards, and ending cards are to be fed into the computer.

If there are no errors made in programming, one can collect the results on the computer printout. However, a single error in arranging the cards, programming, or

[1] W. J. Dixon, ed., *BMDP: Medical Computer Programs* (Berkeley: University of California Press, 1975).

[2] N. Nie, D. Bent, and C. H. Hull, *Statistical Package for the Social Sciences,* 2nd ed., (New York: McGraw-Hill, 1975).

preparing the control cards will result in failure of the computer to perform the necessary operation. Then one needs to go back and check to find the problem that has caused the computer to fail to perform.

A word of caution is in order here. The results that are printed are only as good as the information that is fed into the computer. The computer does not make computational mistakes, but if errors of logic are fed into the computer by means of programming errors set up by the researcher, the computer will blindly, but efficiently, turn out "garbage" for results. There are two kinds of errors that can be made in programming. Language errors, such as misspelled instructions, will be detected by the computer, in which case the job will not be accepted. Errors of logic, such as incorrect instructions, will be accepted by the computer and will result in a very expensive output of meaningless data.

Finally, we want to make these recommendations in relation to computer usage:

1. Take full advantage of computers in your data processing, but make a critical evaluation of the computer's product. Though computers do not make mistakes, they also never correct mistakes made in programming or in preparing the data for processing.

2. Do not blindly use whatever program you can find in program manuals. You must decide for yourself what kind of statistical procedure is most appropriate for a given set of data.

Principles of Interpretation

Once the research data have been collected and the statistical analysis has been made, the researcher can proceed to the challenging task of interpreting the results. Adding to knowledge has been the principal focus of the research endeavor. When the interpretation stage is reached, the researcher can show what has been learned in the project and how this knowledge fits into the general body of knowledge in the field.

THE ROLE OF THE PROPOSAL IN FACILITATING INTERPRETATION

The proper foundation for interpreting the results of a study should have been laid systematically through each stage of the development of the proposal, even before the actual research began. By bearing in mind throughout the study what their data will consist of and may tell them, researchers prepare themselves for interpreting their data and fitting those data into the body of knowledge.

A carefully thought-out plan expressed as a thorough and complete proposal can be expected to generate results that can be easily and meaningfully interpreted. If the study has been laid out in such a way that the consequences of the hypotheses will be expressed in reliable observations, then the interpretation and value of the observations should be obvious.

THE IMPORTANCE OF KEEPING TO THE ORIGINAL PLAN

Once the proposal has been accepted and the project set in motion, the study must be carried out exactly as planned. This rule has ethical as well as practical implications.

To illustrate the ethical implications, let us suppose that Mr. Williams, a foreign-language teacher, has developed, with a great expenditure of time and effort, a system of teaching French that he believes to be greatly superior to existing methods. To test the efficacy of this method, he establishes an experimental group that is taught by his method and a control group, taught by another method. He devises a series of weekly French achievement tests to serve as the dependent variable. Suppose that he discovers in the first few weeks that the mean test scores for the two groups are almost identical. Having a big investment in his own method, he finds it hard to believe that it is no better than the other, so he decides to sit in on the two classes to see what has "gone wrong." He discovers that the experimental group seems to show much greater knowledge and appreciation of French life and culture. Since he is anxious to find a difference between scores, he decides to change his dependent variable to scores on tests on French life and culture.

Such a change would be unethical. Given two random groups one can always find a superiority in either group if one looks long enough. If the experimental group had not appeared superior on French life and culture, it might have been superior on English grammar or Latin or deportment or some other variable. The language teacher *must* carry out the experiment as planned rather than change his dependent variable after he has noted a difference. It is legitimate for him to note somewhere in his report that the experimental group seemed superior in understanding French life and culture and that it might be worthwhile to use that variable in another experiment with another group of subjects. It is unethical to abandon independent or dependent variables that do not seem to be "working out" or add promising new ones. Such changes must be left for future studies.

The addition of new variables is also unwise from a practical standpoint. Such a tactic can confuse the results of a study and obscure the meaning of the results. Researchers are often tempted to add interesting new variables that crop up in their study. However, the theoretical base for interpreting these variables has not been laid and again the best advice to researchers is to leave them for later studies.

INTERPRETATION OF EXPECTED RESULTS

Understandably researchers are pleased when the results of a study fit into the previously constructed framework and interpretation can proceed as expected. The study has "worked" and there is an agreement between rationale and results.

Only a few words of caution need apply in such a case:

1. Do not make interpretations that go beyond the information. This may seem a patently obvious injunction, but researchers often get so excited when results are as expected that they draw conclusions that do not have a valid basis in the data. Even

in published research one frequently finds more interpretations than the data warrant.

2. Do not forget the limitations of the study. These limitations, of course, should have been previously identified in the study—limitations inherent in the less-than-perfect reliability and validity of the instruments, limitations due to the restriction in sampling, the internal validity problems, and so forth.

3. Ethics require that the researcher report internal validity problems that could account for the results. If, despite the researcher's best efforts, the nonexperimental variables were particularly benign for the experimental group and those for the control group were particularly malign, these conditions must be reported and taken into account in interpreting results. (For example, despite random assignment of teachers to groups, the experimental group may have mostly experienced teachers and the control group may have mostly inexperienced teachers.)

4. Remember that statistical significance means only that for the appropriate degrees of freedom the results are unlikely to be a function of chance. Statistical significance does not mean that the results are significant in the generally accepted meaning of the word—that is, important, meaningful, or momentous. Do not assume that statistical significance guarantees momentous import to your findings.

Let us suppose that two equivalent groups have been subjected to two different systems of learning spelling over a two-year period. Those using System A show a mean gain equivalent of 2.15 years of growth on standardized tests during the experiment, while those using System B show a gain of 2.20 in the same period. If the groups are large and/or if the differences within groups are small, the differences between the means would be statistically significant. But a difference of half a month over a two-year period is relatively meaningless in practical terms. If System B is more expensive in terms of student time, teacher time, or materials, teachers would be unwise to adopt it simply because statistically it produced significantly greater gains than System A. If, on the other hand, System B is the less expensive, teachers would be inclined to favor it since its results *are* so similar to those of System A in practical terms.

The potential importance or meaningfulness of results must be established in the proposal before the study begins. A study is not important if it does not provide meaningful information to be added to the existing body of knowledge no matter how statistically significant the results may be.

INTERPRETATION OF NEGATIVE RESULTS

Researchers who find results opposite to those hypothesized often develop sudden revelations concerning the shortcomings of their study. Their interpretation of results reads like a confession. The instruments were inadequate for measuring the variables involved; the sample was too small and was so unrepresentative that results cannot be validly generalized to a meaningful target population, and so on. Hindsight reveals internal validity problems that explain why the study did not come out as it "should have."

Of course, any or all of these things could be true, and the shortcomings of any study should be reported no matter what the results. However, research is always a venture into the unknown, so there is no ultimate "should be." An investigator predicts the expected results of a study on the basis of theory, deduction, and the results of previous research. If these are so conclusive that there can be absolutely no doubt as to the results of this study, then the study is pointless in the first place.

When we undertake a study, we implicitly state that the outcome is a matter of conjecture, not a matter of certainty. When we complete our proposal, it is understood that we declare that we will impartially seek to determine the true state of affairs with the best instruments and procedures available to us for that purpose. Therefore we are obliged to accept and interpret our data no matter how the data stand. When the results contradict the theoretical rationale of the study, the discussion section of our report should include a reconsideration of the original theory in the light of the findings. Researchers are often reluctant to present and interpret data that conflict with previous research or with well-established theory. However, it may be that their results are right and previous results wrong. The progress of the science of education will be retarded if investigators are reluctant to report findings that do not agree with those reported in earlier studies. Contradictory results indicate that a question is not settled, and may stimulate further research. Additional research or theory formation may eventually reconcile seemingly contradictory results. Theory is tentative and should not deter investigators from giving a straightforward interpretation of what was found.

The reconsideration of the theoretical base of a study belongs in the discussion section. One must *not* go back and rewrite the related literature and hypothesis sections of the report.

INTERPRETATION OF RESULTS WHEN THE NULL HYPOTHESIS IS RETAINED

Since a null hypothesis may be retained for a variety of reasons, interpreting such a result can be particularly difficult. A retained null hypothesis may occur because: (1) The null hypothesis is, in fact, true. There may be no relationship between variables. The experimental treatment may be no more effective than the control treatment. (2) The null hypothesis is false, but internal validity problems contaminated the investigation so badly that the actual relationship between variables could not be observed. (3) The null hypothesis is false, but the research design lacked the *power* to reject it.

Any of these states of affairs may be the case, but the investigator does not know which is true and therefore should not claim any one of them as the explanation for the results.

It is incorrect to present a retained null hypothesis as evidence of no relationship between variables. A retained null hypothesis must be interpreted as lack of evidence for either the truth or falsity of the hypothesis. A widely used toothpaste commercial states that tests show a particular toothpaste to be unsurpassed in reducing tooth decay. Interpreting the term *unsurpassed* to mean *no significant difference,* we can imagine a test in which a very small number of subjects were used and/or numerous internal validity problems were present. If a retained null hypothesis is the desired result of an experiment, it is remarkably easy to arrange for such an outcome.

Of course, if one is studying a small population and can do a complete census of that population, a retained null hypothesis can legitimately be interpreted as a lack of relationship between variables within that particular population. A retained null hypothesis also acquires credibility when a very large sample is involved. For example, the Coleman report, with over 600,000 subjects, provides such a large base that we are willing to accept an observed lack of relationships between variables as evidence of an actual lack of relationships in this case. However, in most studies the retained null hypothesis must be interpreted as a lack of evidence and no more.

There is a danger that investigators who become too enamored of their experimental hypothesis may be tempted to interpret a retained null hypothesis as if it were not there. They cite internal validity problems and declare that the results would certainly have been significant if only those unanticipated problems had not ruined the experiment. Of course one should report all internal validity problems that arise in a study, but one should not use them to explain away disappointing results. One may suggest additional research, planned in such a way as to avoid the internal validity problems encountered, but still one must report a retained null hypothesis as lack of evidence and no more.

The *power* of an experiment refers to the statistical ability to reject a null hypothesis when it is, in fact, false. This power is a function of the size of the sample, the heterogeneity of subjects with reference to the dependent variable, the reliability of the measuring instruments used, and the nature of statistical procedure used to test the hypothesis. Researchers should take these factors into account when planning an experiment. A number of statistics textbooks explain how to plan experiments in such a way that meaningful relationships will be expressed as statistically significant observations. The power of an experiment should be considered in planning the study. It must not be brought in at the end of a study to explain away lack of statistical significance. For example, one should not say, ''The results would have been statistically significant if the sample had been larger.''

With rare exceptions the only legitimate interpretation of a retained null hypothesis is that *evidence for a conclusion has not been observed*.

INTERPRETATION OF UNHYPOTHESIZED RELATIONSHIPS

We emphasized earlier that a researcher should not abandon a hypothesis during the conduct of a study in order to pursue more promising avenues that present themselves during the course of the study. This does not mean that any unhypothesized relationships that may be observed in the conduct of a study should be ignored. On the contrary, they should be recorded and analyzed with the same rigor that is employed in pursuing hypothesized relationships. Throughout the history of science serendipitous discoveries have often proved to be important.

However, such findings should always be viewed with more suspicion than findings directly related to the hypothesis, since there is a relatively great possibility that a spurious unhypothesized relationship will appear in a study. Such relationships should be reported, but they should be considered as incidental to the main thrust of the investigation. They should be made the subject of a study specifically designed to investigate them before they can be employed as the basis for conclusions.

The Research Report

The results of a research project are of little value unless they can be communicated to others. Therefore a knowledge of the procedures involved in writing a research report is important to all researchers. The purpose of this section is to give a general guide to the organization and presentation of a report. For specific rules on style and format a style manual should be consulted and several are listed at the end of this chapter.

In a research report the investigator communicates both the procedures and the findings of the research and also discusses the implications of the findings and their relationship to other knowledge in the field.

Since the report will be read by busy professionals, it should be as concise and as logically organized as possible. Anecdotes, stories of personal experiences, and argumentative discourses are out of place in a research report. This does not mean that the report has to be dull and pedantic. If the researcher has approached the study with a spirit of enthusiasm, this spirit tends to be conveyed between the lines.

Since the purpose of the report is to present the research rather than the personality of the author, the tone of the report should be impersonal. In keeping with this, first-person pronouns are never used. Thus one would not write, ''I randomly assigned subjects to the two treatment groups,'' but rather, ''Subjects were randomly assigned to the two treatment groups.'' Despite a natural enthusiasm about the importance of the work, the author should not brag about it but should leave its evaluation to readers and to posterity.

A formal and uniform method of presenting research reports has been evolved. Although at first glance these formalities may seem inhibiting, in practice they serve a useful purpose. It is important to have research reports arranged in such a way that readers know exactly where to find those specific parts of a report they may be seeking. In chapter 3 you were advised to read through the summary section of a journal article first when gathering related research. If an article does not have a summary section, you are forced to spend additional time reading it through before determining whether it is relevant.

In addition the presence of established format eliminates the need for devising one's own. As this topic is discussed, it will be seen that the established format follows logically the steps in a research project presented in earlier chapters.

A research report may be presented as (1) a thesis or dissertation, (2) a journal article, or (3) a conference paper. A different approach is required in each of these cases.

THE THESIS OR DISSERTATION

Most universities have a preferred manual that describes in detail the form the university requires. For those students who are free to choose, several style manuals are listed at the end of this chapter. Once a manual has been chosen, the entire report should be styled according to its recommendations.

The outline lists the sequence and general components described in most style manuals:

I. Preliminary pages
   A. Title page
   B. Acceptance page
   C. Acknowledgments or preface
   D. Table of contents
   E. List of tables
   F. List of figures

II. Text
   A. Introductory section
      1. Statement of the problem and rationale for the study
      2. Objectives
      3. Definitions of terms
      4. Related literature
   B. Methods and results section
      1. Subjects
      2. Procedures
      3. Instruments
      4. Presentation and analysis of data
   C. Discussion of results
      1. Interpretation of findings
      2. Implications
      3. Applications
   D. Conclusions and summary
      1. Conclusions
      2. Summary

III. Supplementary pages
   A. Bibliography
   B. Appendices
   C. Vita (if required)
   D. Abstract

I. Preliminary Pages

The preparation of the preliminary pages is largely a matter of following the rules of the style manual. However, one aspect of these pages that needs additional explanation at this point is the title of the study itself.

The title should describe, as briefly as possible, the specific nature of the study. For example, consider (a) a study of culturally disadvantaged children that compares the reading readiness of those who have participated in a Project Head Start program with that of a matched group of children with no formal preschool experience, and (b) the title, "A Comparison of Reading Readiness Test Scores of Disadvantaged Children Who Have Attended Head-Start Classes for Six Weeks or More with Similar Children with No Preschool Experience." While this title does convey what the study is about, it is too long. Such phrases as "a comparison of," "a study of," "an investigation into" are usually superfluous. Furthermore most prospective readers will know that Project Head Start is a preschool experience designed for culturally disadvantaged children. However, to go to the other extreme by providing a title that is too brief or too vague to convey the nature of the study is a much more serious mistake. With vague or overly brief titles one must search out the article in order to determine what it is about. Titles such as "Head Start and Readiness" or "Reading among the Disadvantaged" illustrate this shortcoming. *The title should identify the major variables and the populations of interest.* The operational definitions of the major variables and the description of the samples need not be included in the title.

Since correct titling will insure correct indexing, a useful strategy is for researchers first to decide under what key words they want their studies to be indexed, working from there to a concise title. In our example the important key words for indexing would be *reading readiness* and *Project Head Start*. So an appropriate title might be "Reading Readiness of Project Head Start and Non-Head Start Children." This title is reasonably brief yet it gives the prospective reader a valid indication of what the study is about.

Emotion-laden titles, such as "We Must Expand the Head Start Programs" or "Don't Let the Disadvantaged Become Poor Readers," should be avoided at all costs. The prospective reader will not expect research findings under such titles but rather armchair articles attempting to sell a point of view.

II. Text

A. *Introductory Section.* The introductory section includes everything that took place in laying the groundwork for the research. It typically consists of materials already prepared for the proposal with relatively minor alterations. The statement of the problem and the justification for the study remain the same as do the statement of objectives, definition of terms, and review of related research. However, here the brief account of the sources of the data and the methods used is written in the past tense rather than in the future tense used in the wording of the original proposal. The review of the related research is usually presented as a separate chapter of the introductory section.

B. *Methods and Results.*   Four categories of information are included in this part of the report:

1. *Subjects:* A detailed description of the sample should be presented, preferably at the beginning. This enables the reader to judge the potential external validity of the research. The population from which the sample was drawn should be defined and the method of sampling should be specified. The kind of information given in the description of the sample will vary from study to study, but in general one can determine what information to include by considering what variables might influence the criterion scores in the study. In the chemistry example considered in chapter 12, the subjects would probably be described in terms of age, grade level, previous science training, IQ, and socioeconomic status.

2. *Procedures:* The report on procedures of the study should be complete enough so that anyone wanting to replicate the study would find all the necessary information there. One of the characteristics of the scientific approach is the possibility of confirming findings by repeating the procedures and observational information necessary for replication. The design of the study, the number of groups (if the study is an experiment), the treatment of subjects, and other pertinent information are included in this section.

3. *Instruments:* A research report should specify all the measuring instruments and observational systems used in carrying out the study. The specifications can be brief when previously established measures, such as ACS-NSTA chemistry examinations, have been used since the references will contain the relevant information about such instruments. If special instruments have been developed for the study, a detailed description of these instruments must be provided along with evidence of reliability and validity and a discussion of scoring procedures.

4. *Presentation and analysis of data:* A recommended technique for the presentation and statistical analysis of data is to organize the discussion around the hypotheses; that is, to restate the first hypothesis and present findings concerning it, repeating this procedure for each hypothesis in turn.

Tables and figures may be profitably employed to present the data more clearly and more concisely than would be possible if the same information were presented in text form. Most style manuals provide examples of commonly used types of tables and figures and instructions for their construction. A well-constructed table can give the reader a concise overview of the data.

Tables constructed in the conduct of the study cannot usually be incorporated directly into the report. For example, on completion of a study one may have an alphabetical list of the subjects in one's study and their scores on criterion measures. Rather than present this list as it stands, one would construct a table of the information in summary form. (Basic raw data tables may be included in the appendices if it is felt they can contribute to understanding.) The first table in the report usually summarizes the descriptive data such as means, standard deviations, correlations, percentages. Later tables present the results of applying inferential statistics and tests of significance to the data. For example, a summary table would be used to present the results of an analysis of variance.

It is desirable to arrange the tables in such a way that they illustrate the relationship of the data to the hypotheses of the study. Beginning researchers are frequently tempted to include the data in both forms, and in so doing merely make their reports longer and more tedious. A better approach is to present the data in tables and figures accompanied by sufficient text to point out the most important and interesting findings. It is especially important to relate the information in the tables to the hypotheses.

The statistical foundation of the analysis of results must be clearly stated. It is convenient to integrate statistical treatment with the presentation of data.

C. *Discussion of Results*.   The findings are interpreted again in relation to the hypotheses (or questions), and the implications and applications of the study are discussed.

1. *Interpretation of findings:* Probably the most difficult, but also the most rewarding, part of the report, the researcher's interpretation of the results relates these findings to the theory and research in the area and to the research procedures.

2. *Implications:* The contribution of the results to knowledge in the general field of study is a matter that should also be discussed in this part. The researcher explains here how the results may modify relevant theories and suggests further studies that logically follow.

3. *Applications:* A statement regarding the application of the findings helps readers of the report to know the extent to which the findings can be applied in practice.

The sections on implications and applications of the results are often not sufficiently developed because it is assumed that these will be as obvious to the reader as they are to the researchers. In fact, in the conduct of the study the investigators should have gained insights into the problem that are deeper than those which most of their readers can be assumed to have. Therefore one would expect their interpretations to be more meaningful than those that readers might make for themselves.

D. *Conclusions and Summary*.   The conclusions and summary sections together form the capstone of the report.

1. *Conclusion:* The discussion of the conclusions indicated by the research findings should be limited to those conclusions that have direct support in the research findings. Researchers are often tempted to conclude too much. The hypotheses provide a convenient framework for stating conclusions; that is, researchers should indicate in this section whether or not the findings support the hypotheses.

It is important to distinguish between results and conclusions. A result is a direct observation. A conclusion is an inference based on results. For example, a study might result in the observation that the mean spelling test scores of students taught spelling by Method A is significantly higher than the mean of students taught by Method B. The conclusion that Method A is more effective than Method B is not a direct result of the study but rather is an inference based on the results of the study.

Researchers may include a brief discussion of their ideas on the implications of their findings and recommendations for possible applications of the findings. They may also suggest any new questions for research that grew out of their study.

2. *Summary:* Since the summary will be more widely read than other sections of the report, its wording must be particularly clear and concise. The summary usually includes a brief restatement of the problem(s), the main features of the methods, and the most important findings. Upon completing a draft of this section, the author should check it carefully to determine whether it gives a concise but reasonably complete description of the study and its findings. One should also check to ascertain that no information has been introduced here that had not been included in the appropriate preceding sections. It is a good idea to have a colleague read the conclusions section to see if one is communicating as well as one intended to do.

III. Supplementary Pages

A. *Bibliography.*   The bibliography must include all sources mentioned in the text or footnotes. Most universities insist that only these be listed, but a few ask that pertinent references not specifically mentioned also be listed. The style manual previously selected will give complete details on the method of listing references. It is important to follow these rules rigorously and completely. In fact, it is a good strategy to learn them before carrying out the search through the literature for the proposal. By listing each reference in the correct form as it is encountered, one can avoid the extra time involved in finding the references again in order to have them in complete form for the bibliography. It is advisable to list them on cards so that they can be filed in alphabetical order.

B. *Appendices.*   The appendices contain pertinent materials that are not important enough to be included in the body of the report but may be of value to some readers. Such materials may include complete copies of locally devised tests or questionnaires, together with the instructions and scoring keys for such instruments, item analysis data for measurements used, verbatim instructions to subjects, and tables that are very long or of only minor importance to the study.

C. *Vita.*   The authors of research reports are sometimes asked to include brief accounts of their training, experience, professional memberships, and previous contributions.

D. *Abstract.*   Most institutions require a separate abstract of the dissertation, which should include a definitive statement of the problem and concise descriptions of the research methods, major findings, conclusions, and implications. The abstract must be limited in length (typically 600 words or less). The abstract pages are numbered separately and placed either at the very beginning or the very end of the dissertation.

THE JOURNAL ARTICLE

In preparing a research article for publication in a journal, a good first step is to look through one's bibliography to determine which journal has published the greatest amount of work in one's area of interest. Information concerning the procedure for submission of manuscripts will usually be found on the inside of a journal's front cover. Many journals will specify which style manual should be used, for example, the *Publication Manual of the American Psychological Association* or the *NEA Style Manual*. If a manual is not specified, the preferred style, method of referencing, and so on, may be determined from a study of the articles included in a recent issue of the journal.

A research article follows the same general outline as a dissertation, but it must be much shorter. A thesis or dissertation functions to demonstrate a student's competence and requires full setting forth of the related research, complete description of the procedures, complete tabulation of results, and reflective elaboration. The journal article, on the other hand, requires only communication of the author's contribution to knowledge. For the sake of economy of journal space and readers' time, the article must be concise. The related literature section contains only those results and arguments that provide the basis for the problem. The general statement of the problem is given in one paragraph, or possibly even omitted, in which case the article would begin with the hypothesis. The procedures section is also presented very briefly, although all the information needed to replicate the experiment should be included if at all possible. The results section will be of greatest interest to the reader and therefore will represent a greater proportion of the article than it would in a dissertation. Only the most important findings should be discussed in any detail.

A brief covering letter should accompany the manuscript along with stamps for its return if it is not accepted for publication. The editor will usually send the author a postcard acknowledging receipt of the manuscript and circulate copies of it among the appropriate members of the editorial board for review. From this point, considerable time usually elapses before the author is informed whether or not the article has been accepted (six weeks is probably typical). After an article is accepted, it is usually many months before it appears in print.

When a manuscript is rejected by a journal, the rejection notice is sometimes accompanied by a statement of the reasons for this rejection. A rejection by one journal does not necessarily mean that the article is unworthy of publication. A number of factors such as competition for space, changes in editorial policy, or bias of reviewers can influence the decision on publication. An article that has been rejected by one journal may be revised and submitted to another. Many articles make the rounds of several journals before finding a home. It is not ethical to submit an article to more than one journal at a time.

THE CONFERENCE

Many researchers find that hearing papers read at professional conventions is a good way to keep up to date in their field. The reason for this is that there is a great lapse of time between the completion of a research project and its appearance in print. This time lag is often so long that professional journals have sometimes been described as being archival in nature.

Papers presented at professional meetings are prepared in much the same manner as journal articles. They are not necessarily always reports of completed research but may be progress reports of ongoing projects. The read paper is less formal than a journal article and can usually be more precisely geared to its audience. The audience can generally be expected to be familiar with details of related research and methods of measurement.

The paper will frequently be organized as follows:

1. Direct statement of the hypothesis
2. Brief description of the procedures
3. Findings, conclusions, and implications

The time allowed for reading a paper is usually quite brief, frequently less than 15 minutes. Therefore, the paper should focus on the most important aspects of one's study. A convenient rule of thumb is to allow 2½ to 3 minutes for each page of double-spaced typed copy.

If figures or tables will assist in the presentation, copies should be available for the audience. Some speakers also distribute copies of the text of their paper to the audience. However, since the audience reads the paper silently more rapidly than the author can read it aloud, there may be a gap in attention. It is preferable to have a complete description of the study mimeographed for those who request it after the paper is presented.

Common Errors in Research Reports

In studying nearly 18,000 reports in business education, Dvorak compiled a long list of shortcomings that provides us with a useful checklist.[3] Writers of research reports would do well to study this list.

The title of the research report. Overly long. Does not reflect accurately the problem solved; that is, it is broader or narrower than the problem stated.

The problem. Statement and analysis of the problem, delimitations, definitions, and purpose(s) of the study are omitted.

Statement and analysis of the problem, delimitations, definitions, and purpose(s) of the study are treated so lightly or are so widely scattered in the report that it is extremely difficult to determine what problem the researcher set out to solve.

Statement and analysis of the problem, delimitations, definitions, and purpose(s) of the study are reported in organized form but serious shortcomings are observable:

The problem is too big to permit solution by one person with limited resources.

The merit of the problem is nil or negligible (the impression is that the person was interested only in meeting a degree requirement, not in having a worthwhile professional experience).

[3]Earl A. Dvorak, ''Shortcomings of Graduate Research in Business Education,'' *Ohio Business Teacher,* 23 (April 1963):19–22.

Statement of the problem is ambiguous, wordy, too long and involved (carries items that might well be included in the delimitations), or not in keeping with the findings reported.

Analysis fails to round out concept of problem; bodies of data necessary as the basis for the solution of the problem are not identified or are not clearly indicated. Explanation of a problem rather difficult to grasp is poorly written or omitted.

Major delimitations necessary to setting clearly the boundaries of the study are omitted, are not placed where they will do the reader the most good, or are poorly stated. Related delimitations are not placed in proximity to one another.

Definitions of terms necessary to a clear understanding of the study are omitted.

Related literature. Related literature is omitted.

Related literature is reported but certain shortcomings are observable:

Some of the items reported as related actually are not related or are remotely so. One gets the impression that this section of the report is "padded."

The relationships of the items to the study undertaken are not reported.

Little more than a list of summaries is presented; that is, no sound pattern of organization is discernible. In other words, even though classification is possible, no attempt is made to do so.

The volume and the pertinency of the literature are not indicated at the outset; one has to read all of the related literature and then judge for himself.

Something less than the original of a related item is used even though the original may be relatively easy to obtain.

Complete bibliographical information for each of the related items is omitted.

Methods of research and the procedure. The methods of research and the procedure followed are not reported.

The methods of research and the procedure followed are so sketchily or ambiguously reported that the worthwhileness of the completed research is difficult to discern.

The methods of research and the procedure followed are reported but serious shortcomings are observable:

The appropriateness of the methods of research used is open to question.

The methods of research used are incorrectly identified.

The procedure followed is badly scattered; that is, a lack of organization prevents easy comprehension of the total plan followed.

The nature of the data used in the solution of the problem is not described, or the description is merely a repetition of the elements of the problem.

The sources of data are not identified, or they are inadequate in terms of the problem set out to be solved. Dates of published materials are not revealed.

Bases for preparation of data-collection devices are not indicated; copies of the devices are not included in the report. Poorly prepared devices are used, devices which have not had the benefit of a trial run. The devices are inappropriate for collection of the types of data desired.

Bases for selection of cases are not indicated. The number of cases is too small or unnecessarily large.

Tests for amount, validity, and reliability of data are not undertaken; or indefensible ones are used.

Unnecessary detail is included—that is, the unimportant is not weeded out from the important—making reading of the procedure laborious and difficult to detect the major steps taken.

The steps taken in processing and interpreting the data and in making generalizations are omitted or are so poorly developed that it is difficult to determine what the researcher did.

Statistical devices are used incorrectly.

In experimental studies, factors are not controlled carefully.

Findings. Findings are reported based on data which are not accounted for in the statement and analysis of the problem and in the procedure followed.

Unprocessed data are presented, the form used being too rough for the reader to gain the maximum benefit from the results of the study. It may be said that "data" are not distinguished from "findings."

Findings are incomplete; that is, data from some of the cases included in the study are not accounted for.

Bias of the researcher is obvious.

Findings of a secondary nature are overemphasized; that is, they are not placed in proper perspective.

Findings by subgroups are not revealed.

The format for presentation of the findings blocks insight.

Interpretation of findings is confused with summarization of findings.

Summarization is lacking at strategic points.

Generalizations. A distinction is not made between findings and generalizations. Summaries of findings are called "conclusions," for example.

No generalizations are made, though the basis for them is clear.

Generalizations beyond the data collected are made.

The premises for drawing the generalization are questionable.

Bias of the researcher is obvious.

Generalizations are based on the related literature rather than on the findings of the study.

A distinction is not made between conclusions and recommendations.

Summary

With electronic computation facilities available on almost all university campuses, many researchers are able to take advantage of these facilities in their data processing. The use of computers saves time and energy and guarantees a great degree of precision in very involved and complex computations.

To use computers for data processing the researcher needs to transform the data into a form that can be read into a computer and to provide instructions for the computer to act on the data by means of an appropriate program.

Writing computer programs requires training, but the researcher can often use available programs prepared for use in data analysis.

The interpretation of the results of a study is a straightforward task if, in the proposal, the researcher has laid a proper foundation for the research study. The following cautions should be kept in mind: (1) interpretation should be strictly based on the data derived from the study, (2) internal- and external-validity problems and other limitations of the study should be considered, and (3) conclusions must be presented as probability statements rather than as facts.

Negative results deserve the same respect and interpretation as do positive results. A retained null hypothesis is interpreted as the result of insufficient evidence and no more. Unhypothesized results deserve attention as sources of future hypotheses.

Formal procedures have been developed for preparing theses, journal articles, and papers. Mastering and employing these procedures assist researchers in communicating with one another and with practicing educators. Several style manuals provide details on these procedures.

References

STYLE MANUALS

The following are widely used manuals detailing general form and style for theses and dissertations:

American Psychological Association, *Publication Manual,* 2nd ed. Washington, D.C.: American Psychological Association, 1974.

Campbell, William G., and Stephen V. Ballou, *Form and Style: Theses, Reports, Term Papers,* 4th ed. Boston: Houghton Mifflin, 1974.

Dugdale, Kathleen, *A Manual of Form for Theses and Term Reports,* 3rd rev. ed. Bloomington, Ind.: Indiana University Bookstore, 1967.

University of Chicago Press, *A Manual of Style,* 12th ed. Chicago: University of Chicago Press, 1969.

U.S. Government Style Manual, rev. ed. Washington, D.C.: Government Printing Office, 1959.

GUIDES FOR PREPARING RESEARCH PROPOSALS

Guba, Egon, "Guides for the Writing of Proposals," in Jack A. Culbertson and Stephen P. Hencly, eds., *Educational Research: New Perspectives.* Danville, Ill.: Interstate Printers & Publishers, 1963, ch. 18.

Krathwohl, David R., *How to Prepare a Research Proposal.* Syracuse: Syracuse University Bookstore, 1965.

Smith, Gerald R., "A Critique of Proposals Submitted to the Cooperative Research Program," in Jack A. Culbertson and Stephen P. Hencly, eds., *Educational Research: New Perspectives.* Danville, Ill.: Interstate Printers & Publishers, 1963, ch. 17.

Veldman, David J., *Writing a Thesis or Dissertation Proposal in the Behavioral Sciences.* Fort Worth, Tex.: American Continental Publishing Co., 1971.

Exercises

1. What changes has the computer made in the practice of educational research?
2. Your study includes the variables sex, marital status, age, economic level, and IQ scores. What procedure would be followed to prepare data for computer processing?
3. Name two sources of computer programs for statistical analysis.
4. What kinds of errors are associated with the use of computers in research?
5. Explain the difference between *statistical significance* of the results and the *significance of the study*.
6. What states of affairs can lead to a retained null hypothesis?
7. Decide whether each title is acceptable or unacceptable and give reasons for your choices:
   a. Grade-Point Average and Driver Education
   b. The Effects of Individualized Tutoring by Sixth Grade Students Three Times a Week on Reading Performance of Below-Average Second Grade Readers
   c. Children Should Be Taught the New Math!
   d. Relationship between Personality Characteristics and Attitudes toward Achievement of Good and Poor Readers
8. What are the differences in format for research reported in dissertation form, in journal form, and in a paper to be read at a conference?
9. Should one discuss research results that do not agree with one's hypothesis?
10. Find a recent article on education research. Critique it using Dvorak's list of shortcomings.

Answers

1. The computer has made it possible to design and conduct research studies without regard for the number of variables or the complexity of the analysis. The data from studies having large numbers of subjects, using multivariate techniques, or requiring sophisticated statistics can now be analyzed with speed and accuracy.
2. Data for each subject would be coded and recorded in data roster form. Each level of sex, marital status, and economic status would be assigned an arbitrary numerical code; for example, married = 1, divorced = 2, separated = 3. Age and IQ could be recorded directly or could be categorized; for example, 20–25 years = 1, 26–30 years = 2. Coded data are ready for input into the computer.
3. The Statistical Package for the Social Sciences (SPSS) and the Biomedical Series (BIMED) are two sources of prepared computer programs.
4. The computer will do exactly as it is told with the information it is given. It can recognize errors of language and these will usually cause the program to stop running until the computer receives new instructions. The computer cannot recognize errors in the information it is supplied nor can it recognize errors in logic made by the researcher during programming. Any data entry errors, programming errors, or logical errors will result in errors in output from the computer.
5. Statistical significance means only that the results are not likely to be a function of chance; the significance of the study is determined by the importance of the findings in regard to theory testing or practical implications.

6. A retained null hypothesis could result from the null hypothesis's actually being true in nature; or it could result from contamination by internal validity problems which obscure treatment effects, from lack of statistical power of the design used in the study, or from inability of the instruments to measure accurately the effects of treatment on the dependent variable.

7. a. unacceptable: no statement of relationship is given
   b. unacceptable: too wordy
   c. unacceptable: emotion-laden titles are not appropriate for research articles
   d. acceptable: meets criteria for title

8. Dissertation form is the most formal and detailed in presentation; it follows the specifics of a particular style manual. The journal article is a more concise presentation, with a brief statement of problem, related literature, and methodology; a greater proportion of the article is devoted to major results and a discussion of their significance. A paper that is to be read at a conference is the most informal; geared to its audience, it states the hypothesis, briefly describes the procedure, and emphasizes the most important findings.

9. Yes, results contrary to one's expectations are as legitimate as any other results and should be interpreted as such.

Appendix

Table A.1: Squares and Square Roots of Numbers from 1 to 1000

Table A.1 may be expanded to permit one to find the square root of numbers larger than 1000. This may be done by either of two methods:

1. Note the relationship between the first column (N, the number) and the second column (N^2, the square) in the table. If the second column contains the square of the number, then the first column contains the number one started with, which would be the square root of the product listed in the second column. If 6 squared is 36 (second column), then the square root of 36 is 6 (first column). If we find 2500 in the square column, then we can look back at the number column and see that the square root of 2500 is 50.

Thus, if we wish to know the square root of a number greater than 1000, we can find it by working backward from the square column. For example, assume that we want the square root of 1700. We begin by moving down the square column until we find the number as close as possible to 1700. It is 1681; then looking back at the number column, we see that 41 is its square root. To approximate the square root of 1700 more closely, we must multiply 41 by 10 and turn to 410 in the first column. Proceeding down this column, we find that the square of 412 is equal to 169,744; so 41.2 is a reasonable approximation of the square root of 1700.

2. An alternative approach is to change the decimal point in the number and square root columns. Assume that we want the square root of 1700: 1700 is equal to 17×100 and its square root is equal to $\sqrt{17} \times \sqrt{100}$ or $\sqrt{17} \times 10$. The table gives the square root of 17 as 4.1231. So $4.1231 \times 10 = 41.231$, which is the square root of 1700.

Similarly, the square root of 55,100 (or 551×100) is equal to $\sqrt{551} \times \sqrt{100}$, or $23.4734 \times 10 = 234.734$.

Let us assume that we want the square root of 6.50. This number is equivalent to $650 \times 1/100$ and its square root is $\sqrt{650} \times 1/\sqrt{100}$ or $25.4951 \times 1/10$, which equals 2.54951 or about 2.55.

Table A.1 Squares and Square Roots

N	N²	√N	N	N²	√N	N	N²	√N	N	N²	√N
1	1	1.00 000	50	2 500	7.07 107	100	10 000	10.00 00	150	22 500	12.24 74
2	4	1.41 421	51	2 601	7.14 143	101	10 201	10.04 99	151	22 801	12.28 82
3	9	1.73 205	52	2 704	7.21 110	102	10 404	10.09 95	152	23 104	12.32 88
4	16	2.00 000	53	2 809	7.28 011	103	10 609	10.14 89	153	23 409	12.36 93
5	25	2.23 607	54	2 916	7.34 847	104	10 816	10.19 80	154	23 716	12.40 97
			55	3 025	7.41 620	105	11 025	10.24 70	155	24 025	12.44 99
6	36	2.44 949	56	3 136	7.48 331	106	11 236	10.29 56	156	24 336	12.49 00
7	49	2.64 575	57	3 249	7.54 983	107	11 449	10.34 41	157	24 649	12.53 00
8	64	2.82 843	58	3 364	7.61 577	108	11 664	10.39 23	158	24 964	12.56 98
9	81	3.00 000	59	3 481	7.68 115	109	11 881	10.44 03	159	25 281	12.60 95
10	100	3.16 228	60	3 600	7.74 597	110	12 100	10.48 81	160	25 600	12.64 91
11	121	3.31 662	61	3 721	7.81 025	111	12 321	10.53 57	161	25 921	12.68 86
12	144	3.46 410	62	3 844	7.87 401	112	12 544	10.58 30	162	26 244	12.72 79
13	169	3.60 555	63	3 969	7.93 725	113	12 769	10.63 01	163	26 569	12.76 71
14	196	3.74 166	64	4 096	8.00 000	114	12 996	10.67 71	164	26 896	12.80 62
15	225	3.87 298	65	4 225	8.06 226	115	13 225	10.72 38	165	27 225	12.84 52
16	256	4.00 000	66	4 356	8.12 404	116	13 456	10.77 03	166	27 556	12.88 41
17	289	4.12 311	67	4 489	8.18 535	117	13 689	10.81 67	167	27 889	12.92 28
18	324	4.24 264	68	4 624	8.24 621	118	13 924	10.86 28	168	28 224	12.96 15
19	361	4.35 890	69	4 761	8.30 662	119	14 161	10.90 87	169	28 561	13.00 00
20	400	4.47 214	70	4 900	8.36 660	120	14 400	10.95 45	170	28 900	13.03 84
21	441	4.58 258	71	5 041	8.42 615	121	14 641	11.00 00	171	29 241	13.07 67
22	484	4.69 042	72	5 184	8.48 528	122	14 884	11.04 54	172	29 584	13.11 49
23	529	4.79 583	73	5 329	8.54 400	123	15 129	11.09 05	173	29 929	13.15 29
24	576	4.89 898	74	5 476	8.60 233	124	15 376	11.13 55	174	30 276	13.19 09
25	625	5.00 000	75	5 625	8.66 025	125	15 625	11.18 03	175	30 625	13.22 88
26	676	5.09 902	76	5 776	8.71 780	126	15 876	11.22 50	176	30 976	13.26 65
27	729	5.19 615	77	5 929	8.77 496	127	16 129	11.26 94	177	31 329	13.30 41
28	784	5.29 150	78	6 084	8.83 176	128	16 384	11.31 37	178	31 684	13.34 17
29	841	5.38 516	79	6 241	8.88 819	129	16 641	11.35 78	179	32 041	13.37 91
30	900	5.47 723	80	6 400	8.94 427	130	16 900	11.40 18	180	32 400	13.41 64
31	961	5.56 776	81	6 561	9.00 000	131	17 161	11.44 55	181	32 761	13.45 36
32	1 024	5.65 685	82	6 724	9.05 539	132	17 424	11.48 91	182	33 124	13.49 07
33	1 089	5.74 456	83	6 889	9.11 043	133	17 689	11.53 26	183	33 489	13.52 77
34	1 156	5.83 095	84	7 056	9.16 515	134	17 956	11.57 58.	184	33 856	13.56 47
35	1 225	5.91 608	85	7 225	9.21 954	135	18 225	11.61 90	185	34 225	13.60 15
36	1 296	6.00 000	86	7 396	9.27 362	136	18 496	11.66 19	186	34 596	13.63 82
37	1 369	6.08 276	87	7 569	9.32 738	137	18 769	11.70 47	187	34 969	13.67 48
38	1 444	6.16 441	88	7 744	9.38 083	138	19 044	11.74 73	188	35 344	13.71 13
39	1 521	6.24 500	89	7 921	9.43 398	139	19 321	11.78 98	189	35 721	13.74 77
40	1 600	6.32 456	90	8 100	9.48 683	140	19 600	11.83 22	190	36 100	13.78 40
41	1 681	6.40 312	91	8 281	9.53 939	141	19 881	11.87 43	191	36 481	13.82 03
42	1 764	6.48 074	92	8 464	9.59 166	142	20 164	11.91 64	192	36 864	13.85 64
43	1 849	6.55 744	93	8 649	9.64 365	143	20 449	11.95 83	193	37 249	13.89 24
44	1 936	6.63 325	94	8 836	9.69 536	144	20 736	12.00 00	194	37 636	13.92 84
45	2 025	6.70 820	95	9 025	9.74 679	145	21 025	12.04 16	195	38 025	13.96 42
46	2 116	6.78 233	96	9 216	9.79 796	146	21 316	12.08 30	196	38 416	14.00 00
47	2 209	6.85 565	97	9 409	9.84 886	147	21 609	12.12 44	197	38 809	14.03 57
48	2 304	6.92 820	98	9 604	9.89 949	148	21 904	12.16 55	198	39 204	14.07 12
49	2 401	7.00 000	99	9 801	9.94 987	149	22 201	12.20 66	199	39 601	14.10 67
50	2 500	7.07 107	100	10 000	10.00 000	150	22 500	12.24 74	200	40 000	14.14 21
N	N²	√N	N	N²	√N	N	N²	√N	N	N²	√N

Table A.1 Squares and Square Roots (cont.)

N	N²	√N
200	40 000	14.14 21
201	40 401	14.17 74
202	40 804	14.21 27
203	41 209	14.24 78
204	41 616	14.28 29
205	42 025	14.31 78
206	42 436	14.35 27
207	42 849	14.38 75
208	43 264	14.42 22
209	43 681	14.45 68
210	44 100	14.49 14
211	44 521	14.52 58
212	44 944	14.56 02
213	45 369	14.59 45
214	45 796	14.62 87
215	46 225	14.66 29
216	46 656	14.69 69
217	47 089	14.73 09
218	47 524	14.76 48
219	47 961	14.79 86
220	48 400	14.83 24
221	48 841	14.86 61
222	49 284	14.89 97
223	49 729	14.93 32
224	50 176	14.96 66
225	50 625	15.00 00
226	51 076	15.03 33
227	51 529	15.06 65
228	51 984	15.09 97
229	52 441	15.13 27
230	52 900	15.16 58
231	53 361	15.19 87
232	53 824	15.23 15
233	54 289	15.26 43
234	54 756	15.29 71
235	55 225	15.32 97
236	55 696	15.36 23
237	56 169	15.39 48
238	56 644	15.42 72
239	57 121	15.45 96
240	57 600	15.49 19
241	58 081	15.52 42
242	58 564	15.55 63
243	59 049	15.58 85
244	59 536	15.62 05
245	60 025	15.65 25
246	60 516	15.68 44
247	61 009	15.71 62
248	61 504	15.74 80
249	62 001	15.77 97
250	62 500	15.81 14
N	N²	√N

N	N²	√N
250	62 500	15.81 14
251	63 001	15.84 30
252	63 504	15.87 45
253	64 009	15.90 60
254	64 516	15.93 74
255	65 025	15.96 87
256	65 536	16.00 00
257	66 049	16.03 12
258	66 564	16.06 24
259	67 081	16.09 35
260	67 600	16.12 45
261	68 121	16.15 55
262	68 644	16.18 64
263	69 169	16.21 73
264	69 696	16.24 81
265	70 225	16.27 88
266	70 756	16.30 95
267	71 289	16.34 01
268	71 824	16.37 07
269	72 361	16.40 12
270	72 900	16.43 17
271	73 441	16.46 21
272	73 984	16.49 24
273	74 529	16.52 27
274	75 076	16.55 29
275	75 625	16.58 31
276	76 176	16.61 32
277	76 729	16.64 33
278	77 284	16.67 33
279	77 841	16.70 33
280	78 400	16.73 32
281	78 961	16.76 31
282	79 524	16.79 29
283	80 089	16.82 26
284	80 656	16.85 23
285	81 225	16.88 19
286	81 796	16.91 15
287	82 369	16.94 11
288	82 944	16.97 06
289	83 521	17.00 00
290	84 100	17.02 94
291	84 681	17.05 87
292	85 264	17.08 80
293	85 849	17.11 72
294	86 436	17.14 64
295	87 025	17.17 56
296	87 616	17.20 47
297	88 209	17.23 37
298	88 804	17.26 27
299	89 401	17.29 16
300	90 000	17.32 05
N	N²	√N

N	N²	√N
300	90 000	17.32 05
301	90 601	17.34 94
302	91 204	17.37 81
303	91 809	17.40 69
304	92 416	17.43 56
305	93 025	17.46 42
306	93 636	17.49 29
307	94 249	17.52 14
308	94 864	17.54 99
309	95 481	17.57 84
310	96 100	17.60 68
311	96 721	17.63 52
312	97 344	17.66 35
313	97 969	17.69 18
314	98 596	17.72 00
315	99 225	17.74 82
316	99 856	17.77 64
317	100 489	17.80 45
318	101 124	17.83 26
319	101 761	17.86 06
320	102 400	17.88 85
321	103 041	17.91 65
322	103 684	17.94 44
323	104 329	17.97 22
324	104 976	18.00 00
325	105 625	18.02 78
326	106 276	18.05 55
327	106 929	18.08 31
328	107 584	18.11 08
329	108 241	18.13 84
330	108 900	18.16 59
331	109 561	18.19 34
332	110 224	18.22 09
333	110 889	18.24 83
334	111 556	18.27 57
335	112 225	18.30 30
336	112 896	18.33 03
337	113 569	18.35 76
338	114 244	18.38 48
339	114 921	18.41 20
340	115 600	18 43 91
341	116 281	18.46 62
342	116 964	18.49 32
343	117 649	18.52 03
344	118 336	18.54 72
345	119 025	18.57 42
346	119 716	18.60 11
347	120 409	18.62 79
348	121 104	18.65 48
349	121 801	18.68 15
350	122 500	18.70 83
N	N²	√N

N	N²	√N
350	122 500	18.70 83
351	123 201	18.73 50
352	123 904	18.76 17
353	124 609	18.78 83
354	125 316	18.81 49
355	126 025	18.84 14
356	126 736	18.86 80
357	127 449	18.89 44
358	128 164	18.92 09
359	128 881	18.94 73
360	129 600	18.97 37
361	130 321	19.00 00
362	131 044	19.02 63
363	131 769	19.05 26
364	132 496	19.07 88
365	133 225	19.10 50
366	133 956	19.13 11
367	134 689	19.15 72
368	135 424	19.18 33
369	136 161	19.20 94
370	136 900	19.23 54
371	137 641	19.26 14
372	138 384	19.28 73
373	139 129	19.31 32
374	139 876	19.33 91
375	140 625	19.36 49
376	141 376	19.39 07
377	142 129	19.41 65
378	142 884	19.44 22
379	143 641	19.46 79
380	144 400	19.49 36
381	145 161	19.51 92
382	145 924	19.54 48
383	146 689	19.57 04
384	147 456	19.59 59
385	148 225	19.62 14
386	148 996	19.64 69
387	149 769	19.67 23
388	150 544	19.69 77
389	151 321	19.72 31
390	152 100	19.74 84
391	152 881	19.77 37
392	153 664	19.79 90
393	154 449	19.82 42
394	155 236	19.84 94
395	156 025	19.87 46
396	156 816	19.89 97
397	157 609	19.92 49
398	158 404	19.94 99
399	159 201	19.97 50
400	160 000	20.00 00
N	N²	√N

Table A.1   Squares and Square Roots *(cont.)*

N	N²	√N	N	N²	√N	N	N²	√N	N	N²	√N
400	160 000	20.00 00	**450**	202 500	21.21 32	**500**	250 000	22.36 07	**550**	302 500	23.45 21
401	160 801	20.02 50	451	203 401	21.23 68	501	251 001	22.38 30	551	303 601	23.47 34
402	161 604	20.04 99	452	204 304	21.26 03	502	252 004	22.40 54	552	304 704	23.49 47
403	162 409	20.07 49	453	205 209	21.28 38	503	253 009	22.42 77	553	305 809	23.51 60
404	163 216	20.09 98	454	206 116	21.30 73	504	254 016	22.44 99	554	306 916	23.53 72
405	164 025	20.12 46	455	207 025	21.33 07	505	255 025	22.47 22	555	308 025	23.55 84
406	164 836	20.14 94	**456**	207 936	21.35 42	**506**	256 036	22.49 44	**556**	309 136	23.57 97
407	165 649	20.17 42	457	208 849	21.37 76	507	257 049	22.51 67	557	310 249	23.60 08
408	166 464	20.19 90	458	209 764	21.40 09	508	258 064	22.53 89	558	311 364	23.62 20
409	167 281	20.22 37	459	210 681	21.42 43	509	259 081	22.56 10	559	312 481	23.64 32
410	168 100	20.24 85	460	211 600	21.44 76	510	260 100	22.58 32	560	313 600	23.66 43
411	168 921	20.27 31	**461**	212 521	21.47 09	**511**	261 121	22.60 53	**561**	314 721	23.68 54
412	169 744	20.29 78	462	213 444	21.49 42	512	262 144	22.62 74	562	315 844	23.70 65
413	170 569	20.32 24	463	214 369	21.51 74	513	263 169	22.64 95	563	316 969	23.72 76
414	171 396	20.34 70	464	215 296	21.54 07	514	264 196	22.67 16	564	318 096	23.74 87
415	172 225	20.37 15	465	216 225	21.56 39	515	265 225	22.69 36	565	319 225	23.76 97
416	173 056	20.39 61	**466**	217 156	21.58 70	**516**	266 256	22.71 56	**566**	320 356	23.79 08
417	173 889	20.42 06	467	218 089	21.61 02	517	267 289	22.73 76	567	321 489	23.81 18
418	174 724	20.44 50	468	219 024	21.63 33	518	268 324	22.75 96	568	322 624	23.83 28
419	175 561	20.46 95	469	219 961	21.65 64	519	269 361	22.78 16	569	323 761	23.85 37
420	176 400	20.49 39	470	220 900	21.67 95	520	270 400	22.80 35	570	324 900	23.87 47
421	177 241	20.51 83	**471**	221 841	21.70 25	**521**	271 441	22.82 54	**571**	326 041	23.89 56
422	178 084	20.54 26	472	222 784	21.72 56	522	272 484	22.84 73	572	327 184	23.91 65
423	178 929	20.56 70	473	223 729	21.74 86	523	273 529	22.86 92	573	328 329	23.93 74
424	179 776	20.59 13	474	224 676	21.77 15	524	274 576	22.89 10	574	329 476	23.95 83
425	180 625	20.61 55	475	225 625	21.79 45	525	275 625	22.91 29	575	330 625	23.97 92
426	181 476	20.63 98	**476**	226 576	21.81 74	**526**	276 676	22.93 47	**576**	331 776	24.00 00
427	182 329	20.66 40	477	227 529	21.84 03	527	277 729	22.95 65	577	332 929	24.02 08
428	183 184	20.68 82	478	228 484	21.86 32	528	278 784	22.97 83	578	334 084	24.04 16
429	184 041	20.71 23	479	229 441	21.88 61	529	279 841	23.00 00	579	335 241	24.06 24
430	184 900	20.73 64	480	230 400	21.90 89	530	280 900	23.02 17	580	336 400	24.08 32
431	185 761	20.76 05	**481**	231 361	21.93 17	**531**	281 961	23.04 34	**581**	337 561	24.10 39
432	186 624	20.78 46	482	232 324	21.95 45	532	283 024	23.06 51	582	338 724	24.12 47
433	187 489	20.80 87	483	233 289	21.97 73	533	284 089	23.08 68	583	339 889	24.14 54
434	188 356	20.83 27	484	234 256	22.00 00	534	285 156	23.10 84	584	341 056	24.16 61
435	189 225	20.85 67	485	235 225	22.02 27	535	286 225	23.13 01	585	342 225	24.18 68
436	190 096	20.88 06	**486**	236 196	22.04 54	**536**	287 296	23.15 17	**586**	343 396	24.20 74
437	190 969	20.90 45	487	237 169	22.06 81	537	288 369	23.17 33	587	344 569	24.22 81
438	191 844	20.92 84	488	238 144	22.09 07	538	289 444	23.19 48	588	345 744	24.24 87
439	192 721	20.95 23	489	239 121	22.11 33	539	290 521	23.21 64	589	346 921	24.26 93
440	193 600	20.97 62	490	240 100	22.13 59	540	291 600	23.23 79	590	348 100	24.28 99
441	194 481	21.00 00	**491**	241 081	22.15 85	**541**	292 681	23.25 94	**591**	349 281	24.31 05
442	195 364	21.02 38	492	242 064	22.18 11	542	293 764	23.28 09	592	350 464	24.33 11
443	196 249	21.04 76	493	243 049	22.20 36	543	294 849	23.30 24	593	351 649	24.35 16
444	197 136	21.07 13	494	244 036	22.22 61	544	295 936	23.32 38	594	352 836	24.37 21
445	198 025	21.09 50	495	245 025	22.24 86	545	297 025	23.34 52	595	354 025	24.39 26
446	198 916	21.11 87	**496**	246 016	22.27 11	**546**	298 116	23.36 66	**596**	355 216	24.41 31
447	199 809	21.14 24	497	247 009	22.29 35	547	299 209	23.38 80	597	356 409	24.43 36
448	200 704	21.16 60	498	248 004	22.31 59	548	300 304	23.40 94	598	357 604	24.45 40
449	201 601	21.18 96	499	249 001	22.33 83	549	301 401	23.43 07	599	358 801	24.47 45
450	202 500	21.21 32	500	250 000	22.36 07	550	302 500	23.45 21	600	360 000	24.49 49
N	N²	√N	N	N²	√N	N	N²	√N	N	N²	√N

Table A.1   Squares and Square Roots *(cont.)*

N	N²	√N	N	N²	√N	N	N²	√N	N	N²	√N
600	360 000	24.49 49	**650**	422 500	25.49 51	**700**	490 000	26.45 75	**750**	562 500	27.38 61
601	361 201	24.51 53	651	423 801	25.51 47	701	491 401	26.47 64	751	564 001	27.40 44
602	362 404	24.53 57	652	425 104	25.53 43	702	492 804	26.49 53	752	565 504	27.42 26
603	363 609	24.55 61	653	426 409	25.55 39	703	494 209	26.51 41	753	567 009	27.44 08
604	364 816	24.57 64	654	427 716	25.57 34	704	495 616	26.53 30	754	568 516	27.45 91
605	366 025	24.59 67	655	429 025	25.59 30	705	497 025	26.55 18	755	570 025	27.47 73
606	367 236	24.61 71	**656**	430 336	25.61 25	**706**	498 436	26.57 07	**756**	571 536	27.49 55
607	368 449	24.63 74	657	431 649	25.63 20	707	499 849	26.58 95	757	573 049	27.51 36
608	369 664	24.65 77	658	432 964	25.65 15	708	501 264	26.60 83	758	574 564	27.53 18
609	370 881	24.67 79	659	434 281	25.67 10	709	502 681	26.62 71	759	576 081	27.55 00
610	372 100	24.69 82	660	435 600	25.69 05	710	504 100	26.64 58	760	577 600	27.56 81
611	373 321	24.71 84	**661**	436 921	25.70 99	**711**	505 521	26.66 46	**761**	579 121	27.58 62
612	374 544	24.73 86	662	438 244	25.72 94	712	506 944	26.68 33	762	580 644	27.60 43
613	375 769	24.75 88	663	439 569	25.74 88	713	508 369	26.70 21	763	582 169	27.62 25
614	376 996	24.77 90	664	440 896	25.76 82	714	509 796	26.72 08	764	583 696	27.64 05
615	378 225	24.79 92	665	442 225	25.78 76	715	511 225	26.73 95	765	585 225	27.65 86
616	379 456	24.81 93	**666**	443 556	25.80 70	**716**	512 656	26.75 82	**766**	586 756	27.67 67
617	380 689	24.83 95	667	444 889	25.82 63	717	514 089	26.77 69	767	588 289	27.69 48
618	381 924	24.85 96	668	446 224	25.84 57	718	515 524	26.79 55	768	589 824	27.71 28
619	383 161	24.87 97	669	447 561	25.86 50	719	516 961	26.81 42	769	591 361	27.73 08
620	384 400	24.89 98	670	448 900	25.88 44	720	518 400	26.83 28	770	592 900	27.74 89
621	385 641	24.91 99	**671**	450 241	25.90 37	**721**	519 841	26.85 14	**771**	594 441	27.76 69
622	386 884	24.93 99	672	451 584	25.92 30	722	521 284	26.87 01	772	595 984	27.78 49
623	388 129	24.96 00	673	452 929	25.94 22	723	522 729	26.88 87	773	597 529	27.80 29
624	389 376	24.98 00	674	454 276	25.96 15	724	524 176	26.90 72	774	599 076	27.82 09
625	390 625	25.00 00	675	455 625	25.98 08	725	525 625	26.92 58	775	600 625	27.83 88
626	391 876	25.02 00	**676**	456 976	26.00 00	**726**	527 076	26.94 44	**776**	602 176	27.85 68
627	393 129	25.04 00	677	458 329	26.01 92	727	528 529	26.96 29	777	603 729	27.87 47
628	394 384	25.05 99	678	459 684	26.03 84	728	529 984	26.98 15	778	605 284	27.89 27
629	395 641	25.07 99	679	461 041	26.05 76	729	531 441	27.00 00	779	606 841	27.91 06
630	396 900	25.09 98	680	462 400	26.07 68	730	532 900	27.01 85	780	608 400	27.92 85
631	398 161	25.11 97	**681**	463 761	26.09 60	**731**	534 361	27.03 70	**781**	609 961	27.94 64
632	399 424	25.13 96	682	465 124	26.11 51	732	535 824	27.05 55	782	611 524	27.96 43
633	400 689	25.15 95	683	466 489	26.13 43	733	537 289	27.07 40	783	613 089	27.98 21
634	401 956	25.17 94	684	467 856	26.15 34	734	538 756	27.09 24	784	614 656	28.00 00
635	403 225	25.19 92	685	469 225	26.17 25	735	540 225	27.11 09	785	616 225	28.01 79
636	404 496	25.21 90	**686**	470 596	26.19 16	**736**	541 696	27.12 93	**786**	617 796	28.03 57
637	405 769	25.23 89	687	471 969	26.21 07	737	543 169	27.14 77	787	619 369	28.05 35
638	407 044	25.25 87	688	473 344	26.22 98	738	544 644	27.16 62	788	620 944	28.07 13
639	408 321	25.27 84	689	474 721	26.24 88	739	546 121	27.18 46	789	622 521	28.08 91
640	409 600	25.29 82	690	476 100	26.26 79	740	547 600	27.20 29	790	624 100	28.10 69
641	410 881	25.31 80	**691**	477 481	26.28 69	**741**	549 081	27.22 13	**791**	625 681	28.12 47
642	412 164	25.33 77	692	478 864	26.30 59	742	550 564	27.23 97	792	627 264	28.14 25
643	413 449	25.35 74	693	480 249	26.32 49	743	552 049	27.25 80	793	628 849	28.16 03
644	414 736	25.37 72	694	481 636	26.34 39	744	553 536	27.27 64	794	630 436	28.17 80
645	416 025	25.39 69	695	483 025	26.36 29	745	555 025	27.29 47	795	632 025	28.19 57
646	417 316	25.41 65	**696**	484 416	26.38 18	**746**	556 516	27.31 30	**796**	633 616	28.21 35
647	418 609	25.43 62	697	485 809	26.40 08	747	558 009	27.33 13	797	635 209	28.23 12
648	419 904	25.45 58	698	487 204	26.41 97	748	559 504	27.34 96	798	636 804	28.24 89
649	421 201	25.47 55	699	488 601	26.43 86	749	561 001	27.36 79	799	638 401	28.26 66
650	422 500	25.49 51	700	490 000	26.45 75	750	562 500	27.38 61	800	640 000	28.28 43
N	N²	√N	N	N²	√N	N	N²	√N	N	N²	√N

Table A.1   Squares and Square Roots (*cont.*)

N	N²	√N	N	N²	√N	N	N²	√N	N	N²	√N
800	640 000	28.28 43	**850**	722 500	29.15 48	**900**	810 000	30.00 00	**950**	902 500	30.82 21
801	641 601	28.30 19	851	724 201	29.17 19	901	811 801	30.01 67	951	904 401	30.83 83
802	643 204	28.31 96	852	725 904	29.18 90	902	813 604	30.03 33	952	906 304	30.85 45
803	644 809	28.33 73	853	727 609	29.20 62	903	815 409	30.05 00	953	908 209	30.87 07
804	646 416	28.35 49	854	729 316	29.22 33	904	817 216	30.06 66	954	910 116	30.88 69
805	648 025	28.37 25	855	731 025	29.24 04	905	819 025	30.08 32	955	912 025	30.90 31
806	649 636	28.39 01	**856**	732 736	29.25 75	**906**	820 836	30.09 98	**956**	913 936	30.91 92
807	651 249	28.40 77	857	734 449	29.27 46	907	822 649	30.11 64	957	915 849	30.93 54
808	652 864	28.42 53	858	736 164	29.29 16	908	824 464	30.13 30	958	917 764	30.95 16
809	654 481	28.44 29	859	737 881	29.30 87	909	826 281	30.14 96	959	919 681	30.96 77
810	656 100	28.46 05	860	739 600	29.32 58	910	828 100	30.16 62	960	921 600	30.98 39
811	657 721	28.47 81	**861**	741 321	29.34 28	**911**	829 921	30.18 28	**961**	923 521	31.00 00
812	659 344	28.49 56	862	743 044	29.35 98	912	831 744	30.19 93	962	925 444	31.01 61
813	660 969	28.51 32	863	744 769	29.37 69	913	833 569	30.21 59	963	927 369	31.03 22
814	662 596	28.53 07	864	746 496	29.39 39	914	835 396	30.23 24	964	929 296	31.04 83
815	664 225	28.54 82	865	748 225	29.41 09	915	837 225	30.24 90	965	931 225	31.06 44
816	665 856	28.56 57	**866**	749 956	29.42 79	**916**	839 056	30.26 55	**966**	933 156	31.08 05
817	667 489	28.58 32	867	751 689	29.44 49	917	840 889	30.28 20	967	935 089	31.09 66
818	669 124	28.60 07	868	753 424	29.46 18	918	842 724	30.29 85	968	937 024	31.11 27
819	670 761	28.61 82	869	755 161	29.47 88	919	844 561	30.31 50	969	938 961	31.12 88
820	672 400	28.63 56	870	756 900	29.49 58	920	846 400	30.33 15	970	940 900	31.14 48
821	674 041	28.65 31	**871**	758 641	29.51 27	**921**	848 241	30.34 80	**971**	942 841	31.16 09
822	675 684	28.67 05	872	760 384	29.52 96	922	850 084	30.36 45	972	944 784	31.17 69
823	677 329	28.68 80	873	762 129	29.54 66	923	851 929	30.38 09	973	946 729	31.19 29
824	678 976	28.70 54	874	763 876	29.56 35	924	853 776	30.39 74	974	948 676	31.20 90
825	680 625	28.72 28	875	765 625	29.58 04	925	855 625	30.41 38	975	950 625	31.22 50
826	682 276	28.74 02	**876**	767 376	29.59 73	**926**	857 476	30.43 02	**976**	952 576	31.24 10
827	683 929	28.75 76	877	769 129	29.61 42	927	859 329	30.44 67	977	954 529	31.25 70
828	685 584	28.77 50	878	770 884	29.63 11	928	861 184	30.46 31	978	956 484	31.27 30
829	687 241	28.79 24	879	772 641	29.64 79	929	863 041	30.47 95	979	958 441	31.28 90
830	688 900	28.80 97	880	774 400	29.66 48	930	864 900	30.49 59	980	960 400	31.30 50
831	690 561	28.82 71	**881**	776 161	29.68 16	**931**	866 761	30.51 23	**981**	962 361	31.32 09
832	692 224	28.84 44	882	777 924	29.69 85	932	868 624	30.52 87	982	964 324	31.33 69
833	693 889	28.86 17	883	779 689	29.71 53	933	870 489	30.54 50	983	966 289	31.35 28
834	695 556	28.87 91	884	781 456	29.73 21	934	872 356	30.56 14	984	968 256	31.36 88
835	697 225	28.89 64	885	783 225	29.74 89	935	874 225	30.57 78	985	970 225	31.38 47
836	698 896	28.91 37	**886**	784 996	29.76 58	**936**	876 096	30.59 41	**986**	972 196	31.40 06
837	700 569	28.93 10	887	786 769	29.78 25	937	877 969	30.61 05	987	974 169	31.41 66
838	702 244	28.94 82	888	788 544	29.79 93	938	879 844	30.62 68	988	976 144	31.43 25
839	703 921	28.96 55	889	790 321	29.81 61	939	881 721	30.64 31	989	978 121	31.44 84
840	705 600	28.98 28	890	792 100	29.83 29	940	883 600	30.65 94	990	980 100	31.46 43
841	707 281	29.00 00	**891**	793 881	29.84 96	**941**	885 481	30.67 57	**991**	982 081	31.48 02
842	708 964	29.01 72	892	795 664	29.86 64	942	887 364	30.69 20	992	984 064	31.49 60
843	710 649	29.03 45	893	797 449	29.88 31	943	889 249	30.70 83	993	986 049	31.51 19
844	712 336	29.05 17	894	799 236	29.89 98	944	891 136	30.72 46	994	988 036	31.52 78
845	714 025	29.06 89	895	801 025	29.91 66	945	893 025	30.74 09	995	990 025	31.54 36
846	715 716	29.08 61	**896**	802 816	29.93 33	**946**	894 916	30.75 71	**996**	992 016	31.55 95
847	717 409	29.10 33	897	804 609	29.95 00	947	896 809	30.77 34	997	994 009	31.57 53
848	719 104	29.12 04	898	806 404	29.96 66	948	898 704	30.78 96	998	996 004	31.59 11
849	720 801	29.13 76	899	808 201	29.98 33	949	900 601	30.80 58	999	998 001	31.60 70
850	722 500	29.15 48	900	810 000	30.00 00	950	902 500	30.82 21	1000	1000 000	31.62 28
N	N²	√N	N	N²	√N	N	N²	√N	N	N²	√N

Table A.2   Areas of the Normal Curve

(1) z	(2) AREA BETWEEN THE MEAN AND Z	(3) AREA IN THE SMALLER PORTION	(1) z	(2) AREA BETWEEN THE MEAN AND Z	(3) AREA IN THE SMALLER PORTION
0.00	.0000	.5000	0.35	.1368	.3632
0.01	.0040	.4960	0.36	.1406	.3594
0.02	.0080	.4920	0.37	.1443	.3557
0.03	.0120	.4880	0.38	.1480	.3520
0.04	.0160	.4840	0.39	.1517	.3483
0.05	.0199	.4801	0.40	.1554	.3446
0.06	.0239	.4761	0.41	.1591	.3409
0.07	.0279	.4721	0.42	.1628	.3372
0.08	.0319	.4681	0.43	.1664	.3336
0.09	.0359	.4641	0.44	.1700	.3300
0.10	.0398	.4602	0.45	.1736	.3264
0.11	.0438	.4562	0.46	.1772	.3228
0.12	.0478	.4522	0.47	.1808	.3192
0.13	.0517	.4483	0.48	.1844	.3156
0.14	.0557	.4443	0.49	.1879	.3121
0.15	.0596	.4404	0.50	.1915	.3085
0.16	.0636	.4364	0.51	.1950	.3050
0.17	.0675	.4325	0.52	.1985	.3015
0.18	.0714	.4286	0.53	.2019	.2981
0.19	.0753	.4247	0.54	.2054	.2946
0.20	.0793	.4207	0.55	.2088	.2912
0.21	.0832	.4168	0.56	.2123	.2877
0.22	.0871	.4129	0.57	.2157	.2843
0.23	.0910	.4090	0.58	.2190	.2810
0.24	.0948	.4052	0.59	.2224	.2776
0.25	.0987	.4013	0.60	.2257	.2743
0.26	.1026	.3974	0.61	.2291	.2709
0.27	.1064	.3936	0.62	.2324	.2676
0.28	.1103	.3897	0.63	.2357	.2643
0.29	.1141	.3859	0.64	.2389	.2611
0.30	.1179	.3821	0.65	.2422	.2578
0.31	.1217	.3783	0.66	.2454	.2546
0.32	.1255	.3745	0.67	.2486	.2514
0.33	.1293	.3707	0.68	.2517	.2483
0.34	.1331	.3669	0.69	.2549	.2451

Table A.2   Areas of the Normal Curve *(cont.)*

(1) z	(2) AREA BETWEEN THE MEAN AND z	(3) AREA IN THE SMALLER PORTION	(1) z	(2) AREA BETWEEN THE MEAN AND z	(3) AREA IN THE SMALLER PORTION
0.70	.2580	.2420	1.05	.3531	.1469
0.71	.2611	.2389	1.06	.3554	.1446
0.72	.2642	.2358	1.07	.3577	.1423
0.73	.2673	.2327	1.08	.3599	.1401
0.74	.2704	.2296	1.09	.3621	.1379
0.75	.2734	.2266	1.10	.3643	.1357
0.76	.2764	.2236	1.11	.3665	.1335
0.77	.2794	.2206	1.12	.3686	.1314
0.78	.2823	.2177	1.13	.3708	.1292
0.79	.2852	.2148	1.14	.3729	.1271
0.80	.2881	.2119	1.15	.3749	.1251
0.81	.2910	.2090	1.16	.3770	.1230
0.82	.2939	.2061	1.17	.3790	.1210
0.83	.2967	.2033	1.18	.3810	.1190
0.84	.2995	.2005	1.19	.3830	.1170
0.85	.3023	.1977	1.20	.3849	.1151
0.86	.3051	.1949	1.21	.3869	.1131
0.87	.3078	.1922	1.22	.3888	.1112
0.88	.3106	.1894	1.23	.3907	.1093
0.89	.3133	.1867	1.24	.3925	.1075
0.90	.3159	.1841	1.25	.3944	.1056
0.91	.3186	.1814	1.26	.3962	.1038
0.92	.3212	.1788	1.27	.3980	.1020
0.93	.3238	.1762	1.28	.3997	.1003
0.94	.3264	.1736	1.29	.4015	.0985
0.95	.3289	.1711	1.30	.4032	.0968
0.96	.3315	.1685	1.31	.4049	.0951
0.97	.3340	.1660	1.32	.4066	.0934
0.98	.3365	.1635	1.33	.4082	.0918
0.99	.3389	.1611	1.34	.4099	.0901
1.00	.3413	.1587	1.35	.4115	.0885
1.01	.3438	.1562	1.36	.4131	.0869
1.02	.3461	.1539	1.37	.4147	.0853
1.03	.3485	.1515	1.38	.4162	.0838
1.04	.3508	.1492	1.39	.4177	.0823

Table A.2   Areas of the Normal Curve *(cont.)*

(1) z	(2) Area between the Mean and z	(3) Area in the Smaller Portion	(1) z	(2) Area between the Mean and z	(3) Area in the Smaller Portion
1.40	.4192	.0808	1.75	.4599	.0401
1.41	.4207	.0793	1.76	.4608	.0392
1.42	.4222	.0778	1.77	.4616	.0384
1.43	.4236	.0764	1.78	.4625	.0375
1.44	.4251	.0749	1.79	.4633	.0367
1.45	.4265	.0735	1.80	.4641	.0359
1.46	.4279	.0721	1.81	.4649	.0351
1.47	.4292	.0708	1.82	.4656	.0344
1.48	.4306	.0694	1.83	.4664	.0336
1.49	.4319	.0681	1.84	.4671	.0329
1.50	.4332	.0668	1.85	.4678	.0322
1.51	.4345	.0655	1.86	.4686	.0314
1.52	.4357	.0643	1.87	.4693	.0307
1.53	.4370	.0630	1.88	.4699	.0301
1.54	.4382	.0618	1.89	.4706	.0294
1.55	.4394	.0606	1.90	.4713	.0287
1.56	.4406	.0594	1.91	.4719	.0281
1.57	.4418	.0582	1.92	.4726	.0274
1.58	.4429	.0571	1.93	.4732	.0268
1.59	.4441	.0559	1.94	.4738	.0262
1.60	.4452	.0548	1.95	.4744	.0256
1.61	.4463	.0537	1.96	.4750	.0250
1.62	.4474	.0526	1.97	.4756	.0244
1.63	.4484	.0516	1.98	.4761	.0239
1.64	.4495	.0505	1.99	.4767	.0233
1.65	.4505	.0495	2.00	.4772	.0228
1.66	.4515	.0485	2.01	.4778	.0222
1.67	.4525	.0475	2.02	.4783	.0217
1.68	.4535	.0465	2.03	.4788	.0212
1.69	.4545	.0455	2.04	.4793	.0207
1.70	.4554	.0446	2.05	.4798	.0202
1.71	.4564	.0436	2.06	.4803	.0197
1.72	.4573	.0427	2.07	.4808	.0192
1.73	.4582	.0418	2.08	.4812	.0188
1.74	.4591	.0409	2.09	.4817	.0183

Table A.2   Areas of the Normal Curve *(cont.)*

(1) z	(2) AREA BETWEEN THE MEAN AND z	(3) AREA IN THE SMALLER PORTION	(1) z	(2) AREA BETWEEN THE MEAN AND z	(3) AREA IN THE SMALLER PORTION
2.10	.4821	.0179	2.45	.4929	.0071
2.11	.4826	.0174	2.46	.4931	.0069
2.12	.4830	.0170	2.47	.4932	.0068
2.13	.4834	.0166	2.48	.4934	.0066
2.14	.4838	.0162	2.49	.4936	.0064
2.15	.4842	.0158	2.50	.4938	.0062
2.16	.4846	.0154	2.51	.4940	.0060
2.17	.4850	.0150	2.52	.4941	.0059
2.18	.4854	.0146	2.53	.4943	.0057
2.19	.4857	.0143	2.54	.4945	.0055
2.20	.4861	.0139	2.55	.4946	.0054
2.21	.4864	.0136	2.56	.4948	.0052
2.22	.4868	.0132	2.57	.4949	.0051
2.23	.4871	.0129	2.58	.4951	.0049
2.24	.4875	.0125	2.59	.4952	.0048
2.25	.4878	.0122	2.60	.4953	.0047
2.26	.4881	.0119	2.61	.4955	.0045
2.27	.4884	.0116	2.62	.4956	.0044
2.28	.4887	.0113	2.63	.4957	.0043
2.29	.4890	.0110	2.64	.4959	.0041
2.30	.4893	.0107	2.65	.4960	.0040
2.31	.4896	.0104	2.66	.4961	.0039
2.32	.4898	.0102	2.67	.4962	.0038
2.33	.4901	.0099	2.68	.4963	.0037
2.34	.4904	.0096	2.69	.4964	.0036
2.35	.4906	.0094	2.70	.4965	.0035
2.36	.4909	.0091	2.71	.4966	.0034
2.37	.4911	.0089	2.72	.4967	.0033
2.38	.4913	.0087	2.73	.4968	.0032
2.39	.4916	.0084	2.74	.4969	.0031
2.40	.4918	.0082	2.75	.4970	.0030
2.41	.4920	.0080	2.76	.4971	.0029
2.42	.4922	.0078	2.77	.4972	.0028
2.43	.4925	.0075	2.78	.4973	.0027
2.44	.4927	.0073	2.79	.4974	.0026

Table A.2   Areas of the Normal Curve *(cont.)*

(1) z	(2) AREA BETWEEN THE MEAN AND Z	(3) AREA IN THE SMALLER PORTION	(1) z	(2) AREA BETWEEN THE MEAN AND Z	(3) AREA IN THE SMALLER PORTION
2.80	.4974	.0026	3.15	.4992	.0008
2.81	.4975	.0025	3.16	.4992	.0008
2.82	.4976	.0024	3.17	.4992	.0008
2.83	.4977	.0023	3.18	.4993	.0007
2.84	.4977	.0023	3.19	.4993	.0007
2.85	.4978	.0022	3.20	.4993	.0007
2.86	.4979	.0021	3.21	.4993	.0007
2.87	.4979	.0021	3.22	.4994	.0006
2.88	.4980	.0020	3.23	.4994	.0006
2.89	.4981	.0019	3.24	.4994	.0006
2.90	.4981	.0019	3.30	.4995	.0005
2.91	.4982	.0018	3.40	.4997	.0003
2.92	.4982	.0018	3.50	.4998	.0002
2.93	.4983	.0017	3.60	.4998	.0002
2.94	.4984	.0016	3.70	.4999	.0001
2.95	.4984	.0016			
2.96	.4985	.0015			
2.97	.4985	.0015			
2.98	.4986	.0014			
2.99	.4986	.0014			
3.00	.4987	.0013			
3.01	.4987	.0013			
3.02	.4987	.0013			
3.03	.4988	.0012			
3.04	.4988	.0012			
3.05	.4989	.0011			
3.06	.4989	.0011			
3.07	.4989	.0011			
3.08	.4990	.0010			
3.09	.4990	.0010			
3.10	.4990	.0010			
3.11	.4991	.0009			
3.12	.4991	.0009			
3.13	.4991	.0009			
3.14	.4992	.0008			

Table A.3   Table of *t* Values

Degrees of freedom	Probability			
	.1	.05	.01	.001
1	6.314	12.706	63.657	636.619
2	2.920	4.303	9.925	31.598
3	2.353	3.182	5.841	12.924
4	2.132	2.776	4.604	8.610
5	2.015	2.571	4.032	6.869
6	1.943	2.447	3.707	5.959
7	1.895	2.365	3.499	5.408
8	1.860	2.306	3.355	5.041
9	1.833	2.262	3.250	4.781
10	1.812	2.228	3.169	4.587
11	1.796	2.201	3.106	4.437
12	1.782	2.179	3.055	4.318
13	1.771	2.160	3.012	4.221
14	1.761	2.145	2.977	4.140
15	1.753	2.131	2.947	4.073
16	1.746	2.120	2.921	4.015
17	1.740	2.110	2.898	3.965
18	1.734	2.101	2.878	3.922
19	1.729	2.093	2.861	3.883
20	1.725	2.086	2.845	3.850
21	1.721	2.080	2.831	3.819
22	1.717	2.074	2.819	3.792
23	1.714	2.069	2.807	3.767
24	1.711	2.064	2.797	3.745
25	1.708	2.060	2.787	3.725
26	1.706	2.056	2.779	3.707
27	1.703	2.052	2.771	3.690
28	1.701	2.048	2.763	3.674
29	1.699	2.045	2.756	3.659
30	1.697	2.042	2.750	3.646
40	1.684	2.021	2.704	3.551
60	1.671	2.000	2.660	3.460
120	1.658	1.980	2.617	3.373
∞	1.645	1.960	2.576	3.291

SOURCE: Abridged from Table II in R. A. Fisher and F. Yates, *Statistical Tables for Biological, Agricultural, and Medical Research* (New York: Hafner, 1974). Reprinted by permission.

Table A.4 The 5 (Roman Type) and 1 (Boldface Type) Percent Points for the Distribution of F

n_1 degrees of freedom (for greater mean square)

n_2	1	2	3	4	5	6	7	8	9	10	11	12	14	16	20	24	30	40	50	75	100	200	500	∞
1	161 **4,052**	200 **4,999**	216 **5,403**	225 **5,625**	230 **5,764**	234 **5,859**	237 **5,928**	239 **5,981**	241 **6,022**	242 **6,056**	243 **6,082**	244 **6,106**	245 **6,142**	246 **6,169**	248 **6,208**	249 **6,234**	250 **6,258**	251 **6,286**	252 **6,302**	253 **6,323**	253 **6,334**	254 **6,352**	254 **6,361**	254 **6,366**
2	18.51 **98.49**	19.00 **99.00**	19.16 **99.17**	19.25 **99.25**	19.30 **99.30**	19.33 **99.33**	19.36 **99.34**	19.37 **99.36**	19.38 **99.38**	19.39 **99.40**	19.40 **99.41**	19.41 **99.42**	19.42 **99.43**	19.43 **99.44**	19.44 **99.45**	19.45 **99.46**	19.46 **99.47**	19.47 **99.48**	19.47 **99.48**	19.48 **99.49**	19.49 **99.49**	19.49 **99.49**	19.50 **99.50**	19.50 **99.50**
3	10.13 **34.12**	9.55 **30.82**	9.28 **29.46**	9.12 **28.71**	9.01 **28.24**	8.94 **27.91**	8.88 **27.67**	8.84 **27.49**	8.81 **27.34**	8.78 **27.23**	8.76 **27.13**	8.74 **27.05**	8.71 **26.92**	8.69 **26.83**	8.66 **26.69**	8.64 **26.60**	8.62 **26.50**	8.60 **26.41**	8.58 **26.35**	8.57 **26.27**	8.56 **26.23**	8.54 **26.18**	8.54 **26.14**	8.53 **26.12**
4	7.71 **21.20**	6.94 **18.00**	6.59 **16.69**	6.39 **15.98**	6.26 **15.52**	6.16 **15.21**	6.09 **14.98**	6.04 **14.80**	6.00 **14.66**	5.96 **14.54**	5.93 **14.45**	5.91 **14.37**	5.87 **14.24**	5.84 **14.15**	5.80 **14.02**	5.77 **13.93**	5.74 **13.83**	5.71 **13.74**	5.70 **13.69**	5.68 **13.61**	5.66 **13.57**	5.65 **13.52**	5.64 **13.48**	5.63 **13.46**
5	6.61 **16.26**	5.79 **13.27**	5.41 **12.06**	5.19 **11.39**	5.05 **10.97**	4.95 **10.67**	4.88 **10.45**	4.82 **10.27**	4.78 **10.15**	4.74 **10.05**	4.70 **9.96**	4.68 **9.89**	4.64 **9.77**	4.60 **9.68**	4.56 **9.55**	4.53 **9.47**	4.50 **9.38**	4.46 **9.29**	4.44 **9.24**	4.42 **9.17**	4.40 **9.13**	4.38 **9.07**	4.37 **9.04**	4.36 **9.02**
6	5.99 **13.74**	5.14 **10.92**	4.76 **9.78**	4.53 **9.15**	4.39 **8.75**	4.28 **8.47**	4.21 **8.26**	4.15 **8.10**	4.10 **7.98**	4.06 **7.87**	4.03 **7.79**	4.00 **7.72**	3.96 **7.60**	3.92 **7.52**	3.87 **7.39**	3.84 **7.31**	3.81 **7.23**	3.77 **7.14**	3.75 **7.09**	3.72 **7.02**	3.71 **6.99**	3.69 **6.94**	3.68 **6.90**	3.67 **6.88**
7	5.59 **12.25**	4.74 **9.55**	4.35 **8.45**	4.12 **7.85**	3.97 **7.46**	3.87 **7.19**	3.79 **7.00**	3.73 **6.84**	3.68 **6.71**	3.63 **6.62**	3.60 **6.54**	3.57 **6.47**	3.52 **6.35**	3.49 **6.27**	3.44 **6.15**	3.41 **6.07**	3.38 **5.98**	3.34 **5.90**	3.32 **5.85**	3.29 **5.78**	3.28 **5.75**	3.25 **5.70**	3.24 **5.67**	3.23 **5.65**
8	5.32 **11.26**	4.46 **8.65**	4.07 **7.59**	3.84 **7.01**	3.69 **6.63**	3.58 **6.37**	3.50 **6.19**	3.44 **6.03**	3.39 **5.91**	3.34 **5.82**	3.31 **5.74**	3.28 **5.67**	3.23 **5.56**	3.20 **5.48**	3.15 **5.36**	3.12 **5.28**	3.08 **5.20**	3.05 **5.11**	3.03 **5.06**	3.00 **5.00**	2.98 **4.96**	2.96 **4.91**	2.94 **4.88**	2.93 **4.86**
9	5.12 **10.56**	4.26 **8.02**	3.86 **6.99**	3.63 **6.42**	3.48 **6.06**	3.37 **5.80**	3.29 **5.62**	3.23 **5.47**	3.18 **5.35**	3.13 **5.26**	3.10 **5.18**	3.07 **5.11**	3.02 **5.00**	2.98 **4.92**	2.93 **4.80**	2.90 **4.73**	2.86 **4.64**	2.82 **4.56**	2.80 **4.51**	2.77 **4.45**	2.76 **4.41**	2.73 **4.36**	2.72 **4.33**	2.71 **4.31**
10	4.96 **10.04**	4.10 **7.56**	3.71 **6.55**	3.48 **5.99**	3.33 **5.64**	3.22 **5.39**	3.14 **5.21**	3.07 **5.06**	3.02 **4.95**	2.97 **4.85**	2.94 **4.78**	2.91 **4.71**	2.86 **4.60**	2.82 **4.52**	2.77 **4.41**	2.74 **4.33**	2.70 **4.25**	2.67 **4.17**	2.64 **4.12**	2.61 **4.05**	2.59 **4.01**	2.56 **3.96**	2.55 **3.93**	2.54 **3.91**
11	4.84 **9.65**	3.98 **7.20**	3.59 **6.22**	3.36 **5.67**	3.20 **5.32**	3.09 **5.07**	3.01 **4.88**	2.95 **4.74**	2.90 **4.63**	2.86 **4.54**	2.82 **4.46**	2.79 **4.40**	2.74 **4.29**	2.70 **4.21**	2.65 **4.10**	2.61 **4.02**	2.57 **3.94**	2.53 **3.86**	2.50 **3.80**	2.47 **3.74**	2.45 **3.70**	2.42 **3.66**	2.41 **3.62**	2.40 **3.60**
12	4.75 **9.33**	3.88 **6.93**	3.49 **5.95**	3.26 **5.41**	3.11 **5.06**	3.00 **4.82**	2.92 **4.65**	2.85 **4.50**	2.80 **4.39**	2.76 **4.30**	2.72 **4.22**	2.69 **4.16**	2.64 **4.05**	2.60 **3.98**	2.54 **3.86**	2.50 **3.78**	2.46 **3.70**	2.42 **3.61**	2.40 **3.56**	2.36 **3.49**	2.35 **3.46**	2.32 **3.41**	2.31 **3.38**	2.30 **3.36**
13	4.67 **9.07**	3.80 **6.70**	3.41 **5.74**	3.18 **5.20**	3.02 **4.86**	2.92 **4.62**	2.84 **4.44**	2.77 **4.30**	2.72 **4.19**	2.67 **4.10**	2.63 **4.02**	2.60 **3.96**	2.55 **3.85**	2.51 **3.78**	2.46 **3.67**	2.42 **3.59**	2.38 **3.51**	2.34 **3.42**	2.32 **3.37**	2.28 **3.30**	2.26 **3.27**	2.24 **3.21**	2.22 **3.18**	2.21 **3.16**

SOURCE: George W. Snedecor and William G. Cochran, *Statistical Methods*, 6th ed. (Ames, Iowa: The Iowa State University Press, 1967). Copyright © 1967 by the Iowa State University Press, Ames, Iowa 50010, and reprinted by permission.

Table A.4   The 5 (Roman Type) and 1 (Boldface Type) Percent Points for the Distribution of F (cont.)

n_1 degrees of freedom (for greater mean square)

n_2	1	2	3	4	5	6	7	8	9	10	11	12	14	16	20	24	30	40	50	75	100	200	500	∞
14	4.60 **8.86**	3.74 **6.51**	3.34 **5.56**	3.11 **5.03**	2.96 **4.69**	2.85 **4.46**	2.77 **4.28**	2.70 **4.14**	2.65 **4.03**	2.60 **3.94**	2.56 **3.86**	2.53 **3.80**	2.48 **3.70**	2.44 **3.62**	2.39 **3.51**	2.35 **3.43**	2.31 **3.34**	2.27 **3.26**	2.24 **3.21**	2.21 **3.14**	2.19 **3.11**	2.16 **3.06**	2.14 **3.02**	2.13 **3.00**
15	4.54 **8.68**	3.68 **6.36**	3.29 **5.42**	3.06 **4.89**	2.90 **4.56**	2.79 **4.32**	2.70 **4.14**	2.64 **4.00**	2.59 **3.89**	2.55 **3.80**	2.51 **3.73**	2.48 **3.67**	2.43 **3.56**	2.39 **3.48**	2.33 **3.36**	2.29 **3.29**	2.25 **3.20**	2.21 **3.12**	2.18 **3.07**	2.15 **3.00**	2.12 **2.97**	2.10 **2.92**	2.08 **2.89**	2.07 **2.87**
16	4.49 **8.53**	3.63 **6.23**	3.24 **5.29**	3.01 **4.77**	2.85 **4.44**	2.74 **4.20**	2.66 **4.03**	2.59 **3.89**	2.54 **3.78**	2.49 **3.69**	2.45 **3.61**	2.42 **3.55**	2.37 **3.45**	2.33 **3.37**	2.28 **3.25**	2.24 **3.18**	2.20 **3.10**	2.16 **3.01**	2.13 **2.96**	2.09 **2.89**	2.07 **2.86**	2.04 **2.80**	2.02 **2.77**	2.01 **2.75**
17	4.45 **8.40**	3.59 **6.11**	3.20 **5.18**	2.96 **4.67**	2.81 **4.34**	2.70 **4.10**	2.62 **3.93**	2.55 **3.79**	2.50 **3.68**	2.45 **3.59**	2.41 **3.52**	2.38 **3.45**	2.33 **3.35**	2.29 **3.27**	2.23 **3.16**	2.19 **3.08**	2.15 **3.00**	2.11 **2.92**	2.08 **2.86**	2.04 **2.79**	2.02 **2.76**	1.99 **2.70**	1.97 **2.67**	1.96 **2.65**
18	4.41 **8.28**	3.55 **6.01**	3.16 **5.09**	2.93 **4.58**	2.77 **4.25**	2.66 **4.01**	2.58 **3.85**	2.51 **3.71**	2.46 **3.60**	2.41 **3.51**	2.37 **3.44**	2.34 **3.37**	2.29 **3.27**	2.25 **3.19**	2.19 **3.07**	2.15 **3.00**	2.11 **2.91**	2.07 **2.83**	2.04 **2.78**	2.00 **2.71**	1.98 **2.68**	1.95 **2.62**	1.93 **2.59**	1.92 **2.57**
19	4.38 **8.18**	3.52 **5.93**	3.13 **5.01**	2.90 **4.50**	2.74 **4.17**	2.63 **3.94**	2.55 **3.77**	2.48 **3.63**	2.43 **3.52**	2.38 **3.43**	2.34 **3.36**	2.31 **3.30**	2.26 **3.19**	2.21 **3.12**	2.15 **3.00**	2.11 **2.92**	2.07 **2.84**	2.02 **2.76**	2.00 **2.70**	1.96 **2.63**	1.94 **2.60**	1.91 **2.54**	1.90 **2.51**	1.88 **2.49**
20	4.35 **8.10**	3.49 **5.85**	3.10 **4.94**	2.87 **4.43**	2.71 **4.10**	2.60 **3.87**	2.52 **3.71**	2.45 **3.56**	2.40 **3.45**	2.35 **3.37**	2.31 **3.30**	2.28 **3.23**	2.23 **3.13**	2.18 **3.05**	2.12 **2.94**	2.08 **2.86**	2.04 **2.77**	1.99 **2.69**	1.96 **2.63**	1.92 **2.56**	1.90 **2.53**	1.87 **2.47**	1.85 **2.44**	1.84 **2.42**
21	4.32 **8.02**	3.47 **5.78**	3.07 **4.87**	2.84 **4.37**	2.68 **4.04**	2.57 **3.81**	2.49 **3.65**	2.42 **3.51**	2.37 **3.40**	2.32 **3.31**	2.28 **3.24**	2.25 **3.17**	2.20 **3.07**	2.15 **2.99**	2.09 **2.88**	2.05 **2.80**	2.00 **2.72**	1.96 **2.63**	1.93 **2.58**	1.89 **2.51**	1.87 **2.47**	1.84 **2.42**	1.82 **2.38**	1.81 **2.36**
22	4.30 **7.94**	3.44 **5.72**	3.05 **4.82**	2.82 **4.31**	2.66 **3.99**	2.55 **3.76**	2.47 **3.59**	2.40 **3.45**	2.35 **3.35**	2.30 **3.26**	2.26 **3.18**	2.23 **3.12**	2.18 **3.02**	2.13 **2.94**	2.07 **2.83**	2.03 **2.75**	1.98 **2.67**	1.93 **2.58**	1.91 **2.53**	1.87 **2.46**	1.84 **2.42**	1.81 **2.37**	1.80 **2.33**	1.78 **2.31**
23	4.28 **7.88**	3.42 **5.66**	3.03 **4.76**	2.80 **4.26**	2.64 **3.94**	2.53 **3.71**	2.45 **3.54**	2.38 **3.41**	2.32 **3.30**	2.28 **3.21**	2.24 **3.14**	2.20 **3.07**	2.14 **2.97**	2.10 **2.89**	2.04 **2.78**	2.00 **2.70**	1.96 **2.62**	1.91 **2.53**	1.88 **2.48**	1.84 **2.41**	1.82 **2.37**	1.79 **2.32**	1.77 **2.28**	1.76 **2.26**
24	4.26 **7.82**	3.40 **5.61**	3.01 **4.72**	2.78 **4.22**	2.62 **3.90**	2.51 **3.67**	2.43 **3.50**	2.36 **3.36**	2.30 **3.25**	2.26 **3.17**	2.22 **3.09**	2.18 **3.03**	2.13 **2.93**	2.09 **2.85**	2.02 **2.74**	1.98 **2.66**	1.94 **2.58**	1.89 **2.49**	1.86 **2.44**	1.82 **2.36**	1.80 **2.33**	1.76 **2.27**	1.74 **2.23**	1.73 **2.21**
25	4.24 **7.77**	3.38 **5.57**	2.99 **4.68**	2.76 **4.18**	2.60 **3.86**	2.49 **3.63**	2.41 **3.46**	2.34 **3.32**	2.28 **3.21**	2.24 **3.13**	2.20 **3.05**	2.16 **2.99**	2.11 **2.89**	2.06 **2.81**	2.00 **2.70**	1.96 **2.62**	1.92 **2.54**	1.87 **2.45**	1.84 **2.40**	1.80 **2.32**	1.77 **2.29**	1.74 **2.23**	1.72 **2.19**	1.71 **2.17**
26	4.22 **7.72**	3.37 **5.53**	2.98 **4.64**	2.74 **4.14**	2.59 **3.82**	2.47 **3.59**	2.39 **3.42**	2.32 **3.29**	2.27 **3.17**	2.22 **3.09**	2.18 **3.02**	2.15 **2.96**	2.10 **2.86**	2.05 **2.77**	1.99 **2.66**	1.95 **2.58**	1.90 **2.50**	1.85 **2.41**	1.82 **2.36**	1.78 **2.28**	1.76 **2.25**	1.72 **2.19**	1.70 **2.15**	1.69 **2.13**

Table A.4   The 5 (Roman Type) and 1 (Boldface Type) Percent Points for the Distribution of F (cont.)

n_1 degrees of freedom (for greater mean square)

n_2	1	2	3	4	5	6	7	8	9	10	11	12	14	16	20	24	30	40	50	75	100	200	500	∞
27	4.21 **7.68**	3.35 **5.49**	2.96 **4.60**	2.73 **4.11**	2.57 **3.79**	2.46 **3.56**	2.37 **3.39**	2.30 **3.26**	2.25 **3.14**	2.20 **3.06**	2.16 **2.98**	2.13 **2.93**	2.08 **2.83**	2.03 **2.74**	1.97 **2.63**	1.93 **2.55**	1.88 **2.47**	1.84 **2.38**	1.80 **2.33**	1.76 **2.25**	1.74 **2.21**	1.71 **2.16**	1.68 **2.12**	1.67 **2.10**
28	4.20 **7.64**	3.34 **5.45**	2.95 **4.57**	2.71 **4.07**	2.56 **3.76**	2.44 **3.53**	2.36 **3.36**	2.29 **3.23**	2.24 **3.11**	2.19 **3.03**	2.15 **2.95**	2.12 **2.90**	2.06 **2.80**	2.02 **2.71**	1.96 **2.60**	1.91 **2.52**	1.87 **2.44**	1.81 **2.35**	1.78 **2.30**	1.75 **2.22**	1.72 **2.18**	1.69 **2.13**	1.67 **2.09**	1.65 **2.06**
29	4.18 **7.60**	3.33 **5.42**	2.93 **4.54**	2.70 **4.04**	2.54 **3.73**	2.43 **3.50**	2.35 **3.33**	2.28 **3.20**	2.22 **3.08**	2.18 **3.00**	2.14 **2.92**	2.10 **2.87**	2.05 **2.77**	2.00 **2.68**	1.94 **2.57**	1.90 **2.49**	1.85 **2.41**	1.80 **2.32**	1.77 **2.27**	1.73 **2.19**	1.71 **2.15**	1.68 **2.10**	1.65 **2.06**	1.64 **2.03**
30	4.17 **7.56**	3.32 **5.39**	2.92 **4.51**	2.69 **4.02**	2.53 **3.70**	2.42 **3.47**	2.34 **3.30**	2.27 **3.17**	2.21 **3.06**	2.16 **2.98**	2.12 **2.90**	2.09 **2.84**	2.04 **2.74**	1.99 **2.66**	1.93 **2.55**	1.89 **2.47**	1.84 **2.38**	1.79 **2.29**	1.76 **2.24**	1.72 **2.16**	1.69 **2.13**	1.66 **2.07**	1.64 **2.03**	1.62 **2.01**
32	4.15 **7.50**	3.30 **5.34**	2.90 **4.46**	2.67 **3.97**	2.51 **3.66**	2.40 **3.42**	2.32 **3.25**	2.25 **3.12**	2.19 **3.01**	2.14 **2.94**	2.10 **2.86**	2.07 **2.80**	2.02 **2.70**	1.97 **2.62**	1.91 **2.51**	1.86 **2.42**	1.82 **2.34**	1.76 **2.25**	1.74 **2.20**	1.69 **2.12**	1.67 **2.08**	1.64 **2.02**	1.61 **1.98**	1.59 **1.96**
34	4.13 **7.44**	3.28 **5.29**	2.88 **4.42**	2.65 **3.93**	2.49 **3.61**	2.38 **3.38**	2.30 **3.21**	2.23 **3.08**	2.17 **2.97**	2.12 **2.89**	2.08 **2.82**	2.05 **2.76**	2.00 **2.66**	1.95 **2.58**	1.89 **2.47**	1.84 **2.38**	1.80 **2.30**	1.74 **2.21**	1.71 **2.15**	1.67 **2.08**	1.64 **2.04**	1.61 **1.98**	1.59 **1.94**	1.57 **1.91**
36	4.11 **7.39**	3.26 **5.25**	2.86 **4.38**	2.63 **3.89**	2.48 **3.58**	2.36 **3.35**	2.28 **3.18**	2.21 **3.04**	2.15 **2.94**	2.10 **2.86**	2.06 **2.78**	2.03 **2.72**	1.98 **2.62**	1.93 **2.54**	1.87 **2.43**	1.82 **2.35**	1.78 **2.26**	1.72 **2.17**	1.69 **2.12**	1.65 **2.04**	1.62 **2.00**	1.59 **1.94**	1.56 **1.90**	1.55 **1.87**
38	4.10 **7.35**	3.25 **5.21**	2.85 **4.34**	2.62 **3.86**	2.46 **3.54**	2.35 **3.32**	2.26 **3.15**	2.19 **3.02**	2.14 **2.91**	2.09 **2.82**	2.05 **2.75**	2.02 **2.69**	1.96 **2.59**	1.92 **2.51**	1.85 **2.40**	1.80 **2.32**	1.76 **2.22**	1.71 **2.14**	1.67 **2.08**	1.63 **2.00**	1.60 **1.97**	1.57 **1.90**	1.54 **1.86**	1.53 **1.84**
40	4.08 **7.31**	3.23 **5.18**	2.84 **4.31**	2.61 **3.83**	2.45 **3.51**	2.34 **3.29**	2.25 **3.12**	2.18 **2.99**	2.12 **2.88**	2.07 **2.80**	2.04 **2.73**	2.00 **2.66**	1.95 **2.56**	1.90 **2.49**	1.84 **2.37**	1.79 **2.29**	1.74 **2.20**	1.69 **2.11**	1.66 **2.05**	1.61 **1.97**	1.59 **1.94**	1.55 **1.88**	1.53 **1.84**	1.51 **1.81**
42	4.07 **7.27**	3.22 **5.15**	2.83 **4.29**	2.59 **3.80**	2.44 **3.49**	2.32 **3.26**	2.24 **3.10**	2.17 **2.96**	2.11 **2.86**	2.06 **2.77**	2.02 **2.70**	1.99 **2.64**	1.94 **2.54**	1.89 **2.46**	1.82 **2.35**	1.78 **2.26**	1.73 **2.17**	1.68 **2.08**	1.64 **2.02**	1.60 **1.94**	1.57 **1.91**	1.54 **1.85**	1.51 **1.80**	1.49 **1.78**
44	4.06 **7.24**	3.21 **5.12**	2.82 **4.26**	2.58 **3.78**	2.43 **3.46**	2.31 **3.24**	2.23 **3.07**	2.16 **2.94**	2.10 **2.84**	2.05 **2.75**	2.01 **2.68**	1.98 **2.62**	1.92 **2.52**	1.88 **2.44**	1.81 **2.32**	1.76 **2.24**	1.72 **2.15**	1.66 **2.06**	1.63 **2.00**	1.58 **1.92**	1.56 **1.88**	1.52 **1.82**	1.50 **1.78**	1.48 **1.75**
46	4.05 **7.21**	3.20 **5.10**	2.81 **4.24**	2.57 **3.76**	2.42 **3.44**	2.30 **3.22**	2.22 **3.05**	2.14 **2.92**	2.09 **2.82**	2.04 **2.73**	2.00 **2.66**	1.97 **2.60**	1.91 **2.50**	1.87 **2.42**	1.80 **2.30**	1.75 **2.22**	1.71 **2.13**	1.65 **2.04**	1.62 **1.98**	1.57 **1.90**	1.54 **1.86**	1.51 **1.80**	1.48 **1.76**	1.46 **1.72**
48	4.04 **7.19**	3.19 **5.08**	2.80 **4.22**	2.56 **3.74**	2.41 **3.42**	2.30 **3.20**	2.21 **3.04**	2.14 **2.90**	2.08 **2.80**	2.03 **2.71**	1.99 **2.64**	1.96 **2.58**	1.90 **2.48**	1.86 **2.40**	1.79 **2.28**	1.74 **2.20**	1.70 **2.11**	1.64 **2.02**	1.61 **1.96**	1.56 **1.88**	1.53 **1.84**	1.50 **1.78**	1.47 **1.73**	1.45 **1.70**

Table A.4 The 5 (Roman Type) and 1 (Boldface Type) Percent Points for the Distribution of F (cont.)

n_1 degrees of freedom (for greater mean square)

n_2	1	2	3	4	5	6	7	8	9	10	11	12	14	16	20	24	30	40	50	75	100	200	500	∞
50	4.03 **7.17**	3.18 **5.06**	2.79 **4.20**	2.56 **3.72**	2.40 **3.41**	2.29 **3.18**	2.20 **3.02**	2.13 **2.88**	2.07 **2.78**	2.02 **2.70**	1.98 **2.62**	1.95 **2.56**	1.90 **2.46**	1.85 **2.39**	1.78 **2.26**	1.74 **2.18**	1.69 **2.10**	1.63 **2.00**	1.60 **1.94**	1.55 **1.86**	1.52 **1.82**	1.48 **1.76**	1.46 **1.71**	1.44 **1.68**
55	4.02 **7.12**	3.17 **5.01**	2.78 **4.16**	2.54 **3.68**	2.38 **3.37**	2.27 **3.15**	2.18 **2.98**	2.11 **2.85**	2.05 **2.75**	2.00 **2.66**	1.97 **2.59**	1.93 **2.53**	1.88 **2.43**	1.83 **2.35**	1.76 **2.23**	1.72 **2.15**	1.67 **2.06**	1.61 **1.96**	1.58 **1.90**	1.52 **1.82**	1.50 **1.78**	1.46 **1.71**	1.43 **1.66**	1.41 **1.64**
60	4.00 **7.08**	3.15 **4.98**	2.76 **4.13**	2.52 **3.65**	2.37 **3.34**	2.25 **3.12**	2.17 **2.95**	2.10 **2.82**	2.04 **2.72**	1.99 **2.63**	1.95 **2.56**	1.92 **2.50**	1.86 **2.40**	1.81 **2.32**	1.75 **2.20**	1.70 **2.12**	1.65 **2.03**	1.59 **1.93**	1.56 **1.87**	1.50 **1.79**	1.48 **1.74**	1.44 **1.68**	1.41 **1.63**	1.39 **1.60**
65	3.99 **7.04**	3.14 **4.95**	2.75 **4.10**	2.51 **3.62**	2.36 **3.31**	2.24 **3.09**	2.15 **2.93**	2.08 **2.79**	2.02 **2.70**	1.98 **2.61**	1.94 **2.54**	1.90 **2.47**	1.85 **2.37**	1.80 **2.30**	1.73 **2.18**	1.68 **2.09**	1.63 **2.00**	1.57 **1.90**	1.54 **1.84**	1.49 **1.76**	1.46 **1.71**	1.42 **1.64**	1.39 **1.60**	1.37 **1.56**
70	3.98 **7.01**	3.13 **4.92**	2.74 **4.08**	2.50 **3.60**	2.35 **3.29**	2.23 **3.07**	2.14 **2.91**	2.07 **2.77**	2.01 **2.67**	1.97 **2.59**	1.93 **2.51**	1.89 **2.45**	1.84 **2.35**	1.79 **2.28**	1.72 **2.15**	1.67 **2.07**	1.62 **1.98**	1.56 **1.88**	1.53 **1.82**	1.47 **1.74**	1.45 **1.69**	1.40 **1.62**	1.37 **1.56**	1.35 **1.53**
80	3.96 **6.96**	3.11 **4.88**	2.72 **4.04**	2.48 **3.56**	2.33 **3.25**	2.21 **3.04**	2.12 **2.87**	2.05 **2.74**	1.99 **2.64**	1.95 **2.55**	1.91 **2.48**	1.88 **2.41**	1.82 **2.32**	1.77 **2.24**	1.70 **2.11**	1.65 **2.03**	1.60 **1.94**	1.54 **1.84**	1.51 **1.78**	1.45 **1.70**	1.42 **1.65**	1.38 **1.57**	1.35 **1.52**	1.32 **1.49**
100	3.94 **6.90**	3.09 **4.82**	2.70 **3.98**	2.46 **3.51**	2.30 **3.20**	2.19 **2.99**	2.10 **2.82**	2.03 **2.69**	1.97 **2.59**	1.92 **2.51**	1.88 **2.43**	1.85 **2.36**	1.79 **2.26**	1.75 **2.19**	1.68 **2.06**	1.63 **1.98**	1.57 **1.89**	1.51 **1.79**	1.48 **1.73**	1.42 **1.64**	1.39 **1.59**	1.34 **1.51**	1.30 **1.46**	1.28 **1.43**
125	3.92 **6.84**	3.07 **4.78**	2.68 **3.94**	2.44 **3.47**	2.29 **3.17**	2.17 **2.95**	2.08 **2.79**	2.01 **2.65**	1.95 **2.56**	1.90 **2.47**	1.86 **2.40**	1.83 **2.33**	1.77 **2.23**	1.72 **2.15**	1.65 **2.03**	1.60 **1.94**	1.55 **1.85**	1.49 **1.75**	1.45 **1.68**	1.39 **1.59**	1.36 **1.54**	1.31 **1.46**	1.27 **1.40**	1.25 **1.37**
150	3.91 **6.81**	3.06 **4.75**	2.67 **3.91**	2.43 **3.44**	2.27 **3.14**	2.16 **2.92**	2.07 **2.76**	2.00 **2.62**	1.94 **2.53**	1.89 **2.44**	1.85 **2.37**	1.82 **2.30**	1.76 **2.20**	1.71 **2.12**	1.64 **2.00**	1.59 **1.91**	1.54 **1.83**	1.47 **1.72**	1.44 **1.66**	1.37 **1.56**	1.34 **1.51**	1.29 **1.43**	1.25 **1.37**	1.22 **1.33**
200	3.89 **6.76**	3.04 **4.71**	2.65 **3.88**	2.41 **3.41**	2.26 **3.11**	2.14 **2.90**	2.05 **2.73**	1.98 **2.60**	1.92 **2.50**	1.87 **2.41**	1.83 **2.34**	1.80 **2.28**	1.74 **2.17**	1.69 **2.09**	1.62 **1.97**	1.57 **1.88**	1.52 **1.79**	1.45 **1.69**	1.42 **1.62**	1.35 **1.53**	1.32 **1.48**	1.26 **1.39**	1.22 **1.33**	1.19 **1.28**
400	3.86 **6.70**	3.02 **4.66**	2.62 **3.83**	2.39 **3.36**	2.23 **3.06**	2.12 **2.85**	2.03 **2.69**	1.96 **2.55**	1.90 **2.46**	1.85 **2.37**	1.81 **2.29**	1.78 **2.23**	1.72 **2.12**	1.67 **2.04**	1.60 **1.92**	1.54 **1.84**	1.49 **1.74**	1.42 **1.64**	1.38 **1.57**	1.32 **1.47**	1.28 **1.42**	1.22 **1.32**	1.16 **1.24**	1.13 **1.19**
1000	3.85 **6.66**	3.00 **4.62**	2.61 **3.80**	2.38 **3.34**	2.22 **3.04**	2.10 **2.82**	2.02 **2.66**	1.95 **2.53**	1.89 **2.43**	1.84 **2.34**	1.80 **2.26**	1.76 **2.20**	1.70 **2.09**	1.65 **2.01**	1.58 **1.89**	1.53 **1.81**	1.47 **1.71**	1.41 **1.61**	1.36 **1.54**	1.30 **1.44**	1.26 **1.38**	1.19 **1.28**	1.13 **1.19**	1.08 **1.11**
∞	3.84 **6.64**	2.99 **4.60**	2.60 **3.78**	2.37 **3.32**	2.21 **3.02**	2.09 **2.80**	2.01 **2.64**	1.94 **2.51**	1.88 **2.41**	1.83 **2.32**	1.79 **2.24**	1.75 **2.18**	1.69 **2.07**	1.64 **1.99**	1.57 **1.87**	1.52 **1.79**	1.46 **1.69**	1.40 **1.59**	1.35 **1.52**	1.28 **1.41**	1.24 **1.36**	1.17 **1.25**	1.11 **1.15**	1.00 **1.00**

Table A.5   Table of χ^3

Degrees of Freedom	P = .99	.98	.95	.90	.80	.70	.50	.30	.20	.10	.05	.02	.01
1	.000157	.000628	.00393	.0158	.0642	.148	.455	1.074	1.642	2.706	3.841	5.412	6.635
2	.0201	.0404	.103	.211	.446	.713	1.386	2.408	3.219	4.605	5.991	7.824	9.210
3	.115	.185	.352	.584	1.005	1.424	2.366	3.665	4.642	6.251	7.815	9.837	11.341
4	.297	.429	.711	1.064	1.649	2.195	3.357	4.878	5.989	7.779	9.488	11.668	13.277
5	.554	.752	1.145	1.610	2.343	3.000	4.351	6.064	7.289	9.236	11.070	13.388	15.086
6	.872	1.134	1.635	2.204	3.070	3.828	5.348	7.231	8.558	10.645	12.592	15.033	16.812
7	1.239	1.564	2.167	2.833	3.822	4.671	6.346	8.383	9.803	12.017	14.067	16.622	18.475
8	1.646	2.032	2.733	3.490	4.594	5.527	7.344	9.524	11.030	13.362	15.507	18.168	20.090
9	2.088	2.532	3.325	4.168	5.380	6.393	8.343	10.656	12.242	14.684	16.919	19.679	21.666
10	2.558	3.059	3.940	4.865	6.179	7.267	9.342	11.781	13.442	15.987	18.307	21.161	23.209
11	3.053	3.609	4.575	5.578	6.989	8.148	10.341	12.899	14.631	17.275	19.675	22.618	24.725
12	3.571	4.178	5.226	6.304	7.807	9.034	11.340	14.011	15.812	18.549	21.026	24.054	26.217
13	4.107	4.765	5.892	7.042	8.634	9.926	12.340	15.119	16.985	19.812	22.362	25.472	27.688
14	4.660	5.368	6.571	7.790	9.467	10.821	13.339	16.222	18.151	21.064	23.685	26.873	29.141
15	5.229	5.985	7.261	8.547	10.307	11.721	14.339	17.322	19.311	22.307	24.996	28.259	30.578
16	5.812	6.614	7.962	9.312	11.152	12.624	15.338	18.418	20.465	23.542	26.296	29.633	32.000
17	6.408	7.255	8.672	10.085	12.002	13.531	16.338	19.511	21.615	24.769	27.587	30.995	33.409
18	7.015	7.906	9.390	10.865	12.857	14.440	17.338	20.601	22.760	25.989	28.869	32.346	34.805
19	7.633	8.567	10.117	11.651	13.716	15.352	18.338	21.689	23.900	27.204	30.144	33.687	36.191
20	8.260	9.237	10.851	12.443	14.578	16.266	19.337	22.775	25.038	28.412	31.410	35.020	37.566
21	8.897	9.915	11.591	13.240	15.445	17.182	20.337	23.858	26.171	29.615	32.671	36.343	38.932
22	9.542	10.600	12.338	14.041	16.314	18.101	21.337	24.939	27.301	30.813	33.924	37.659	40.289
23	10.196	11.293	13.091	14.848	17.187	19.021	22.337	26.018	28.429	32.007	35.172	38.968	41.638
24	10.856	11.992	13.848	15.659	18.062	19.943	23.337	27.096	29.553	33.196	36.415	40.270	42.980
25	11.524	12.697	14.611	16.473	18.940	20.867	24.337	28.172	30.675	34.382	37.652	41.566	44.314
26	12.198	13.409	15.379	17.292	19.820	21.792	25.336	29.246	31.795	35.563	38.885	42.856	45.642
27	12.879	14.125	16.151	18.114	20.703	22.719	26.336	30.319	32.912	36.741	40.113	44.140	46.963
28	13.565	14.847	16.928	18.939	21.588	23.647	27.336	31.391	34.027	37.916	41.337	45.419	48.278
29	14.256	15.574	17.708	19.768	22.475	24.577	28.336	32.461	35.139	39.087	42.557	46.693	49.588
30	14.953	16.306	18.493	20.599	23.364	25.508	29.336	33.530	36.250	40.256	43.773	47.962	50.892

SOURCE: R. A. Fisher, *Statistical Methods for Research Workers*, 14th ed. (New York: Hafner, 1973), Table III. Reprinted by permission.

Table A.6 Table of Random Numbers

<table>
<tr><td rowspan="2">Row</td><td colspan="8" align="center">Column Number</td></tr>
<tr><td>00000
01234</td><td>00000
56789</td><td>11111
01234</td><td>11111
56789</td><td>22222
01234</td><td>22222
56789</td><td>33333
01234</td><td>33333
56789</td></tr>
<tr><td colspan="9" align="center">1st Thousand</td></tr>
<tr><td>00</td><td>23157</td><td>54859</td><td>01837</td><td>25993</td><td>76249</td><td>70886</td><td>95230</td><td>36744</td></tr>
<tr><td>01</td><td>05545</td><td>55043</td><td>10537</td><td>43508</td><td>90611</td><td>83744</td><td>10962</td><td>21343</td></tr>
<tr><td>02</td><td>14871</td><td>60350</td><td>32404</td><td>36223</td><td>50051</td><td>00322</td><td>11543</td><td>80834</td></tr>
<tr><td>03</td><td>38976</td><td>74951</td><td>94051</td><td>75853</td><td>78805</td><td>90194</td><td>32428</td><td>71695</td></tr>
<tr><td>04</td><td>97312</td><td>61718</td><td>99755</td><td>30870</td><td>94251</td><td>25841</td><td>54882</td><td>10513</td></tr>
<tr><td>05</td><td>11742</td><td>69381</td><td>44339</td><td>30872</td><td>32797</td><td>33118</td><td>22647</td><td>06850</td></tr>
<tr><td>06</td><td>43361</td><td>28859</td><td>11016</td><td>45623</td><td>93009</td><td>00499</td><td>43640</td><td>74036</td></tr>
<tr><td>07</td><td>93806</td><td>20478</td><td>38268</td><td>04491</td><td>55751</td><td>18932</td><td>58475</td><td>52571</td></tr>
<tr><td>08</td><td>49540</td><td>13181</td><td>08429</td><td>84187</td><td>69538</td><td>29661</td><td>77738</td><td>09527</td></tr>
<tr><td>09</td><td>36768</td><td>72633</td><td>37948</td><td>21569</td><td>41959</td><td>68670</td><td>45274</td><td>83880</td></tr>
<tr><td>10</td><td>07092</td><td>52392</td><td>24627</td><td>12067</td><td>06558</td><td>45344</td><td>67338</td><td>45320</td></tr>
<tr><td>11</td><td>43310</td><td>01081</td><td>44863</td><td>80307</td><td>52555</td><td>16148</td><td>89742</td><td>94647</td></tr>
<tr><td>12</td><td>61570</td><td>06360</td><td>06173</td><td>63775</td><td>63148</td><td>95123</td><td>35017</td><td>46993</td></tr>
<tr><td>13</td><td>31352</td><td>83799</td><td>10779</td><td>18941</td><td>31579</td><td>76448</td><td>62584</td><td>86919</td></tr>
<tr><td>14</td><td>57048</td><td>86526</td><td>27795</td><td>93692</td><td>90529</td><td>56546</td><td>35065</td><td>32254</td></tr>
<tr><td>15</td><td>09243</td><td>44200</td><td>68721</td><td>07137</td><td>30729</td><td>75756</td><td>09298</td><td>27650</td></tr>
<tr><td>16</td><td>97957</td><td>35018</td><td>40894</td><td>88329</td><td>52230</td><td>82521</td><td>22532</td><td>61587</td></tr>
<tr><td>17</td><td>93732</td><td>59570</td><td>43781</td><td>98885</td><td>56671</td><td>66826</td><td>95996</td><td>44569</td></tr>
<tr><td>18</td><td>72621</td><td>11225</td><td>00922</td><td>68264</td><td>35666</td><td>59434</td><td>71687</td><td>58167</td></tr>
<tr><td>19</td><td>61020</td><td>74418</td><td>45371</td><td>20794</td><td>95917</td><td>37866</td><td>99536</td><td>19378</td></tr>
<tr><td>20</td><td>97839</td><td>85474</td><td>33055</td><td>91718</td><td>45473</td><td>54144</td><td>22034</td><td>23000</td></tr>
<tr><td>21</td><td>89160</td><td>97192</td><td>22232</td><td>90637</td><td>35055</td><td>45489</td><td>88438</td><td>16361</td></tr>
<tr><td>22</td><td>25966</td><td>88220</td><td>62871</td><td>79265</td><td>02823</td><td>52862</td><td>84919</td><td>54883</td></tr>
<tr><td>23</td><td>81443</td><td>31719</td><td>05049</td><td>54806</td><td>74690</td><td>07567</td><td>65017</td><td>16543</td></tr>
<tr><td>24</td><td>11322</td><td>54931</td><td>42362</td><td>34386</td><td>08624</td><td>97687</td><td>46245</td><td>23245</td></tr>
</table>

SOURCE: M. G. Kendall and B. B. Smith, "Randomness and Random Sampling Numbers," *Journal of the Royal Statistical Society* 101 (1938): 164–66. Reprinted by permission of the Royal Statistical Society and the authors.

Table A.6 Table of Random Numbers *(cont.)*

Row	00000 01234	00000 56789	11111 01234	11111 56789	22222 01234	22222 56789	33333 01234	33333 56789
				2nd Thousand				
00	64755	83885	84122	25920	17696	15655	95045	95947
01	10302	52289	77436	34430	38112	49067	07348	23328
02	71017	98495	51308	50374	66591	02887	53765	69149
03	60012	55605	88410	34879	79655	90169	78800	03666
04	37330	94656	49161	42802	48274	54755	44553	65090
05	47869	87001	31591	12273	60626	12822	34691	61212
06	38040	42737	64167	89578	39323	49324	88434	38706
07	73508	30908	83054	80078	86669	30295	56460	45336
08	32623	46474	84061	04324	20628	37319	32356	43969
09	97591	95549	36630	35106	62069	92975	95320	57734
10	74012	31955	59790	96982	66224	24015	96749	07589
11	56754	26457	13351	05014	90966	33674	69096	33488
12	49800	49908	54831	21998	08528	26372	92923	65026
13	43584	89647	24878	56670	00221	50193	99591	62377
14	16653	79664	60325	71301	35742	83636	73058	87229
15	48502	69055	65322	58748	31446	80237	31252	96367
16	96765	54692	36316	86230	48296	38352	23816	64094
17	38923	61550	80357	81784	23444	12463	33992	28128
18	77958	81694	25225	05587	51073	01070	60218	61961
19	17928	28065	25586	08771	02641	85064	65796	48170
20	94036	85978	02318	04499	41054	10531	87431	21596
21	47460	60479	56230	48417	14372	85167	27558	00368
22	47856	56088	51992	82439	40644	17170	13463	18288
23	57616	34653	92298	62018	10375	76515	62986	90756
24	08300	92704	66752	66610	57188	79107	54222	22013

Table A.6 Table of Random Numbers *(cont.)*

COLUMN NUMBER

3rd Thousand

Row	00000 01234	00000 56789	11111 01234	11111 56789	22222 01234	22222 56789	33333 01234	33333 56789
00	89221	02362	65787	74733	51272	30213	92441	39651
01	04005	99818	63918	29032	94012	42363	01261	10650
02	98546	38066	50856	75045	40645	22841	53254	44125
03	41719	84401	59226	01314	54581	40398	49988	65579
04	28733	72489	00785	25843	24613	49797	85567	84471
05	65213	83927	77762	03086	80742	24395	68476	83792
06	65553	12678	90906	90466	43670	26217	69900	31205
07	05668	69080	73029	85746	58332	78231	45986	92998
08	39302	99718	49757	79519	27387	76373	47262	91612
09	64592	32254	45879	29431	38320	05981	18067	87137
10	07513	48792	47314	83660	68907	05336	82579	91582
11	86593	68501	56638	99800	82839	35148	56541	07232
12	83735	22599	97977	81248	36838	99560	32410	67614
13	08595	21826	54655	08204	87990	17033	56258	05384
14	41273	27149	44293	69458	16828	63962	15864	35431
15	00473	75908	56238	12242	72631	76314	47252	06347
16	86131	53789	81383	07868	89132	96182	07009	86432
17	33849	78359	08402	03586	03176	88663	08018	22546
18	61870	41657	07468	08612	98083	97349	20775	45091
19	43898	65923	25078	86129	78491	97653	91500	80786
20	29939	39123	04548	45985	60952	06641	28726	46473
21	38505	85555	14388	55077	18657	94887	67831	70819
22	31824	38431	67125	25511	72044	11562	53279	82268
23	91430	03767	13561	15597	06750	92552	02391	38753
24	38635	68976	25498	97526	96458	03805	04116	63514

Table A.6   Table of Random Numbers (*cont.*)

	COLUMN NUMBER							
Row	00000 01234	00000 56789	11111 01234	11111 56789	22222 01234	22222 56789	33333 01234	33333 56789
				4th Thousand				
00	02490	54122	27944	39364	94239	72074	11679	54082
01	11967	36469	60627	83701	09253	30208	01385	37482
02	48256	83465	49699	24079	05403	35154	39613	03136
03	27246	73080	21481	23536	04881	89977	49484	93071
04	32532	77265	72430	70722	86529	18457	92657	10011
05	66757	98955	92375	93431	43204	55825	45443	69265
06	11266	34545	76505	97746	34668	26999	26742	97516
07	17872	39142	45561	80146	93137	48924	64257	59284
08	62561	30365	03408	14754	51798	08133	61010	97730
09	62796	30779	35497	70501	30105	08133	00997	91970
10	75510	21771	04339	33660	42757	62223	87565	48468
11	87439	01691	63517	26590	44437	07217	98706	39032
12	97742	02621	10748	78803	38337	65226	92149	59051
13	98811	06001	21571	02875	21828	83912	85188	61624
14	51264	01852	64607	92553	29004	26695	78583	62998
15	40239	93376	10419	68610	49120	02941	80035	99317
16	26936	59186	51667	27645	46329	44681	94190	66647
17	88502	11716	98299	40974	42394	62200	69094	81646
18	63499	38093	25593	61995	79867	80569	01023	38374
19	36379	81206	03317	78710	73828	31083	60509	44091
20	93801	22322	47479	57017	59334	30647	43061	26660
21	29856	87120	56311	50053	25365	81265	22414	02431
22	97720	87931	88265	13050	71017	15177	06957	92919
23	85237	09105	74601	46377	59938	15647	34177	92753
24	75746	75268	31727	95773	72364	87324	36879	06802

Table A.6   Table of Random Numbers (*cont.*)

COLUMN NUMBER

5th Thousand

Row	00000 01234	00000 56789	11111 01234	11111 56789	22222 01234	22222 56789	33333 01234	33333 56789
00	29935	06971	63175	52579	10478	89379	61428	21363
01	15114	07126	51890	77787	75510	13103	42942	48111
02	03870	43225	10589	87629	22039	94124	38127	65022
03	79390	39188	40756	45269	65959	20640	14284	22960
04	30035	06915	79196	54428	64819	52314	48721	81594
05	29039	99861	28759	79802	68531	39198	38137	24373
06	78196	08108	24107	49777	09599	43569	84820	94956
07	15847	85493	91442	91351	80130	73752	21539	10986
08	36614	62248	49194	97209	92587	92053	41021	80064
09	40549	54884	91465	43862	35541	44466	88894	74180
10	40878	08997	14286	09982	90308	78007	51587	16658
11	10229	49282	41173	31468	59455	18756	08908	06660
12	15918	76787	30624	25928	44124	25088	31137	71614
13	13403	18796	49909	94404	64979	41462	18155	98335
14	66523	94596	74908	90271	10009	98648	17640	68909
15	91665	36469	68343	17870	25975	04662	21272	50620
16	67415	87515	08207	73729	73201	57593	96917	69699
17	76527	96996	23724	33448	63392	32394	60887	90617
18	19815	47789	74348	17147	10954	34355	81194	54407
19	25592	53587	76384	72575	84347	68918	05739	57222
20	55902	45539	63646	31609	95999	82887	40666	66692
21	02470	58376	79794	22482	42423	96162	47491	17264
22	18630	53263	13319	97619	35859	12350	14632	87659
23	89673	38230	16063	92007	59503	38402	76450	33333
24	62986	67364	06595	17427	84623	14565	82860	57300

Table A.7   Critical Values of the Pearson Correlation Coefficient

df	Level of significance for one-tailed test			
	.05	.025	.01	.005
	Level of significance for two-tailed test			
	.10	.05	.02	.01
1	.988	.997	.9995	.9999
2	.900	.950	.980	.990
3	.805	.878	.934	.959
4	.729	.811	.882	.917
5	.669	.754	.833	.874
6	.622	.707	.789	.834
7	.582	.666	.750	.798
8	.549	.632	.716	.765
9	.521	.602	.685	.735
10	.497	.576	.658	.708
11	.576	.553	.634	.684
12	.458	.532	.612	.661
13	.441	.514	.592	.641
14	.426	.497	.574	.623
15	.412	.482	.558	.606
16	.400	.468	.542	.590
17	.389	.456	.528	.575
18	.378	.444	.516	.561
19	.369	.433	.503	.549
20	.360	.423	.492	.537
21	.352	.413	.482	.526
22	.344	.404	.472	.515
23	.337	.396	.462	.505
24	.330	.388	.453	.496
25	.323	.381	.445	.487
26	.317	.374	.437	.479
27	.311	.367	.430	.471
28	.306	.361	.423	.463
29	.301	.355	.416	.486
30	.296	.349	.409	.449
35	.275	.325	.381	.418
40	.257	.304	.358	.393
45	.243	.288	.338	.372
50	.231	.273	.322	.354
60	.211	.250	.295	.325
70	.195	.232	.274	.303
80	.183	.217	.256	.283
90	.173	.205	.242	.267
100	.164	.195	.230	.254

SOURCE: Abridged from R. A. Fisher and F. Yates, *Statistical Tables for Biological, Agricultural, and Medical Research* (New York; Hafner, 1974). By permission.

Name Index

Subject Index